International Protection of Traditional Knowledge under the Law of Trademarks and Geographical Indications

World Trade Institute Advanced Studies

VOLUME 18

The titles published in this series are listed at *brill.com/wtia*

International Protection of Traditional Knowledge under the Law of Trademarks and Geographical Indications

A Case Study on Persian Carpets

By

Hojjat Khademi

BRILL | NIJHOFF

LEIDEN | BOSTON

The open access publication of this book has been published with the support of the Swiss National Science Foundation.

The Library of Congress Cataloging-in-Publication Data is available online at https://catalog.loc.gov
LC record available at https://lccn.loc.gov/2025006564

Typeface for the Latin, Greek, and Cyrillic scripts: "Brill". See and download: brill.com/brill-typeface.

ISSN 2405-9331
ISBN 978-90-04-72135-7 (hardback)
ISBN 978-90-04-72136-4 (e-book)
DOI 10.1163/9789004721364

This book is printed on acid-free paper and produced in a sustainable manner.

To Thomas Cottier, whose wisdom has illuminated not just my academic path but also brought light to my personal life. Words are not enough to express my appreciation for your guidance and support.
Thank you for everything.

Contents

Acknowledgement

My journey in the road to reach this point began during an international meeting on protection of genetic resources, traditional knowledge and folklore which was held in Geneva at WIPO headquarters. I was lucky to be able to attend one of the side events of the meeting and listen to the presentation made by Professor Thomas Cottier on the rights to plant genetic resources and traditional knowledge. That particular presentation gave me a prime motive to focus on different issues which he raised at the time. Later with his fruitful guidance, I chose my topic of this dissertation. In fact, from the very early steps of my decision to write on the issue of Traditional Knowledge to the final stage in this journey, I have been enjoying his full supports and help, not only as supervisor of my academic work, but also in mine and my family daily life in Bern, Switzerland. We never felt alone midst the problems of living in a different country. He also gave me the chance to experience work with the World Trade Institute (WTI) family and professionally gain more than I ever did before. The very diverse culture of distinguished scholars and researchers working with and in the Institute afforded me a unique opportunity to find myself in a place with no limitation of legal and economic aspects of trade from various theories, coming from all over the world. I *shall* express my gratitude to all supports and friendship of Thomas to me. Moreover, Thomas gave me a great chance to work with brilliant colleagues of mine in the NCCR research working group on innovation and creativity in international trade. My profound thanks to Dr Michelangelo Temmerman, Dr Mira Burri, Dr Dannie Jost, Dr Georg Karlaganis, Dr Maria Anna Corvaglia, Mrs Rachel Liechti, Dr Adamu Pam, Dr Arno Hold and Dr Judith Schäli for their *esprit de corps* and togetherness. I will never forget the cooperation and supportive manner of them and their very fruitful discussions and instructive suggestions to improve my studies and work.

Besides, I shall not forget the most kind and amazing people of the Institute of European and International Economic Law (IEW) whose assist and cooperation made it possible for me to do my work in my best situation. In particular, I shall name Dr Shaheeza Lalani as Programme Director of the Doctoral School; Mrs Rosemarie Cöppicus as IEW Administration Officer; Mrs Margrit Vetter as WTI Director of Administration; Dr Melanie Mettler as Academic Writing Advisor; Mrs Susan Plattner and Mrs Susan Kaplan as Scientific editors; Mr Wulfhard Stahl as Librarian and Mr Christian Steiger as IT Manager.

I also wish to express my sincere gratitude to my thesis second reviewer, Professor Cyrill P. Rigamonti, for his insightful and constructive comments on my doctoral work. I am equally thankful to Professors Henning Grosse

Ruse-Khan and Mira Burri for their valuable feedback. My thanks also go to Professor Pamela Andanda, with whom I co-authored a chapter in *Indigenous Knowledge & Intellectual Property* (JUTA, 2016), for our stimulating discussions on the protection of traditional knowledge.

With consideration to the vital social and cultural role of hand-woven Carpets in lives of thousands of Iranian, and with leaning to my earlier experiences in cooperation with centres, groups and people linked to this issue, I have done my best to use the diverse points of views in a way to cover all important facts, needs, expectations and theories of them. To do so, I enjoyed kindly helps and supports from authorities and experts who have hands in the area of Intellectual Property Rights and Persian hand-woven carpets. In particular, I have to name Mr Mohammad Hassan Kiani, Director General, Iran Intellectual Property Centre, Dr Sey'yed Hassan Mirhosseini, a retired judge of Iran Supreme Court and Professor of IP Law in Tehran. Also, in Iran National Centre of Carpet, Mr. Ebrahim Azizi Haris, Deputy Director; Mr Mohsen Hassan Zadeh, Deputy of Research and Education; Mr Sey'yed Mohammad Veysian, Manager of Researches and Mrs Mansoureh Mohammad Hossein Doulabi, Librarian. Also, Dr Nazila Daryaie, Researcher on Iranian Carpets in Iran Encyclopaedia Foundation.

Additionally, I must express my gratitude to key figures at Brill who have been instrumental in this publication process: Ms Marie Sheldon, Publishing Director of International Law; Ms Beth Derr, Associate Editor of International Law; Ms Dove Morissette, production editor; and Mr Kan Wai Min, Open Access Coordinator. Their unwavering support and expertise have been vital in making this publication possible.

Furthermore, I would like to extend my profound appreciation to the Swiss National Science Foundation for its financial support, which has enabled the publication of this work as an open access resource.

Although my great sensitive care to collect most current and very accurate information, I won't be able to claim that this work is coming to an end without any mistakes whatever from my understanding of the other researchers, authors or scholars or for providing the information from the reliable sources. Therefore, I welcome any criticism, recommendations or suggestions for amendments or improvements of this work. Finally, the book encompasses a comprehensive analysis of Iran's Industrial Property Law up to the end of 2023. Subsequent developments are not included, in particular impending legislation.

Disclaimer: All images used in this book are included solely for scholarly and illustrative purposes. The inclusion of any brand names, labels, or geographic terms does not imply endorsement, affiliation, or legal judgment. No claim is made regarding ownership or commercial association, and all rights remain with their respective holders.

Figures and Tables

Figures

Tables

Cases

Anheuser-Busch Inc v Budějovický Budvar, národní podnik [2004] ECJ C-245/02, 2004 I-10989
Ansul BV v Ajax Brandbeveiliging BV [2003] ECJ C-40/01, ECR I-2439
Belmora LLC v Bayer Consumer Care AG [2016] 4th Cir 15-1335, 819 F3d 697
Federal Court Case 4C229/2003/lma
Feist Publications, Inc, v Rural Tel Serv Co [1991] Sup Ct 89-1909, 499 US 340
Foster v Mountford (1976) 29 FLR 233 (Austl)
George M, Payunka, Marika & Others v Indofurn Pty Ltd* [1994] FCA 1215
Hamid v Arman Co [2014] Tehran Civil Inferior Court 9209980226300930
John Bulun Bulun & Anor v R & T Textiles Pty Ltd. [1998] Federal Court of Australia FCA 0975, DG3 of 1996
Mehrdad & Reza v Saeed [2016] Tehran Civil Court of Appeal 93099802263916
Milpurrurru, G & Ors v Indofurn P/L & Ors [1994] FCA 1082, DG4 of 1993
Municipality of Oslo ("Vigeland") [2017] EFTA Court Case E-5/16
Navajo Nation v Urban Outfitters, Inc (2019) 379 F Supp 3d 783
Phillip Morris Inc v Reilly [2000] F Supp 2d 142, 113 129
Piazza's Seafood World LLC v Bob Odom [2006] USA Court of Appeals, 5 Circuit 448 F. 3d 744, 448 Federal Reporter 744
Religious Technology Center v Wollersheim (1992) 971 F2d 364 (9th Cir)
Smith v Dravo Corp (1953) 203 F2d 369 (Ct App 7th Cir)
Trader Joe's Company v Hallat [2016] 9th Cir 14-35035, 835 F3d 960
United States – Measure Affecting Imports of Woven Wool Shirts and Blouses from India [1997] World Trade Organization (Appellate Body)
Wagner Asia Equipment LLC v Borogchin LLC [2001] The Sukhbaatar District Court Decision No. 452

Abbreviations

ABS	Access and Benefit Sharing
AO	Appellations of Origin
ARIPO	African Regional Intellectual Property Organization
BIRPI	Bureaux Internationaux Réunis pour la Protection de la Propriété Intellectuelle (French for "United International Bureau for the Protection of Intellectual Property")
CBD	Convention on Biological Diversity
ECOTA	Economic Cooperation Organization Trade Agreement
EFTA	European Free Trade Association
EU	European Union
EUIPO	European Union Intellectual Property Office
FAO	Food and Agriculture Organization of the United Nations
FTA	Free Trade Agreement
GIS	Geographical Indications
GRS	Genetic Resources
IACA	Indian Arts and Crafts Act
IGC	Intergovernmental Committee on Intellectual Property and Genetic Resources, Traditional Knowledge and Folklore
IGC-GRTKF	Intergovernmental Committee on Intellectual Property and Genetic Resources, Traditional Knowledge and Folklore
IGE | IPI	Swiss Federal Institute of Intellectual Property
INCC	Iran National Carpet Centre
IOC	International Olympic Committee
ITC	International Trade Centre UNCTAD/WTO
ITPGRFA	International Treaty on Plant Genetic Resources for Food and Agriculture
IP	Intellectual Property
IPC	Intellectual Property Centre of Iran
IPRS	Intellectual Property Rights
OAPI	African Intellectual Property Organization
OECD	Organisation for Economic Co-Operation and Development
PCS	Persian Carpets
PGRS	Plant Genetic Resources
PIC	Prior Informed Consent
TCE	Traditional Cultural Expression
TIP-rights	Traditional Intellectual Property Rights

TK	Traditional Knowledge
TK-RI	Traditional Knowledge-Related Indication
TK-RS	Traditional Knowledge-Related Signs
TKDL	Traditional Knowledge Digital Library
TKHS	Traditional Knowledge Holders
TKU	Traditional Knowledge User
TRIPS	Trade-Related Aspects of Intellectual Property Rights
UC	Unfair Competition
UN	United Nations
UNEP	United Nations Environment Programme
UNESCO	United Nations Educational, Scientific and Cultural Organization
UPOV Convention	International Convention for the Protection of New Varieties of Plants
USPTO	United States Patent and Trademark Office
WCT	WIPO Copyright Treaty
WHO	World Health Organization
WIPO	World Intellectual Property Organization
WPPT	WIPO Performances and Phonograms Treaty
WTO	World Trade Organization

Introduction

1 Background on Persian Carpets and Traditional Knowledge

Original Persian Carpets (PCs) have been one of the foremost expressions of Iranian culture, sold and traded in the region and worldwide for centuries. Recent decades have witnessed increased copying of patterns and fabric abroad, sold at low prices and undercutting the reputation and quality of the long tradition of hand-made high quality and enduring PCs. The law has not been able to address these developments properly, neither domestically nor internationally. The present book seeks to explore potential approaches and answers, mainly in international law by investigating the options available under the Agreement on Trade-Related Aspects of Intellectual Property Rights (TRIPS Agreement),[1] incorporating the Paris Convention on the Protection of Industrial Property (Paris Convention).[2] It primarily investigates the extent to which and traditional knowledge (TK) can be protected under law of trademarks and geographical indications (GIs). While this study does not extensively cover other forms of intellectual property rights (IPRs), it provides a concise evaluation of the strengths and limitations of copyright, unfair competition (UC), and trade secrets laws. These areas, however, are not the central focus of this research. It explore the potential of Article 10bis of the Paris Convention and its general clauses and obligations on UC law. To this effect, the study is able to refer to the work of Christian Riffel.[3] He explored the potential of Article 10bis Paris Convention and found that it offers a basis for the protection of TK, but that additional regulatory efforts are required. The present work builds upon this effort and seeks to find new insights in examining the problem of protecting the sector of PCs as a particular expression of TK.

In doing so, the linkage between TK and PCs has to be clarified. TK is the information which has been developed over time by the people of a community, based on experience and adaptation to a local culture and environment.[4]

1 Agreement on Trade-Related Aspects of Intellectual Property Rights 1994 (1869 UNTS 299 (entered into force 1 January 1995)).

2 Paris Convention for the Protection of Industrial Property, as last revised at Stockholm 1967 (828 UNTS 305 (entered into force 26 April 1970)).

3 Christian Riffel, *Protection Against Unfair Competition in the WTO TRIPS Agreement; the Scope and Prospects of Article 10bis of the Paris Convention for the Protection of Industrial Property* (BRILL | NIJHOFF 2016) Pages 134–249.

4 Stephen A Hansen and Justin W van Fleet, 'Traditional Knowledge and Intellectual Property: A Handbook on Issues and Options for Traditional Knowledge Holders in Protecting Their

TK is now more fully and carefully defined, as the understanding or skill of indigenous peoples or local communities that relates to technologies and cultural expressions;[5] and may use as a base for creativity and innovation.[6] PCs are illuminating examples of TK based products. PCs precedent goes back 2500 years and have a rich tradition. Two main types of PCs are known Local Woven and Nomadic Woven Carpets. Nomadic Carpets use improvised geometric design which makes each of them unique. Nomadic carpets are using lambs' wool and organic colour extracted from vegetable dyes. Local woven are made typically from silk and wool. The pre-determined designs usually floral patterns are used for local woven carpets. With combination of skill, the best materials and traditions PCs are the best made and the most famous woven carpets all over the world. Everything from the fibres to the dyes is made from genetic materials of the region from which they originate. The quality and global reputation of PCs are directly related to the strong knowledge of local communities of how to provide the best raw materials such as herbal colours from local races[7] of plants and the proper wool from local animals. It also depends on to special skills of the weaver in the issues such as row-counting, type of knot and number of wefts.[8] This kind of knowledge offers the local communities the potential to produce the high quality and resistant carpets which contrary to expectation will increase in value over time. In every and each part of Iran, PCs' features such as designs, textures, colouring, and knots are distinctly attributed with certain characteristics of the geography. Therefore, as a general rule, PCs are called with the well-known names of their geographical places to give the customers a general view what they could expect from different carpets.

As another significant factor, Iran is a big country which occupies almost 1.65 million square kilometres.[9] PCs are a common production in all different

---

Intellectual Property and Maintaining Biological Diversity' (American Association for the Advancement of Science 2003) Page 3.

5 Stephen R Munzer and Kal Raustiala, 'The Uneasy Case for Intellectual Property Rights in Traditional Knowledge' (2009) 27 Cardozo Arts & Entertainment Law Journal 37, Page 38.

6 Carlos M Correa, *Traditional Knowledge and Intellectual Property – Issues and Options Surrounding the Protection of Traditional Knowledge* (The Quaker United Nations Office 2001) Page 3.

7 The knowledge on colours is very special as the term "Abrash" is used to describe it. The concept of Abrash is changes on the natural and variable of colours of the rugs and carpets over the times when different dyes are using. For more information see: Houghton Mifflin Company, 'The American Heritage Dictionary.'

8 Javad Yasavoli, مقدمه ای بر شناخت قالی ایران (*An Introduction to the Study of Persian Rugs*) (2nd edn, Farhangsara 1996).

9 Glenn E Curtis and Eric Hooglund, *Iran: A Country Study* (5th edn, Government Printing Office 2008) xxv.

geographical places of Iran which includes the social, spiritual, cultural, ecological, economic, intellectual, scientific, technological and educational values of Iranian local communities. Iranians admire PCs as a cultural phenomenon and their ancestor's legacy. PCs are the result of thousands of years' civilization and one of the most important principal symbols of Iran's culture and history. PCs play the role of cultural ambassador of Iran before other nations from the ancient time to the present. PCs have been used as a tool to safeguard Iranian culture and identity amid the invasion of the invaders through history. PCs connect local communities within the nation. PCs form a very important part of Iran folklore and its cultural civilization and represent local communities' folklore and their cultural heritage. The position of PCs as a part of Iranian daily life and its importance to the Iranian culture and the nomadic, rural and urban subcultures are very well known. While PCs are tied with the history of the country; its roots go back through the deepest part of Iranian customs, beliefs and faiths. Iranians' ancestors preserved PCs as their priceless treasure from the past to the present, and it has to be transferred to the future generations.

2 The Value of TK and PCs for Local Communities

TK is of great value for commercial exploitation in various fields such as industry, sciences, agriculture, literature and artistic works. It is widely recognized that there is a growing interest in the various values inherent to TK.[10] There is a strong believe that the effective preservation, protection and exploitation of TK will depend upon a true understanding of these inherent values of TK, including its economic, social, cultural and environmental components, and how they relate to the protection of IPRs. The Contracting Parties of the Convention on Biological Diversity (CBD) requested World Intellectual Property Organization (WIPO) to consider the impact of IPRs on "the value of knowledge, innovations and practices of indigenous and local communities embodying traditional lifestyles relevant for the conservation and sustainable use of biological diversity."[11] And following this demand, during the negotiations within the framework of WIPO 'Intergovernmental Committee on Intellectual Property and Genetic

10 See delegation of Japan on behalf of Group B: WIPO Secretariat, 'Report' (World Intellectual Property Organization 2000) WIPO Doc WO/GA/26/10 Page 10.

11 UNEP-CBD, 'Decisions Adopted by the Conference of the Parties to the Convention on Biological Diversity at Its Fifth Meeting' (2000) UNEP Doc UNEP/CBD/COP/5/23 Annex III para 15(e), Page 199.

Resources, Traditional Knowledge and Folklore' (IGC-GRTKF), negotiators emphasised the importance to recognize value of TK and to promote respect "for the dignity, cultural integrity and spiritual values of the TK."[12] In the same vein, contracting parties of the Swakopmund Protocol recognized "the intrinsic social, cultural, spiritual, economic, intellectual, scientific, ecological, agricultural, medical, technological, commercial and educational values" of TK.[13]

In accordance with the draft guidelines on the protection of the cultural heritage of indigenous peoples, 'users of elements of indigenous peoples' cultural heritage beyond its traditional context shall make every endeavour to identify the source and origin of the elements and seek to return them to the people concerned.[14] Some scholars suggest respecting TK includes 'valuing' it. They demand "indigenous peoples' customs, rules and practices, should not only be recognized and respected, but also valued."[15] As one of the important criteria, protection of cultural heritage shall not only underline indigenous peoples' intrinsic values;[16] It should also include the objective of protection responding to these values.[17] Any legal protection mechanism must consider distinct traits of TK and its values.[18]

But, before considering whether such recognition can have any real impact on the protection of PCs, it is important to discuss what exactly the term 'value' means. "The significance, desirability, or utility of something"[19] or its "worth in usefulness or importance to the possessor"[20] is known as *value* of the thing. Value is also defined as "the contribution of an action or object to

12 IGC-GRTKF Secretariat, 'The Protection of Traditional Knowledge: Draft Articles Rev. 2' (World Intellectual Property Organization 2014) WIPO Doc WIPO/GRTKF/IC/28/5 Annex 2.

13 Swakopmund Protocol on the Protection of Traditional Knowledge and Expressions of Folklore 2010 (entered into force 11 May 2015) Paragraph 4 of Preamble.

14 Yozo Yokota, 'Standard-Setting: Future Priorities for Standard-Setting Activities; Draft Guidelines on the Protection of the Cultural Heritage of Indigenous Peoples' (UN Commission on Human Rights, Sub-Commission on the Promotion and Protection of Human Rights, Working Group on Indigenous Populations 2006) UN ESC, 24th sess, Item 5(a), UN Doc E/CN.4/Sub.2/AC.4/2006/5 8, Section III, paragraph C(10).

15 Erica-Irene Daes, 'Principles and Guidelines for the Protection of the Heritage of Indigenous People' (UN Commission on Human Rights, Sub-Commission on the Promotion and Protection of Human Rights 2000) UN ESC Doc E/CN.4/Sub.2/2000/26 Page 6.

16 Yozo Yokota (n 14) Page 5, Section II, Paragraph (f).

17 *ibid Page 4, Section I, Paragraph (n).*

18 Swakopmund Protocol Preamble.

19 Bryan A Garner, 'Black's Law Dictionary' Page 1690.

20 Houghton Mifflin Company (n 7).

user-specified goals, objectives or conditions."[21] In like manner, *value* is called "the process of expressing a value for a particular good or service, usually in terms of something that can be counted, often money, but also through methods and measures from other disciplines (sociology, ecology, etc.)"[22]

In accordance with these concepts, undoubtedly, TK is one of the most valuable assets for communities which are in the possession of TK. It has always been playing a critical role as a vital resource to develop lives of indigenous peoples and local farming communities. This essential role is recognized widely in different area of human life. To recognize the significance, desirability, utility and contribution of the PCs in Iranian life and civilization it will worth to review PCs different aspects of value.

2.1 *TK, Economy and International Trade*

TK is a valuable property for 'Traditional Knowledge Holders' (TKHs)[23] which is in its all forms a significant source for economic and commercial boost. Traditional and rural based industries such as handicraft play an important role in the economic self-reliance and development of TKHs and this important factor shall be recognized by the concerned governments.[24] PCs is an essential economic source of millions of peoples in different ethnic groups of Iran. It is a main foundation for business and trade in raw materials, final products and related services. This business includes the supply and demand for TK based carpet products both in domestic and international markets.

Conserving markets and expansion of marketing opportunities for the TKHs' genuine products and industries constitute the commercial actual values of TK. Moreover, utilization of TK aiming to produce a final product is another commercial value. Also "enhancing market access for environmentally preferable products could be linked to the promotion of protection of TK by granting

21 Secretariat of the Convention on Biological Diversity, Global Mechanism of the United Nations Convention to Combat Desertification, and OSLO consortium, 'Valuing the Biodiversity of Dry and Sub-Humid Lands' (Secretariat of the Convention on Biological Diversity 2013) Peer reviewed 71 Page 11.

22 *ibid.*

23 For the purposes of this research the term 'Traditional Knowledge Holders' (TKHs) will be used as a general term to refer the various traditional knowledge holders (indigenous people, local communities, rural and nomadic people, etc.). Detailed explanations will be given in the first chapter of this research under the discussion "who are beneficiaries?."

24 Convention Concerning Indigenous and Tribal Peoples in Independent Countries (ILO No. 169) 1989 (1650 UNTS 383 (entered into force 5 September 1991)) Art 23(1).

facilitated market access for such products."[25] Crafts are TK based products and important for cultural preservation, and economic growth. In 2004, according to Flower "Artisan handicrafts represent an estimated US$30 billion world market."[26] PCs are outstanding examples of commercial advantages of TK. This local traditional industry plays a key and vital role in economy of local communities and the country in general. As TK based products and after oil, PCs are the second largest and most important export production of Iran. PCs are exported to more than 103 countries, the most important being the USA, Switzerland and EU countries.[27] In 1996 about 7 million square meters PCs with the value of 1.257.142.857 $ were produced in Iran, and the export incomes of it reached to 642.449.578 $.[28]

Based on the first and second 'Iran Five Years Economic, Social and Cultural Development Program Acts,' it was predicted that the amount of foreign income from exported PCs should reach to 4.4 and 7.5 billion dollars orderly at the end of those development programs. Those figures were 24.7% and 27.2% of total exports income. However, in practice they touched 38% and 22.5% of total export revenue.[29]

2.2 *TK and Employment*

Any type of TK product or service has an inherent value dedicated to its nature. This value generally is commercialized by market forces and impact on income distribution in each community. In this regard, PCs include a lot of job opportunities such as knitter/weaver, and establishment of the individual guilds[30] and unit guilds.[31] This industry plays an important role in the daily life of many Iranians. Almost 7% of the population is engaged in this sector.[32] Accounting

25 Thomas Cottier, 'WTO Negotiations on Environmental Goods and Services: A Potential Contribution to the Millennium Development Goals' (United Nations 2009) UNCTAD/DITC/TED/2008/4 Page 27.

26 Betsy J Fowler, 'Preventing Counterfeit Craft Designs' in J Michael Finger and Philip Schuler (eds), *Poor People's Knowledge, Promoting Intellectual Property in Developing Countries* (The World Bank and Oxford University Press 2004) Page 114.

27 SH Khodadad Hosseini and MA Sham Abadi, 'Export Marketing of Persian Hand-Woven Carpet, Analysing Impact Factors and Damages' (2007) 43 Iranian Journal of Trade Studies 1, Paragraph 3.

28 Shahbaz Shams'Oldini, 'Iran Place in Hand-woven Carpets Global Exports' in Iran National Carpet Centre (ed), *1st National Seminar on Researches of Persian Hand-Woven Carpets*, vol 2 (Iran National Carpet Centre 2003) Page 344.

29 *ibid.*

30 Iran – Act on Country's Guild System 2004 Art 2.

31 *ibid Art 3.*

32 Khodadad Hosseini and Sham Abadi (n 27) Paragraph 3.

for linked industries, around 8 million individuals, equivalent to 13.3% of total population of the country were engaged in this art/industry.[33]

2.3 TK and Sustainable Development

TK has the potential to boost community based economic development and is acknowledged as a key tool for achieving human development too.[34] TK has the possibility to fulfill human needs[35] and sustain the livelihoods of families and individuals and their identities.[36] There are many ingredients included in the term 'development' but "the most critical ones are to lead a long and healthy life, to be educated and to enjoy a decent standard of living."[37] Following this view, TK has not only a close relation and critical contribution in communities' development; but also in the first place as a type of local science it is a tool for development. Moreover, TK and its different facets make an important contribution to sustainability, defined as a careful balance of social, economic and environmental values and concerns.[38] Because of such critical contribution, TK plays a distinctly important role in achieving the Sustainable Development Goals[39] (SDGs). Dhir points out TK is essential to achieving multiple goals especially through:

> Ensuring the sustainable management and use of natural resources such as forests or marine resources
>
> Enhancing sustainable agricultural practices and food security
>
> Achieving effective climate change mitigation and adaptation to build resilient communities

33 Shams'Oldini (n 28) Page 344.

34 UNDP defines human development as "a process of enlarging people's choices." See: UNDP, *Human Development Report 1990* (Oxford University Press 1990) Page 10.

35 Martin Khor, *Intellectual Property, Biodiversity and Sustainable Development: Resolving Difficult Issues* (Zed Books; Third World Network 2002) Page 16.

36 IGC-GRTKF Secretariat, 'Revised Provisions for the Protection of Traditional Knowledge: Policy Objectives and Core Principles' (World Intellectual Property Organization 2011) WIPO Doc WIPO/GRTKF/IC/18/5 Annex Page 3.

37 UNDP (n 34) Page 10.

38 See: Simone Heri and others, *International Instruments Influencing the Rights of People Facing Investments in Agricultural Land* (ILC 2011) Pages 97–100.

39 The SDGs were adopted on 25 September 2015 by the world leaders. As the agenda for sustainable development, the SDGs include 17 sustainable development goals and 169 targets that cover actions over the years by 2030 in areas of critical importance for humanity and the planet. See: 'Transforming Our World: The 2030 Agenda for Sustainable Development' (2015) GA Res 70/1, UN GAOR, 70th sess, 4th plen mtg, UN Doc A/RES/70/1.

Enhancing sustainable forms of livelihood, creating green jobs and spurring climate-sensitive innovation, entrepreneurship and businesses

Achieving gender equality and the greater participation of women, including in decision-making and natural resource management

Raising productivity and economic growth while taking into account environmental considerations

Securing the peaceful and stable societies necessary for inclusive social and economic development

Establishing strong monitoring and accountability mechanisms so as to ensure that no one is left behind

Enhancing knowledge-sharing and collaboration to implement and achieve the ambitious 2030 Agenda for Sustainable Development.[40]

Overall, TK bears to potential, if properly managed and protected, to make an important contribution in realising the principle of sustainable development.

2.4 *TK, Social and Gender Value*

If something has significance, desirability, or utility to the general public it would be considered as of social value to the public.[41] Satisfaction of life, religious and spiritual beliefs, attitudes towards current affairs, views on environment, gender equality and children upbringing have been seen as a core part of this type of values.[42] They maintain certain qualities that are shared within a particular group of people and shape their approaches towards culture, economy and politics. Rural and nomadic women have a vital role in preserving the community social values as they are the most important part of the producing chain of PCs. So, if this industry fails on any reason, this will decrease their participation in social activities of traditional communities.

2.5 *TK, Cultural Value and Diversity*

TKHs have been educated and trained within a social process. The process is shaped by exclusive beliefs and cultural values which are in close connection with their natural world. They believe this process maintains their knowledge

---

40 Rishabh Kumar Dhir, 'Sustainable Development Goals: Indigenous Peoples in Focus' (ILO 2016) Page 10.

41 Garner (n 19) Page 1690.

42 See: Science Policy Research Group, 'Social Values, Science and Technology' (European Commission 2005) EUR Series 22062 EN.

system and give their TK a distinction character.[43] Therefore, TKHs' contribution to the cultural diversity of humankind is a distinctive character of TK.[44] Culture includes arts and letters and also traditions and beliefs. It is a complex of spiritual, material, intellectual and emotional features.[45] The cultural values of TK are very significant, because these processes will help TKHs to endure their knowledge systems.[46]

Having considered the importance of TK, it is also reasonable for TKHs to look for protection of TK as a way to avoid the persons outside their communities from access and usage of TK. This is particularly important when TKHs engage with industrial processes other than neighbouring communities in cultural exchange. Cultural values of a community must be respected.[47] Therefore, governments are required to provide effective mechanisms for prevention of actions which would eventuate in depriving indigenous peoples from their cultural values.[48] Traditional communities' industries such as handicrafts shall be recognized as an important component for continuation of the TKHs cultural values.[49] In Iran, designating June 10th as National Handwoven Carpet Day symbolizes a commitment to the cultural continuation of PCs, reflecting their significant cultural importance. This initiative underscores the foundational principles of the Iran National Council for Public Culture, emphasizing the pivotal role that PCs play in shaping the cultural identity of Iranians on a national scale.[50]

2.6 *TK and Ecological Values*

TK has a key role in the preservation and protection of biological diversity[51] and thus, there is a long-term interest in preservation and protection of TK in

43 UNEP-CBD Executive Secretary, 'Development of Elements of Sui Generis Systems for the Protection of Traditional Knowledge, Innovations and Practices' (UNEP 2005) CBD WG8J, 4th mtg, Agenda Item 8, UNEP Doc, UNEP/CBD/WG8J/4/INF/18 Page 3.

44 Indigenous and Tribal Peoples Convention Paragraph 7 of Preamble.

45 UNESCO, 'World Conference on Cultural Policies Final Report' (1982) UNESCO Doc CLT/MD/1 Page 41.

46 UNEP-CBD Executive Secretary (n 43) Page 3.

47 Swakopmund Protocol Section 19(2).

48 'United Nations Declaration on the Rights of Indigenous Peoples' (2007) GA Res 61/295, UN GAOR, 61st sess, 107th plen mtg, Supp No 49, UN Doc A/RES/61/295 Art 8(2)(1).

49 Indigenous and Tribal Peoples Convention Art 23(1).

50 Iran – Designating June 10th as the National Day of Hand-Woven Carpets 2021 (Resolution 753).

51 "Biological diversity means the variability among living organisms from all sources including, inter alia, terrestrial, marine and other aquatic ecosystems and the ecological

developing and least developed countries. Therefore, recognizing and rewarding the contributions made by TKHs to the conservation of the environment need to be kept in mind.[52] Environment and TK as tangible and intangible components of human's life cannot be detached from each other and need to co-exist together. TKHs and the environment are inseparable in nature. Therefore, "the importance of the TK for the conservation of biological diversity and the sustainable use of its components, and for the sustainable livelihoods of these communities,"[53] has been recognized. Besides, TK plays a key role in the preservation and protection of biological diversity.[54] This function is realized by means of crucial environmental management by TKHs[55] and their know-how to use and maintain ecological agents and their ecosystems. In fact, TK is valuable knowledge in the process of exploitation of biological diversity in coexistence with the eco-system. Access to natural resources, cultivar selection, pest infestations, and nutritional status can all be addressed with TK. Even when the nature and body of TK does not match the end products, TK as an indicator often leads to the potential use of the Genetic Resources (GRs) and producing final products. By the knowledge of identifying GRs and their potential uses, TK adds value and efficiency to the biodiversity properties.[56] Any decision of governments on development activities and implementation shall be taken to protect the environment of the territories they inhabit.[57]

2.7 *TK's Role in Decreasing the Pollution of Ecosystems*

The industrial revolution in different sectors is characterized by recourse to new and efficient technologies which, at the same time, in increasing dependence often have produced uncontrollable ecological damage. The utilitarian

---

complexes of which they are part; this includes diversity within species, between species and of ecosystems." See: Convention on Biological Diversity 1992 (1760 UNTS 79 (entered into force 29 December 1993)) Art 2.

52 Swakopmund Protocol Paragraph 6 of Preamble.

53 Nagoya Protocol on Access to Genetic Resources and the Fair and Equitable Sharing of Benefits Arising from Their Utilization to the Convention on Biological Diversity 2010 (3010 UNTS 118 (entered into force 12 October 2014)) Paragraph 21 of Preamble.

54 See: CBD Art 2.

55 See: Susette Biber-Klemm and Danuta Szymura Berglas, 'Problems and Goals' in Susette Biber-Klemm and Thomas Cottier (eds), *Rights to Plant Genetic Resources and Traditional Knowledge: Basic Issues and Perspectives* (CABI 2006) Page 3.

56 UNEP-CBD, 'Report of the Meeting of the Group of Technical and Legal Experts on Traditional Knowledge Associated with Genetic Resources in the Context of the International Regime on Access and Benefit-Sharing' (2009) CBD AHWG, 8th mtg, Agenda Item 32, UNEP Doc UNEP/CBD/WG-ABS/8/2 Annex Page 8, Paragraph 13.

57 Indigenous and Tribal Peoples Convention Art 7(4).

approach of multinational corporations and modern industries are essentially focused on profits and financial returns, financial interests and such an attitude often went along with irresponsible exploitation of the ecosystem. Chemical and industrial pollutions and climate change are clear examples of demolition of this process. On the other hand, TKHs who are directly in connect with their ecosystems are learnt to use and exploit the resources in a way to control the ecological consequences of exploitation make the least pollution to the ecosystem.

2.8 *TK and Agriculture*

The agricultural sector is an outcome of a tight relation with farmers and their ecosystem. "Clearly, there is a very close relationship between biodiversity and the livelihoods and well-being of agricultural communities."[58] Traditional farmers hold in trust very precious and rich traditional information and knowledge of the environment in the places they live in and use this knowledge to cultivate the best agricultural products compatible with the specific environmental features. They also use this knowledge to produce the best seasonal products. They have a proper understanding of the limitations of their ecosystem. They practice their rich experiences to reduce the biological costs of their activities. Local agricultural systems are mostly reliable and less risky compared with the imported exotic styles, as their methods have been originated and promoted based on the 'trial and error procedure' and 'environmental and cultural evolution' across the decades and centuries of practical life.

2.9 *Scientific and Technological Values*

TK has equal scientific value as other knowledge systems.[59] It has been playing a critical role not only next to local communities and indigenous people, but also for the modernized societies and to international co-operation and co-understanding.[60] The advent of the knowledge-based economy within a globalized information society has recited all forms of humankind innovation and creativities including TK even more valuable.[61] TK is not only a type of

---

58 Stewart Lockie and David Carpenter, 'Agriculture, Biodiversity and Markets' in Stewart Lockie and David Carpenter (eds), *Agriculture, Biodiversity and Markets: Livelihoods and Agroecology in Comparative Perspective* (Earthscan 2010) Page 1.

59 IGC-GRTKF Secretariat, 'The Protection of Traditional Knowledge: Draft Articles Rev. 2' (n 12) Page 2.

60 Indigenous and Tribal Peoples Convention Paragraph 7 of Preamble.

61 IGC-GRTKF Secretariat, 'Report of Intergovernmental Committee on Intellectual Property and Genetic Resources, Traditional Knowledge and Folklore' (World Intellectual Property Organization 2001) WIPO Doc WIPO/GRTKF/IC/1/13 Paragraph 6.

local technology but also an aspiration of modern technology. In 2011, a team of Japanese researchers visited the Chaharmahal and Bakhtiari region in Iran, known for its distinguished PCs production. They engaged in local carpet dyeing workshops, conducted comprehensive studies on the unique carpet dyes and traditional dyeing techniques, and collected relevant data directly from the source. This research visit took place shortly after the Chaharmahal and Bakhtiari Handmade Carpet was honoured with the World Colour Originality Award at Germany's Domotex exhibition.[62]

In the age of modern knowledge and technology, TK has been reconsidered as an important tool to meet communities' economic and social challenges and "to promote global economic development."[63] TK is a base for biotechnology[64] and biotechnological inventions.[65] "In the broad sense the definition of biotechnology covers many of the tools and techniques that are commonplace in agriculture and food production."[66]

3 Description of the Problem

The industrial revolution was a big step forward to modernization and improvement of human life. Yet, at the same time, it not only unsettled the social order and cultural context of traditional communities, but also it increased poverty and their decline and erosion among them. In this process, traditional communities did not completely leave their identities behind and have always been endeavouring to preserve and guard their cultures and customs. Across

62 IRNA News Agency, 'Japanese researchers document the tradition of dyeing Chaharmahal and Bakhtiari hand-woven carpets' (*Database of the Iran National Carpet Centre*, 28 May 2011) <https://www.irna.ir/news/4044758/پژوهشگران-ژاپنی-سنت-رنگرزی-فرش-چهارمحال-وبختیاری-رامستند سازی>.

63 Charles R McManis, 'Biodiversity, Biotechnology and Traditional Knowledge Protection: Law, Science and Practice' in Charles R McManis (ed), *Biodiversity and the Law: Intellectual Property, Biotechnology and Traditional Knowledge* (Earthscan 2007) Page 1.

64 Biotechnology means "any technological application that uses biological systems, living organisms, or derivatives thereof, to make or modify products or processes for specific use." See: CBD Art 2; and Nagoya Protocol Art 2.

65 "Biotechnological invention concerns a product consisting of or containing biological material or a process by means of which biological material is produced, processed or used" See: Directive 98/44/EC of the European Parliament and of the Council of 6 July 1998 on the Legal Protection of Biotechnological Inventions 1998 (OJ L 213/13) Art 3(1).

66 FAO, 'FAO Statement on Biotechnology' (*Agricultural Biotechnologies in Crops, Forestry, Livestock, Fisheries and Agro-Industry*, 2000) <http://www.fao.org/biotech/fao-statement-on-biotechnology/en/> accessed 13 August 2014.

thousands of years towards today, they created, promoted, preserved and transferred this knowledge among generations and have been trying to keep this knowledge alive and constant alongside with its due biodiversity. TK is the raw material for creativity and innovation. Therefore, it plays a vital role in modern societies for producing and distributing wealth and extracting benefits from using biodiversity, and as well as in using different forms of IPRs for protection their modern knowledge.

Importantly, this development caused an imbalance between accessible protection for modern knowledge while TK by and large remained without appropriate protection. Remuneration went to holder of IP based upon innovation while does contributing TK to this process end up empty-handed. What part of this wealth should be paid back to the TKHs? And how this should be done? To make it possible to distribute the wealth originated from using TK through a fair mechanism, there is a need to build a rebalanced system of IPRs which can support, enhance and recuperate the TKHs' rights. Moreover the lack of recognition of traditional territories, resources and customary authorities; markets pressure, extension of government control; unjust land policies; cultural modification policies and inappropriate conservation management are the main threats to the cultural diversity. Besides, the problem is being intensified even more with globalization.[67]

TK in the process of industrialization is already being lost at huge rates, even greater than the disappearance of languages. Although immense knowledge of TKHs has been acquiring through their constant interaction with the natural environment, still their TK is disappearing rapidly. It has been estimated that 80% of all cultural diversity will have disappeared in 100 years' time.[68] There are different reasons for such a lost, among them, the loss of biodiversity and the steady crawl of world to become more uniform culturally, socially and economically.

Recourse of so-called western industries to use TK as raw materials to develop and exploit products and marketing them which has been begun in 19th century is taking place today even in larger scale, considering the fact that nowadays markets are growing to the global scales.[69] In products like PCs,

---

67 See: Darrell A Posey, *Indigenous Peoples and Sustainability: Cases and Actions* (International Books 1997). Pages 59–74.

68 IGC-GRTKF Secretariat, 'Report of Intergovernmental Committee on Intellectual Property and Genetic Resources, Traditional Knowledge and Folklore' (World Intellectual Property Organization 2004) WIPO Doc WIPO/GRTKF/IC/6/14 7.

69 Silke Von Lewinski, 'Introduction' in Silke von Lewinski (ed), *Indigenous Heritage and Intellectual Property: Genetic Resources, Traditional Knowledge, and Folklore* (2nd edn, Kluwer Law International 2008) Page 2.

local communities as TKHs today are faced with the appearance of competitors from other countries who are exporting their products in ways that seem to be unfair to the TKHs. These competitors are producing their carpets using of knowledge, methods, designs, and motifs of PCs and marketing them in the name and with misappropriation of PCs reputation. In fact, they mislead the consumers into believing that their products have been made with the same knowledge and quality as PCs have. As a result, the TKHs on PCs are facing challenges such as decreasing exports, jobs cut and immigration of community members to big cities, loss of knowledge and disappearance of cultural and spiritual ritual. Therefore, local communities are asking for legal protection for their TK on PCs to prevent competitors from use the PCs designs, motifs and reputation in unfair ways and without their prior consent.

4 Methodology

This study will scrutinize the texts of the international treaties together with their interpretations and cases, and the domestic laws and judicial precedents in the EU Region, the USA and Switzerland, as the main markets for PCs. As a first step, this study will review the state of the art, definitions, descriptions, classifications, technical and artistic characteristics, and also human, natural and geographical specialties in PCs production; to assess the possibility of comparison of the above-mentioned elements with protection mechanisms under legal regimes of Trademarks and GIs. It will investigate trademark provisions under the Paris Convention and the TRIPS Agreement, whereas the use of similar signs for similar goods by competitors may lead to confusion of consumers as to the designation of origin and quality of PCs. Especially, the specific roles of collective marks and certification marks on protection of PCs in the aimed markets legal system will be considered. It will study GIs mechanisms such as indications of source which is used in Articles 1(2) and 10 of the Paris Convention and in the text of Madrid Agreement for the Repression of False or Deceptive Indications of Source on Goods (1891); and appellations of origin that is used in Article 1(2) of the Paris Convention and Article 2 of Lisbon Agreement for the Protection of Appellations of Origin and their International Registration (1958) and Articles 22 to 24 TRIPS Agreement relating to the protection of GIs to discover whether GIs may prohibit any designation or presentation that is false or misleading as to the true place of origin of the PCs. It will continue by examining Traditional Intellectual Property Rights (TIP-rights) to protect TK on PCs, based on the IP protection and normative standards and principles such as prior informed consent (PIC) which are recognized by international community.

To do such I will try to clarify seven main questions:

- Concept of protection with respect to PCs as TK manifestation,
- Protection mechanisms under existing IPRs,
- The rights claimed for protection,
- Challenges for protection under existing IPRs,
- Beneficiaries of protection,
- Protection period.

The research output will include practical recommendations on how to offer a better solution to the problem of protection of TK on PCs at the national and international levels. It is expected to be used as a model for protection of other types of TK and to help national policy-makers to promote the legal mechanisms on issues related to UC regulations to cover the TK misappropriation cases. The other important outlets for disseminating the project's results will be international negotiations, such as WIPO, WTO and CBD. And as most important audience of this study what countries like Iran shall take as effective and appropriate measures in different area of legislative, administrative or policy measures in order to make proper preservation and utilization of TK.

CHAPTER 1

Concepts of Traditional Knowledge

1 Brief Review of International Instruments regarding TK

Although TK is created, preserved and governed by local communities and indigenous peoples, it is demanded to be protected not only locally and nationally, but globally to the extent that such knowledge is employed in international economic relations and trade. The TKHs face challenges to preserve and protect their local interest in the global context, thus, they also need global solutions. Moreover, there is a wide world interest in TK as fruitful asset and protection of TK represents a common concern of the international community. Therefore, TK has been receiving high level of attention in the last three decades. Countries and TKHs worldwide have been engaged in the debates of how to find the best way to address TK issues in different international institutions. These discussions range from organization to organization and across different forums. The multi-dimensional and complex nature of TK has brought it to the attention of every concerned organization within its area of expertise and interests. Regarding IPRs, the WIPO and the WTO today are two main international institutions which deal with protection of TK on the global level.[70]

The first initiative for providing a TK protection model was taken jointly by WIPO and the United Nations Educational, Scientific and Cultural Organization (UNESCO) in 1978. The fruit of cooperation between these two organizations was the 'Model Provisions for National Law on the Protection of Expressions of Folklore Against Illicit Exploitation and Other Prejudicial Action of 1982.'[71] Since then, more attempts were initiated by the international community through international bodies dealing with human rights,

70 Christoph Beat Graber and Martin A Girsberger, 'Traditional Knowledge at the International Level: Current Approaches and Proposals for a Bigger Picture That Includes Cultural Diversity' in Jörg Schmid and Paul Richli (eds), *Recht des ländlichen Raums: Festgabe der Rechtswissenschaftlichen Fakultät der Universität Luzern für Paul Richli zum 60. Geburtstag* (Schulthess 2006) Page 267.

71 The Committee of Governmental Experts and WIPO, 'Model Provisions for National Laws on the Protection of Expressions of Folklore Against Illicit Exploitation and Other Prejudicial Actions' (UNESCO, WIPO 1983) UNESCO/WIPO/FOLK/AFR/2.

 | DOI:10.1163/9789004721364_003

environment and IPRs to protect TK and TKHs.[72] Gradually, as a result of such efforts, the international community began to establish institutions, norms and rules addressing protection of TK.

1.1 *International Agreements and Soft Law*

1.1.1 Convention Concerning Indigenous and Tribal Peoples

The Convention Concerning Indigenous and Tribal Peoples in Independent Countries, also known as International Labour Organization Convention No. 169 of 1989,[73] is a human rights instrument addressing indigenous and tribal peoples' rights over their lands and their rights to self-identification. Member States of the convention are committed to "respect the special importance for the cultures and spiritual values of the peoples concerned."[74] In this regard, states shall "promote the full realization of the social, economic and cultural rights of these peoples with respect for their social and cultural identity; their customs and traditions and their institutions."[75] They shall recognize and protect "social, cultural, religious and spiritual values and practices" of these peoples.[76] Although the convention neither defines TK nor directly calls for the protection of TK, it recognizes indigenous peoples' rights over their lands, traditions, customs and institutions. Governmental activities and measures shall be taken in a way to preserve and protect the communities, inhabitants and environment.[77]

1.1.2 Convention on Biological Diversity

Negotiations for the codification of the 1992 Convention on Biological Diversity (CBD) took place in Nairobi, Kenya, and the final draft was signed the same year on June 5th in Rio de Janeiro, Brazil. Among the goals of the Convention range appropriate access to genetic resources, appropriate transfer of related technologies, and to move toward a fair and equitable sharing of benefits obtained from the application of genetic resources.[78] The CBD calls upon its Member States to "respect, preserve and maintain knowledge, innovation and practices of indigenous and local communities."[79] It recognizes a possible

72 Surinder Kaur Verma, 'Protecting Traditional Knowledge, Is a Sui Generis System an Answer?' (2004) 7 The Journal of World Intellectual Property 765, Page 771.
73 Indigenous and Tribal Peoples Convention.
74 *ibid Article 13.*
75 *ibid Article 2(2).*
76 *ibid Article 5(a).*
77 *ibid Art 7(4).*
78 CBD Article 1.
79 *ibid Article 8(j).*

influence of IPRs on implementation of the convention and obliges the contracting parties to cooperate at national or international level to ensure that IPRs are "supportive of and do not run counter" to the convention objectives.[80] Iran ratified the Convention in 1996.

1.1.3 Bonn Guidelines

The Bonn Guidelines are voluntary guide to assist governments in developing access and benefit-sharing (ABS) policy. The first draft of the guidelines was prepared during the intergovernmental meeting on October 2001 in Bonn, Germany. The final text of the Bonn Guidelines were eventually adopted in April 2002, in the Hague during the sixth meeting of the Conference of the Parties of the CBD. The guidelines were prepared in implementing Article 15 of the CBD on 'Access to Genetic Resources.'[81] The scope of the guidelines with the exclusion of human genetic resources are "All genetic resources and associated traditional knowledge, innovations and practices covered by the Convention on Biological Diversity and benefits arising from the commercial and other utilization of such resources."[82] Regarding the ABS, among other things, it includes provisions on roles and responsibilities in ABS, the participation of stakeholders, and necessary steps in ABS procedures. With respect to the IPRs, the guidelines recommend governments to apply it in a "coherent and mutually supportive manner with the work of WIPO,"[83] take measures to encourage the disclosure of the origin of TK and innovations and practices of indigenous and local communities in applications for IPRs,[84] use of IP terms and conditions in the mutually agreed terms of the ABS,[85] and steps of national monitoring on application for IPRs.[86] Moreover, the Guidelines in its appendix I, suggest IP elements in the material transfer agreements.

1.1.4 The Nagoya Protocol

The Nagoya Protocol on Access to Genetic Resources and the Fair and Equitable Sharing of Benefits Arising from their Utilization to the Convention

---

80 *ibid Article 16(5).*

81 Secretariat of the Convention on Biological Diversity, *Bonn Guidelines on Access to Genetic Resources and Fair and Equitable Sharing of the Benefits Arising out of Their Utilization* (Secretariat of the Convention on Biological Diversity 2002).

82 Bonn Guidelines on Access to Genetic Resources and Fair and Equitable Sharing of the Benefits Arising out of their Utilization 2002 (CBD COP Dec VI/24, Item A, 6th mtg, UNEP Doc UNEP/CBD/COP/6/20 Annex) I(C).

83 *ibid I(D)(10).*

84 *ibid II(C)(16)(d)(ii).*

85 *ibid IV(D)(43)(c) & (d).*

86 *ibid V(C)(55)(c).*

on Biological Diversity was adopted in 2010 during the 10th Conference of Parties (COP) of the CBD, following up on the Bonn Guidelines. According to Article 1 of the Protocol, its objective is "the fair and equitable sharing of the benefit arising from the utilization of GRs." Besides GRs, the Protocol recognizes the importance of TK[87] and considers the term "traditional knowledge associated with genetic resources" in several different Articles.[88] The principal activities of the protocol include inter alia access to TK and sharing of benefits arising from the utilization of such knowledge.[89]

1.1.5 United Nations Convention to Combat Desertification

'The United Nations Convention to Combat Desertification in Those Countries Experiencing Serious Drought and/or Desertification, Particularly in Africa (UNCCD)'[90] is a Convention aiming to combat desertification and mitigate the effects of drought. It was adopted on 17 June 1994 in France (Paris) following the recommendations of the Rio Agenda 21. It requests its Member States to grant protection of "traditional and local technology, knowledge, know-how and practices,"[91] Moreover, the convention parties shall undertake policies and legislation to facilitate access to technologies taking into account the need to protect IPRS.[92] They shall also take appropriate measures "conducive to development, transfer, acquisition and adaptation of suitable technology, knowledge, know-how and practices, including measures to ensure adequate and effective protection of intellectual property rights."[93] Iran joined the convention in 1996.

1.1.6 International Treaty on Plant Genetic Resources for Food and Agriculture

The International Treaty on Plant Genetic Resources for Food and Agriculture (ITPGRFA)[94] was signed in 2001. It was negotiated in harmony with the CBD objectives[95] and adopted by the Conference of the Food and Agricultural

87 Nagoya Protocol Preamble Paragraph 21.

88 *ibid Preamble Paragraphs* 12bis, *20, 22, 23, 24; and Articles 3(1), 4(4),* 5bis, 7bis, *9, 10(b),* $12^{bis}(1)$, *14, 17, 18(5)(J).*

89 *ibid Article 3.*

90 United Nations Convention to Combat Desertification in those Countries Experiencing Serious Drought and/or Desertification, Particularly in Africa (UNCCD) 1994 (1954 UNTS 3 (entered into force 26 December 1996)).

91 *ibid Article 18(2).*

92 *ibid Article 18(1)(b).*

93 *ibid Article 18(1)(e).*

94 International Treaty on Plant Genetic Resources for Food and Agriculture (ITPGRFA) 2001 (2400 UNTS 303 (entered into force 29 June 2004)).

95 *ibid Article 1.*

Organization (FAO). The objective of the treaty is the protection of sustainable use and dissemination of PGRs while securing fair and equitable benefit sharing from use of them.[96] The contracting parties of the treaty are committed to take measures for "protection of traditional knowledge relevant to plant genetic resources for food and agriculture."[97] ITPGRFA Contracting Parties agree on their responsibilities to take measures to protect and promote farmers' rights including protection of TK relevant to PGRs for food and agriculture.[98] Farmers' rights are based on recognition of TKHs and farmers' contributions for the conservation and development of PGRs.

1.1.7 United Nations Declaration on the Rights of Indigenous Peoples

Declaration on the Rights of Indigenous Peoples[99] is a resolution of the United Nations General Assembly which declares that:

> Indigenous peoples are entitled to the recognition of the full ownership, control, and protection of their cultural and intellectual property. They have the right to special measures to control, develop and protect their sciences, technologies and cultural manifestations, including human and other genetic resources, seeds, medicines, knowledge of the properties of fauna and flora, oral traditions, literatures, designs and visual and performing arts.[100]

In this regard, "States shall take effective measures to recognize and protect" indigenous peoples' rights over their TK.[101] States are required to protect the integrity, cultural values and ethnic identities of indigenous peoples as distinct peoples.[102]

1.1.8 Intangible Cultural Heritage Convention

The Convention for the Safeguarding of the Intangible Cultural Heritage (also known as Intangible Cultural Heritage Convention) was signed during the 32nd session of the general conference of the UNESCO which was held in Paris, from 29 September to 17 October 2003. In accordance with the convention, "the practices, representations, expressions, knowledge, skills – as well as the

96 *ibid.*
97 *ibid Article 9(2)(a).*
98 *ibid Article 9(2).*
99 'United Nations Declaration on the Rights of Indigenous Peoples' (n 48).
100 *ibid Article 31(1).*
101 *ibid Article 31(2).*
102 *ibid Article 8(2)(a).*

instruments, objects, artefacts and cultural spaces associated therewith" are recognized as the 'Intangible Cultural Heritage' of communities and in some cases of individuals.[103] These people, in reaction to the environment, nature and history recreate their heritage continuously and transmit it from one generation to the next generation; and it forms a part of their identity and continuity. The manifestations of the 'intangible cultural heritage' are – among others – "knowledge and practices concerning nature and universe."[104]

1.1.9 The TRIPS Agreement

The TRIPS has been seen to amount to the strongest binding instrument ever adopted in order to protect IPRS globally due to its integration in the WTO and its powerful enforcement mechanism. TRIPS by incorporating 'Berne Convention for the Protection of Literary and Artistic Works' (Berne Convention)[105] and Paris Convention, has become a comprehensive agreement on IPRS regimes including copyrights and related rights, trademarks, GIS, industrial designs, patents, layout-designs (topographies) of integrated circuits as well as the protection against UC and the procedural norms which have been an obligatory part of commercial law and trade multilateral system. It binds Member States to harmonizing IPRS in terms of minimal standards and simultaneously to subject it to WTO dispute settlement.[106] TK was never a subject matter of negotiations during the Uruguay Round. The topic came up in the Committee on Trade and Environment as of June 1995.[107] Since then, interest in involvement of TK in the WTO debates increased. It was assumed that TKHS may use the TRIPS Agreement as a coherent platform to achieve a worldwide protection capability.

Given the strong connotation of TK to human rights values, as expressed in the Declaration on Indigenous Rights above, and the absence of TRIPS to refer to human rights values, the question arises as to how TRIPS could be linked to TK and such values.

---

103 Convention for the Safeguarding of the Intangible Cultural Heritage 2003 (2368 UNTS 3 (entered into force 20 April 2006)) Article 2(1).

104 *ibid Article* 2(2).

105 Berne Convention for the Protection of Literary and Artistic Works, as revised at Paris 1971 (1161 UNTS 3 (entered into force 15 December 1972)).

106 Thomas Cottier, Matthias Oesch and Thomas M Fischer, *International Trade Regulation: Law and Policy in the WTO, the European Union and Switzerland: Cases, Materials and Comments* (Staempfli Publishers 2005) Page 916.

107 Graham Dutfield, 'TRIPS-Related Aspects of Traditional Knowledge' (2001) 33 Case Western Reserve Journal of International Law 233, Pages 269–271.

In response to this, Cottier and Germann argue that IPRS, despite their utilitarian foundations, also include human rights values in some areas such as copyrights which are highly important to the protection of individual rights. Furthermore, IPRS need to take into consideration human rights in the process of shaping the scope of rights. Finally, the development and extension of IPRS to the protection of issues such as TK in WIPO or other international organization such as FAO and World Health Organization (WHO), each dealing with different perspectives of IPRS in their respective functions, could also allow linking TK to the WTO negotiations.[108]

TK has not been referred to as an IP category among those subjects of Sections 1 through 7 of Part II of the existing TRIPS Agreement. However, it should be noted that for progressive elaboration of IPRS globally TK may be dealt with and even enhanced as an IP subject matter to meet the trade aspects of the TRIPS Agreement rules, including marketing and licensing.[109] The Doha Ministerial Declaration at paragraph 19 introduces the subject and requires the TRIPS Council in pursuing its work program to review Article 27.3(b) and Article 71.1 to examine, inter alia, the relationship between the TRIPS Agreement and the protection of TK and folklore:

> We instruct the Council for TRIPS, in pursuing its work programme including under the review of Article 27.3(b), the review of the implementation of the TRIPS Agreement under Article 71.1 and the work foreseen pursuant to paragraph 12 of this Declaration, to examine, inter alia, the relationship between the TRIPS Agreement and the Convention on Biological Diversity, the protection of traditional knowledge and folklore, and other relevant new developments raised by Members pursuant to Article 71.1. In undertaking this work, the TRIPS Council shall be guided by the objectives and principles set out in Articles 7 and 8 of the TRIPS Agreement and shall take fully into account the development dimension.[110]

108 Thomas Cottier and Christophe Germann, 'Agreement on Trade-Related Aspects of Intellectual Property Rights: The TRIPS Agreement Is Annex 1C of the Marrakesh Agreement Establishing the World Trade Organization, Signed in Marrakesh, Morocco on 15 April 1994.' in Thomas Cottier and Pierre Véron (eds), *Concise International and European IP Law: TRIPS, Paris Convention, European Enforcement and Transfer of Technology*, vol 4 (2nd edn, Kluwer Law International 2008) Pages 7 and 9.

109 *ibid Pages 9 and 34.*

110 WTO, 'Doha Ministerial Declaration' WTO Doc WTO Doha Ministerial Conference, 4th sess, WTO Doc WT/MIN(01)/DEC/1 (20 November 2001 Adopted on 14 November 2001) Article 19.

Most of the developing countries are sceptical about the benefits of TRIPS for their development policy[111] and NGOs believe that implementation of the substantial rules of TRIPS will have a negative impact on the daily life of their people.[112] Notwithstanding this negative opinion, it seems that all possible avenues to achieve the protection of TK goals and objectives need to be considered. One might argue that if there would not be a worldwide system such as TRIPS as a tool for harmonization IPRS standards among countries, how world trade would develop in the face of fragmentation in implementing IPRS.

It should be mentioned that main competitors in the global markets of hand-woven carpets are Iran, China, India, Pakistan, Türkiye, Afghanistan and Nepal.[113] Except for Iran, these countries are Member States of the World Trade Organization (WTO). Iran's Working Party was established on 26 May 2005. The Working Party has not yet met.[114] Accession negotiations will give the advantage to those states to exploit WTO and TRIPS mechanism for exporting and marketing carpets and to eventually address these issues in WTO dispute settlement.

1.1.10 World Intellectual Property Organization

In its 26th session from September 25 to October 3, 2000, the WIPO General Assembly decided to establish an intergovernmental committee on intellectual property and genetic resources, traditional knowledge and folklore (IGC).[115] The IGC serves as a forum for discussing and debating IPRS issues regarding:

(i) access to genetic resources and benefit sharing;
(ii) protection of traditional knowledge, whether or not associated with those resources; and
(iii) the protection of expressions of folklore.[116]

Trying to involve all stakeholders, the IGC is composed of WIPO Member States and representatives of indigenous and local communities, international

111 Carlos M Correa, *Intellectual Property Rights, the WTO and Developing Countries: The TRIPS Agreement and Policy Options* (Zed Books; Third World Network 2000).

112 Khor (n 35) Page 10.

113 See: Fatemeh Rostami, 'بررسی رقبای بین المللی برای صادرات فرش دست باف (A Study on International Competitors in the Export of Persian Hand-Woven Carpets)' (Science and Art University of Ardakan 2015).

114 'Members and Observers' (*World Trade Organization*, 1 April 2024) <https://www.wto.org/english/thewto_e/acc_e/a1_iran_e.htm>.

115 Dutfield, 'TRIPS-Related Aspects of Traditional Knowledge' (n 107) Pages 266–269.

116 WIPO Secretariat, 'Matters Concerning Intellectual Property and Genetic Resources, Traditional Knowledge and Folklore' (2000) WIPO GA Dec WO/GA/26/6 Page 4.

organizations, non-governmental organizations and research and education institutions.[117]

The IGC has carried out different tasks to address all concerns and opinions of delegations raised, such as the examination of IP protection regarding TK documentation, TK databases and IPRS terms in the bilateral accession agreements. Moreover, debates continued as other subject matters have remained unsolved. All delegations and observers repeatedly reached a consensus that the committee's work should be extended to push ahead the IGC mandate for another two years. In consequence, in October 2003, WIPO General Assembly agreed to renew the mandate of the IGC and authorized "the possible development of an international instrument or instruments" for an additional two years. While developing countries had been emphasizing and pushing for an international treaty for protection of TK, Traditional Cultural Expressions (TCES) and GRS within WIPO system, Industrialized countries showed their desire for a more gradual approach to IGC work.[118] Therefore, due to lack of agreement on nature and procedure of protection among IGC participants, the General Assembly decided to renew its mandate several times. So far, the IGC has held meetings for more than two decades at WIPO's headquarters in Geneva. The goal of the IGC negotiations over the past two decades has been to develop international IP legal instruments on GRS, TK, and TCES. These efforts aim to narrow existing gaps and reach a consensus on core issues including: definitions, subject matter of protection, objectives and beneficiaries of protection, scope of rights and public domain.[119]

Under the 2022–2023 biennial mandate approved by the WIPO General Assembly in 2021,[120] the IGC convened in June 2022. The meeting resulted in

117 Ulia Popova-Gosart, *Traditional Knowledge & Indigenous Peoples* (World Intellectual Property Organization 2009) Page 105.

118 Antonella Ingrassia, Daniele Manzella and Elzbieta Martyniuk, *The Legal Framework for the Management of Animal Genetic Resources* (Food and Agriculture Organization of the United Nations 2005) Pages 30–31.

119 WIPO Secretariat, 'Report of the Assemblies of the Member States of WIPO' (2017) WIPO GA Doc A/57/11 ADD.6.

120 The WIPO General Assembly, at its Fifty-Fourth (25th Ordinary) Session in October 2021, agreed on the mandate for the IGC for the 2022/2023 biennium, to expedite its work, building on existing work carried out by the Committee, to narrow existing gaps and reach common understanding on core issues, with the objective of finalizing an agreement on an international legal instrument(s) which will ensure the balanced and effective protection of GRS, TK and TCES. See: WIPO Secretariat, 'Report on the Intergovernmental Committee on Intellectual Property and Genetic Resources, Traditional Knowledge and Folklore (IGC)' (World Intellectual Property Organization 2021) WIPO GA Doc WO/GA/54/10.

a committee report that detailed the outcomes of its 42nd and 43rd sessions held earlier that year and offered recommendations to the General Assembly. Notably, the report discussed the 'Draft International Legal Instrument Relating to Intellectual Property, Genetic Resources and Traditional Knowledge Associated with Genetic Resources,' known informally as the Chair's Text, prepared by Mr. Ian Goss (former Chair of the IGC).[121] Both sessions made considerable progress and achieved significant convergence around the Chair's text as a "focused, effective, and balanced basis for further engagement." Contrary to the expectations that the General Assembly would merely review the report and renew the IGC's mandate, the Assembly, acting on a proposal from the African Group, decided to convene a diplomatic conference on GRs and associated TK in 2024.[122] This decision was notably taken by vote rather than consensus, diverging from the usual procedures of the Assembly. In preparation for the diplomatic conference, a Preparatory Committee met from September 11 to 13, 2023, in Geneva to establish the conference's modalities, including the agenda, timeline, and procedural rules. Additionally, an initial proposal for the treaty's administrative and final provisions was drafted. Prior to this, a special session of the IGC convened from September 4 to 8, aiming to bridge any significant gaps in preparation for the conference.[123]

The Diplomatic Conference on the Proposed Treaty on Intellectual Property, Genetic Resources, and Associated Traditional Knowledge was held in May 2024 at WIPO's Geneva Headquarters. The central proposition mandated that patent applications concerning inventions derived from GRs and associated TK must incorporate detailed information regarding the source or origin of these elements. Currently, such disclosure is not typically required within patent applications, as it does not generally pertain to the assessment of an invention's patentability. Certain GRs are linked to TK by virtue of their utilization and preservation by TKHs across generations.[124] This TK occasionally aids in scientific research, potentially leading to the creation of protected inventions. Additionally, outside the domain of IPRs, these GRs and the TK associated with

121 See: Chair of the IGC Mr Ian Goss, 'Chair's Text of a Draft International Legal Instrument Relating to Intellectual Property, Genetic Resources and Traditional Knowledge Associated with Genetic Resources' (2022) WIPO Doc WIPO/GRTKF/IC/43/5.

122 WIPO Secretariat, 'Proposal to Advance WIPO Normative Agenda on the Subjects of Genetic Resources Associated with Traditional Knowledge, and the Design Law Treaty' (World Intellectual Property Organization 2022) WIPO GA Doc WO/GA/55/11 Annex.

123 WIPO Secretariat, 'Summary Report of Assemblies of the Member States of WIPO' (2022) WIPO GA Doc A/63/9 Page 6, Note 27.

124 Chair of the IGC Mr Ian Goss (n 121).

them are governed by ABS agreements, as delineated in the CBD, the Nagoya Protocol, and other pertinent international accords.[125]

On 24 May 2024, WIPO member states adopted a historic new treaty, expected to primarily address the issue of biopiracy, marking only a modest advance in the broader efforts to combat the misappropriation of TK. This outcome will likely close a chapter on one aspect of TK misappropriation, yet it leaves unanswered a central question explored in this book: whether PCs are protectable under trademark and GIs regimes. This unresolved issue remains crucial for the comprehensive protection and recognition of TCEs.

1.2 *Regional Agreements*

The dispersion of TK does not necessarily follow the geopolitical borders of countries or countries' internal geographical divisions. As the geopolitical borders often do not match the cultural borders, there are many local communities divided between different countries but united in culture identities and share the same TK. In fact, TKHs with the same identity have been separated by today borders of neighbouring countries through the ages; but, they share the same values and rights over TK among themselves in transnational communities. Those countries must address the coherent policies and legal measures for protecting the TKHs' rights in cooperation not only with their neighbour states but the traditional peoples as well. An important role of regional organizations and their competent national authorities would be to cooperate and make a common recognized system for protection of shared TK among their local communities. The importance of the regional cooperation has been reflected in the IGC negotiations and documents in accordance with them if the same TK is common and shared among several states, they are called to cooperate for protection of that TK.[126] Two examples of such regional cooperation are reflected in Swakopmund Protocol, and The Economic Cooperation Organization Trade Agreement (ECOTA).

1.2.1 Swakopmund Protocol

On August 9th, 2010, during its diplomatic conference in Namibia, (Swakopmund), the African Regional Intellectual Property Organization (ARIPO)[127]

125 Wend Wendland, 'Is an International Agreement on IP, Genetic Resources and Associated Traditional Knowledge Finally in Sight?' [2023] *WIPO Magazine.*

126 See: IGC-GRTKF Secretariat, 'The Protection of Traditional Knowledge: Draft Articles Rev. 2' (n 12) Article 12.

127 The ARIPO was established in 1976 under Lusaka Agreement. Members of the African Union (AU) or members of the United Nations Economic Commission for Africa (ECA) can be member of the ARIPO. At present, 19 states are members of the Lusaka Agreement and therefore members of ARIPO. These states are Botswana, The Gambia, Ghana, Kenya,

adopted the text of "Swakopmund Protocol on the Protection of Traditional Knowledge and Expressions of Folklore."[128] The Swakopmund Protocol distinguishes between TK and TCEs as subject matters of protection in parts II and III, and addresses directly several issues regarding TK. It includes: protection criteria, formalities, beneficiaries, rights of TKHs, exceptions and limitations, compulsory licenses, duration of protection, administration and enforcement and access to TK.[129]

1.2.2 ECOTA

Iran is a diverse society with different cultural and ethnic groups such as Azerbaijanis, Arabs, Kurds and Balochs with many other minorities.[130] These groups share the identical knowledge and cultures within themselves and some neighbour countries. For example, Azerbaijanis live in the North-West region of Iran in provinces named West Azerbaijan, East Azerbaijan and Ardabil which are in borders with Republic of Azerbaijan.[131] The Iranian Balochs inhabit in Iranian Sistan and Balochistan province in border with Pakistani' Balochistan. Therefore, the Iran Government attached great importance to conclude the regional arrangements with its neighbours. ECOTA is a regional agreement for promotion in regional cooperation, support for the accession of Economic Cooperation Organization members to the WTO, harmonization of economic policies, and more engagement with economic development. The general principles governing this agreement are national treatment, equitable access of the contracting parties to the benefits of the agreement, and exchange in multilateral concessions.[132] The goals of the agreement are the promotion,

---

Lesotho, Malawi, Mozambique, Namibia, Sierra Leone, Liberia, Rwanda, São Tomé and Príncipe, Somalia, Sudan, Swaziland, Tanzania, Uganda, Zambia and Zimbabwe. For more information. See: ARIPO, 'About Us | ARIPO' (*IP ARIPO*, 2017) <https://www.aripo.org/member-states>.

128 Swakopmund Protocol.

129 *ibid Sections 4–15.*

130 Laura Etheredge, *Iran* (Britannica Educational Pub in association with Rosen Educational Services 2011) Page 14.

131 'Admission of the Republic of Azerbaijan to Membership in the United Nations' (1992) Res 742, UN SCOR, 3052nd mtg, SC Res S/RES/742(1992); "Historically, the geographical entity known as Azerbaijan covered a much larger area than the present-day Iranian provinces of the same name, extending to the north and to the west across the boundaries of several contemporary nation states." See: John Henry Lorentz, *Historical Dictionary of Iran* (Scarecrow Press 2007) Page 41.

132 The agreement was signed by Economic Cooperation Organization (ECO) members in Islamabad, Pakistan and subsequently ratified by five countries: Afghanistan, Iran, Pakistan, Tajikistan, and Türkiye. See: Economic Cooperation Organization Trade Agreement (ECOTA) 2003 (entered into force 24 April 2008) Preamble and Articles 2(1),(2) and (3).

support, and advancement of regional trade based on shared principles, and solidification of economic cooperation between Member States, accordingly:

a. to promote through the expansion of trade the harmonious development of the economic relations among the Contracting Parties;
b. to provide fair conditions of competition for trade among the Contracting Parties;
c. to contribute in this way to intra-regional trade, to the smooth flow of commodities and the expansion of world trade; and
d. to increase substantially trade-related investment opportunities in the territories of the Contracting Parties.[133]

The agreement includes commitment of members to protect IPRS. Members shall grant and enforce protection of copyrights, comprising computer programs and databases, neighbouring rights, archaeological heritage, trademarks, GIS, industrial designs, patents, plant varieties as well as traditional knowledge, undisclosed information and know-how on a non-discriminatory basis. Besides, they shall hold expert consultations on IPRS and in particular on activities relating to the harmonization, administration and enforcement of international conventions and on activities in international organizations. Concerning cooperation related to WTO, members "shall extend to any other Contracting Party, not a member state of WTO, a treatment no less favorable than that extended to the WTO member states in relation to protection of IPRS falling within the scope of the Agreement." As a general exception, agreement shall not preclude the prohibitions or restrictions on, inter alia, the protection of IPRS if such measures are made effective in conjunction with restrictions on domestic production or consumption.[134] Although, this regional agreement provides a good ground for regional cooperation on protection of TK, yet not a single measure has been taken by member states to utilize such protection mechanism. It offers a suitable platform to take up, and integrate, the protection of TK, in particular, in relation to PCS.

1.3 *Bilateral Agreements*

TK is going to be a very important subject matter between trade partners. For instance, Colombia and Peru have been known very pursuant actors in international negotiations for the establishment of legal frameworks to protect TK. In the 'understanding regarding biodiversity and traditional knowledge' both Colombia and Peru attached a letter to their Free Trade Agreements (FTAS) with the USA and highlighted the TK contribution to their cultural, social

133 *ibid Article 2(4).*
134 See: *ibid Articles 4(3), 15(A)(1), 19(1), (2) and (4).*

and economic developments. Also, they recognized that access and benefit sharing of TK "can be adequately addressed through contracts that reflect mutually agreed terms between users and providers."[135] This approach is fostering the position of TK in bilateral trade agreements as countries following the principle of 'most favoured nations' try to achieve the same advantage in respective agreements. A very good example of such an approach is reflected in the understanding letter of the 'United States – Panama Trade Promotion Agreement.' In the course of IPRs negotiations under Chapter Fifteen, the two countries reached a promise that they recognize the importance of TK and Folklore for their people. They also agreed that if the USA and a third country sign an FTA that contains provisions addressing TK or folklore, "the United States and Panama shall promptly consult after that agreement enters into force on whether to apply similar provisions, as appropriate, between the United States and Panama."[136] These bilateral agreements have not prevented Colombia, Peru and Panama from demanding a multilateral solution for the protection of TK in the context of ongoing negotiations in the other international arrangements like WIPO IGC or WTO Doha Round.

Iran has concluded about 18 bilateral agreements on IPRs, Amity, Trade, Customs, Economic and Industrial Cooperation, Cultural and Artistic Affairs, Scientific and Technological Cooperation which directly or indirectly refer to protection of IPRs between parties.[137] Also, by the end of 2019, Iran concluded 68 Bilateral Investment Treaties (52 of them in force) with other countries in which IPRs including copyrights, patent, utility models, industrial designs, trademarks, service marks, trade names, and know-how are counted as investors' protectable property in the territory of other parties.[138] Unfortunately, none of these agreements consider TK as a subject matter of the IPRs regimes protection. Therefore, Iran and its contracting parties only may rely on the existing IPRs for protection of TK which will depend on common interpretation of both parties on applicability of those regimes to the protection of TK.

135 The United States – Colombia Trade Promotion Agreement 2006 (entered into force 15 May 2012); and The United States – Peru Trade Promotion Agreement 2006 (entered into force 14 December 2007).

136 The United States – Panama Trade Promotion Agreement 2007 (entered into force 31 October 2012).

137 These agreements are concluded with Algeria, Armenia, Cuba, Georgia, Germany, Italy, Japan, Lebanon, Macedonia, Nigeria, Poland, Qatar, Russia, Spain, Sweden, Syria, USA and Venezuela and an agreement with International Atomic Energy Agency (IAEA).

138 'Islamic Republic of Iran – Bilateral Investment Treaties (BITs)' (*UNCTAD Investment Policy Hub*, 25 October 2016) <http://investmentpolicyhub.unctad.org/IIA/CountryBits/98#iiaInnerMenu>.

2 What Is Traditional Knowledge?

2.1 *Definition of Traditional Knowledge*

Despite an increasing recognition of the importance of TK, the international community has not been able to reach an agreement on the necessity of establishing a definition, nor on how to define TK in a manner that covers all aspects of their needs, expectations, and concerns. In brief, discussions on TK begin with consideration of TK definition at the first stage, and the scope and concept of TK subject matters at the second stage. Therefore, further discussion is needed on the purpose of a definition for TK.[139]

During the international debates on TK issues, two main approaches to a definition of TK exist. Considering the fact that it is difficult to find a clear definition of TK,[140] and because of TK manifestations of diverse characteristics, conceptual discussions on TK may be useful helping to achieve solid results, but no firm conclusion on concepts and definitions should be established, as a condition for the beginning of discussions on the legal framework under the first approach.[141] In contrast, the second attitude argues with precise definition, distinguishes different subjects and seeks to clarify the concept. Each of these theoretical positions makes a significant contribution to our understanding of TK and need to be analyzed.

Achieving an exhaustive and comprehensive definition of IPRs has never been the main concern of the international IP conventions or agreements. Instead, they have sought to establish minimum standards, harmonization of specific rights of IP regimes and guarantees of national treatment of reciprocal rights, giving more flexibility to national legal systems for determinations of the boundaries of protectable subject matters.[142]

The lack of a precise definition of TK and its subject matters is not a barrier to effective protection and enforcement of the rights of TKHs. Historically, terms

139 See European Community statement: IGC-GRTKF Secretariat, 'Report of Intergovernmental Committee on Intellectual Property and Genetic Resources, Traditional Knowledge and Folklore' (n 61) Page 7.

140 Thomas Cottier and Andrea Nascimento Müller, 'The Case for Protecting Geographical Indications and Traditional Knowledge in Agricultural Trade' Page 440; in Thomas Cottier, *Trade and Intellectual Property Protection in WTO Law: Collected Essays* (Cameron May 2005).

141 See statement of Brazil delegation: IGC-GRTKF Secretariat, 'Report of Intergovernmental Committee on Intellectual Property and Genetic Resources, Traditional Knowledge and Folklore' (n 61) Page 17, Paragraph 27.

142 IGC-GRTKF Secretariat, 'Traditional Knowledge – Operational Terms and Definitions' (World Intellectual Property Organization 2002) WIPO Doc WIPO/GRTKF/IC/3/9 Page 2.

such as 'trademarks' or 'unfair competition' have not been defined in the Paris Convention and the convention only refers to 'industrial property' as a broad term. Generally speaking, any and each international IP regime approach has been to create coordination and harmonization among its members on the basis of minimal standards and to compel them to establish effective legal protection in their jurisdictions and grant exclusive rights to applicants independently from the other members' jurisdiction. Even on the national level, offering and use of precise definitions is not a concern as long as the national law is capable of granting IPRs within an identical legal scope.[143] Moreover, TK is notably diverse and dynamic and no single definition could cover all of its features and "it would be difficult to obtain a specific and complete definition of TK."[144] "However, such a singular definition may not be necessary in order to delimit the scope of subject matter for which protection is sought."[145]

On the other hand, proponents of having a precise definition argue that definitions help countries clarify their proposition on the same topic. They assert that without clear definitions of the subject-matter at hand, it seems impossible to reach a shared understanding on a particular idea. They refer to the WIPO experience of promoting a working definition of TK which proved to be helpful for facilitating the discussions.[146] In the same spirit, "the EU Delegation welcomed the opportunity to constructively participate in discussions on the purpose of a definition of the term *traditional knowledge*."[147]

Before investigating both views, there is a need to understand what we expect from a definition. Kelley in his book 'The Art of Reasoning' points out that definition is "a statement that gives the meaning of a concept"[148] and explains "concepts serve as mental file folders we use to organize our knowledge about classes of similar things. Definitions tell us what is in the folder."[149] It can be seen from Kelly's opinion that no definition of TK can meet those

143 *ibid Page 3.*

144 IGC-GRTKF Secretariat, 'Report of Intergovernmental Committee on Intellectual Property and Genetic Resources, Traditional Knowledge and Folklore' (World Intellectual Property Organization 2002) WIPO Doc WIPO/GRTKF/IC/3/17 Page 71.

145 Government of Switzerland, 'Draft Guidelines on Access and Benefit Sharing Regarding the Utilisation of Genetic Resource' (World Intellectual Property Organization 2001) WIPO Doc WIPO/GRTKF/IC/1/9 Page 22.

146 UNEP-CBD, 'Report of the Meeting of the Group of Technical and Legal Experts on Traditional Knowledge Associated with Genetic Resources in the Context of the International Regime on Access and Benefit-Sharing' (n 56) Page 10.

147 IGC-GRTKF Secretariat, 'Report of Intergovernmental Committee on Intellectual Property and Genetic Resources, Traditional Knowledge and Folklore' (n 61) Page 7.

148 David Kelley, *The Art of Reasoning* (Norton 1988) Page 32.

149 *ibid.*

expectations. Because even if we assume that a definition can serve a meaning for TK to organize our knowledge about it; as it was accepted widely by different scholar, TK has dynamic nature and therefore neither can it construct classes of similar things nor it can tell us what is contained within it.

Another significant aspect is the relation between the definition of TK and the legal protection of TK. To provide such a link, a set of concepts needs to be considered in which TK could be characterized as eligible object for the enjoyment of legal protection. While characterizing of TK might be possible, this would lead us to a *vicious circle*[150] between the definition and characterization of TK. And finally, the protection of TK is not constrained by consensus on a definition.

As it was explained before, at present, there is no globally accepted definition of TK or a comprehensive consensus on the notion and scope of the term, which may influence the legal impact on protection. Instead, the main approaches have to discuss the merits and subject matters of protection which is more important than seeking a definition of TK.

2.2 *The Subject Matter of Traditional Knowledge*

The term 'Traditional Knowledge' is composed of two words: 'knowledge' and 'tradition.' As the Japan delegation raised the question when discussing IPRS, it is important to clarify what 'traditional' and 'knowledge' mean, as well as what should be protected?[151] Regarding etymology, the origin of the word 'knowledge' comes from Middle English, derived irregularly from the word 'known' and it means among others "the fact or condition of knowing something with familiarity gained through experience or association, acquaintance with or understanding of a science, art, or technique."[152] In accordance with the American Heritage Dictionary 'Knowledge' is defined as, "The state or fact of knowing; familiarity, awareness, or understanding gained through

150 Vicious Circle is defined as: "a situation in which an attempt to resolve one problem creates new problems that lead back to the original situation. It is also a fallacy in reasoning in which the premise is used to prove the conclusion, and the conclusion used to prove the premise. For example, A depends on B and B depends on A. The conclusion is that A depends on A. It is the circularity in argument or proof." See: 'Vicious Circle' (*Islamic Quest Net*, 16 March 2013) <http://www.islamquest.net/en/archive/keyword/vicious%20 circle> accessed 17 March 2014.

151 See the statement of the Japan Delegation: IGC-GRTKF Secretariat, 'Revised Draft Report of Intergovernmental Committee on Intellectual Property and Genetic Resources, Traditional Knowledge and Folklore' (World Intellectual Property Organization 2008) WIPO Doc WIPO/GRTKF/IC/11/15 Prov 2. Paragraph 296.

152 Encyclopaedia Britannica, 'Knowledge,' *Britannica Online Encyclopaedia* (2014) <http://www.britannica.com/bps/dictionary?query=knowledge> accessed 23 January 2014.

experience or study; the sum or range of what has been perceived, discovered, or learned ..."[153] This definition refers to two main elements of knowledge consisting of 'what is known' and 'what has been acquired through study or experiences.'[154] The term 'knowledge' as described above is a general term which covers a wide range of issues, while in this study only the knowledge with a tradition character is regarded. In other words, knowledge has to be 'traditional' to be considered in the discussion of TK.

The term 'tradition' refers to "past customs and usages that influence or govern present acts or practices."[155] In the context of TK, 'traditional' means that "the TK is developed according to the rules, protocols and customs of a certain community, and not that it is old."[156] Also, 'traditional context' refers to the way of using TK in the proper artistic framework based on continuous usage by the community.[157] According to Pires de Carvalho, the adjective 'traditional' qualifies the method of creating TK and not the knowledge itself.[158] Given the mentioned concept of the term 'tradition,' TK is traditional as it is the result of customs and traditions of a specific community. Thereupon, 'traditional' refers neither to the nature of knowledge nor to the time or duration of creation of knowledge.

While this is correct that traditional is not an adjective concerning the nature of knowledge but relates to the way knowledge has been created, Munzer and Raustiala point out that TK passes from one generation to the next generation and evolves over ages.[159] Equally, Cobo when describing indigenous communities and people, notes the 'historical continuity' of these societies:

> [t]hose which, having historical continuity with pre-invasion and precolonial societies that developed on their territories, consider themselves distinct from other sectors of the society now prevailing in those territories or parts of them.[160]

---

153 Houghton Mifflin Company (n 7).

154 *ibid.*

155 Garner (n 19).

156 IGC-GRTKF Secretariat, 'Elements of a Sui Generis System for the Protection of Traditional Knowledge' (World Intellectual Property Organization 2002) WIPO Doc WIPO/GRTKF/IC/4/8 Page 11.

157 The Committee of Governmental Experts and WIPO (n 71) Part III (42).

158 Nuno Pires de Carvalho, 'From the Shaman's Hut to the Patent Office: A Road Under Construction' in Charles R McManis (ed), *Biodiversity and the Law: Intellectual Property, Biotechnology and Traditional Knowledge* (Earthscan 2007) Page 244.

159 Munzer and Raustiala (n 5) Page 58.

160 See Dr Martinez Cobo quoted in: Michael Blakeney, 'What Is Traditional Knowledge? Why Should It Be Protected? Who Should Protect It? For Whom? Understanding the Value

Therefore, it is generally conceded that the factor of time cannot be entirely denied in describing TK. After all, in the context of PCs, both the manner of creation and the historical background can be identified.

Beyond the traditional description of knowledge, another important aspect of TK is to identify the criteria of protectable subject matter. In this regard, two main views are considered: TK as *stricto sensu* and TK as *lato sensu.*

2.2.1 Traditional Knowledge Subject Matter in Narrow Sense (TK *stricto sensu*)

TK in the narrow sense is attributed to knowledge as such. In particular, it refers to "the knowledge resulting from intellectual activity in a traditional context, and includes know-how, practices, skills, and innovations."[161] This approach to TK is evident in the United Nations Convention to Combat Desertification which mentions "relevant traditional and local technology, knowledge, know-how and practices."[162] In the same way, the CBD refers to "knowledge, innovations and practices."[163] In the IGC's work TK *stricto sensu* is used to refer to knowledge itself:

> content or substance of knowledge resulting from intellectual activity in a traditional context, [including] the know-how, skills, innovations, practices and learning that form part of traditional knowledge systems, and knowledge embodying traditional lifestyles of indigenous and local communities, or contained in codified knowledge systems passed between generations.[164]

In like manner, the Swakopmund Protocol defines TK in the narrow sense as:

> [a]ny knowledge originating from a local or traditional community that is the result of intellectual activity and insight in a traditional context,

---

Chain' (World Intellectual Property Organization 1999) WIPO Doc, WIPO/IPTK/RT/99/3 Pages 3–4.

161 IGC-GRTKF Secretariat, 'Glossary of Key Terms Related to Intellectual Property and Genetic Resources, Traditional Knowledge and Traditional Cultural Expressions' (World Intellectual Property Organization 2014) WIPO Doc WIPO/GRTKF/IC/28/INF/7 Annex Page 40.

162 UNCCD Article 18(2).

163 CBD 8(j).

164 IGC-GRTKF Secretariat, 'Revised Provisions for the Protection of Traditional Knowledge: Policy Objectives and Core Principles' (World Intellectual Property Organization 2010) WIPO Doc WIPO/GRTKF/IC/17/5 Annex Page 32.

> including know-how, skills, innovations, practices and learning, where the knowledge is embodied in the traditional lifestyle of a community, or contained in the codified knowledge systems passed on from one generation to another. The term shall not be limited to a specific technical field, and may include agricultural, environmental or medical knowledge, and knowledge associated with genetic resources.[165]

The term TK is not limited to a specific field, and may include agricultural, scientific, technical, ecological, medicinal, biodiversity-related and other technical knowledge.[166] In the same way, Githaiga separates TK and folklore as aspects of heritage and refers to knowledge as "all kinds of scientific, agricultural, technical and ecological knowledge, including cultigens, medicines and the rational use of flora and fauna."[167]

2.2.2 Traditional Knowledge Subject Matter in Broader Sense (TK as *lato sensu*)

Opposing the approach for defining the subject matter of TK in a narrow sense, TK in *lato sensu* – or in a broad portrayal – includes the content of knowledge, associated genetic resources and traditional expressions of the knowledge. Since TK is strictly interrelated with TCEs and GRs, in a way, it cannot be considered without addressing corresponding aspects of the two others.[168]

> Traditional Knowledge as a broad description of subject matter, generally includes the intellectual and intangible cultural heritage, practices and knowledge systems of traditional communities, including indigenous and local communities (traditional knowledge in a general sense or lato sensu). In other words, traditional knowledge in a general sense

---

165 Swakopmund Protocol Section 2.

166 WIPO, *Intellectual Property Needs and Expectations of Traditional Knowledge Holders: WIPO Report on Fact-Finding Missions on Intellectual Property and Traditional Knowledge (1998–1999)* (WIPO 2001) Page 25.

167 Joseph Wambugu Githaiga, 'Intellectual Property Law and the Protection of Indigenous Folklore and Knowledge' (1998) 5 Murdoch University Electronic Journal of Law 53, Page 2.

168 For the same reason, WIPO general assembly decided to establish intergovernmental committee on genetic resources, traditional knowledge and folklore as a forum in which discussions on intellectual property issues that arise in the terms of the theses three themes could proceed together. For more information see documents: WIPO Secretariat, 'Matters Concerning Intellectual Property and Genetic Resources, Traditional Knowledge and Folklore' (n 116) Paragraph 14; and WIPO Secretariat, 'Report of General Assembly' (2000) WIPO GA Dec WO/GA/26/10 Paragraph 71.

> embraces the content of knowledge itself as well as traditional cultural expressions, including distinctive signs and symbols associated with traditional knowledge.[169]

With this in mind, some countries believe that a broad definition should be adopted for TK.[170] This approach is supported by scholars such as Munzer & Raustiala who point out, "TK is the understanding or skill possessed by indigenous peoples pertaining to their culture and folklore, their technologies, and their use of native plants for medicinal purposes."[171] In their view, TK is firstly possessed by peoples and secondly, it relates to the culture and folklore, technologies and use of plants. In like manner, Lewinski divides knowledge of traditional communities into four main sections including genetic resources, traditional knowledge, indigenous names and designations, and folklore.[172] In the same way, Hansen and van Fleet identify TK as peoples' information "based on the experience and adaptation to a local culture and environment, have developed over the time and continue to develop."[173] Another debate which supports the notion of TK in its broader concept is the difference between TKHs and indigenous communities. While all indigenous peoples and communities are TKHs, not all TKHs are recognized as indigenous.[174] In this debate, TK includes both TK *stricto sensu* as well as TCE. Given these interpretations, I allow myself to conclude that TK must be regarded in its broader concept and include not only knowledge but also TCEs and GRs.

Regarding TCEs, TK aims to cover TCEs as forms of TK. Some forms that have embodied TK are:

- traditional designs, icons, and symbols that are representative of specific indigenous and local communities or of groups within these;[175]
- traditional music, arts, performances, rituals and traditional fabrication and use of instruments or products that are identified with particular indigenous and local communities;

---

169 WIPO, *Intellectual Property Needs and Expectations of Traditional Knowledge Holders* (n 166) Page 25.

170 See Asian Group statement: IGC-GRTKF Secretariat, 'Report of Intergovernmental Committee on Intellectual Property and Genetic Resources, Traditional Knowledge and Folklore' (n 61) Page 9.

171 Munzer and Raustiala (n 5) Page 38.

172 Lewinski (n 69) Page 4.

173 Hansen and van Fleet (n 4) Page 3.

174 WIPO, *Intellectual Property Needs and Expectations of Traditional Knowledge Holders* (n 166) Page 26.

175 *ibid Page 25.*

- traditional dress, customs, and corporeal accessories identified with particular indigenous and local communities;
- traditional material culture and handicrafts production; and artifacts;
- traditional designs and methods in jewellery, stonework, metalwork, woodwork, etc;[176]

Concerning GRs, they are inseparable in nature from TK. Different reasons support their integrated natures:
- landraces and traditional varieties are products of farmers' knowledge who have conserved and developed them through generations.
- according to the TKHs, intangible and tangible components of TK have been used and transmitted together and cannot be separated.
- conservation of the TK depends on the customary use of GRs.[177]

Besides, the term TK, among others, refers to the "ways and means by which individuals or communities identify and improve GRs over time, including processes related to their extraction from nature and their preparation for human usage."[178] As the term implies, an important part of TK is the TKHs' information of using GRs. As Cottier states:

> We are now essentially dealing with the appropriation of information. Such information, genetically encoded, is either exclusively contained in nature, yet untouched by man, or it exists in combination with human knowledge as how to make good use of such information or know-how with or without knowledge of the gene code.[179]

Other scholars, while accepting this linkage between TK and GRs, provide a list of TK associated with GRs in different categories including:
- knowledge of current, previous, or potential use of plant and animal species,
- know-how concerning preparation, processing, or storage of useful species,
- knowledge of individual species,

176 *ibid.*

177 UNEP-CBD Executive Secretary (n 43) Page 3.

178 Thomas Cottier and Marion Panizzon, 'Legal Perspectives on Traditional Knowledge: The Case for Intellectual Property Protection' in Keith E Maskus and Jerome H Reichman (eds), *International Public Goods and Transfer of Technology under a Globalized Intellectual Property Regime* (First, Cambridge University Press 2005) Page 566.

179 Thomas Cottier, 'The Protection of Genetic Resources and Traditional Knowledge: Towards More Specific Rights and Obligations in World Trade Law' (1998) 1 Journal of International Economic Law 555, Page 558.

– knowledge of ecosystem conservation,
– classification systems of knowledge such as traditional plant taxonomies,[180]

In the same manner, Gupta lists technological fields in relation to GRs. This list includes, *inter alia*, crop protection and production, animal husbandry, grain storage, leather industry, organic farming and local varieties of seeds.[181] Having considered these categories, we will be able to understand how TK plays an important role for the "conservation of biological diversity and the sustainable use of its components and for the sustainable livelihoods" of TKHs.[182] This role is already recognized in the Nagoya Protocol as associated TK.[183] Furthermore, according to some experts, even when TK associated with GRs does not match the final products, it adds value to GRs by indicating the potential value of GRs.[184] Even regarding biopiracy, it has been widely accepted by different stakeholders that biopiracy is the illegitimate appropriation or commercialization of TK and GRs.[185]

2.2.3 Which Approach Is More Feasible for the Protection of TK?

The clarification of TK and identification of its subject matter are key elements for analyzing the relationship between TK and IP protection systems. TK has a miscellaneous nature and a wide spectrum of issues, which could be addressed as its different expressions. At the same time, these varied and dynamic expressions are clearly distinct from each other and individualized. Traditional customs and customary laws and institutions;[186] health and medicine; traditional agriculture and farming; traditional use of environment and biodiversity; traditional usage of natural resources such as water and land; traditional know-how for production, preservation and conservation of foods; and traditional architecture and building techniques; and traditional designs, paints, symbols and icons, arts and music are parts of the TK different

180 Darrell A Posey and Graham Dutfield, *Beyond Intellectual Property: Toward Traditional Resource Rights for Indigenous Peoples and Local Communities* (International Development Research Centre 1996) Page 12.

181 Quoted from: Graham Dutfield, 'Harnessing Traditional Knowledge and Genetic Resources for Local Development and Trade' (WIPO 2005) Pages 9–10.

182 See: Nagoya Protocol Preamble, Recital 21.

183 *ibid Article 12.*

184 UNEP-CBD, 'Report of the Meeting of the Group of Technical and Legal Experts on Traditional Knowledge Associated with Genetic Resources in the Context of the International Regime on Access and Benefit-Sharing' (n 56) Page 8, Paragraph 13.

185 Miguel N Alexiades and Sarah A Laird, 'Laying the Foundation: Equitable Biodiversity Research Relationships' in Sarah A Laird (ed), *Biodiversity and Traditional Knowledge: Equitable Partnerships in Practice* (Earthscan Publications 2002) Page 8.

186 See for example: Indigenous and Tribal Peoples Convention.

faces.[187] This gives TK diverse holistic conceptions with a dynamic and evolving nature.[188] To address all mentioned areas, different terminologies have been hired regarding TK subject matters. Among these terminologies, Terms such as Folklore,[189] Expression of Folklore,[190] Traditional Cultural Expression,[191] Traditional Ecological Knowledge,[192] Traditional Environmental Knowledge[193]

---

187 For more information on the forms of TK see: IGC-GRTKF Secretariat, 'List and Brief Technical Explanation of Various Forms in Which Traditional Knowledge May Be Found' (World Intellectual Property Organization 2010) WIPO Doc WIPO/GRTKF/IC/17/INF/9 Annex Page 2–3.

188 Swakopmund Protocol Section 1(2)–(3).

189 Discussions around traditional communities' intellectual creativities were oriented under the notion of Folklore; but other scholars gradually generated other terms such as TK to challenge concept of Folklore. Blakeney notes that Folklore reflects the cultural and social identity of the communities in different forms such as rituals, customs, architecture, handicrafts and all kind of arts. And according to Githaiga, Folklore refers to "all kinds of literary and artistic works such as music, dance, song, ceremonies, symbols and designs, narratives and poetry." See: Blakeney, 'What Is Traditional Knowledge? Why Should It Be Protected? Who Should Protect It? For Whom? Understanding the Value Chain' (n 160) Page 2; And Githaiga (n 167) Page 2.

190 In accordance with the WIPO-UNESCO Model Provisions Expressions of Folklore are "productions consisting of characteristic elements of the traditional artistic heritage developed and maintained by a community of a country or by individuals reflecting the traditional artistic expectations of such a community, in particular: (i) Verbal expressions, (ii) Musical expressions, (iii) Expressions by action, (iv) Tangible expressions." Also, Swakopmund Protocol defines Expressions of Folklore as: "[a]ny forms, whether tangible or intangible, in which traditional culture and knowledge are expressed, appear or are manifested." It puts the forms of EoF in same categories of WIPO-UNESCO Model Provisions and offers example of some forms of expressions or combinations of them. According to the both documents, words, signs, names and symbols are examples of verbal expressions; and drawings, designs, paintings, carpets and handicrafts categorized under tangible expressions. See: The Committee of Governmental Experts and WIPO (n 71) Section 2; and Swakopmund Protocol Section 2(1).

191 WIPO's IGC use Traditional Cultural Expressions and Expressions of Folklore alternatively and as synonyms to refer the intangible and tangible forms of TK and Cultures. See: IGC-GRTKF Secretariat, 'Glossary of Key Terms Related to Intellectual Property and Genetic Resources, Traditional Knowledge and Traditional Cultural Expressions' (n 161) Pages 13, 14 and 39.

192 Berkes considering different concepts of traditional ecological knowledge defines TEK as: "a cumulative body of knowledge and beliefs, handed down through generations by cultural transmission, about the relationship of living beings (including humans) with one another and with their environment." See: Fikret Berkes, 'Traditional Ecological Knowledge in Perspective' in Julian T Inglis (ed), *Traditional Ecological Knowledge: Concepts and Cases* (International Program on Traditional Ecological Knowledge: International Development Research Centre 1993) Page 3.

193 The Dene Cultural Institute defines Traditional Environmental Knowledge as "a body of knowledge and beliefs transmitted through oral tradition and first-hand observation. It includes a system of classification, a set of empirical observations about the local

have been used more than others in the context of international debates on protection of TK. Again, besides the area in which TK may be found, the diverse technical methods of classification of TK have been hired to explain its nature and importance for the related communities. For instance, TK is technically organized as: formal and informal, fixed or not fixed[194] (whether documented or non-documented, verbally or manifested by actions, recorded or unrecorded, written or non-written), codified and non-codified,[195] disclosed and undisclosed[196] and exclusive and publicly available.[197]

Having considered the vast array of different terms, and although each terminology tries to add a set of values to a given type of TK, it is important to avoid fruitless disputes over which terminology could represent TK correctly and truly. Instead, it is significant to properly consider a broader concept of TK which enables us to develop a context-sensitive use of the term and facilitate proper responses to needs and expectations raised by stakeholders and to gain deeper understanding of TK by considering it from different viewpoints. Moreover, the creation of international IPRS protection has never been dependent on one harmonized, standard, comprehensive and exhaustive definition of the protection of subject matter. Instead the attitude towards globalization of IPRS protection has been focused on establishing a common policy at an international level in order to give national authorities enough space to determine the boundaries of protectable issues and subject matters.

A general definition of TK, particularly at the international level, may allow national authorities to use a general concept of terminology to promote more precise definitions for TK subject matters at the national level, based on

environment, and a system of self-management that governs resource use. Ecological aspects are closely tied to social and spiritual aspects of the knowledge system." See: Marc G Stevenson, 'Indigenous Knowledge in Environmental Assessment' (1996) 49 Arctic Institute of North America 278, Page 281.

194 Some scholars point out protection of TK is not conditioned to fixation in a tangible form such as writing or drawing. See: Munzer and Raustiala (n 5) Page 53.

195 Codified TK is "traditional knowledge which is in some systematic and structured form, in which the knowledge is ordered, organized, classified and categorized in some manner." See: IGC-GRTKF Secretariat, 'List and Brief Technical Explanation of Various Forms in Which Traditional Knowledge May Be Found' (n 187) Pages 6–7.

196 Undisclosed TK or Secret TK are important for communities in accordance with their customary law and practices. See: IGC-GRTKF Secretariat, 'Glossary of Key Terms Related to Intellectual Property and Genetic Resources, Traditional Knowledge and Traditional Cultural Expressions' (n 161) Page 37; Something is secret if it is "kept from the knowledge of others or shared only with those concerned." See: Garner (n 19).

197 IGC-GRTKF Secretariat, 'List and Brief Technical Explanation of Various Forms in Which Traditional Knowledge May Be Found' (n 187) Pages 3–4.

national law. "[f]or most categories of IP protection, the approach taken to defining subject matters is more general and remains open to distinct interpretation and application at the national level."[198] Furthermore, the broad definition of TK could be used by local legal systems to determine TK subject matter separately, and to specify their eligibility for the enjoyment of legal protection as a subset of TK. Equally, portioning out TK to its subject matters which are eligible to be protected might serve as a tool for national policy makers to determine the criteria for protection on a case-by-case approach on one side and to select and grant protection to those TKs which are important and vital for their concerned communities. In contrast, the concrete determination and setting of the boundaries for the scope of protection will increase the risk of delimitation of subject matters.[199] And also, it may deprive some communities of the legal protection of their associated TK.

TK has different manifestations and different meanings for different communities in different areas. Differentiation among diverse types of TK will "artificially disaggregate components of single reality and make it more difficult to enforce a viable system of legal protection for TK"[200] in general, and for PCs in particular. Therefore, for the purposes of this study, the broader concept of TK is chosen as follows to discuss:

- PCs in the context of knowledge *per se*.
- PCs as manifestation of traditional cultural expressions.
- PCs associated to genetic resources.

2.3 *Persian Carpets as Subject Matter of Traditional Knowledge*

In the Persian language, carpet is named 'Farsh' and 'Qali.' In the historical texts in the Pahlavi Language,[201] the words 'Namat,' 'Vistarg' and 'bop/bup' were used to name 'Farsh,' and 'Qali' as a precious type of 'Farsh.' Farsh literally means whatever is used for spreading on the ground. It consists any ground cloth woven form natural materials such as wool, silk, fibres and cottons.

198 IGC-GRTKF Secretariat, 'Traditional Knowledge – Operational Terms and Definitions' (n 142) Page 3.

199 *ibid Pages 8–9.*

200 Cottier and Panizzon, 'Legal Perspectives on Traditional Knowledge: The Case for Intellectual Property Protection' (n 178) Page 583.

201 Pahlavi or Pehlevi language was a Middle Iranian language during Sassanid times (224–654 CE). For more information see: Rüdiger Schmitt, *Compendium Linguarum Iranicarum* (L Reichert 1989).

Although Kilim[202] (Kelim or Gelim), Zilu,[203] Jajim[204] (Jijim, Djidim, Cicim), Palas (Pallas), Namat,[205] Farsh[206] and Qali[207] and other like objects are different types of Farsh, but the word Farsh is normally used to specifically refer to Qali.[208] In international instruments, carpets have been addressed as tangible expression of Folklore.[209]

Raw materials used to produce carpets are sourced from the local fauna and flora of the regions and include wool, hair, silk, thread, yarn, and dyes. Understanding the methods for exploiting, processing as well as procedures for use of these materials would be vital when establishing a unique linkage between the TK of the producers and the production itself, which results in a quality unmatched in other regions of the world or even within the country.

2.3.1 PCs and Knowledge

2.3.1.1 *Knowledge of Making Dyes*

The history of making dye in Iran is several thousands of years old. The enamel tiles of 'Persian Immortals Soldiers' discovered in Persepolis, held at the Louvre Museum, indicate that Iranians have long recognized the secret of access to these magical colours. The bright and pleasant colours of these tiles are the best indicators of the taste and manner of Iranians in the preparation of different colours and the methods of their use. The tiles that adorn the doors and walls of the historic buildings of Isfahan and the palaces of the Safavid Dynasty Kings are of great beauty. Soulful colours and harmony in applying these colours together make each viewer wonder how these colours are still magic and eye-catching after more than 300 years. The profession of glazing is due to the technical work and the use of hidden knowledge that others have not been able to achieve and has always been shrouded in secrecy and ambiguity. The secret of making magical colours was only passed on if the son followed in his father's footsteps, otherwise it would go to the grave with the death of the father.

Today, carpet dyeing, due to ownership of this latent knowledge and applying of the old skills and techniques to provide beautiful and pleasant colours,

202 Short-napped coarse carpet.

203 Pileless carpet.

204 Woollen cloth.

205 Felt.

206 Carpet.

207 Rug.

208 Ahmad Daneshgar, فرهنگ جامع فرش یادواره – دانشنامه ایران (*Yadvareh Comprehensive Encyclopaedia of Carpet – Iran Encyclopaedia*), vol 1 (2nd edn, Yadvareh Asadi 2011).

209 Swakopmund Protocol Section 2(1)[6](iv).

and despite the introduction of various types of chemical dyes into the industries, is an indelible factor in the structure and overall composition of the carpet of Iran. Although the making of these colours is not the same in different parts of the country, the overall construction for making them is the same from native plants. These colours do not lose their appearance against sunlight or when rinsing. The stability of traditional organic colours against the sunlight and alkaline materials during washing, although it creates somewhat roughness in the carpet, preserves the carpet's integrity for a long time and does not lose its colour at all. Only gradual passing of the time and the slow effect of alkali materials on the carpet causes it to gradually diminish its colour over time and its colours become more delicate and interspersed, and in harmony with each other, giving rise to a natural and striking sparkle. In this case, the colours are no longer crude, and their identical luminosity creates a special coherence which cannot be limited to any border.[210]

Dyeing the materials needed for carpet weaving is a task that requires both artistic taste and sophistication, and demands precision and efficiency. Masters of carpet dyeing, using traditional dyeing materials such as walnut shells, grape leaves, and rhinos and other similar materials, create consistent staining colours that have been resistant to light and other natural factors for hundreds of years, and as the life and the aging and erosion of the carpet is increased, its shine and gloss increase rather than diminish.

In many areas of the world where carpets are produced, the use of industrial colours is commonplace in terms of time and cost savings and speed of operation in time and cost. In Iran, PCs' companies and some famous manufacturers have continued to use traditional techniques in carpet dyeing and have maintained this tradition. Obviously, if the traditional methods in PCs' dyeing are not pursued with systematic planning, it can be argued that the PCs will suffer irreparable damage, as the knowledge of the traditional colouring techniques which are especially in hands of Iranians' dyeing masters, would be lost. Since artificial colours are produced and used in all carpet-producing countries, there would be no significant difference between the PCs and the carpets produced in other countries

2.3.1.2 *Knowledge of Weaving*

Carpet weaving, particularly the weaving of high-quality carpets, requires deep know-how and skills. These types of carpets are mostly woven in specific regions such as Qum, Naein, Isfahan, Tabriz, Kashan.[211]

---

210 Yasavoli (n 8).

211 Daneshgar (n 208).

The steps to start the weaving of a carpet are as follows:

- Preparing the raw and original materials;
- Arranging the loom and other tools;
- Designing;
- Setting up the warping frame;
- Weaving the Kilim;
- Knotting the warps;[212]
- Knotting based on the design (coloured checkered);
- Weaving the weft and the process of beating;
- Securing the selvages and fringes;
- Beating the course (Raj) and trimming excess piles;
- Taking careful precautions to avoid damage;
- Removing from the loom.[213]

2.3.1.3 *Producing Tools*

After procuring the initial materials using the traditional and indigenous knowledge of the people, carpet weaving can begin. However, this process would not be possible without using the practical tools that manufacturers and weavers from various regions utilize, each tailored to their specific style of production. In this section, these tools are briefly described:

2.3.1.3.1 Carpet Loom

The device used for carpet weaving is called Carpet Loom. It is based on a framework consisting of two vertical posts and two horizontal timbers that are fastened together by means of joints. The way of working with such devices and the way weavers stand against them is not only effective in the texture and quality of the carpet, but also important for the health of weavers.[214] The beams used in Iran for the construction of carpets are made from Poplar[215]

---

212 It should be explained that in a carpet, the density of the knots and their elegance represents the quality of the carpet. This means that the higher the number of knots and the so-called 'carpet weighing,' the higher its quality. In general, PCs weaving is in two common types: the Turkish knot (symmetric) of Tabriz, Hamedan, Fars tribes and so on. Farsi knot (asymmetric) of Arak, Isfahan, Mashhad, Birjand, Kerman, Naein, Kashan, Qum and others.

213 'Process of Weaving' (*Iran Carpet Co.*, 2015) <http://en.irancarpet.ir/CarpetEncyclopedia/TheProcessofWeaving.aspx>.

214 In Persian Bafandeh. See: Peter F Stone, *Oriental Rugs: An Illustrated Lexicon of Motifs, Materials, and Origins* (Tuttle Publishing 2013).

215 In Persian Tabrizi or Sepidar.

Trees which are relatively straightforward. In Iran, four types of Carpet Looms are used:

- Horizontal Loom: Rug wrapped with horizontal beams will cover most of the small pieces, as the size of the wooden beams will make it difficult to transport them.
- Vertical Loom: It has three types: Rural, Tabriz and Battalion-style.

2.3.1.3.2 Other Tools

Apart from loom, carpet weavers use other tools. These tools, each of which has a particular role in weaving process, started with different structures from what we use today. However, the defects and imperfections of this tool have gradually been addressed, resulting in their present form. These tools include hooks, combs,[216] beaters, and scissors.

2.3.2 PCs' Designs, Words, Signs, Names and Symbols

Designs and drawings that can be produced, expressed or manifested as forms of tangible expressions, shall be protected regardless of their mode or form of expression.[217] The designs, motifs and colours of the PCs are among the components that have played a major role in shaping the cultural and artistic identity of the PCs. Importantly, the placement of design and motif and colour along with other qualitative aspects of the carpet, combine to make it materially and spiritually valuable. What produces the variety and diversity in the imagination of the carpet is the original pattern and colours that a variety of producers (weaver, designer) can create. In fact, the design and role of the flow in the permanent and evolving carpet have transformed throughout its life. From this continuous cycle in motion, there have always been many designs left out and sometimes forgotten, and others which have become luckier and have been given more time and scope to manifest themselves.

On the other hand, terms such as designs, motifs, patterns, carpets, and rugs are used interchangeably, while each has a distinct definition. For example, Lachak Toranj carpets, Lachak Toranj drawing, Lachak Toranj designs, and Lachak Toranj motifs are used in place of each other, while some of them are principally incorrect. Therefore, the structure must be known precisely to avoid such mistakes. From this perspective, the motifs are the same forms while their composition and positioning together establish the differences

---

216 "A weighted comb is used to beat down wefts over rows of knots in weaving pile rugs. An image of a comb is often used as a filler motif in tribal and nomadic rugs." Excerpt from: Stone (n 214).

217 See: Swakopmund Protocol Sections 2(1)[6](iv) and 16(b).

from other patterns. In this manner, the term Lachak Toranj of Shah Abbasi in Isfahan, means a pattern with the structure of Lachak Toranj which constitutes the main and dominant element of the Shah Abbasi Patterns which belongs to Isfahan region. The main designs or structures are: Shah Abbasi, Vase Design, In and out Fish Design, Bandi, Moharamat, Historical Monuments Design, Celebrities,[218] Golfarang, Eslimi Design, Boteh, Tree,[219] Prayer-niche Design,[220] Overall Flower Design, Talfighi, Derivatives.[221]

2.3.3 PCs and Genetic Resources

Producing PCs has a direct relation to the use and exploitation of biological resources[222] belonging to the geographical spots of production.

2.3.3.1 *Animal Genetic Resources*

2.3.3.1.1 Sheep Wool

Most PCs produced by villagers and tribes are made of wool because of the ease of access to wool in Iran. Wool quality depends directly on the delicacy of the fibre, its thin diameter, the length of the wool blade, its strength, wave, natural colour, the ability to dye and elasticity. Regardless of these factors, reversibility, transparency and odour are also important in the wool structure. Regarding the elegance of the fibres, the quality of the wool is not the same over the whole body of the sheep. Wool of the shoulder is the best part, and wool from the area of the ribs is graded as second, while third grade wool comes from the thighs and under the abdomen. Obviously, if the wool is a mix of different parts, the desired uniformity and the elegance of the texture cannot be achieved. As for the diameter of the wool fibre, the lesser it is, the thinner and of higher-quality is the wool. Also, the higher the warp lengths, the better. This length can even reach seven centimetres in first-grade wool fibres. The wool strength has direct relation with the animal's nutrition where the wool will become dry and fragile in the case of improper nutrition. Furthermore, waved wool will cause problems in the weaving process, and as the straightening of

218 In Persian: Shakhsiatha.

219 In Persian Derakhti.

220 In Persian Mihrabi.

221 In Persian Eghtebasi.

222 "Biological resources include genetic resources, organisms or parts thereof, populations, or any other biotic component of ecosystems with actual or potential use or value for humanity." See: CBD Article 2; also, it has been defined as "individuals, organisms or parts of them, populations or any biotic component of value or of real or potential use that contains a genetic resource or its by-products." See: ANDEAN Decision No. 391 – Common Regime on Access to Genetic Resources 1996 (entered into force 17 July 1996) Article 1.

the fibres involves chemical operations, wool durability is reduced, regardless of increasing the costs. The natural colour of the wool can be white, yellow, grey, brown and black. The best qualities and the most expensive wools are white. White wools are easily coloured without involving any chemical process which could decrease the quality and durability of the wool. In terms of commercial value, this type is called first-grade wool. In brief, dyeability of the wool depends on the following factors:

- the original colour of the wool;
- the amount of fat that should be removed or minimized by proper washing;
- the diameter of the wool fibres.

The best and brightest wool is made from the sheep which are fed on the mountainside pastures. For example, Kurdish, Sarkhsi and Sistani sheep raised in Khorasan Province bear the best types of wools. In the eastern and western Azerbaijan provinces, breeding sheep of Maku and Harki races prevail.[223]

2.3.3.1.2 Silkworm

Silk is one of the important materials for producing high-quality carpets. It is a type of natural protein fibre. Silk originates mainly from silkworm larvae which form cocoons.[224] Silk is usually used for making bluish rugs, and sometimes also for making fine rugs. Sometimes they use it for flowers and paints and carpet paintings. This kind of carpet is called 'silk carpet.' A carpet made entirely of silk is not commonly used for flooring and mostly it is used to decorate the walls and the tables. Producing silk carpets needs expertise and currently only a few countries are capable of producing such carpets. In Iran, these types of carpets are mostly woven in Qum, Naein, Isfahan, Tabriz, Kashan, and, of course, as it was said, its texture is considered very low compared to other carpets. In the provinces of Khorasan and Gilan, and some other places, there are some silkworm breeding factories.[225]

2.3.3.1.3 Coccus laccae[226]

One of the most expensive natural colours of PCs is red. Cochineal is the main source of the red colours. Cochineal "usually describes dye made from the dried bodies of the female coccus cacti."[227] The insect lives in the branches

---

223 See: Yasavoli (n 8).

224 See: Iranian Company of Breeding of Silkworm, پرورش کرم ابریشم (*Silkworm Breeding*) (Iranian Company of Breeding of Silkworm 1997).

225 Daneshgar (n 208).

226 In Persian 'Ghermez Daneh.'

227 Stone (n 214).

of the fig tree family and absorbs sap from the plants. It dyed wool in various shades of red from bright red to purple. In Iran, Cochineal is called 'Lac.'[228]

2.3.3.2 *Plant Genetic Resources*

2.3.3.2.1 Cotton

Cotton is an essential material for providing the carpet's warp and weft. In the past, wool was predominantly used in the production of warp. Still in many parts of Shiraz and also by Qashqai tribes, and some other places, warp is made of wool. Nowadays, because of the cost of wool and some technical issues, weavers prefer to make carpet from cotton. Cotton is a fibre plant, and the diameter, length and strength of cotton fibres are as important as wool. Cotton is cultivated in most parts of Iran. Iranian cotton includes diverse varieties. Each variety has special physical and natural characteristics, and this variation depends on the breeding environment and its climatic conditions. Therefore, choosing the most applicable breed of cotton is very important.[229]

2.3.3.2.2 Organic Colour

The most important of PGRs for organic colouring are Madder, Weld (sometimes known as Dyer's Mignonette), Indigo (NIL), Dyer's Woad (*isatis tinctoria*), Pomegranate Skin, Walnut Skin, Sumac and Safflower, which are used in dyeing.

2.4 *Matching TK Criteria for PCs*

Although TK as local knowledge systems are diverse in nature, some definite common characteristics are known among them. It is important to know these common characteristics of TK, because they will help clarify whether a special subject matter could be considered under TK manifestation. These characteristics also serve to identify the scope of TK that would be eligible for legal protection.[230] Three common characteristics have been identified among them, including:

- TK is generated, preserved and transmitted in a traditional and intergenerational context;
- TK is distinctively associated with a local or traditional community; and
- TK is integral to the cultural identity of a local or traditional community.[231]

---

228 See: Yasavoli (n 8).

229 Daneshgar (n 208).

230 IGC-GRTKF Secretariat, 'The Protection of Traditional Knowledge: Draft Articles' (World Intellectual Property Organization 2016) WIPO Doc WIPO/GRTKF/IC/31/4 Annex Page 7, Article 1.

231 See: WIPO, *Intellectual Property and Genetic Resources, Traditional Knowledge and Traditional Cultural Expressions: Overview.* (World Intellectual Property Organization 2015) Page 13; and Swakopmund Protocol Section 4.

These three aspects are considered in different facets of TK. For instance, Daes, talking about heritage, points out, "the heritage of indigenous people has a collective character and is comprised of all objects, sites and knowledge ... the nature or use of which has been transmitted from generation to generation, and which is regarded as pertaining to a particular people or its territory of traditional natural use." She also points out that the heritage includes creation such as biodiversity-related knowledge and symbols and designs.[232] These elements have been reflected in PCs as a manifestation of TK.

2.4.1 Intergenerational Aspect of PCs

The nature of knowledge is to be gained through experiences or studies, but it does not stipulate whether the factor of time plays a critical role in attaining experiences and studies, but the term 'traditional' – as an adjective to the knowledge – has been used to emphasise the important of time in defining TK. Moreover, traditional issues are elements of a culture passing down from generation to generation. They are modes of thoughts or behaviours, customs or usages which are continuously followed from generation to generation.[233] TK is rarely frozen in time and evolves over ages. It is passing from one generation to the next, carrying the information and knowledge. "Indeed, it is implicit in the very concept of TK that the knowledge in question is fairly old."[234]

Regarding the element of time, PCs have an old background. The history of PCs goes back to the time when the first tribal and nomadic communities took shape on ancient land of Persia. Iran is the land of early agriculture communities, whose farming skills provide cotton from the fields, and wool from local sheep and goats, and also silk, which became available later. The most ancient sign of hand-woven carpet in Iran goes back to the Bronze Age, when a carpet weaving knife was found in an excavated grave in north of Iran. More evidence from 3500–2800 BC, was found in the Burnt City[235] that in today Sistan and Balochistan[236] Province.

Again, the oldest hand-woven carpet dates back 500–400 BC which is believed it was made in Persia in the Achaemenian or Parthian era. Its designs and motifs were popular in their age. It is named as Pazyryk and at present, is being kept in the Hermitage Museum in St. Petersburg in Russia.

232 Erica-Irene Daes, 'Principles and Guidelines for the Protection of the Heritage of Indigenous People' (UN Commission on Human Rights, Sub-Commission on the Promotion and Protection of Human Rights 2000) UN ESC Doc E/CN.4/Sub.2/2000/26 Annex I Notes 12 and 13.
233 Houghton Mifflin Company (n 7).
234 Munzer and Raustiala (n 5) Page 58.
235 Shahr-e-Soukhteh.
236 Also, Sistan-Baluchistan.

The most famous Carpet in the history of Persia is Baharestan Carpet. It was a property of the last king of Sassanid Dynasty and materials such as silk, gold, silver and precious stones were used in it. It is said that the Baharestan was torn apart by the Islamic Conqueror around 637–651 AD. During the Safavid Dynasty (1501–1736 AD), PCs reached their heights. In the period of Shah Ismaeil, the dynasty's founder, he established the first carpet weaving workshop in his capital city of Tabriz. His successor, Shah Tahmasb also encouraged the production and the art of hand-woven carpets. Probably, Ardabil Carpets are the most famous carpets of this time. They were made in pair to be laid in Sheikh Safi al-Din Ardabili Shrine. At present one of them is being kept by Victoria & Albert Museum in London and the other by the Los Angeles Museum of Arts. The region of Shah Abbas the first (1587–1629 AD), he made Isfahan the new capital of the Safavid Dynasty. He did a great attempt to organize and modernize tribal and rural crafts. Therefore, enormous workshops were established in Isfahan. Moreover, other regions of the country were persuaded to remain faithful to their local designs and weaving methods to safeguard the originality of their works designs. Also, his ruling set new standards for raw materials such as silk, wool and cotton. In his time, workshops began to receive orders from foreign traders which caused great improvement in carpet producing either from artisanal angle or economical aspects. Moreover, foreign traders – mostly from Europe – established their merchant houses in Iran to directly control the trade of carpets.

In 1736, Afsharit Dynasty was founded by Nader Shah, who ousted the Safavid Dynasty. He chose the holy city of Mashhad in north-eastern province of Khorasan as the new Capital city of Iran; and Mashhad became the new capital of PCs weaving activities and Afshari designs and motifs became the new mark in the art of PCs. The PCs of Mashhad and its subordinate cities possess their distinctive characteristics and are known by warm colours, robust structures and long life but also cheaper values.

Zandieh Dynasty was the next ruler of Iran, and during their era, Shiraz was chosen as the new capital city of Iran. During Zandieh artisanal work directly and the art of carpet weaving indirectly were encouraged.

The art and economy of PCs continued during the Qajar era well into the twentieth century from 1785 to 1925. This is the period in which commercialization of PCs experienced its most significant development; in particular trade with European countries. In this period, trading offices from England, France, Italy, Germany, Austria and the Netherlands were established in cities such as Tabriz, Isfahan and Kerman. They initiated direct trade with major PCs producing centres. For example, Companies such as Ziegler & Co invested heavily in the PCs' industry in order to meet the developing need of wealthy European markets.

Since the twentieth century, extensive advances in the preparation of raw materials as wool, cotton and silk and dyes; and forming new designs and patterns were made. Also, new standards on size and quality of PCs were set. During this time, new institutions were established to organize and support the production of PCs. Nowadays many higher education institutions and universities offer academic courses on PCs from providing high quality materials to the weaving techniques and art of designing.

In brief, the art and economy of PCs is a never-ending magical story of Iranian TKHs who, generation after generation, put forth innovative efforts to create what are called The Magic Carpets.[237]

2.4.2 PCs Associated with Local Community

When we speak of TK, the main approach focuses on a particular community with a particular geographic perimeter. Iran's vast plateau, with its special climate and geography, and its hard-working people, has long been a land suitable for agriculture and animal husbandry. The inhabitants of Iran's land – as history attests – were among the first of peoples who have made handicrafts, especially the weaving of various Rugs, Carpets, Kilim and Felts from sheep' wool and the evolution of this industry over its long life, is an indication of the people's desire for carpet weaving. Iran's carpet is first and foremost a popular product. This pleasant effect is due to the work of every single anonymous artist who is scattered throughout this land and has dedicated their life to this end. It is this geographic extent that has paved the way for Iran's carpet to have diverse designs and outstanding features. This diversity has a complete and unbreakable bond with the beliefs, and desires of the people who cherish it and strive toward this goal.[238]

2.4.3 PCs and the Identity of a Local Communities

Mountain people in this area, following their hard-working life, are weaving thick and broken geometric lines, because the structure of their life and their tireless struggle and their solidarity with the heights, lines, and surfaces of rocks, have raised them in such a manner. The inhabitants of the plains apply delicate and beautiful designs such as flowers, leaves, branches and spinning lines, and they use fine, and soft fibres for carpet weaving and use bright colours in their works and weave large carpets. Nomads that have less

---

237 See for more details: Sayed Ali Mojabi, *An Introduction on the History of Persian Carpet – Since Genesis until the Late 19th Century* (1st edn, Persian Carpet Research Centre (PCRC) 2003) 6–30; and 'History | Iran Carpet Co.' (*Iran Carpet Co.*, 2015) <http://en.irancarpet.ir/IranCarpetCo/History.aspx>.

238 Daneshgar (n 208).

space to live in, weave smaller carpets to lighten their load while travelling. Women transfer what they know about the courage of the lion and the dignity of the horse to the carpet and put it on the walls of their houses, so the men and other members of the family can share in such moods. Such features in the carpet, have traditionally made this handmade item an ancestral art and made it public in Iran.[239]

Although carpet weaving is an ancestral art and industry in this land and it is common in every corner of Iran, the geographical situation of some parts of this land is more favorable for further development of this industry. In some parts of Iran, in every house and shop, there are devices for carpet weaving, and the general public, especially those near their main businesses, is also engaged in carpet weaving. These centres have been developed today in view of the positive impact of carpet weaving on strengthening the families' finances.

3 Who Are the Beneficiaries?

One of the problems regarding the protection of TK is identifying who the beneficiaries of protection of different elements of TK are and what the legal relation is between beneficiaries and other actors in regard to a given TK, and in our case PCs. Therefore, clear rights and obligations of diverse actors must be set. In the second step, there is a need to clarify how to distribute the benefits between them in an equitable way. Although both steps are of equal importance, identifying beneficiaries of TK protection is more critical. Then the rights and obligations of the different involved actors can eventually be defined whenever misappropriation of TK is at issue.[240]

As stated above, no universal definition of beneficiaries of protection of TK has been accepted yet. Although, it has been argued that since TK is collectively originated and held, the beneficiaries of the rights will be communities, other than in some cases where individuals might be recognized as beneficiaries of protection.[241] In the IGC negotiations, beneficiaries are defined as "all persons who create, originate, develop and preserve TK in a traditional

239 *ibid.*

240 Grethel Aguilar, 'Access to Genetic Resources and Protection of Traditional Knowledge in the Territories of Indigenous Peoples' (2001) 4 Environmental Science & Policy 241, Page 243.

241 IGC-GRTKF Secretariat, 'Draft Report of Intergovernmental Committee on Intellectual Property and Genetic Resources, Traditional Knowledge and Folklore' (World Intellectual Property Organization 2011) WIPO Doc WIPO/GRTKF/IC/17/12 PROV. 2.

setting and context."[242] In the context of TK, the term beneficiaries is an issue which could include a wide range of terminology. Terms such as indigenous peoples, indigenous communities, local communities, traditional communities, cultural communities,[243] nations,[244] groups, families, and minorities[245] and individuals, have been referred to.[246] Also, terms such as local population, tribal communities,[247] nomadic people,[248] people concerned, social group, ethnic group, and practitioners might be considered related to the beneficiaries. Importantly, it is not limited to indigenous people but extends to all kind of communities, mainly but not exclusively rural.

Although, no universal definition has been agreed upon regarding terminology, 'Indigenous and Local Community' has attracted more attention and

---

242 IGC-GRTKF Secretariat, 'Glossary of Key Terms Related to Intellectual Property and Genetic Resources, Traditional Knowledge and Traditional Cultural Expressions' (n 161) Page 41.

243 Cultural community is "a tightly knit social unit whose members experience strong feelings of unity and solidarity and which is distinguished from other communities by its own culture or cultural design, or by a variant of the generic culture." The term includes the nationals of an entire country. See: UNESCO, 'DRAFT GLOSSARY – Proposed by a Group of Dutch Experts Convened by the Bureau of the Netherlands National Commission for UNESCO' (2002) International Meeting of Experts on Intangible Cultural Heritage: Establishment of a Glossary UNESCO Doc, TER/CH/2002/WD/4.

244 The term 'nation' is defined as "a large group of people having a common origin, language, and tradition and usually constituting a political entity." See: Garner (n 19); It carries "connotations of a community shaped by common descent, culture and history and often by a common language as well." See: Dieter Kugelmann, 'The Protection of Minorities and Indigenous Peoples Respecting Cultural Diversity' in Armin von Bogdandy, Rüdiger Wolfrum and Christiane Philipp (eds), *Max Planck Yearbook of United Nations Law*, vol 11 (Max-Planck-Institut für Ausländisches Öffentliches Recht und Völkerrecht 2007) Page 235.

245 The term 'minority' refers to "a group that is different in some respect from the majority and that is sometimes treated differently as a result." See: Garner (n 19); According to Capotorti "a minority is a group which is numerically inferior to the rest of the population of a State and in a nondominant position, whose members possess ethnic, religious or linguistic characteristics which differ from those of the rest of the population, and who if only implicitly, maintain a sense of solidarity directed towards preserving their culture, traditions, religion or language." See the definition developed in 1979 by Francesco Capotorti, the former Special Rapporteur of the United Nations; Quoted in: Kugelmann (n 244) Page 237.

246 IGC-GRTKF Secretariat, 'Glossary of Key Terms Related to Intellectual Property and Genetic Resources, Traditional Knowledge and Traditional Cultural Expressions' (n 161) Page 2.

247 Tribal peoples are distinguished from other sections of national community because of their social, cultural and economic conditions and by their own traditions or customs. See: Indigenous and Tribal Peoples Convention Article 1(1)(a).

248 See: *ibid Article 14(1)*.

generated considerable discussions. In particular, the CBD refers to the "knowledge, innovation and practices of indigenous and local communities."[249] The Convention uses the term 'indigenous and local communities' in recognition of communities that have a long association with the resources that they have traditionally lived on or used.[250] The same term is used in different articles of the Nagoya Protocol.[251] This term is also used in the FAO Treaty on Plant Genetic Resources for Food and Agriculture in which member states shall recognize the enormous contribution that the 'local and indigenous communities' of all regions of the world have made and will continue to make for the conservation and development of PGRs.[252] The Treaty demands its member states to "promote or support, as appropriate, 'farmers and local communities' efforts to manage and conserve on-farm their plant genetic resources for food and agriculture ..."[253]

But what is the difference between indigenous peoples/communities and local communities? In reply to this question, plenty of definitions have been suggested by different institutions.[254] And yet, there is no unique universal acceptance of those definitions. Riffel points out that the privilege of TK is not limited to indigenous people.[255] Besides, as it has been mentioned before in explaining the concept of TK, the scope of TK is broader than the scope of indigenous peoples. Although there is no doubt that indigenous peoples are TKHS, not all TKHS are recognized as indigenous.[256] Therefore, to embrace as many communities as possible under the TK protection systems and also to avoid any misinterpretation on identification of related communities and

249 See: CBD Article 8(j).

250 See: Secretariat of the Permanent Forum on Indigenous Issues, 'Who Are Local Communities?' (UNEP 2006) UNEP Doc, UNEP/CBD/WS-CB/LAC/1/INF/5.

251 See: Nagoya Protocol Preamble and Articles 5, 6, 7, 11, 12, 13, 14, 16, 21, 22 and 25.

252 ITPGRFA Article 9(1).

253 *ibid Article 5(1)(c).*

254 See for instance: UNDP, 'The UNDP and Indigenous Peoples: A Policy of Engagement' (United Nations Development Program 2001); and UNESCO, 'DRAFT GLOSSARY – Proposed by a Group of Dutch Experts Convened by the Bureau of the Netherlands National Commission for UNESCO' (n 243); and UNEP, *Glossary of Terms for Negotiators of Multilateral Environmental Agreements* (UNEP 2007) Page 49; and UNEP-CBD Executive Secretary (n 43); and World Bank, 'Indigenous Peoples' (2005) Operational Policies: OP 4.10; and IFAD, 'Engagement with Indigenous Peoples: Policy' (The International Fund for Agricultural Development 2009); and UNEP-CBD Executive Secretary, 'Identification of Common Characteristics of Local Communities' (UNEP 2011) UNEP Doc, UNEP/CBD/AHEG/LCR/INF/1.

255 Riffel (n 3) Page 135.

256 WIPO, *Intellectual Property Needs and Expectations of Traditional Knowledge Holders* (n 166) Page 26.

assigning rights to them, I chose the term 'Traditional Knowledge Holders' to refer to the groups or individuals as beneficiaries of PCs. Although the definition of 'holder' might be different in various jurisdictions because of the history and political, economic and stage of development in each of them,[257] in general, it refers to communities and individuals who conserve, develop and maintain TK system.[258] In this regard, Swakopmund Protocol, trying to identify the concept of 'holder,' refers to forms of "custodianship, guardianship, collective and cultural ownership and responsibilities."[259] It calls for recognition the rights of TKHs, empowering TKHs to exercise due control over their knowledge, protecting TKHs against infringement of their rights, registering or recording of knowledge, relevant policies and laws and procedures of TKHs.[260] The protocol also refers to the rights conferred to holders of TK.[261]

TKHs are assumed to be the owner of rights. The term 'owner' is referred to in the Swakopmund Protocol in which the owner of rights shall be the TKHs whether indigenous and local communities or individuals recognized within those communities who create, preserve and transmit knowledge in a traditional and intergenerational context.[262] Some suggest using the term 'stewardship' rather than the term 'ownership'[263] In summary, TKHs are owners of rights and therefore beneficiaries of TK. Beneficiaries of TK either communities or individuals linked to concerned communities shall have right to attain, right to exercise, and enforce their rights:

> The peoples concerned shall be safeguarded against the abuse of their rights and shall be able to take legal proceedings, either individually or through their representative bodies, for the effective protection of these rights.[264]

257 William O Hennessey, *Toward A Conceptual Framework for Recognition of Rights for the Holders of Traditional Knowledge and Folklore* (University of New Hampshire School of law 2002) Page 8.

258 IGC-GRTKF Secretariat, 'Revised Provisions for the Protection of Traditional Knowledge: Policy Objectives and Core Principles' (n 36) Page 3.

259 Swakopmund Protocol Section 4(iii).

260 See: *ibid Preamble Paragraphs 9 and 14 and Sections 1 and 5(2).*

261 *ibid Section 7.*

262 *ibid Sections 6, 7(1),(2),(4), 8(1), 17(4) and 18.*

263 See: Kristen A Carpenter, Sonia K Katyal and Angela R Riley, 'In Defense of Property' (2009) 118 The Yale Law Journal 1022.

264 Indigenous and Tribal Peoples Convention Article 12.

4 Who Are the Beneficiaries of PCs?

Production of carpets in Iran is done either individually by home producers or in workshops. In addition, many jobs are dependent on the carpet industries. It is estimated that about 28 professions relating to the carpet weaving exist, including livestock breeding, cutting wool, spinning wool, scouring, classification and distribution, yarn, selling colours, dyeing, painter and designer, skein cutter, carpet weaving, carpet sellers, marketer and merchant. Each of these businesses acts as part of the production chain and has their own definitions and characteristics.[265] Recognition of these beneficiaries is important because, after defining PCs as subject matter of protection, the recognition of those who can benefit from the protection, or in other words, those who have the right to be protected, is of great importance.

4.1 *Communities as Persian Carpets' Beneficiaries*

In Iran, identification of local communities is directly linked with the laws and regulation regarding the country's divisions. Therefore, in this study, these divisions and their indicators are used for the analysis of PCs' communities.[266] The main divisions are: villages, rural districts, districts, cities, counties, and provinces.[267]

4.1.1 Rural Community

'Rural Knowledge' is among the various terms used for referencing TK and for describing the rural communities' knowledge on different and diverse issues like botany, zoology, agriculture, and know-how, which all of them are born as a result of creativities and innovations of rural life in their ecosystems and typically include the best and the most compatible methods and mechanisms to live within all the elements of the natural life in their given place.[268] In this regard, strengthening and promotion of rural activities have been emphasized in the 'Indigenous and Tribal Peoples convention,' and governments shall

265 Hassan Azarpad and Fazlol'lah Heshmati Razavi, فرش نامه ایران (*Persian Carpet-Nama*) (Institute for Humanities and Cultural Studies (IHCS) 2005).

266 The idea of links between the Iranian system of administrative divisions and the identity of local communities was put forward by Mr Motamedi in his Master thesis on national protection of TK. See: Gholamreza Motamedi, 'تبیین نظام ملی حمایت حقوقی از دانش سنتی در پرتو حقوق بین الملل (Identification of the National Regime for the Legal Protection of the Traditional Knowledge in Light of International Law)' (Master Thesis, Islamic Azad University – Tehran Central Branch 2005) Page 11–15.

267 Iran – Law on Definitions and Criteria of Country Divisions 1983 Article 1.

268 See: Robert Chambers, *Rural Development: Putting the Last First* (Longman 1989).

recognize rural communities' activities such as handicrafts and community-based industries.[269]

Taking the same approach, the importance of the rural areas is reflected in Iran's national laws and regulations, according to which the village is the smallest geographic unit in the country's divisions, and its indicators are:

- Environmentally homogeneous in terms of natural, social, cultural, and economic status,
- Independent customary or formal sovereignty,
- Including at least 20 households or 100 people, whether centralized or dispersed,
- Occupation of residents is directly or indirectly engaged in agriculture, animal husbandry, horticulture in general, and rural industries and fishing activities.[270]

4.1.2 Cities

Besides TKHs who might live in remote areas, some individual members of their communities may inhabit cities and still carry the same TK while they may lose their connection with the originating societies.[271] Also, rural areas may change to the city because of changes in their entity. A city is a place with a legal entity within the geographical boundaries and has a structure with its own characteristics in terms of construction, employment and other factors. And the majority of its permanent residents are employed in business, trading, industry, agriculture, services and administrative activities. And in the field of urban services, it has a relative affinity and it is the center of social, economic, cultural and political exchanges and has at least 10,000 residents. Any dismemberment, integration, conversion, creation and consolidation, as well as the determination and modification of the centralization and renaming of the divisions of the country other than the provinces will be based on the proposal of the Ministry of Interior and the approval of the Cabinet of Ministers.[272]

The differences between the legal definitions and criteria of villages and cities are not only significant but also impactful in the context of TK and PCs and the application of protection mechanisms to them. For instance, changing the number of residents could lead to the conversion of a village's identity

---

269 Indigenous and Tribal Peoples Convention Article 23(1).

270 Iran – Law on Definitions and Criteria of Country Divisions Article 2.

271 Graham Dutfield, 'Legal and Economic Aspects of Traditional Knowledge' in Keith E Maskus and Jerome H Reichman (eds), *International Public Goods and Transfer of Technology under a Globalized Intellectual Property Regime* (First, Cambridge University Press 2005) Page 498.

272 Iran – Law on Definitions and Criteria of Country Divisions Article 13.

to a new city which would have severe legal impacts, and consequently, the overall changes in the local authorities, representatives and administrative institutions.

4.1.3 Nomadic People

In addition to rural and urban communities, nomadic societies have been an important part of Iran's social, cultural and economic life. Their TK and hand-woven carpets are well-known all over the world. The designs and patterns of nomadic and rural rugs are amongst the richest reservoirs of designs and patterns that need to be preserved, not only to preserve them as ancient objects, but also because they are national heritage and an important cultural and historical change to assets. Therefore, their maintenance is necessary.[273]

According to a survey of the status of Iran's nomadic people during the past few decades, it has been observed that a decrease in the proportion of nomadic population in the country has taken place compared to the total population of the country. In accordance with historical sources, in 1866, about 38.6 percent of Iran population were nomads, which decreased to 9.6 percent in 1967. The latest official nomadic census conducted by the Iranian Statistics Centre, the ratio of the nomadic population to the total population has decreased to 1.68%, which indicates a deep decrease in the proportion of the nomadic population of the country. However, from 1987 to 1998 the number of nomads was growing again while its proportion decreased compared to whole population of the country. Again, this trend reversed, with the nomadic population declining to 1,186,398 in 2008 and to 1,115,041 in 2020. This relates, on the one hand, to various nomadic settlement programs and, on the other hand, to the migration and control of the population of this community.[274]

Therefore, it is vital to consider the legal situation of nomadic peoples in Iran. They have a migratory tribal life and their life depends on livestock, animal husbandry and pastoral activities.[275] Besides, the law on definitions and criteria of country divisions and its by-law recognize the regional, geographical and administrative criteria of Iran's nomadic people. In accordance with this law, nomads in the various seasons are under the governorate of the authorities

---

273 Mohammad Ali Espanani, 'آسیب شناسی احیای طرح ها ونقشه های قالی عشایری و روستایی (Difficulties in Reviving the Designs and Patterns of Nomadic and Rural Carpets)' (2007) 6 and 7 Goljaam, Iranian Carpet Scientific Society Quarterly 35, Page 36.

274 'جمعیت عشایری ایران (The Nomadic Population of Iran)' (*Organization for Nomads Affairs*, 2024) <https://ashayer.ir/جمعیت-عشایر-کشور>.

275 Iran – Decree on Establishment of Iran's Nomads High Council 1986 (A Decree of Iran Council of Ministers) Article 1.

of the area in which they reside at the very same time.[276] Also, the districts which are located in the passage of nomads during their seasonal movements are recognized as 'nomadic districts' and those districts will be responsible for providing the services and administrative supports for nomads. In addition, the identification of these districts will be proposed by the Ministry of Interior and approved by the Cabinet of Ministers.[277]

4.1.4 Well-Known Communities of PCs

In the following table, some well-known regions of PCs are briefly introduced:[278]

TABLE 1 Well-known centres of Persian carpets

Province	Communities
Markazi	– Cities: Arak, Mahalat, Khomeyn, Farahan, Sarough, Sarband.
Ardabil	– Cities: Ardabil, Sarab, Meshgin Shahr.
Azerbaijan (East & West)	– Cities: Tabriz, Marand, Maragheh, Khoy, Kalibar. – Villages: Haris, Guravan, Bakhshayesh, Sharabian, Mehraban. – Nomads: Shahsevan, Arasbaran.
Chaharmahal and Bakhtiari	– Cities: Chaleshtar, Saman, Eshkaftak, Borujen, Vardanjan, Boldaji, Farrokhshahr, Hiregan, Faradonbeh, Ardal, Babaheydar, Shalamzar. – Nomads: Bakhtiari and Qashqai.
Fars	– Cities: Shiraz. – Nomads: Qashqai and Lor.
Qum	– City: Qum.
Golestan	– Cities: Gorgan, Gonbad-e Kavous, Aqqala, Bandar-e Torkman, Bandar-e Gaz, Aliabad-e Katul. – Villages: Atabay and Jafarbay in Maraveh Tappeh.
Hamedan	– Cities: Hamedan, Dargazin, Toyserkan, Kabudarahang, Bozchelou.
Isfahan	– Cities: Isfahan, Falavarjan, Qomsheh, Naein, Najafabad, Natanz, Kashan, Khansar, Golpayegan.

276 *Law on Definitions and Criteria of Country Divisions*, *supra* note 246 at Article 5.

277 Iran – Regulation of Law on Definitions and Criteria of Country Divisions 1984 (A Decree of Iran Council of Ministers) Article 11.

278 See: Daneshgar (n 208).

TABLE 1 Well-known centres of Persian carpets (*cont.*)

Province	Communities
Kerman	– Cities: Kerman, Ravar, Rafsanjan, Sirjan, Baft, Shahre Babak, Rabor, Jiroft. – Villages: Ravar Outskirts Villages, Mahan and Golbaf Region. – Nomads: Afshar Tribe, Pichaghchi Tribe, Jebal Barezi Tribes, Mehni Tribes.
Kermanshah	– Cities: Kermanshah. – Nomads: Nomadic Groups of Kermanshah.
Khorasan Razavi	– Cities: Gonabad, Mashhad, Neyshabur, Quchan, Sabzevar, Kashmar, Torbate Heydarieh, Torbate Jam.
Khorasan North	– Cities: Shirvan, Bojnourd.
Khorasan South	– Cities: Birjand, Tabas.
Kordestan	– Cities: Sanandaj, Bijar, Ghorveh, Baneh. – Nomads: Nomadic Groups of Saqez, Baneh, Marivan, Divandareh and Uramanat.
Yazd	– Cities: Yazd.

4.2 PCs *Individual Beneficiaries*

A wide range of beneficiaries, including individuals, cooperatives, associations, and communities, are included under the concept of TKHs. As Cottier and Panizzon point out "given the strong intergenerational component of TK, it will be difficult to identify a single holder."[279] To understand the role and position of individuals with regard to the clarification of the beneficiaries is a key issue, in particular, in application of TKHs rights and protection and the role of communities or their representatives to recognize individuals.[280] As noted before, there are a wide range of businesses that rural, urban and nomadic people are engaging in these businesses and play a role in the production process from procurement of raw materials to exporting the carpets to foreign markets. However, the carpet weavers should be recognized as the most important part in this context.

279 Cottier and Panizzon, 'Legal Perspectives on Traditional Knowledge: The Case for Intellectual Property Protection' (n 178) Page 583.

280 See statement of the delegation of Colombia: IGC-GRTKF Secretariat, 'Revised Provisions for the Protection of Traditional Knowledge: Policy Objectives and Core Principles' (n 36) Page 5.

4.2.1 Domestic Producers

In the PCs' industry, both natural persons and legal entities are active, and the first group is mainly engaged in weaving at their own homes. Weavers at home are those who weave in their homes and decide when to weave the carpet, and most family members are often employed in the process. Domestic production is categorized into two types: producers on their own accounts and producers on the order by others. Domestic producers on their own account are those who provide the carpet's raw materials themselves, own the carpet weaving tools, and sell the carpet after weaving. Many carpet designers fall into this category. Domestic producers on the order by others are producers who weave carpets at home by order of others. In this arrangement, the client supplies the raw materials, and after weaving, gives a share to the weaver and takes the carpet. One example of this type is decentralized weaving carpet workshops which are collections of weavers at home working under a single management.[281]

4.2.2 Workshops Production

Workshop production refers to a distinct style. In this style, carpets production takes place in the workshops. Workshops owners employ weavers as contractors and weavers must work from 7 AM to 6 PM in the workshop for gaining wages. Carpet weavers are actually organized weavers whose main place of work is the workshops of carpet industries. This method has been prevalent across the country since the past. Also, some major PCs producers such as 'Iran Carpet Company' and 'Astan-e-ghods-e-Razavi Carpet Co' operates such workshops in different regions of the country.

One of the important differences between home producers and workshop producers is the size of carpets they weave. While household production produces small size carpets (6 m^2 or less), workshops mostly weave larger size. Another dissimilarity of these two methods is the quality of woven carpets. In the workshops, the quality of carpets is expected to be higher because of the better raw materials, texture and constant monitoring on weavers' works. Besides, workshops usually engage more experienced weavers. However, workshop production increases the cost and eventually the price of carpets. Therefore, it is essential to support and maintain the production of carpets in workshops to assist the constant quality and distinctive features of the PCs.[282]

---

281 See: Nourallah Pasha, 'مطالعه ویژگیهای اجتماعی شیوه تولید خانگی وکارگاهی در تولید فرش دستباف دراستان همدان (A Study on Social Features of Domestic and Workshop Production Methods in Producing Hand-Woven Carpets in Hamadan Province)' (Iran National Carpet Centre 2003).

282 *ibid.*

Therefore, government policy has been focused on promoting this method. In this regard, in 2003, the 'Act for Supporting Establishment and Administration of Large and Centred Carpet Weaving Complexes' was enacted.[283] According to the by-law of the Act, complexes shall apply the quality criteria which are set by Iran National Carpet Centre (INCC). These criteria cover a wide range of issues such as using specific raw materials, the methods of weaving, washing mechanisms, and the standards of tools.[284] If these criteria are violated, the INCC, after two written notices, will proceed with the suspension of the establishment license.[285]

4.2.3 Well-Known Producers of PCs

In the following table, some well-known producers of PCs are briefly introduced:[286]

TABLE 2 Well-known producers

Region	Well-known producers
Arak	– Peoples: Moshtaghi and Madani. – Companies: Salim Shahanian Co., Telfenian Co., Navsahandchian Co.
Azerbaijan	– Peoples: Haj Jalili, Haj Hasan Aalabaf, Sedghiani, Alinasab Brothers, Nezamidoost, Tabatabaei.
Isfahan	– Peoples in Isfahan: Seirafian, Safdarzadeh Haghighi, Dardashti, Mahdiei. – Peoples in Kashan: Mohtasham, Miralavi, Farshchi, Ataei, Dabir-al-Sanaye, Mola Mahmoud, Tavakoli, Esfahanian, Kashi, Etminan, Sedghiani. – Peoples in Naein: Habibian, Mofidi, Ghanbari, Haj Bandeh Ali.

283 See: Iran – Act for Supporting Establishment and Administration of Large and Centred Carpet Weaving Complexes 2002.

284 Iran – By-Law of the Act for Supporting Establishment and Administration of Large and Centred Carpet Weaving Complexes 2006 (A Decree of Iran Council of Ministers) Article 6.

285 *ibid Article 7.*

286 Daneshgar (n 208).

TABLE 2 Well-known producers (*cont.*)

Region	Well-known producers
Khorasan	– Peoples in Mashhad: Amoughli, Makhmalbaf, Khamenei, Saber, Akhavan Nasaj, Madad, Sheikh Bour Rangi, Momeni, Khadivi, Heidar Kafi Pour, Sheshgelani, Ghazi Khani. – Peoples in Birjand: Derakhshi, Abdolali Ahmadi, Jamshidi, Khamenei, Kamyabi, Malek, Bazargan, Farasat, Amini. – Companies in Birjand: Shargh Co. – Peoples in Kashmar: Tork, Golestani, Vazan, Abedini, Moshtaghi, Mosafer. – Peoples in Tabas: Attari, Nakhaiee, Ghasemnia, Meghdari, Gholami, Nasiri, Rasoulof. – Peoples in Sabzevar: Cheshmi, Feizabadi, Taghadosi, Soufian. – Peoples in Neishabour: Golabetouni, Fakour, Mazdourkar.

4.2.4 Well-Known Designers of PCs

In the following table, some well-known designers of PCs are briefly introduced:[287]

TABLE 3 Well-known designer in each region

Region	Well-known designers
Arak	– Asadollah Daghighi, Jafar Chegini, Zabiholah Abtahi, Eshghi Golbaz, Ezzatollah Ebrahimi and Mohammad Astaneh.
Azerbaijan	– Rassam Arzhangi, Habibollah Amin Afshar, Ahmad Emad, Abbas Ali Aalabaf, Taghi Khiabani, Gholamhossein Habibi, Shirfard and Khouban Fard.
Hamedan	– Shahab-al-din Kosari, Eshagh Mirzapour, Mirza Reza Yeganeh, Ali Asghar Hasankhani, Ahmad Ghafari, Hasan Shahidi, Mahmoud Ahmad Shahidi, Asadollah Shakhesi, Mohammad Gilani.

287 *ibid.*

TABLE 3 Well-known designer in each region (*cont.*)

Region	Well-known designers
Isfahan	– Ahmad Archang, Seyed Jafar Rashtian, Reza Shakeri, Abbas Karbasioun, Issa Bahadori, Ahmad Shokrani, Asghar Bayat and Akbar Mahdiei in Isfahan. – Seyed Reza Khan Sanei, Mirza Nasrollah Naghashzadeh, Mohammad Afsari, Nezam Afsari, Mohammad Sanei, Hossein Taghdisi, Abbas Mohtashamzadeh and Amir Karimpour in Kashan. – Sheikh Hasan Motevalli, Akhavan Mofidi, Jahan Mofidi, Reza Yousef Pour, Mohammad Ali Rahnian Mohammadi, Hasan Talhani and Jahangir Talhani in Naein.
Khorasan	– Mirza Hasan Zarrin Kalak, Mirza Hasan Tarhchi, Abdolhamid Sanatkar, Haj Seyed Mehdi Javaherghalam, Haj Seyed Mehdi Yazdi and Mohammad Hossein Fakhr-al-Vaezin Mahdavi in Mashhad. – Mohammad Ali Samimi, Mahmoud Karim Kermani, Mohammad Hasan Lotfi in Birjand. – Tavakol Fathi, Abdollah Fathi, Mohammad Safarzadeh, Mohammad Reza Sheibani, Masha'allah Hadi, Hasan Soltani and Hossein Fathi in Tabas.

5 Who Might Represent Beneficiaries?

To manage TKHs' rights and to help the government in the administration of its duty to promote and protect those rights, specific representatives and agencies have to be established as focal points of the TKHs concerned. Governments shall consult THKs through their representatives.[288] Secondly, TKHs' representatives shall be fully included in the decision making process regarding their TK.[289] For instance they shall participate in any process regarding the documentation of TK.[290] Thirdly, TKHs shall be able to take legal proceedings against the abuse of their rights – including use, management and conservation

288 Indigenous and Tribal Peoples Convention Article 6(1); and also: 'United Nations Declaration on the Rights of Indigenous Peoples' (n 48) Article 32.

289 United Nations, 'What Can We Do? Activity Guide for the Implementation of the Second International Decade of the World's Indigenous People, 2005–2014' (Department of Economic and Social Affairs 2010) Page 9.

290 WIPO, 'The World Intellectual Property Organization Traditional Knowledge Documentation Toolkit' (World Intellectual Property Organization 2012) Page 12.

of their resources – through their representatives.[291] For example, TKHs' representatives could apply for IPRs on behalf of their respected communities. Representative also have an important role on awareness-raising campaigns for informing their respected communities of their existing rights and structures and to support the recognition and protection of the rights of communities. This could be implemented through a reporting and monitoring system.[292] However, further points need to be considered. Firstly, determining who can act on behalf of TKHs in PCs. And secondly, identifying the political and commercial nature of these representatives:

5.1 *Commercial Representatives*

5.1.1 Associations

Unions play a significant role in protecting TK. The primary approach and the ultimate goal of the unions, particularly, and guilds in general, are to protect the rights of their members. In the context of TK, the most prominent right of TKHs is to maintain the collective rights of the communities' members over TK. For example, Rurales' and nomads' unions may support their members to use and practice their TK, including irrigation and farming practices, the use of natural fertilizers, pest control practices, plant and animal breeding, coping with unexpected coldness and hundreds of other practical knowledge. In area of PCs, hand-woven carpet associations play a critical role in the process of production to the final stage of trading. They act as representatives of producers and merchants alongside the national authorities, particularly, with regards to the implementation and administration of recognized rights of PCs actors. The competence of the unions includes organization's affairs, duties, powers, limits and rights of unions and their members. Crafts and traders in the similar occupational activities may form their union. These unions are independent and they have non-profit legal personality.[293] The authorities and obligations of the unions are accounted for as:

- Submission of the proposal for the preparation, regulation or modification of the criteria for issuing business licenses and work permits to the Council of Trade Unions,
- Implementation of the resolutions and directives of the Supreme Supervisory Board and the Supervisory Commission,
- Submission of the proposals regarding trade unions' affairs to the council of trade unions,

291 Indigenous and Tribal Peoples Convention Article 12 and 15(1).

292 United Nations (n 289) Pages 27 and 33.

293 Iran – Act on Country's Guild System Articles 1 and 21(note 1).

- Issuance of business license in accordance with applicable laws and regulations,
- Revocation of licenses and suspending the businesses which disobey the law and regulations and preventing unauthorised business activities of traders that are not licensed or whose licenses are cancelled,
- Creating the necessary facilities for the training of unions and their members,
- Establishment of Commissions for hearing complaints, dispute settlements, inspection of business units, technical and educational offices. …[294]

The rules and regulations of the guild system, in particular, have paid special attention to the businesses in the field of hand-woven carpets and in the mechanisms in which associations operate in the production and supply of handmade carpets. The law and its regulations have established the appropriate capacities to create PCs production and trade associations. According to this law, emphasizing the importance of PCs, the lawmaker allowed the establishment of provincial or local associations of hand-woven carpets weavers or related professions in order to support hand-woven carpets professions.[295] Some important associations that are active in the PCs professions are:

- Iran Carpet Manufacturers and Exporters Association
- Iran Rural Hand-Woven Carpet Central Association
- Iran Nation-Wide Union of Carpet Producing Cooperatives
- East Azerbaijan Union of Carpet Producing Cooperatives
- Tehran Carpet Sellers Association
- Carpet Manufacturers & Weavers Union of Tabriz
- Qum Hand-Woven Carpet Exporters Association
- Isfahan Hand-Woven Carpet Producers Association
- Shiraz Hand-Woven Carpet Weavers Association
- Khorasan Razavi Hand-Woven Carpet Exporters Association
- Mashhad Hand-Woven Carpet Weavers and Producers Association
- Yazd Hand-Woven Carpet Sellers Association

Considering the extensive list of associations of hand-woven carpets, a very rich capacity is available for TKHs of PCs in different regions in Iran to serve as their representatives.

5.1.2 Merchants

Merchants play a key role, among others, for continuing the production of PCs. In the absence of PCs merchants or ineffective trade practicing, carpet as a

294 *ibid Article 30.*

295 *ibid Article 77.*

commodity will face an unavoidable misfortune and the gradual destruction. Therefore, merchants are also considered as an important part of the production chain. In this regard, 'Act for Protection of Geographical Indications' refers to traders as producers:

> "Producer" means any person who is engaged in production and processing of agricultural, livestock and food products or produces industrial tools and handmade articles or manipulates natural materials for the purpose of production or a trader of the said products.[296]

According to last part of this recital, a trader of handmade articles counts as producer. Therefore, merchants of PCs are member of communities concerned. These traders can be natural persons or legal entities. Amongst the most important legal entities involved in the trading of PCs are the hand-woven carpet cooperative companies and Iran Carpet Company.[297] At the same time, as will be pointed out in later sections, PCs' merchants can be considered as beneficiary only in case they can provide evidences of a kind of dependence on carpet production areas. Hence, provincial units of each of these companies can be considered as traders if they have an independent legal personality.

5.2 *Public Representatives*

In Iran, two types of public representatives consisting of governmental institutions and elected institutions for TKHs of PCs are recognized.

5.2.1 Governmental Institutions

Regarding governments obligations, TKHs expect a wide range of activities to be undertaken by governments among them:

- designate an appropriate authority as a body or an agency which is authorized by the State or entrusted with the responsibility to supervise and administer the rules and regulations,[298]

---

296 Iran – Act for Protection of Geographical Indications 2005 Article 1(d).

297 Iran Carpet Co. was established in 1935 and possesses over 80 years of rich experiences of weaving, producing and commercialization of PCs. It is a major public company and the biggest hand-woven carpet companies across the country. It has 100 branches in the major cities and 500 branches in the rural areas with 10.000 weavers. Besides, providing wide-range of carpets in different size, design and dyeing, the Company participates in the national and international fairs and exhibitions, and taking orders for producing unique carpets for specific places and consumers. See: 'History | Iran Carpet Co.' (n 237).

298 Swakopmund Protocol Section 2(1).

- ensure the existence of appropriate agencies and mechanisms for administrating the programs affecting THKS,[299]
- ensure that activities like handicrafts, rural and community-based industries are strengthened and promoted,[300]
- provide technical and financial assistance for TKHS,[301]
- take necessary action for protecting the rights of TKHS,[302]
- prevent and redress any action which may aim to or affect TKHS' cultural values or their integrity as distinct peoples,[303]
- prevent third parties from unauthorized use of TK,[304]
- mitigate TKHS' difficulties in facing new conditions of life,[305]
- improve TKHS' life and work conditions and levels of health and education,[306]
- carry out studies to assess the social, cultural and environmental impact of development activities on TKHS.[307]

It happens that TK has no identifiable holder or author, therefore, one of the state duties is to identify the beneficiaries, when there is no identifiable holder of TK.[308] The Berne Convention principally has accepted that the works of unknown creators are entitled to be protected. To do so it has recognized those works may be represented by the designated competent national authorities.[309] Such an approach is taken in the USA copyright law in cases where an identifiable person reworks a work of unknown authorship.[310]

Besides all the above-mentioned functions, national authorities can take any other measures which seem to them necessary for protection of TK. Although all of those obligations are of the same value, I assume the first and the most important task of governments is to designate an 'appropriate authority' as a body or an agency which is authorized by the State or entrusted

299 Indigenous and Tribal Peoples Convention Article 33(1).

300 *ibid Article 23(1).*

301 *ibid Article 23(2).*

302 *ibid Article 2(1).*

303 'United Nations Declaration on the Rights of Indigenous Peoples' (n 48) Article 8(2)(a).

304 Indigenous and Tribal Peoples Convention Articles 14–15–16 and 17(3).

305 *ibid Article 5(c).*

306 *ibid Article 7(2).*

307 *ibid Article 7(3).*

308 UNEP-CBD, 'Report of the Meeting of the Group of Technical and Legal Experts on Traditional Knowledge Associated with Genetic Resources in the Context of the International Regime on Access and Benefit-Sharing' (2009) CBD AHWG, 8th mtg, Agenda Item 32, UNEP Doc UNEP/CBD/WG-ABS/8/2 Page 21.

309 Berne Convention Article 15(4).

310 Munzer and Raustiala (n 5) Page 53 Footnote 38.

with the responsibility to supervise and administer the rules and regulations.[311] By the same token, in Iran, some institutions have been designated as responsible agencies for fulfilling such tasks, but of course, these institutions have different approaches. In the first approach, PCs, as manifiestations of TK, are subject matter of protection. In the second, the institutions' obligation is to support TKHs themselves. Therefore, I will consider both types to reach tangible understanding of which approach could be more efficient for the protection of PCs.

5.2.1.1 *Iran National Carpet Centre* (INCC)

Before 2003, policies, administration, supervision and management regarding PCs production and trade were divided across several institutions of different levels such as Ministry of Commerce, Ministry of Agriculture Jihad, the Handicraft Organization, Iran Carpet Company, and others. In 2003, in order to centralize and organize PCs affairs in a unique nation-wide institution, the INCC established.[312] It is affiliated with the Ministry of Industry, Mine, and Commerce. The goals for establishing the Centre are:

- increasing in production,
- enhancing quality,
- organizing the hand-woven carpet industry,
- solving market problems including supply and marketing,
- setting the criteria and technical requirements for production and exports,
- preserving the artistic and cultural aspects of hand-woven carpets,
- reducing government role in production and sales,
- aggregating the tasks of parallel state-owned institutions in one organization,[313]
- investigating and addressing violations of 'Large and Centred Carpet Weaving Complexes' that do not comply with production quality standards, and suspending their licenses.[314]

Establishment of the Centre has provided the possibility of an integrated management of PCs across the country. Accordingly, all issues regarding PCs including policy making, planning, conduction, supervision, support and protection of hand-woven carpets, as well as researches and education, setting

311 Swakopmund Protocol Section 2(1).

312 Iran – Resolution on Increasing of Production, Enhancing of Quality and Organizing Hand-Woven Carpet Industry 2003 (Resolution of High Council of Administrative Affairs).

313 *ibid Note 1.*

314 Iran – By-Law of the Act for Supporting Establishment and Administration of Large and Centred Carpet Weaving Complexes Article 7.

the criteria and technical requirements regarding production and export of the hand-woven carpets have been transferred from other organizations and institutions and assigned to the Centre. On the other hand, government involvement in producing and trade of carpets has been delegated to the private sector.[315] The INCC provides the necessary legal ground and capacity for the use of law for protection of PCs such as IPRS. INCC functions and obligations are to support and protect PCs itself as subject matter of TK. It does not protect and support TKHs themselves.

5.2.1.2 *Iran High Council of Nomads*

The establishment of the 'High Council of Nomads' was suggested for the first time in the era of 'Muzaffar ad-Din Shah' who was the fifth Qajar Monarch of Persia and reigned from 1896 to 1907. But in practice, Council was created in 1946 during the next dynasty, the Pahlavi, with the goal to regulate Nomads affairs.[316] After Islamic Revolution of 1979, the Council was restructured under the Ministry of Internal Affairs to settle Nomads' problems and improve their levels of life as well as the restoration of indigenous and tribal cultures and traditions, and support them by providing social services such as education and health.[317] Soon it was realized that the Ministry of Internal Affairs did not have enough capacity to manage all aspects of Nomads needs and expectations and more institutions should be engaged to meet Nomadic Peoples' requirements. Therefore, in 1986, the Council was reformed again under the Iran Presidency Office. The duties of the Council are:

- Policy making, long-term, and short-term planning,
- Coordinating with various operational responsible organizations and monitoring their programs and operations,
- Providing facilities for the improvement and development of animal husbandry and handicraft products of nomads,
- Addressing the status of the nomadic community of Iran,
- Improving the living conditions and reviving traditional and nomadic cultures,
- Proper use of their potential and talents.[318]

---

315 Iran – Resolution on Increasing of Production, Enhancing of Quality and Organizing Hand-Woven Carpet Industry Note 2.

316 See: 'تاریخچه سازمان امور عشایر ایران (History of Nomad Affairs Organization)' (*Organization for Nomads Affairs*, 2008) <http://ashayer.ir/index.aspx?fkeyid=&siteid=1&pageid=135>.

317 See: Iran – Reconstruction of Iran High Council of Nomads in the Ministry of Internal Affairs 1980 (A Resolution of Iran Revolutionary Council).

318 Iran – Decree on Establishment of Iran's Nomads High Council Article 4.

Although the Council, as a responsible body, has the authority to take necessary measures for supporting and protecting Nomads' TK, its duties regarding the production of handmade carpets have been delegated to the INCC.

5.2.1.3 *Provincial Councils for Planning and Development*

In the Iranian administration system, the 'Provincial Councils for Planning and Development' play a special role in managing local affairs and enjoy relative autonomy. Local governors and other government officials are required to comply with the decisions of the councils, which are made based on the councils' competence.[319] The responsibilities of the Councils, among others, include determining the economic, social, and cultural development policies as well as investment opportunities in each province.[320]

It should be noted that the Councils have technical and professional committees which work as specialized working groups of the Councils and evaluate local communities' needs. The Culture and Art Working Group, which has a special and guided role in supporting TKHs, is one of them. Although the structure of the Council provides a high capacity for the support of TKHs in general and PCs in particular within development programs, it has not yet addressed the issue.

5.2.1.4 *Other State Entities*

In addition to the aforementioned governmental bodies, other organizations also share responsibilities in supporting individuals and legal entities involved in the PCs production. According to the 'Act for Supporting Artists, Artisans, and Handicrafts Practitioners,' PCs are recognized as an innovative and aesthetic manifestation of the artistic and traditional industries. The Ministry of Cultural Heritage, Tourism, and Handicrafts and the Ministry of Industry, Mine, and Commerce bear direct responsibility for supporting the PCs production. Other governmental organizations, indirectly and in cooperation with these two ministries, are also tasked with providing support for PCs and other handicrafts.

These supportive actions encompass a wide range of management and technical assistance, information dissemination, education, promotion, financial support, and the empowerment of non-governmental, cooperative, and private institutions. Notably, Note (D) of Article (4) specifically assigns these two ministries the duties of *coordination* and *planning* regarding the IPRs of

319 *Iran – The Constitution of the Islamic Republic of Iran 1979 Principle 104.*

320 Iran – Law for the Third Development Plan of the I.R. Iran 2000 Article 71 and 73; and Iran – Law on Standing Rules of the Country Development Program 2017 Article 31.

PCs both domestically and internationally. However, it is important to note that none of these responsibilities explicitly includes the representation of artists, craftsmen, and handicrafts practitioners.[321]

5.2.2 Elected Institutions

In Iran, local people elect the members of the 'Village Councils' and 'City Councils' through a direct vote in accordance with the 'Law on Organization, Duties and Election of the Islamic Councils of the Country and Assignment of Mayors.'[322] Unfortunately, nothing in the law refers to the TK of the respected communities. Although, it calls for participation and cooperation of the public in cultural activities.[323] But it seems non-efficient for offering any kind of support for TKHs or their TK. While TK had been considered in the prior abolished laws. For example, the efforts for documenting village historical geography, identity, stories, legends, customs, rituals, poems and local songs were part of rights and obligations of Village Associations, who should cooperate with 'Village House of Culture' and seek guidance from respected elders and local authorities to fulfill these responsibilities[324] or on the duties of the Islamic Councils of Village, the act encourages villagers to engage in handicrafts and rural industries.[325] Although the members of these institutions are representatives of the villagers, in practice their capacity does not include management of the TK or supporting respected communities.[326]

6 Summary

TK is an important subject matter for a wide range of communities known as TKHs across the world. As it was mentioned earlier in Section 1 of this chapter, the vital role of TK is relatively reflected in various international legal instruments which call for respecting the rights of TKHs and the supporting and protection of TK. Although TK has absorbed a lot of interest from different stakeholders, and despite the efforts made by beneficiaries and users of TK, there is no agreement on what the proper legal definition of TK is. Some scholars defend the necessity of reaching a worldwide accepted definition for TK.

---

321 See: Iran – Act for Supporting Artists, Artisans, and Handicrafts Practitioners 2018.
322 See: Iran – Law on Organization, Duties and Election of the Islamic Councils of the Country and Assignment of Mayors 1996.
323 *ibid Article 68(L).*
324 Iran – Act for the Establishment of Village Association and Village's Governor 1975 Article 27(11) and (13).
325 Iran – Act on Establishment of the Country Islamic Councils 1982 Article 26(5).
326 See: Motamedi (n 266).

In contrast, others discuss how TK has a dynamic nature and no definition can fully represent TK. Instead, they suggest we will be better off with identification of what the subject matters of TK are. I could not be more in agreement with the second group and I suppose that an abstract definition of TK will not help to reach an agreement for protection of TK both on international and national levels. Besides, any definition should be left to the national authorities and TKHs to provide their version of definition regarding different faces of TK in the respective communities.

If we accept that no comprehensive definition on TK could and should be reached, then the subject matters of TK need to be identified. We expect to learn what is protectable as TK. Supporters of the no-definition idea are divided among themselves on the issue of subject matter of TK. The first group regards TK in a narrow sense and believes TK only to include knowledge in the form of know-how, practices, skills and innovations in nature, and should be treated and protected as such. The second group accounts the difficulties of such a vision, and considers TK in a broader sense. They argue that TK is not separable from GRs and TCEs in nature and therefore, knowledge, genetic materials and culture of TKHs shall be protected under one umbrella of TK. This approach seems to be more reasonable in relation to PCs. As the knowledge related to the production of raw materials or finished carpet products receives little to no protection for TKHs in the context of handicrafts and PCs, I put PCs under general discussion of protection of TK.

After considering PCs as subject matter of TK, the next important issue is to assess who are the beneficiaries of TK protection in general and PCs protection in particular. The term 'Beneficiaries' encompasses a wide range of concepts. It is concluded from current global debates that local communities, indigenous peoples and individuals of these communities are the most related people to the term beneficiaries. However, in this study TKHs were considered as beneficiaries; because TK includes a broader scope than indigenous people, and it is essential to include as many communities and related individuals as possible as TK beneficiaries.

In the light of the discussion of TK beneficiaries, the analysis of PCs was extended to identify beneficiaries of PCs in the rural and nomadic communities as well as in cities, and related individuals to those communities. Then Iran's laws and regulations were examined to determine who could play the role of representative of TKHs in regards to PCs.

A wide range of beneficiaries is involved in PC production. These beneficiaries include communities and their individual members, cooperatives and associations. Three well-known groups of communities are known to be beneficiaries of PCs.

Iran's rural communities include households that have independent customary or formal sovereignty and are homogeneous in terms of natural, social, cultural and economic status. They engage in rural industries and, in particular, in producing PCs.

Urban areas in Iran are the communities that have emerged from the expansion of the rural regions. Thus, cities carry the cultural, social and economic heritage of Iranian villagers. Moreover, rural migration to cities leads to a continuous cultural, social and economic exchange between rural and urban areas. The production of PCs in cities is therefore under the influence of the surrounding rural areas. Despite the common features between the rural and urban areas, it should be noted that, at the same time, urban communities have unique characteristics that distinguish them from rural areas. For example, unlike in villages where individual producers are more common, workshop productions are more common in cities. Moreover, many professions, especially in services, are also concentrated in cities. The differences between the criteria of the villages and cities are legally significant in the context of PCs and the application of the protection mechanisms. For instance, there are dissimilarities in the local authorities, representatives and administrative institutions.

The third significant group of beneficiaries of PCs is tribal communities. The Iranian legal system officially recognizes their independent identity. Moreover, as nomadic people, they migrate according to the seasons, and, therefore, they are simultaneously under the governance of their various places of residence.

Cities like Tabriz, Isfahan, Kashan, Qum, Mashhad, Bijar and Sarough; rural areas such as Haris, Sharabian, Ravar, Mahan, Golbaf; and the nomads of Shahsevan, Qashqai, Lor and Afshar are some examples of communities well known for producing high-quality PCs.

More than 28 professional disciplines are members of these communities. However, the carpet weavers and designers play the most crucial role in this context. Weavers and designers work either individually as domestic producers or together in workshop productions. Domestic production includes producers on their own accounts and producers who take orders from others. In workshop production, the carpet-producing activities take place in the workshops. Domestic producers are heavily dependent on those individuals who provide them with raw materials. Workshop owners employ weavers and designers as contractors. Production in workshops has been predominant in the PC industry. While workshops produce higher quality carpets, their cost is higher too. Therefore, it is essential to support and maintain the production of carpets in workshops to ensure the consistent quality and distinctive features of the PCs. Some major PC producers such as the 'Iran Carpet Company' and 'Astan-e-ghods-e-Razavi Carpet Co' operate such workshops in different regions of the country. Also, there is a long list of well-known producers and designers.

Other key beneficiaries of PCs are representatives of TKHs. These include:

- commercial representatives including PCs' associations and merchants,
- public representatives including INCC; Iran High Council of Nomads; and Provincial Councils for Planning and Development; and Village and City Councils.

These entities carry out a wide range of activities on behalf of the TKHs. Such activities include documentation of the TK in PCs, awareness-raising, managing, promoting and protecting TKHs' rights, assisting national and local authorities in policy-making, and participation in implementation of the laws and regulations.

CHAPTER 2

Intellectual Property Protection of Traditional Knowledge

1 The Concept of Protection

The term 'protection' in the context of TK and IPRs involves several concepts that must be addressed and distinguished. TK manifestations differ in their nature and functions; thus, common elements of these manifestations need to be identified. Such definitions will help in finding the most appropriate system for meeting the needs and expectations of TKHs for protection. As discussed earlier in my brief review of international instruments, major documents already address, in their respective contexts, the aspirations for protection of TK. In the context of biodiversity, protection may mean conservation, preservation and safeguarding of TK through customary, local, regional, national and international actions and steps. In the context of IPRs, protection of TK may mean a demand for recognition and respect for the exclusive rights of TKHs over TK. It may also mean legal action against misappropriation and unauthorized use and misuse of TK by parties other than TKHs.[327]

Conservation of biological diversity and sustainable development are key goals for TKHs.[328] They are vital because commercial and industrial use of TK will affect the TKHs' endeavours to use and preserve their natural resources and biodiversity. Therefore it is important for them not to be prevented from accessing and using their environment as this will lead TK to extinction.[329] Safeguarding of TK aims at "the adoption of precautionary measures to shield certain cultural practices and ideas which are considered of value."[330] and

327 WIPO, *Intellectual Property, Traditional Knowledge and Traditional Cultural Expressions/ Folklore: A Guide for Countries in Transition* (1st edn, World Intellectual Property Organization 2013) Page 4.

328 CBD Art 1.

329 Anil K Gupta, 'Rewarding Traditional Knowledge and Contemporary Grassroots Creativity: The Role of Intellectual Property Protection,' *A Seminar at Kennedy School* (Harvard University 2000) Page 5.

330 IGC-GRTKF Secretariat, 'Glossary of Key Terms Related to Intellectual Property and Genetic Resources, Traditional Knowledge and Traditional Cultural Expressions' (n 161) Page 37.

"... (e)nsuring the viability of the intangible cultural heritage."[331] The Convention for the Safeguarding of the Intangible Heritage describes the particular steps that are needed to enable the different aspects of heritage to be maintained. These measures include "identification, documentation, research, preservation, protection, promotion, enhancement, transmission ... as well as the revitalization"[332] of such heritage, in particular, by using the formal and non-formal education systems. The goal of preservation is to maintain the cultural and social context of TK and TCEs. It assists in sustaining TK and TCEs for future generations of TKHs.[333] It makes them accessible for public users like researchers conducting studies regarding the importance of TK and TCEs for humanity.[334] Two broad elements characterize the preservation of TK. The first element is the act of the maintaining the customary framework of developing, passing on and governing TK and TCEs, and the second is the act of maintaining TK and TCEs in fixed forms.[335]

To achieve the goals of conservation, safeguarding and preservation of TK is not an easy task. On one hand, different protection mechanisms might be chosen to meet these policies' goals. For example, international organizations like UNEP and UNESCO deal with the preservation, conservation and safeguarding of TK and TCEs in the context of their specific policy.[336] Although the coherence between various protection mechanisms and different policies must be maintained, practical protection systems need to be used to attain the overall objectives of the chosen mechanism for protection. On the other hand, any approach for achieving these goals of protecting TK may increase the already considerable risk of rapid loss and forfeiture of TK. To overcome this risk it needs to consider appropriately the distinct nature and social and economic characteristics of TK through *per se* respecting and strengthening those

331 Intangible Heritage Convention Art 2(3).

332 *ibid.*

333 IGC-GRTKF Secretariat, 'Glossary of Key Terms Related to Intellectual Property and Genetic Resources, Traditional Knowledge and Traditional Cultural Expressions' (n 161) Page 30.

334 *ibid.*

335 IGC-GRTKF Secretariat, 'Overview of Outcomes and Activities of the Intergovernmental Committee' (World Intellectual Property Organization 2003) WIPO Doc WIPO/GRTKF/IC/5/12 Page 7 Para 18. In this context documentation is seen as a form of fixation. Hofman defines 'fixation' as to put the work into material form for example by writing it down or recording it; See: Julien Hofman, *Introducing Copyright: A Plain Language Guide to Copyright in the 21st Century* (Commonwealth of Learning 2009) Pages 30–31.

336 IGC-GRTKF Secretariat, 'Glossary of Key Terms Related to Intellectual Property and Genetic Resources, Traditional Knowledge and Traditional Cultural Expressions' (n 161) Page 30.

distinct features of TK systems. Therefore, it is necessary to choose the protection mechanisms that could best help to halt the rapid loss of TK.[337] In this regard, IPRs have a significant role to play in the protection of TK.

2 Intellectual Property Rights as a Tool for Protection of TK?

TK has been produced by the innovative and creative efforts of TKHs. Thus, TK could be counted as a subject matter of IPRs. As the convention establishing the world intellectual property organization stipulates, IPRs include intellectual activity:

> Intellectual property shall include the rights to: … and all rights resulting from intellectual activity in the industrial, scientific, literary or artistic fields.[338]

The same opinion has been offered by the report of the Organization for Economic Co-operation and Development (OECD)[339] on IPRs which redefines these types of rights as the product of intellectual effort and ingenuity:

> Intellectual property rights are rights granted by state authority for certain products of intellectual effort and ingenuity[340]

The UNESCO Convention on Cultural Diversity "recognizes the importance of IPRs in sustaining those involved in cultural creativity."[341] And finally, The UN declaration on the rights of indigenous peoples recognizes their IPRs over their heritage, knowledge and culture:

> Holders of TK should be entitled to fair and equitable sharing of benefits arising from the use of their knowledge.

---

337 See UNEP-CBD Executive Secretary (n 43).

338 Convention Establishing the World Intellectual Property Organization 1967 (828 UNTS 3 (entered into force 26 April 1970)) Article 2(viii).

339 See: Richard Woodward, *The Organization for Economic Co-Operation and Development (OECD)* (Routledge 2009).

340 See: R Stephen Crespi and Joseph Straus, 'Intellectual Property, Technology Transfer and Genetic Resources: An OECD Survey of Current Practices and Policies' (OECD Publishing 1996) Page 12.

341 Convention on the Protection and Promotion of the Diversity of Cultural Expressions (CPPDCE) 2005 (2440 UNTS 311 (entered into force 18 March 2007)) Preamble.

> … they also have the right to maintain, control, protect and develop their intellectual property over such cultural heritage, traditional knowledge, and traditional cultural expressions.[342]

Having considered the abovementioned relationship between TK and IPRS, however, there is some opposition against protection of TK under IPRS.

During the 11th session of the United Nations Permanent Forum on Indigenous Issues which was held on 7–18 May, 2012, the indigenous peoples' delegations presented the view that WIPO's measures and procedures on the issue of TK, TCES and GRS are immoral and illegal. They advised indigenous peoples and nations to establish their own standards and mechanisms for protection of TK, TCES and GRS.[343] This view is not new, and for many years there have been a substantial number of objections against the negative role of IPRS in preservation and promotion of TK. These arguments include:

First, the conflict between exclusive rights conferred to the private sector by a strong IPRS regime on one side and TKHS' principle rights to use and develop their knowledge on the other side. Speaking, IPRS regimes are not generally designed with features that meet TKHS needs and expectations but rather to respond to the economic requirements of modern industries.[344] The proper goal of IPRS is to concentrate, increase and monopolize the economic power in the hands of right holders, often well-organized rich corporations with strong technological capabilities. This enables them to play a key role in policies on price and access to TK and TK-based products. As a result, there would be no level playing field enabling TKHS, especially in the developing countries, to compete with them.[345]

Second, there is a concern about the lack of appropriate mechanisms to push IPRS holders to transfer the modern technologies for usage of TK to the original local and indigenous communities. This happens either because TKHS are "unaware of their legal options"[346] or IPRS holders do not have any legal

342 'United Nations Declaration on the Rights of Indigenous Peoples' (n 48) Article 31(1).

343 Gale Courey Toensing, 'World Intellectual Property Organization Blasted for "Misappropriation" of Indigenous Knowledge, Resources' (*Indian Country Today Media Network.com*, 16 May 2012).

344 See Thailand statement on behalf of Asian group: IGC-GRTKF Secretariat, 'Report of Intergovernmental Committee on Intellectual Property and Genetic Resources, Traditional Knowledge and Folklore' (n 61) Page 9.

345 Khor (n 35) Page 10.

346 Riffel (n 3) Page 142.

obligation to recognize and respect the fundamental role of local and indigenous communities in creating and promoting TK under TIP.[347]

Third, there is evidence of the role of IPRS in facilitating misappropriation and misuse of different facets of TK through biopiracy. Different regimes of IPRS have a considerable impact on traditional forms of exchange and dissemination of TK. The most important reason for this impact is the emergence of modern technologies. IPRS as a legal foundation could take TK beyond the TKHS' jurisdiction. In this regard, among the basic points of agreement of the COICA/UNDP Regional Meeting on IPRS and Biodiversity, it was accepted that the IP system means legitimation of the misappropriation of indigenous peoples' knowledge and resources.[348]

Fourth, so far, TK *per se* is not covered by specific forms of IPRS. TK is publicly available, so how it could be protected by IPRS?

Fifth, TK does not meet the requirement for novelty as an element of IP protection!

Sixth, as TK is not a new creation, there is no individual creator who can claim protection and we cannot readily identify the TKHS who are to be granted IPRS protection! "especially when, as is the case more often than not, the knowledge is spread across a community or several communities."[349] Therefore, TK has been free for use by third parties.

Seventh, TK is by its nature holistic: it is related to communities' identity and a part of their everyday life, whereas IPRS are commercial. Therefore, IPRS regimes are not generally the most appropriate means to protect TK.

Eighth, preservation is not a function of IPRS.

Moving on to the counter-arguments, some are in favor of IP protection of TK. These arguments are as follows:

First, the rise of the knowledge-based economy expands the vital role of IPRS worldwide. Rapid advance in technology development and increasing trade among countries increase the demand for stronger and more extensive IP protection in the industrialized countries. Therefore, the EU, USA, Switzerland and Japan have put IPRS at the centre of global trade policies as exemplified by the TRIPS Agreement among WTO agreements. The insertion of IPRS into the WTO agenda gave rise to controversy about IPRS policies[350] and many unsuccessful efforts were made to prevent the extension of IPRS as

347 Khor (n 35) Page 11.

348 Posey and Dutfield (n 180) Page 215.

349 Riffel (n 3) Page 142.

350 See: Susan K Sell, *Private Power, Public Law: The Globalization of Intellectual Property Rights* (Cambridge University Press 2003).

western-style rights.[351] Efforts have also been made to adjust IPRs and rebalance them among different actors in the developed and developing world. In this regard, some developing countries have considered TK could be a relevant subject matter for IPRs. Potentially, it could meet the need for rebalancing of the international IP system by considering TK as an IP asset and preventing misappropriation and misuse of TK by industrialized countries.[352] In the same way, as Cottier points out, "enhancing market access for environmentally preferable products could provide the framework to introduce enhanced protection of TK in the field of intellectual property rights."[353] Besides, as IPRs aim to encourage innovation and creativity through financial incentives the regime may include mechanisms for protection of TK if it is able to facilitate and promote financial motivation for TKHs.

Second, the role of TK in enhancing the legitimacy and rebalancing of IPRs is critical. Balanced mechanisms are a core tenet of IPRs.[354] IPRs have the capacity to be used as a tool for protection of TK and biodiversity. The content of TCEs might already be protected via copyright and related rights, GIs and trademarks.[355]

Third, the importance and relevance of IPRs in terms of the management, protection and utilization of TK is increasing all over the world.[356] Proponents of the protection of TK under IPRs argue that the worldwide capability of international IPRs regimes, which have been constantly getting stronger in recent decades, could be a useful tool for achieving TKHs' claims for protection.[357] For example, plant genetic resources are important parts of TK and IPRs have been granted to the users of plants in different forms, such as plant breeders'

351 Munzer and Raustiala (n 5) 50.

352 Josef Drexl and others (eds), 'Intellectual Property Chapters in Free Trade Agreements: Their Significance and Systemic Implications,' *EU Bilateral Trade Agreements and Intellectual Property: For Better or Worse?* (Springer 2014) Page 31.

353 Cottier, 'WTO Negotiations on Environmental Goods and Services' (n 25) Page 27.

354 In fact this balance has been the ultimate goal of objective in TRIPS Agreement as it stipulates: 'The protection and enforcement of intellectual property rights should contribute … in a manner conducive to social and economic welfare, and to a balance of rights and obligations.' See: TRIPS Agreement Article 7.

355 IGC-GRTKF Secretariat, 'Report of Intergovernmental Committee on Intellectual Property and Genetic Resources, Traditional Knowledge and Traditional Cultural Expressions' (World Intellectual Property Organization 2017) WIPO Doc WIPO/GRTKF/IC/33/7 7.

356 See the Delegation of Malaysia statement, speaking on behalf of the Asian Group: IGC-GRTKF Secretariat, 'Report of Intergovernmental Committee on Intellectual Property and Genetic Resources, Traditional Knowledge and Folklore' (n 61) Page 9.

357 Munzer and Raustiala (n 5) Page 57.

rights (PBRs) and trademarks for the names of varieties.[358] Besides IPRs, legal regimes like passing off and disclosure of confidential information may be used to protect TK.

Fourth, even if we suppose that TK has no element of novelty, IPRs aim to protect information and innovation. Therefore, novelty is not necessarily required for TK to be protected under IPRs. It is comparable to trademark protection in this respect. Moreover, we note that undisclosed information also lack novelty.[359] Moreover, TK includes a sense of creativity regarding *in-situ* and *ex-situ* utilization of resources. *Ex-situ* utilization aims to add commercial and economic values to the TK and the associated GRs while the TK has been used *in-situ* by the local and indigenous communities as a source of their own creative activities in an informal manner. Classification of TK as an informal intellectual activity has extended the rationale for counting TK as a specific area with special needs for legal protection, among them *sui generis* IPRs. Such a trend can be seen in the field of plant genetic resources where breeders are recognized as formal innovators and farmers as informal creators in the context of plant breeding.[360]

Fifth, "the term 'intellectual property protection' is taken to mean private property rights covering the intellectual contribution in TK and conferring exclusive rights to (i) control the commercial exploitation of that intellectual contribution and (ii) safeguard the integrity of and attribution to works."[361] Although IPRs are private rights, they might be assigned to the communities. IP regimes such as collective marks, GIs and trade secrets are examples of existing private rights assignable to communities.[362] Some suggest the concept of communities' IPRs which would mean that no third party can use TK without permission of the TKHs.[363] Protection under IPRs could guarantee the survival and productivity of TK for both holders and users.

358 For more information see: *International Convention for the Protection of New Varieties of Plants, as last revised at Geneva*, 19 March 1991, 1861 UNTS 281 (entered into force 24 April 1998) [*UPOV Convention*] at Article 20.

359 Thomas Cottier and Marion Panizzon, 'Legal Perspectives on Traditional Knowledge: The Case for Intellectual Property Protection' (2004) 7 Journal of International Economic Law 371, Page 390.

360 Government of Switzerland (n 145) Paragraph 9.

361 IGC-GRTKF Secretariat, 'Survey of Existing Forms of Intellectual Property Protection for Traditional Knowledge' (World Intellectual Property Organization 2001) WIPO Doc WIPO/GRTKF/IC/2/5 Page 4 Paragraph 11.

362 Cottier and Panizzon, 'Legal Perspectives on Traditional Knowledge' (n 359) Pages 382–383.

363 Anil K Gupta, *WIPO-UNEP Study on the Role of Intellectual Property Rights in the Sharing of Benefits Arising from the Use of Biological Resources and Associated Traditional Knowledge* (World Intellectual Property Organization 2004) Page 51.

Sixth, as well as having cultural value TK is commercially valuable information. IPRS are important to protect commercial aspects of TK.[364] If IPRS protection could be accorded properly to TK, huge potential social benefits could be expected for the communities concerned.[365]

Seventh, utilization of existing IPRS as a tool enables TKHS to enjoy protection at the international and regional levels. In particular, TKHS could benefit from the international and regional legal arrangements for approaching and harmonizing basic standards of protection. This also includes legal and administrative procedures for granting and enforcement of appropriate rights to TK beneficiaries and engagement of the national and international IP institutions to meet this goal.

Eighth, TK as scientific, artistic and/or literary production of TKHS deserves to be protected as IPRS under human rights norms and instruments.[366]

Considering the arguments on both sides, the opponents of IPRS appear to rely on the lack of competency and capability of existing IPRS regimes as an instrument for protection of TK. Although they may be right, it has not been shown that existing IPRS are in fact unable to provide a protection mechanism for TK and thus to rebalance an asymmetry. It is untested to what extent the flexibility of IPRS and their capability to improve protection of intellectual activities could make them suitable to address the concerns captured by TK for PCS' protection. Therefore, it is necessary to evaluate the gaps for protection of TK under the existing IPRS system and the approach available for filling those gaps.

2.1 *The Approaches for Protecting TK within IPRS Systems*

In the debates over setting policies for protection of TK, two principle demands have arisen:

---

364 Cottier and Panizzon, 'Legal Perspectives on Traditional Knowledge' (n 359) Page 374.

365 WIPO Secretariat, 'Matters Concerning Intellectual Property and Genetic Resources, Traditional Knowledge and Folklore' (n 116) Paragraph 14; and WIPO Secretariat, 'Report of General Assembly' (n 168) Page 14.

366 See: United Nations, 'The Universal Declaration of Human Rights' (1948) UN Doc GA Res 217 A (III), 3rd sess, UN Doc A/RES/3/217 A Article 27(2): "Everyone has the right to protection of moral and material interests resulting from any scientific, literary or artistic production of which he [or she] is the author."; and also see: International Covenant on Economic, Social and Cultural Rights (ICESCR) 1966 (993 UNTS 3 (entered into force 3 January 1976)) Article 15(1)(c) "The States Parties to the present Covenant recognize the right of everyone to benefit from the production of the moral and material interests resulting from any scientific, literary or artistic production which he is the author."

- Recognition of TKHs' rights relating to their TK,
- Prevention of unauthorized granting of IP rights over TK to outsiders.[367]

These two demands were crystallized in the legal approaches for protection of TK in the forms of 'positive protection' and 'defensive protection.' During the negotiations in the IGC meetings, many delegations of both countries and NGOs stated that both mechanisms are necessary for protection of TK.[368]

2.1.1 Defensive Protection

Defensive protection is defined in diverse wording such as:

- "Safeguarding against illegitimate IP rights taken out by others over TK subject matter."[369]
- Preventing the grant of improper IPRs to unauthorized persons is one of the core objectives of the protection system.[370]
- Preventing third persons from obtaining illegitimate or groundless IPRs over TK.[371]

In brief, the goal of this type of protection is to halt the misappropriation and misuse of TK by persons other than TKHs. This is necessary since IPRs have failed to prevent unfair exploitation of TK. Also, TKHs rely on defensive protection because some types of TK, such as sacred TK, shall not be owned by outsiders.[372] Moreover, defensive protection might be used as a tool to invalidate outsiders' IPRs or to block the enforcement of their IPRs which have been acquired based on TK used without PIC of the TKHs.[373] Finally, defensive protection is aimed to avoid third parties' taking any measure which "disparages, offends or falsely suggests connection with the community concerned, or brings the community into contempt or disrepute."[374]

---

367 Frederick M Abbott, Thomas Cottier and Francis Gurry, *International Intellectual Property in an Integrated World Economy* (2nd edn, Wolters Kluwer Law & Business 2011) Page 660.

368 IGC-GRTKF Secretariat, 'Overview of Outcomes and Activities of the Intergovernmental Committee' (n 335) Page 7.

369 Abbott, Cottier and Gurry (n 367) Page 660.

370 IGC-GRTKF Secretariat, 'Revised Provisions for the Protection of Traditional Knowledge: Policy Objectives and Core Principles' (n 36) Page 1.

371 IGC-GRTKF Secretariat, 'Overview of Outcomes and Activities of the Intergovernmental Committee' (n 335) Page 11.

372 Munzer and Raustiala (n 5) Page 50.

373 An example of this case is the EPO patent on a Neem-Oil based fungicide in 1994, while Indians have been using Neem as traditional medicine for centuries. Thus, the patent was challenged because it did not meet the 'inventive step' requirement for patenting the product and finally the EPO in 2000 revoked it. See: Bernard O'Connor, *The Law of Geographical Indications* (Cameron May 2004) Pages 363–364.

374 Swakopmund Protocol Section 19(2)(b).

In the context of PCs, TKHs need defensive protection to be recognized in order to prevent any use and avoid any acquisition or exercise of IPRs over words, signs, names, symbols, designs, patterns and motifs which could wrongfully suggest a link between PCs and their reputation with competitors in the global markets.

2.1.1.1 *Prior Informed Consent (PIC)*

In accordance with the principle of PIC, TKHs or their authorized representatives must be informed of any potential use of their TK and should grant consent for such a use. The principle of PIC may be applied and implemented through contracts or permits or upon mutually agreed terms,[375] which means a legal mechanism is needed to stipulate how PIC shall be implemented.[376]

The concept of PIC is derived from the ethics in medical law under which the patient's right to be fully informed of the treatment risks and able to decide whether to undergo the treatment is recognized. The notion of PIC and sometimes 'Free, Prior and Informed Consent' has been addressed in the various international instruments especially in the field of environmental law, which provides a legal basis for the debates. The instruments concerned are:

- Universal Declaration of Human Rights,[377]
- International Covenant on Civil and Political Rights,[378]
- International Covenant on Economic, Social and Cultural Rights,[379]
- Universal Declaration on the Human Genome and Human Rights,[380]
- Indigenous and Tribal Peoples Convention,[381]
- Basel Convention on the Transboundary Movement of Hazardous Wastes,[382]

---

375 See the USA Comment: IGC-GRTKF Secretariat, 'Report of Intergovernmental Committee on Intellectual Property and Genetic Resources, Traditional Knowledge and Folklore' (n 68) Paragraph 76.

376 IGC-GRTKF Secretariat, 'Draft Policy Objectives and Core Principles: Background Information and Discussion' (World Intellectual Property Organization 2004) WIPO Doc WIPO/GRTKF/IC/7/5 Annex II Page 34.

377 United Nations (n 366) Article 16(2).

378 International Covenant on Civil and Political Rights (ICCPR) 1966 (999 UNTS 171 (entered into force 23 March 1976)) Articles 7, 23(3) and 42(1).

379 ICESCR Articles 10 and 11.

380 UNESCO, 'Universal Declaration on the Human Genome and Human Rights' (1997) GA Res 53/152, 26th mtg, UN Doc. Article 5(b): 'In all cases, the prior, free and informed consent of the person concerned shall be obtained. If the latter is not in a position to consent, consent or authorization shall be obtained in the manner prescribed by law, guided by the person's best interest.'

381 Indigenous and Tribal Peoples Convention Articles 6(2) and 16(2).

382 Basel Convention on the Control of Transboundary Movements of Hazardous Wastes and their Disposal 1989 (1673 UNTS 57 (entered into force 5 May 1992)) Article 6(4).

- Convention on Biological Diversity,[383]
- International Treaty on Plant Genetic Resources for Food and Agriculture,[384]
- Nagoya Protocol,[385]
- Declaration on Bioethics and Human Rights,[386]
- Declaration on the Rights of Indigenous Peoples,[387]
- International Convention on the Elimination of All Forms of Racial Discrimination.[388]

Moreover, the application the principle of PIC to TK protection debates was one of the main issues of IGC negotiations and a wide range of delegations supported this approach.[389]

The term 'Free Prior Informed Consent' includes four elements:

1. 'Free' refers to a situation in which there is no coercion or force at the time of 'decision making.'
2. 'Prior' emphasises that time matters and it is important to allow people to have enough time to review the proposals in advance and make their decision.
3. 'Informed' refers to a party who has information and the capacity to make an assessment of the information, which could help that party to make balanced decisions.

383 CBD. See Article 15(5): "Access to genetic resources shall be subject to prior informed consent of the Contracting Party providing such resources, unless otherwise determined by that Party."

384 ITPGRFA Article 10.

385 Nagoya Protocol. See Article 16(1): "[e]ach Party shall take appropriate, effective and proportionate legislative, administrative or policy measures, as appropriate, to provide that traditional knowledge associated with genetic resources utilized within their jurisdiction has been accessed in accordance with prior informed consent or approval and involvement of indigenous and local communities ..."

386 'Universal Declaration on Bioethics and Human Rights' (2005) GA Res, 33rd session, UNESCO Doc. Article 6 requires the "prior, free and informed consent of the person concerned" when it comes to "preventive, diagnostic and therapeutic medical intervention" or "scientific research."

387 'United Nations Declaration on the Rights of Indigenous Peoples' (n 48) Articles 10, 11(2), 19, 28, 29(2) and 32(2).

388 International Convention on the Elimination of All Forms of Racial Discrimination 1966 (660 UNTS 195 (entered into force 4 January 1969)) Article 14(6).

389 See: Brazil, Canada, Iran, Mexico, New Zealand, Norway, Peru, USA and NGOs comments in: IGC-GRTKF Secretariat, 'Report of Intergovernmental Committee on Intellectual Property and Genetic Resources, Traditional Knowledge and Folklore' (n 68).

4. 'Consent' refers to the process in which permission will be given based on communication and trust. Permission shall be given after receiving a clear and transparent explanation.[390]

PIC has also been to referred as 'Approval and Involvement' of TKHs for "sustainable use of biological diversity and promote their wider application."[391]

In respect of words, signs, names and symbols, the relevant communities shall have the right to prevent any use of these manifestations of TK without their PIC. In particular PIC may be refused, if such use "disparages, offends or falsely suggests a connection with the community concerned or bring the community into contempt or disrepute."[392] Therefore, TKHs in the context of PCs demand prevention of such use of the PCs' names, patterns and motifs by third parties without their PIC or their approval and involvement. However, TKHs do not yet know what legal regime may provide the best capacity for offering such protection.

Some analysis suggests that the legal regime of copyright for protection of moral rights of TKHs could be well-fitted to meet the needs and expectations of these communities. In particular, the compensation mechanisms for receiving royalties and damages can fulfill their needs and expectations.[393]

This of course does not seem correct. Firstly, because moral rights are not protected worldwide and may only be granted in particular jurisdictions.[394] Secondly, TKHs are asking for international protection of their moral rights. Although the concept of moral rights has been considered in the Berne Convention, the TRIPS Agreement which is the most important international binding instrument in the context of trade regarding protection of IPRs does not cover moral rights protection under copyrights:

> Members shall comply with Articles 1 through 21 of the Berne Convention (1971) and the Appendix thereto. However, Members shall not have rights

390 Steve Allen and Alexandra Xanthaki, *Reflections on the UN Declaration on the Rights of Indigenous Peoples* (Hart Pub 2011) Page 49; quoted in: IGC-GRTKF Secretariat, 'Glossary of Key Terms Related to Intellectual Property and Genetic Resources, Traditional Knowledge and Traditional Cultural Expressions' (n 161) Page 31.

391 CBD Article 8(j).

392 See: Swakopmund Protocol Section 19(2)(b).

393 WIPO, *Consolidated Analysis of the Legal Protection of Traditional Cultural Expressions/ Expressions of Folklore.* (World Intellectual Property Organization 2003) Page 36.

394 Philippe Cullet and others, 'Intellectual Property Rights, Plant Genetic Resources and Traditional Knowledge' in Susette Biber-Klemm and Thomas Cottier (eds), *Rights to Plant Genetic Resources and Traditional Knowledge: Basic Issues and Perspectives* (CABI 2006) Page 113.

> or obligations under this Agreement in respect of the rights conferred under Article 6bis of that Convention or of the rights derived therefrom.[395]

Even though the integration of the Berne Convention in the TRIPS Agreement was in largely accepted, the United States opposed the entitlement of moral rights for protecting the integrity of works in the final text of agreement. The United States argued that these were not trade-related economic rights. However, Cottier points out:

> [i]t also appears doubtful whether inclusion or exclusion would make a strong practical difference, since jurisdiction to challenge the use of moral rights for protectionist purposes already exists under Article XX(d) of the GATT,[396] which is not limited to the rights protected under the TRIPS Agreement.[397]

Considering the above-mentioned discussions, I am doubtful that moral rights within the copyrights like-minded regime can provide the platform for protection of PCs' names, patterns and designs.

2.1.2 Positive Protection

As opposed to defensive protection, positive protection is aimed at "giving TK holders the right to take action or seek remedies against certain forms of misuse of TK"[398] It includes affirmative measures for protection of TK in one or another form of IPRs.[399] Positive protection within existing IPRs offers two advantages to the TKHs:

---

395 TRIPS Agreement Article 9(1).

396 General Agreement on Tariffs and Trade 1947 (55 UNTS 194 (entered into force 1 January 1948)). Article XX: "General Exceptions: Subject to the requirement that such measures are not applied in a manner which would constitute a means of arbitrary or unjustifiable discrimination between countries where the same conditions prevail, or a disguised restriction on international trade, nothing in this Agreement shall be construed to prevent the adoption or enforcement by any contracting party of measures: (d) necessary to secure compliance with laws or regulations which are not inconsistent with the provisions of this Agreement, including those relating to ... the protection of patents, trademarks and copyrights, and the prevention of deceptive practices."

397 Thomas Cottier, 'Chapter 22 – The Agreement on Trade-Related Aspects of Intellectual Property Rights' in Patrick FJ Macrory, Arthur E Appleton and Michael G Plummer (eds), *The World Trade Organization: Legal, Economic and Political Analysis*, vol 1 (Springer 2005) Page 1082.

398 Abbott, Cottier and Gurry (n 367) Page 660.

399 See: Drexl and others (n 352) Pages 31–32.

- active exploitation of TK by source communities, gives them the power to prevent unauthorized use of TK by third parties;
- non-IP legal protection of TK could be used as complementary mechanisms for protection of TK under existing IPRS.[400]

For instance, in the case of the protection of words, signs, names, symbols, designs, patterns and motifs, and if no false connection with a given community is suggested, any IPRS could be granted lawfully. It may thus prevent outsiders from making illegitimate use of TK.[401]

Even though TKHS, or at least some of them, may prefer to use existing IPRS, they face difficulties in gaining access to IPRS systems and navigating the formalities such as documentation, administration and procedures, which prevent them from enjoying effective protection.[402] Moreover, positive protection may be less accessible than defensive protection, as defensive protection would be based on specific modifications of existing IPRS regimes.[403] To overcome these challenges, both mechanisms should be used in a comprehensive approach complementing each other. TKHS cannot rely solely on one or the other for protection of TK.[404] Some have suggested that positive protection is likely to require a completely new system.[405] Munzer and Raustiala use the term 'offensive protection' to describe the type of legal protection according to which TKHS could control their TK, which is not protected by the existing IP system.[406] The idea of creating a new system is supported by TKHS and other stakeholders. This indicates that besides using existing and modified IPRS standards, the development and establishment of new IPRS standards as a *'sui generis'* system for protection of TK must be top of the agenda.[407] Such a system should be implemented in a manner that supports TK against misuse and misappropriation, and should enable TKHS to effectively exercise their rights and authority over their own knowledge.[408]

400 IGC-GRTKF Secretariat, 'Overview of Outcomes and Activities of the Intergovernmental Committee' (n 335) Pages 8–9.

401 *ibid Page 8.*

402 WIPO, 'Customary Law and Traditional Knowledge' (World Intellectual Property Organization) Background Brief No. 7 Page 2.

403 Dutfield, 'Legal and Economic Aspects of Traditional Knowledge' (n 271) Page 505.

404 Abbott, Cottier and Gurry (n 367) Page 660.

405 Dutfield, 'Legal and Economic Aspects of Traditional Knowledge' (n 271) Page 505.

406 Munzer and Raustiala (n 5) Page 40.

407 WIPO, *Intellectual Property Needs and Expectations of Traditional Knowledge Holders* (n 166) Page 225.

408 IGC-GRTKF Secretariat, 'Revised Provisions for the Protection of Traditional Knowledge: Policy Objectives and Core Principles' (n 36) Page 4.

A *sui generis* system is a system of "its own kind or class; unique or peculiar."[409] In the context of IPRs, this term has already been used for describing a legal protection regime that is outside existing copyright, patent, trademark or trade secret systems. Protection for databases which are not eligible for protection under copyright law is an example of a *sui generis* system designed specifically for databases. Also, a *sui generis* regime for protection of new plant varieties and breeders' IPRs was established by the International Convention on the Protection of New Varieties of Plants.[410] The protection of integrated circuits under the Treaty on Intellectual Property in Respect of Integrated Circuits[411] and the TRIPS Agreement are two other types of *sui generis* IP regimes. Both are specifically designed to deal with specific issues. Each makes an important contribution to our knowledge and understanding of *sui generis* characteristics and subject matters. And each has new IPRs standards to encompass an issue which is not protectable under existing regimes of IPRs. To the extent that TK and TKHs does seem to be able to enjoy protection under IPRs as they currently stand, seeking a new *sui generis* system for TK protection would be essential. Supporting the idea of protection under a *sui generis* system, Thomas Cottier theorized a new concept of a *sui generis* regime for protection of TK, which is known as 'Traditional Intellectual Property Rights' (TIP-rights).[412] This new *sui generis* regime addresses protection of TK and is a "private law entitlement vested in communities and which covers data and information." TIP-rights are supposed to provide protection for all prospective beneficiaries and encompass the entire range of TKHs, either communities or individuals.[413] Dutfield suggests "the *sui generis* system should encourage the registration of right claims but not make this a legal requirement for protection" and such a system could be operated as "either property regimes, liability regimes, or as combined systems containing elements of both."[414] TIP-rights fundamentally build upon the concept of UC.[415] Also, any misappropriation regime includ-

409 Garner (n 19).

410 UPOV Convention.

411 Washington Treaty on Intellectual Property in Respect of Integrated Circuits 1989 (Not yet in force).

412 See: Cottier, 'The Protection of Genetic Resources and Traditional Knowledge' (n 179).

413 Thomas Cottier and Marion Panizzon, 'A New Generation of IPR for the Protection of Traditional Knowledge in PGR for Food, Agricultural and Pharmaceutical Uses' in Susette Biber-Klemm and Thomas Cottier (eds), *Rights to Plant Genetic Resources and Traditional Knowledge: Basic Issues and Perspectives* (CABI 2006) Page 221.

414 Dutfield, 'Legal and Economic Aspects of Traditional Knowledge' (n 271) Page 514.

415 Thomas Cottier, 'Introduction' in Susette Biber-Klemm and Thomas Cottier (eds), *Rights to Plant Genetic Resources and Traditional Knowledge: Basic Issues and Perspectives* (CABI 2006) Page xvii.

ing a liability regime "could and probably should incorporate the concept of unfair competition."[416] Both regimes are expected to promote legal protection and security and to improve trade as well as offer certainty and rebalancing of IPRS to meet the expectations of TKHS. The use of UC and its components, such as protection of names, marks, and GIS is still untested and unclear. As the EU delegation in Geneva noted, it is necessary to study and analyze national and regional IPRS regimes regarding protection of TK as well as to look at how existing IPRS regimes are used to protect TK and the role of trademark, design, copyright, trade secrets and GIS legislation.[417] Therefore, it is crucial to analyze defensive and positive protection in the context of trademark and GIS.

2.2 *Traditional Knowledge Holders' Rights*

Given the varied nature of TK, the priority of rights claimed by TKHS would also vary. It depends on the knowledge, region, people and products. They go beyond IPRS. With this in mind, Aguilar enumerates – avoiding to limit them – basic rights of TKHS, such as the right to self-determination, property rights over land and resources, rights to prior informed consent, human rights, cultural rights and rights to have institutions as the representative of TKHS.[418] Hennessey extends holders' rights to the rights to conservation, preservation, identification, information, participation and sharing of risk and benefit.[419] Therefore, rights over TK should be examined from the perspective of each type of TK and situation. IPRS are one significant aspect of protection of TK among others. In this study, I only highlight those rights that I assume could affect Iranian TKHS or the protection of PCS from an IPRS' perspective. In this regard, I will consider the IPRS which include moral rights and exclusive economic rights. While the first concerns non-economic forms of protection and arrangement of equitable compensation, the second excludes others from carrying out some definite acts.[420]

2.2.1 TKHS' Moral Rights

As a human right, everyone has the right "to benefit from the protection of the moral and material interests resulting from any scientific, literary or artistic

416 Dutfield, 'Legal and Economic Aspects of Traditional Knowledge' (n 271) Page 512.

417 See: The Permanent Delegation of the European Union in Geneva, 'Proposal for the Terms of Reference for a Study' (World Intellectual Property Organization 2016) WIPO Doc WIPO/GRTKF/IC/31/9 Annex.

418 Aguilar (n 240) Page 245.

419 Hennessey (n 257) Page 7.

420 WIPO, *Intellectual Property and Genetic Resources, Traditional Knowledge and Traditional Cultural Expressions* (n 231) Page 20.

production of which he is the author."[421] This principle has been reflected in the context of the international IPRs system, which recognizes the exclusive rights of a rights' holder to exclude third parties from certain acts; and in the copyrights regime it includes protection of moral rights of authors. By the same token, TKHs want their moral and exclusive rights over TK to be protected.

The conception of moral rights as non-economic rights of authors originated prior to human rights protection in the Berne Convention,[422] which requires specific types of rights to be granted to authors to claim:

- Authorship of the work, which means the author has the right to be identified as the author (also known as the right of paternity);
- Object to any distortion, mutilation, modification, or other derogatory action,[423] which would be prejudicial to the honour or reputation of authors (known as the right of integrity).

According to paternity rights, the author can sue third parties, if they do not respect authorship. The paternity right by and large applies if the author claims it. Another significant aspect of moral rights is the author's right to prevent third parties from amending the work or object if it is subject to derogatory treatment, or if the amendment misrepresents the work in a way that is misleading in the context of the work. Because the right of integrity is open to interpretation, there is controversy about what treatment may be interpreted as derogatory.[424] Moral rights are required to be independent from economic rights. The moral rights remain with authors even after transfer of the authors' economic rights.[425]

TKHs' claim for moral rights means firstly that they have the right to be identified and acknowledged as TKHs.[426] Secondly, no one, not even a member of

---

421 ICESCR Article 15(1)(c).

422 Berne Convention Article 6bis (1).

423 Derogatory Action refers to "a prejudice to the honor or reputation." It refers to situations where communication of a work is done in such a manner as to cause the author harm. This term was added to the Brussels Revision of the Bern Convention to cover uses of the work that were prejudicial to the author. See: Sam Ricketson and Jane C Ginsburg, *International Copyright and Neighbouring Rights: The Berne Convention and Beyond*, vol 1 (Oxford University Press 2006) Page 603.

424 Lorna Brazell, *Intellectual Property Protection and Enforcement* (Thorogood Ltd 1998) Page 75.

425 WIPO, *Intellectual Property Reading Material* (2nd edn, WIPO 1998) Page 42.

426 IGC-GRTKF Secretariat, 'Revised Provisions for the Protection of Traditional Knowledge: Policy Objectives and Core Principles' (n 36) Page 3.

their community, will be allowed to distort, mutilate,[427] or otherwise modify[428] their TK in a way which may damage their honour, reputation, and integrity.[429] Also, they believe their cultural heritage should not be used in any product or service which is prejudicial to their reputation as original creators.[430]

2.2.1.1 *Recognition of Traditional Knowledge Holders*

According to the general principle of moral rights, the author of the work has the right to be recognized as such and may assert the wish to be identified as such in accordance with the terms of the copyright.[431] Taking the same approach, TKHs demand to be acknowledged as TKHs by any person who is using TK beyond its traditional context. In this regard, the user shall indicate the source and where possible, the origin of the TK.[432] For example, in the Philippines, all writings, publications and journals related to the results of research on TK shall acknowledge the provider's (indigenous peoples') name as the source.[433] Hennessey illustrates the right to be acknowledged as the source of TK is accordance with Article 6bis of the Berne Convention regarding recognition of the author and Article 4ter of the Paris Convention concerning identification of inventorship, and commercial reputation of the

427 The protection against mutilation is one attribute of the author's moral rights. It refers to "the act of cutting out or excising a part of a thing, especially a book or other document; to change or destroy part of the content or meaning," See: Berne Convention Article 6bis.

428 Modification is a 'change to something.' See: Garner (n 19); This term uses to describe something changes to become suitable to a new or special application or situation. See: Houghton Mifflin Company (n 7); The act of modification on a TK based work in a way to create a new work with a different propose of the original work – which it principally considered to be served for. See: Mihály Ficsor, *Guide to the Copyright and Related Rights Treaties Administered by WIPO and Glossary of Copyright and Related Rights Terms* (WIPO 2003); The notion of modification is principally accepted in the long-running debates over application and wider use of TK; but depends upon the understanding, customary practices, norms, and laws of TK holders and on condition that meet their direct benefit. See: IGC-GRTKF Secretariat, 'Revised Provisions for the Protection of Traditional Knowledge: Policy Objectives and Core Principles' (n 36).

429 See for example: Swakopmund Protocol Section 19(2)(a)(iii).

430 Gupta, *WIPO-UNEP Study on the Role of Intellectual Property Rights in the Sharing of Benefits Arising from the Use of Biological Resources and Associated Traditional Knowledge* (n 363) Page 62.

431 Brazell (n 424) Page 75.

432 See: Swakopmund Protocol Section 10; and WIPO, *Intellectual Property and Genetic Resources, Traditional Knowledge and Traditional Cultural Expressions* (n 231) Page 26.

433 See: Philippines' Administrative Order No.1, 1998, in Gupta, *WIPO-UNEP Study on the Role of Intellectual Property Rights in the Sharing of Benefits Arising from the Use of Biological Resources and Associated Traditional Knowledge* (n 363) Page 45.

trademark owner.[434] Moreover, in order to acknowledge TKHS, TK systems and approaches to conserving, developing and maintaining of those systems have to be known, because it can affect the people who made the systems for their sustainable livelihood.[435] In the case of PCs, there are two sets of problems. Some competitors use the names, designs and patterns of PCs but they mislead consumers about the true origin of the carpets because the providers are not real TKHs. The second type of problem is use of designs, patterns and motifs in products other than PCs. A good example is the fashion industry which uses those elements without acknowledgement of TKHs or without PIC.

2.2.2 TKHs' Economic Rights

Many TKHs do not treat their TK as a property with economic rights, which could be owned by their communities or by individual members of their communities. Instead, they view and implement their TK according to their custom with full respect for the environment or other communities. Therefore, for them, TK is more about relationships and responsibilities than a source of economic rights originating from ownership under a property system.[436] In contrast, it is argued, knowledge in its modern conception is a product of individuals' genuine efforts and deserves to be granted proprietary and economic rights. These economic rights are recognized as IPRs often obtained by individuals, corporations, universities and research institutes.[437]

Considering these two completely different approaches to the economic rights over knowledge, modern societies use TK, for example in bio-prospecting, as source for their innovations to obtain exclusive economic rights, while IPRs, as they are currently conceived, cannot protect TKHs effectively against exploitation by outsiders. Instead, the system is tailored mainly for the benefit of foreigners.[438]

The concept of economic rights in modern IPRs originates from the copyright regime. The Berne Convention clearly refers to the author's economic rights independently from moral rights.[439] In accordance with this type of

434 Hennessey (n 257) Page 8.

435 IGC-GRTKF Secretariat, 'Revised Provisions for the Protection of Traditional Knowledge: Policy Objectives and Core Principles' (n 36) Page 3.

436 Jonathan Curci, *The Protection of Biodiversity and Traditional Knowledge in International Law of Intellectual Property* (Cambridge University Press 2009) Page 92.

437 Posey and Dutfield (n 180) Page 76.

438 Dashaco John Tambutoh, Agus Sardjono and Memunat Dabiri, 'Traditional Medicine and Intellectual Property Rights – a Move Towards Protection in Developing Countries' (WIPO Specialisation Course on Intellectual Property, Turin, 2011) Page 4.

439 Berne Convention Article 6bis.

rights, the owner may use the protected work as he or she wishes and exclude others from exploiting it without the owner's authorization. Economic rights include prevention of copying, reproducing, adapting, performing in public, recording, displaying and communicating to the public.[440] In the same manner, under Iranian copyright law, the exclusive economic rights of authors are recognized and the following activities need the author's permission:

1. Production of films for cinema, television and the like.
2. Stage performances, as in theatre, ballet or other such performances.
3. Recording of a work by sound or vision on tapes, or by any other such means.
4. Broadcast by radio and television, or by any other such means.
5. Translation, reproduction, publication and public presentation of works by means of painting, printing, photography, etching, photogravure, moulding and the like.
6. Use of the work in any scientific, literary, artistic, technical and advertising purposes.
7. Use of the work in producing or creating other works.[441]

Faced with the new situation, TKHs began to be aware and understand the economic and commercial value of their TK and thus they wished to set their own terms regarding use of TK by outsiders.[442] These terms are set out as TKHs' exclusive rights for authorizing or preventing any kind of exploitation of TK by other persons. The term exploitation with respect to TK refers to the acts in relation to TK products, processes or in some cases services related to TK. Where TK is a product, any act of "manufacturing, importing, exporting, offering for sale, selling" or using TK beyond its context or "being in possession of the product for purposes of offering it for sale, selling it or using it beyond the TK"[443] count as exploitation of TK. Where the TK is a process, exploitation means use of the process beyond its traditional context; and carrying out the acts of manufacturing, importing, exporting, offering for sale, selling or using beyond the traditional context with respect to a product that is a direct result of the use of the process.[444] The TKHs' demand for economic rights has been recognized by some national governments. For example, in Venezuelan law, "The State shall recognize and protect the economic rights and traditional

440 Molly Torsen and Jane Anderson, *Intellectual Property and the Safeguarding of Traditional Cultures – Legal Issues and Practical Options for Museums, Libraries and Archives* (World Intellectual Property Organization 2010) Page 10.

441 Iran – Act for Protection of Authors, Composers and Artists' Rights 1970 Article 5.

442 Posey and Dutfield (n 180) Page 12.

443 Swakopmund Protocol Section 7(3)(a)(i) and (ii).

444 *ibid Section 7(3)(b)(i) and (ii).*

knowledge of local communities and indigenous peoples and communities, in relation to biological diversity."[445] In Portuguese law, TK is composed of "intangible elements associated with commercial or industrial utilization," which is developed by a local population and form their cultural and spiritual traditions and includes *inter alia* products, processes and services. In this law, traditional crafts are given as an example of TK.[446] Although in Iran's legal system, no protection of TK has been provided for, "original works based on folklore and national heritage of culture and arts" are protected works under copyrights law.[447]

Unlike moral rights, which remain forever with the authors, economic rights might be assigned,[448] licensed[449] or franchised[450] to others.[451]

2.2.3 Exceptions and Limitation of Rights

TKHs claim that their rights to grant or refuse consent to access and use of their TK should be respected, but like other IPRs regimes, TKHs' rights could not be absolute and should be appraised in the light of the principle of equitable balance of interests of TKHs and traditional knowledge users (TKUs). A central concern, therefore, is that protection of TK should aim not only to respect TKHs' rights but also those of the TKUs. This includes other producers and consumers who seek legal permission to use TK for the promotion of

445 See Article 39 of 'The Law on Biological Diversity' in the Bolivarian Republic of Venezuela quoted in: Rodrigo de la Cruz, 'Customary Law in the Protection of Traditional Knowledge' (Quito 2006) Page 10.

446 The Delegation of Portugal, 'Ministry of Agriculture, Development and Fisheries, Decree-Law No. 118/2002' (World Intellectual Property Organization 2005) WIPO Doc WIPO/GRTKF/IC/8/13 Annex Page 3.

447 Iran – Act for Protection of Authors, Composers and Artists' Rights Article 2(10).

448 Assignment is a method in which rights owner transfers all exclusive rights without any limitation or condition to another person. In such case original owner will have no longer any economic rights over TK. And the assignee will be the owner of economic rights exclusively. This method has been used in existence IPRs such as copyrights and neighbouring rights, patents and trademarks. See: Sell (n 350) Page 45.

449 Licensing mechanism is an agreement in which right holders grant specific use of their TK to others. See: IGC-GRTKF Secretariat, 'Draft Report of Intergovernmental Committee on Intellectual Property and Genetic Resources, Traditional Knowledge and Folklore' (n 241).

450 According to franchising method, franchisor allows franchisee to exploit "any economic activity for which a system can be developed for the manufacture, processing and/or distribution of goods or the rendering of services." See: WIPO, *WIPO Intellectual Property Handbook: Policy, Law and Use* (2nd edn, World Intellectual Property Organization 2008) Page 97.

451 WIPO, *Intellectual Property Needs and Expectations of Traditional Knowledge Holders* (n 166) Page 34.

creativity and innovation and transfer of technology based on shared benefits for both sides.[452] Here when reaching such a balance among different stakeholders' rights and their reasonable interests, the concept of exceptions and limitations to any rights over TK needs to be considered. The idea of exceptions and limitations[453] is already considered in the IPRS system, for example copyrights, patents or plant breeders' rights.

In the context of the copyright law, exceptions are permitted with the aim of sustaining an expedient balance between the interests of stakeholders of a given protected work. Exceptions are embodied as a set of rules in respect of which exclusive rights over protected works in accordance with the owner's monopoly could be removed based on law. Exceptions are not subject to neither authorization nor remuneration of authors.[454] Despite expectations, limitation of economic rights is to allow use of the protected work without the authorization of the rights' owner with or without remuneration.[455] The Berne Convention contains certain provisions regarding free uses of works, such as "quotations from newspaper articles and periodicals in the form of press summaries"[456] and "illustration in publications, broadcasts or sound or visual recordings for teaching."[457] These free uses of works are known as 'fair practice.' To illustrate what measures might be considered 'fair' and to determine the permissibility of exceptions the three-step test will be considered.[458] These steps are:

(i) it may only cover certain special cases;
(ii) it must not conflict with a normal exploitation of the work; and
(iii) it must not unreasonably prejudice the legitimate interests of the authors.[459]

---

452 Swakopmund Protocol Preamble at Paragraph 14.

453 limitation refers to the "act of limiting; the state of being limited, a restriction." See: Garner (n 19); "The word limits, in addition to 'exceptions' refers to boundaries or restrictions." See: Pierre Sirinelli, 'Exceptions and Limits to Copyright and Neighbouring Rights' (WIPO 1999) WIPO Doc WCT-WPPT/IMP/1 Page 2.

454 Sirinelli (n 453) Page 2.

455 IGC-GRTKF Secretariat, 'Glossary of Key Terms Related to Intellectual Property and Genetic Resources, Traditional Knowledge and Traditional Cultural Expressions' (World Intellectual Property Organization 2017) WIPO Doc WIPO/GRTKF/IC/34/INF/7 Annex Page 24.

456 Berne Convention Article 10(1).

457 *ibid Article 10(2).*

458 Also, 'fair dealing' in the common-law tradition, and 'fair use' in national laws are used to refer 'fair practice' concept. See: Ficsor (n 428) Page 289.

459 Berne Convention Article 9(2).

This test has been extended to the TRIPS Agreement, the WIPO Copyright Treaty (WCT) and the WIPO Performances and Phonograms Treaty (WPPT).[460] With respect to patent law, although a patent owner has exclusive power to authorize making, using, distributing or selling the invention commercially, there are possible exceptions and limitations to patent owners' rights such as:

- private and non-commercial use;
- using patented inventions on transportation means like airplanes, ships and land vehicles of other territories which accidentally or temporarily enter the territory of a country;
- experimental and research activities;
- prior users' exception, which allows use of an invention by anybody who has been using it in good faith before the priority/filing date of the patent.[461]

Another example of exceptions is in the context of the international legal regime for the protection of plant breeders, which is reflected in the UPOV Convention.[462] Exceptions and limitations to the breeders' exclusive rights are as follows:

- Private, non-commercial activities with respect to protected varieties,
- Research exemptions for experimental purposes,
- Breeders' exemptions for creating new varieties,
- Farmers' privilege to use on their own holding seeds of new varieties.[463]

These exceptions allow farmers and breeders to use protected new varieties freely and to benefit from them.[464]

Having considered the philosophy and precedent of exceptions and limitations on IPRs, it is also reasonable to look at possible exceptions and limitations on rights over TK reflecting the need for a fair and equitable balance between the rights and interests of different stakeholders. As well as TKHs, TKUs need to be able to exploit TK for their professional non-commercial activities such as research, education, review, criticism, reporting events, legal and court

460 See Article 13 of TRIPS Agreement; and Article 10 of WIPO Copyright Treaty 1996 (2186 UNTS 121 (entered into force 3 March 2002)); and Article 16 WIPO Performances and Phonograms Treaty 1996 (2186 UNTS 203 (entered into force 20 May 2002)).

461 IGC-GRTKF Secretariat, 'List and Brief Technical Explanation of Various Forms in Which Traditional Knowledge May Be Found' (n 187) Pages 8–9.

462 UPOV Convention.

463 Laurence R Helfer, *Intellectual Property Rights in Plant Varieties: International Legal Regimes and Policy Options for National Governments* (FAO 2004) Page 28.

464 Gupta, *WIPO-UNEP Study on the Role of Intellectual Property Rights in the Sharing of Benefits Arising from the Use of Biological Resources and Associated Traditional Knowledge* (n 363) Page 23.

proceedings, archiving and so on.[465] In this regard, any protection system should address the need for bringing together various policy concerns on equitable balance of interests. Hence, states may adopt limitations and exceptions to exclusive rights over TK provided that such limitations and exceptions not only have no conflict with the normal utilization of the TK by the beneficiaries but also do not cause or derogate beneficiaries' rights or prejudice unreasonably the legitimate interests of the beneficiaries.[466] In accordance with the Swakopmund Protocol, protection of TK shall not be prejudicial to the continued availability of TK for practice, exchange, use and transmission by TKHs within its traditional context.[467]

3 Formalities for Protection

Formality is defined as "a small point of practice that, though seemingly unimportant, must usually be observed to achieve a particular legal result." As a general and public concept, protection of TK against misappropriation and misuse shall not be subject to any formality.[468] This concept has already been recognized in the copyright context where it is known as "the principle of formality-free"[469] in which enjoyment and exercise of the rights would not be subject to any formality. The Berne Convention,[470] the WCT[471] and the WPPT[472] are examples of international copyright instruments in which formality is not a condition for protection. The advantage of a protection system without formalities is automatic protection in which measures against misappropriation would not be conditioned to any terms, including registration of TK.

---

465 As an example, a list of such activities has been mentioned in Swakopmund Protocol. See: Swakopmund Protocol Section 20(1)(c).

466 IGC-GRTKF Secretariat, 'The Protection of Traditional Knowledge: Draft Articles Rev. 2' (n 12) Article 6(1).

467 Swakopmund Protocol Section 11.

468 IGC-GRTKF Secretariat, 'The Protection of Traditional Knowledge: Draft Articles' (World Intellectual Property Organization 2017) WIPO Doc WIPO/GRTKF/IC/34/5 Annex Article 11; and Swakopmund Protocol Sections 5(1)–17(1).

469 Ficsor (n 428) Page 41.

470 Berne Convention Article 5(2): 'The enjoyment and the exercise of these rights shall not be subject to any formality.'

471 WCT Article 25(10): 'Contracting Parties will not rely on this Article to devise or implement rights management systems that would have the effect of imposing formalities which are not permitted under the Berne Convention or this Treaty.'

472 WPPT Article 20: 'The enjoyment and exercise of the rights provided for in this Treaty shall not be subject to any formality.'

There are some exceptions to the formality-free rule. For example, national authorities may apply the rule for registration of the TKHs. States may maintain any type of documentation such as registration and recording of the knowledge or to fix TK in case it sounds appropriate. The general policies and law or procedures with respect to the needs and expectations of TKHs, such as the need to ensure transparency and evidence and requirements for preservation, would be respected.[473] In the case of secret TK, registration shall not include undisclosed elements of TK.[474] Or in case of Expressions of Folklore (EoF), national laws may require notification to the appropriate authorities.[475] But such a notification shall have the function of a declaratory note and would establish no rights or obligation for documentation, recording or public disclosure.[476]

3.1 *Registration of TK*

Although it has been emphasized that protection of TK must not be conditioned on formalities, including registration of TK or establishing TK databases or any other kind of registration, some countries are using registration as a condition for protection. Registration of knowledge as a condition for protection or putting the knowledge in a database are the kind of requirements imposed by these countries or communities. The opponents of registration have noted that registration means the necessity for TKHs to take legal steps within defined circumstances and a specific time frame or risk losing the protection. Thus, opponents of registration consider that it may impose a duty on TKHs who already suffer from lack of capacity or resources to take such legal steps.[477]

In contrast, the defendants of registration argue that this system offers more predictability and simpler procedures for enforcement of rights.[478] Moreover, collecting information about TK is critical and without registration would be barely achievable. Also, such a register as a legal institution may have the right

473 Swakopmund Protocol Sections 5(2) and 17(4).

474 See: IGC-GRTKF Secretariat, 'Revised Provisions for the Protection of Traditional Knowledge: Policy Objectives and Core Principles' (n 164) Page 73; Also see: Swakopmund Protocol Section 5(3).

475 Swakopmund Protocol Section 17(2).

476 *ibid Section 17(3).*

477 IGC-GRTKF Secretariat, 'Revised Provisions for the Protection of Traditional Knowledge: Policy Objectives and Core Principles' (n 164) Page 74.

478 *ibid.*

to authorize the use of registered TK. In addition, registered TK may be used as prior art.[479]

Despite their arguments, the defendants do not ignore the TKHs' willingness as the basic requirement for establishing a registration system for TK. For example, The State of Peru "recognizes the rights and power of indigenous peoples and communities to dispose of their collective knowledge as they see fit."[480]

Registers differ in accordance with their legal nature and systems. They could have a declaratory or a constitutive nature. According to a declaratory regime, rights over TK are pre-existing rights and no act of government including registration of TK could affect the existence and practice of TKHs' rights over their TK. Governments might use such a regime to prevent challenges imposed by modern IPRs. For instance, this regime might be used as prior art to block patent claims on products or procedures that directly or indirectly utilize TK. Another function of registers could be facilitation of access and benefit sharing between TK providers and users. Constitutive registers constitute a legal regime for recognizing and granting rights to TKHs and recording those rights in order to ensure TKHs' moral and economic rights are preserved, respected and protected. This model pursues the same goal as positive protection of TK and administration by government institutions.[481] Also, registration might be implemented at different levels:

- Local registers,
- Public national registers,
- Confidential national registers.[482]

Another advantage of registration of TK is the obligation to record all access, authorization, assignment, or licences for TK which make the concerned acts legally enforceable.[483]

---

479 Peter-Tobias Stoll and Anja von Hahn, 'Indigenous Peoples, Indigenous Knowledge and Indigenous Resources in International Law' in Silke von Lewinski (ed), *Indigenous Heritage and Intellectual Property: Genetic Resources, Traditional Knowledge, and Folklore* (2nd edn, Kluwer Law International 2008) Pages 48–49.

480 Peru – Law Introducing a Protection Regime for the Collective Knowledge of Indigenous Peoples Derived from Biological Resources 2002 (Peruvian Law No 27811) Article 1.

481 Merle Alexander and others, 'The Role of Registers and Databases in the Protection of Traditional Knowledge: A Comparative Analysis' (Institute of Advanced Studies, United Nations University 2004) UNU-IAS Page 32.

482 See for example: Peru – Law Introducing a Protection Regime for the Collective Knowledge of Indigenous Peoples Derived from Biological Resources Article 15.

483 Swakopmund Protocol Section 8(2).

One area in which formality shall be obligatory is licensing TK. A license agreement includes terms on reward for the access to TK as well as guarantees for benefits deriving from the distribution of TK.[484] In this case, States may set onerous conditions for issuing advance approval for licensing agreements. However, such a requirement for pre-approval of licensing TK does not match with the reality of marketing and licensing IPRS.[485]

3.2 *TK Databases*

Two polarized approaches towards establishing TK databases are considered in this section.

On one hand, establishment of a database or digital libraries which include information on TK is a precondition for implementing defensive protection and precluding the grant of improper IPRS.[486] For example, in 2011, the database of Official Insignia on Native American Tribes was established by the United States Patent and Trademark Office (USPTO). The database includes comprehensive data of the United States federally recognized native tribes. The USPTO uses the database to check that the proposed marks are not falsely suggesting a link with American tribes and their beliefs, in which case the USPTO may refuse an application for registration of such marks.[487] Another example of a well-known database is Traditional Knowledge Digital Library (TKDL) of India. It is designed to prevent misappropriation of traditional medicinal knowledge in collaboration with the Patent Offices across the world. It exists in local languages such as Sanskrit, Hindi, Arabic, Urdu, Persian, Tamil etc. So far, 359 books on the Indian medicine system are included in this database as prior art and are accessible to the German, Japanese, English, Spanish and French examiners.[488] In addition, establishing TK databases allows TKHS

484 Peru – Law Introducing a Protection Regime for the Collective Knowledge of Indigenous Peoples Derived from Biological Resources Article 7.

485 CIP – The Anton Mostert Chair of Intellectual Property, 'The Winning Choice For Traditional Culture' (20 July 2013) <http://blogs.sun.ac.za/iplaw/2013/07/20/the-winning-choice-for-traditional-culture/> accessed 21 December 2017.

486 IGC-GRTKF Secretariat, 'Revised Provisions for the Protection of Traditional Knowledge: Policy Objectives and Core Principles' (n 36) Page 6.

487 United States Patent and Trademark Office, 'USPTO Establishes Database of Official Insignia of Native American Tribes' (29 August 2001) </about-us/news-updates/uspto-establishes-database-official-insignia-native-american-tribes> accessed 22 December 2016.

488 For more information see: Indian Council of Scientific & Industrial Research, 'About TKDL' (*Traditional Knowledge Digital Library*, March 2012) <http://tkdl.res.in/tkdl/lang default/common/Home.asp?GL=Eng>; and IGC-GRTKF Secretariat, 'Report of the Thirty-First Session of the Committee of Experts of the Special Union for the International

to authorize use of their recording by third parties. Moreover, organizations shall be allowed to create libraries and databases that facilitate the association of peoples with their TK.[489] Archiving TK is a tool for safeguarding and preserving TK, while using modern technologies allows TKHs to document and digitize their TK and assist them to preserve, promote and pass on TK to the next generations. TK databases may help TKHs to address the needs of non-commercial use of TK including reproductions of TK.[490]

On the other hand, despite the advantage of using technology for documenting and digitizing TK, it may leave TKHs with a risk of their TK being vulnerable and easily accessible to third parties.

In the face of such criticism, proponents of establishing TK databases have responded that databases which are original because of the arrangement and/or selection of their content could be protected by copyright. For instance, the TRIPS Agreement places databases as subject matter of existing copyright protection mechanisms. In accordance with section 1 of the TRIPS Agreement "Compilations of data or other material, whether in machine readable or other form, which by reason of the selection or arrangement of their contents constitute intellectual creations shall be protected as such."[491] If protection of copyright is denied for a database which is non-creative, it might be protectable by legislation on UC to some degree.[492] Also a *sui generis* legal regime might be used for protection of TK databases and collections.[493] An example of protection under a *sui generis* regime is reflected in the EU Database Directive for protection of databases.[494] In accordance with the rules of chapter III of the directive, a *sui generis* protection regime is predicted in which if the database maker can demonstrate a substantial qualitative/quantitative investment in "obtaining, verification or presentation of the contents" he or she may prevent unauthorized extraction and/or reutilization of the database.[495]

Patent Classification – Present Status of TKDL Project' (World Intellectual Property Organization 2002) WIPO Doc WIPO/GRTKF/IC/3/13 Appendix II of Annex I.

489 IGC-GRTKF Secretariat, 'Revised Provisions for the Protection of Traditional Knowledge: Policy Objectives and Core Principles' (n 36) Page 10.

490 Swakopmund Protocol Section 20(1)(c).

491 TRIPS Agreement Article 10.2.

492 UNCTAD-ICTSD, *Resource Book on TRIPS and Development* (Cambridge University Press 2005) Pages 45–46.

493 WIPO, 'The World Intellectual Property Organization Traditional Knowledge Documentation Toolkit' (n 290) Page 13.

494 Directive 96/9/EC of the European Parliament and of the Council of 11 March 1996 on the Legal Protection of Databases 1996 (OJ L 077) Chapter III.

495 Daniel Gervais and Mathias Studer, 'Agreement on Trade-Related Aspects of Intellectual Property Rights: Part II. Standards Concerning the Availability, Scope and Use of

Both approaches appear to partially reflect the realities concerning the role and impact of TK databases in promoting and protecting TK. This point is also underlined by the work of Gupta in his Honey Bee Network case study. Gupta points out that in the process of raising awareness of the potential value of TK, it is critical to document TK as a first step.[496] However, he also states that "the degree of openness among different actors in different domains and at different levels in the society may influence the strategies for harnessing the power of cocreation and network management for distributed knowledge system."[497]

As its general strategy in Iran, the government is obliged to collect oral history, dialects, accents, customs, and ceremonies, as well as national and local cultural characters in order to preserve and recognize the historical identities of the country.[498] In the context of PCs, TKHs, their representatives and governmental institutions, the approach is to document as much as possible the know-how, techniques, knowledge, associated GRs and designs, patterns, motifs, names and places. This is the consequence of strong beliefs that documentation of PCs could help original TKHs to preserve and promote PCs as their primary goal and prevent outsiders and competitors from misappropriating and misusing PCs. In this regard, providing and establishing the PCs' Encyclopaedia is top of the agenda in the country. Work on the encyclopaedia by Iran's Carpet Scientific Association began in 2009. They aim to ensure the authenticity, comprehensiveness and authority of the information collected. The ultimate goals for creating this encyclopaedia are:

- Registration of the various aspects of this authentic art and preventing the loss of information and knowledge of PCs;
- Collecting the information; and identification of well-known regions of PCs as well as the characteristics, styles and their methods, and also its GIs within the country and its main hometowns; and the place of PCs in social and economic development;
- Collecting and recording historical data on PCs and the specifications of exquisite carpets in various collections inside and outside the country;

Intellectual Property Rights' in Thomas Cottier and Pierre Véron (eds), *Concise International and European IP Law: TRIPS, Paris Convention, European Enforcement and Transfer of Technology*, vol 4 (2nd edn, Kluwer Law International 2008) Page 42.

496 Anil K Gupta, 'From Sink to Source: The Honey Bee Network Documents Indigenous Knowledge and Innovations in India' (2006) 1 Innovations: Technology, Governance, Globalization 49, Page 50.

497 Anil K Gupta, 'The Honey Bee Network: Linking Knowledge-Rich Grassroots Innovations' Conclusion.

498 Iran – Law for the Fourth Development Plan of the I.R. Iran 2004 Article 109.

- Establishing a credible and scientifically valid and at the same time documented and legally reliable resource for researchers and scholars, and using it in conjunction with the official authorities and agencies to protect intellectual property and economic rights of artists, producers, traders and owners of original designs, motifs and patterns;
- Establishing an authentic collection of knowledge and know-how in order to adopt rural development strategies and macro and micro economic plans for the country;
- Providing a common understanding of the concepts and terminology relating to the PCs and the branches of carpet industries;
- Identification of the scope and extent of the knowledge by PC experts and scholars.[499]

Although these goals are defined to preserve and protect PCs – as subject matter of TK – it is not clear how this information could be protected from misappropriation and misuse while it does not include any strategy concerning the degree of access for different users at different domains and levels.

4 Duration of TK Protection

Modern IPRs are intended to appropriate exclusive rights for a definite period during which innovators will be compensated for their efforts and investment of time and capital to create new knowledge. After that time, that subject matter will be transmitted to the public domain and available freely to others. The IPRs approach towards protection duration raises the question of how long TKHs' rights over their TK should be protected? According to one view, TKHs' rights should survive in perpetuity. Temporal limitations do not suffice for the protection of their TK because TKHs' right over TK is timeless. It is the heritage of their ancestors, it has been held collectively by their communities, it has lasted for centuries among successive generations and it shall be passed down to the next generations.[500] Therefore, they request limitless duration of protection, which in turn is incompatible with modern IPRs that put TK in the public

499 'دانشنامه فرش ایران (Encyclopedia of Persian Carpets)' (*Iran Carpet Scientific Association*, May 2014) <http://icsa.ir>.

500 Ana María Pacón, 'The Peruvian Proposal for Protecting Traditional Knowledge' in Sophia Twarog and Promila Kapoor (eds), *Protecting and Promoting Traditional Knowledge: Systems, National Experiences and International Dimensions* (United Nations 2004) Page 178.

domain.[501] Munzer and Raustiala support and advocate indefinite duration for protection of TK, because normative TK differs from IPRS:

> Indeed, it is implicit in the very concept of "traditional knowledge" that the knowledge in question is fairly old, and in many cases would, as a result, fall outside the bounds of ordinary IP rights. The practical terms of the current debate over TK thus lead us to view indefinite duration as central.[502]

There is also, however, another view to be considered in accordance with which TK protection shall be continued as long as the specific criteria for protection are fulfilled,[503] and governments may regulate the duration of protection of TK as long as it meets the criteria for eligibility for protection.[504] These approaches have already been considered in the discussions on establishment of TIP-rights by Cottier and Panizzon. In their view, one of the requirements for protection of TK, should be active use of TK:

> Rights to TK should only arise so long as the process or information exists within, and is being used by, a particular community. Once it fades into the past, it is no longer of commercial interest to the community and should no longer be granted protection.
>
> When the use of active TK is protected, however, the period of liability for specific uses will have to be determined by law.[505]

The duration of protection of TK under the new TIP-rights regime suggested by Cottier and Panizzon as well as a Compensatory Liability Regime are two main areas in which formal limitations of duration will not be applied. Consequently, they are convenient for meeting TKHS' needs on protection of their inalienable rights on their TK.[506] The applicability of these legal regimes for protection of PCs will be appraised.

---

501 Luo Li, *Intellectual Property Protection of Traditional Cultural Expressions: Folklore in China* (Springer Science & Business 2014) Page 14.

502 Munzer and Raustiala (n 5) Page 58.

503 Swakopmund Protocol Sections 13 and 21.

504 IGC-GRTKF Secretariat, 'The Protection of Traditional Knowledge: Draft Articles' (n 230) Article 7.

505 Cottier and Panizzon, 'Legal Perspectives on Traditional Knowledge: The Case for Intellectual Property Protection' (n 178) Pages 588–589.

506 Curci (n 436) Pages 297–298.

5 TK in the Public Domain

One of the normative theories of IPRS, *inter alia*, is to achieve a balance between private property and public domain. Public domain plays an important role regarding innovation and creativity, as last innovations could derive late ones. Besides, private exclusive control over innovations could prevent free expression and confine economic competition. Therefore, a dynamic public domain system would assist in maintaining the balance between monopolies on innovations and knowledge availability.[507]

Public domain is defined as "[t]he universe of inventions and creative works that are not protected by intellectual property rights and are therefore available for anyone to use without charge."[508] Therefore, as soon as exclusive rights on patents, copyrights, trademarks and trade secrets are gone or have lapsed, the protected IPRS will become an item of public domain and the public could use them without legal restrictions or liability for infringement of the rights.[509] Different views of public domain have been propounded by IPRS scholars.[510] Furthermore, public domain may have different definitions for different purposes based on the context in each of the regimes: patents, copyrights, trademarks and *sui generis*. For instance, in the field of copyrights and related rights, public domain is defined as:

> the scope of those works and objects of related rights that can be used and exploited by everyone without authorization, and without the obligation to pay remuneration to the owners of copyright and related rights concerned.[511]

In the context of patent law:

> public domain consists of knowledge, ideas and innovations over which no person or organization has any proprietary rights. Knowledge, ideas and innovations are in the public domain if there are no legal restrictions

507 Munzer and Raustiala (n 5) Page 53.

508 Garner (n 19).

509 SCP Secretariat, 'Dissemination of Patent Information' (2009) WIPO SCP, 13th sess, Agenda Item 6, WIPO Doc SCP/13/5. Page 27.

510 For example, Pamela Samuelson identifies thirteen faces of public domain, while James Boyle identifies four understandings of its concept. See: Pamela Samuelson, 'Enriching Discourse on Public Domains' (2006) 55 Duke Law Journal 783; and James Boyle, *The Public Domain: Enclosing the Commons of the Mind* (Yale University Press 2008).

511 Ficsor (n 428) Page 305.

> of use. (varying in different legislations and forming, therefore, different public domains), after expiration of patents (regularly 20 years), in consequence of non-renewal, after revocation and after invalidation of patents.[512]

Accepting the existence of the different faces of public domain benefits several subject matters.[513] It would assist both classic IPRS and the new generation of IPRS to take advantage of the public domain concepts. One of the new generation of IPRS is TK.

Public domain is a controversial concept in relation to TK. By its nature, TK in most cases, other than undisclosed TK, has already disclosed among the members of the concerned community and has become public knowledge among them. Also, TK might have been disclosed to the public outside the concerned community either without the consent of the concerned community or with their consent for specific regulated purposes.[514] In such a situation, TK is considered as public domain[515] because in accordance with general principles of existing IPRS regimes, it falls within the general concept of public domain, and any innovator or creator other than the TKHS may use it freely to raise IPRS claims on different aspects of TK. Although TK is a part of the public domain in the view of the conventional IPRS system, this is not so in the eyes of TKHS. They would never abandon their rights and responsibilities just because TK has been put within the concept of the so-called public domain.[516] The concept of public domain does not fit well with TKHS' rights to control and protect TK.[517] Even though TK has been revealed and diffused either by TKHS or unintentionally, this does not mean that third parties are free to use TK without authorization of the TKHS merely because third parties' rights have been recognized by western-made concepts of IPRS outside the customary law of TKHS. In this regard, those who wish to access TK must justify why "they have any

512 SCP Secretariat (n 509) Pages 26–27.

513 Samuelson (n 510) Page 823.

514 IGC-GRTKF Secretariat, 'Revised Provisions for the Protection of Traditional Knowledge: Policy Objectives and Core Principles' (n 36) Page 5.

515 Wend Wendland, 'Intellectual Property, Genetic Resources, Traditional Knowledge and Traditional Cultural Expressions' (Workshop on Intellectual Property and Traditional Knowledge for Economic Development: Empowering Local Communities of Uganda, Kampala, Uganda, 4 July 2017) Page 4.

516 Dutfield, 'Legal and Economic Aspects of Traditional Knowledge' (n 271) Pages 502–503.

517 See the comments of representative of the Indigenous Peoples Council on Biocolonialism in: IGC-GRTKF Secretariat, 'Revised Provisions for the Protection of Traditional Knowledge: Policy Objectives and Core Principles' (n 164) Page 38.

liberty-right or power to access this TK."[518] Conversely, TKHs are attempting to find a way to pull TK out of the western concept of public domain, and to do so in perpetuity.[519] The most compelling evidence of TKHs' efforts to reach this goal is their active participation in the IGC and other fora to discuss public domain and its meaning, role, boundaries and contours regarding TK.[520] They recognize that due to its circumstantial nature, the public domain provides a ground to be attributed to TK outside its western concepts. Thus, other understandings of public domain will not be wrong or misguided.[521] This approach matches completely with the modern conception of TK in which subject matters might come under the scope of public domain in specific respects and outside of it in other respects.

6 A Preliminary Note on Copyright, Unfair Competition and Trade Secret

The main question of this study is to determine the feasibility of protecting PCs against UC from other competitors in its primary markets through the protection mechanisms of the laws of trademark and GIs. To what extent can legal disciplines existing in domestic and international law be mustered to address the imbalance and risk described above, and to what extent can they be employed to halt the process of erosion and thus the loss of diversity and sustainability?

It may prompt inquiry as to why the scope of this study is limited solely to the legal disciplines of trademarks and GIs, considering the range of IP regimes available for the protection of PCs. To address this inquiry, a cursory evaluation of the capabilities and limitations of copyright and UC laws has been conducted, though these areas are not the central focus of the present research.

6.1 *Protection of TK under Copyright Laws*

TK in its broader concept, as explained in chapter 1, Section 2.2 of this book, includes TCEs. In other words, the relationship between TK and TCEs is 'absolute generality and peculiarity.' TK contains cultural expressions which in

518 Munzer and Raustiala (n 5) Page 54.

519 *ibid Page 53.*

520 IGC-GRTKF Secretariat, 'Glossary of Key Terms Related to Intellectual Property and Genetic Resources, Traditional Knowledge and Traditional Cultural Expressions' (n 161) Pages 33–34.

521 Stephen R Munzer, 'Commons, Anticommons, and Community in Biotechnological Assets' (2008) 10 Theoretical Inquiries in Law 271, Page 275.

turn encompass TKHs' symbols, designs, patterns, and cultural goods, known as, among others, cultural intellectual property (cultural IP). PCs with their eye-catching and artistic designs and patterns, as folkloric works, are no exception. TKHs, therefore, consider unauthorized use of their cultural expressions as violating their cultural IP. Therefore, protection of the cultural IP is a critical issue for TKHs. At first glance, copyright law seems the most suitable IP regime to provide legal protection for this aspect of TK. Generally speaking, "copyright protection is above all one of the means of promoting, enriching and disseminating the national cultural heritage."[522]

In the same way, Osei-Tutu suggests "the term cultural IP, as used here, refers to a narrow category of intangible cultural goods that could be protected under modern IP law, more specifically copyright."[523] However, he conditioned the possibility of protection of cultural IP as follows:

> First, it is a type of intangible cultural good that significantly overlaps with traditional IP.
>
> Second, it is protected under national law as a form of cultural heritage. This concept of cultural IP extends to those cultural goods that could be protected by copyrights, if they would have been protectable under copyright law at one point in time.[524]

Thus, it seems that the TKHs could also utilize copyright law to protect their TCES.

During the IGCs' meetings, some delegations suggested that copyright and related rights law could eventually protect some traditional creations.[525] Furthermore, several TKHs worldwide have exploited copyright law to control and protect their TCEs.[526] In Canada, for instance, Aboriginal creators and artists applied the Copyright Act to prevent unauthorized exploitation of their artworks, such as woodcarvings, silver jewelry, songs and sound recordings, and sculptures.[527] In Australia a few court decisions relied on copyright law to protect Aboriginal creations.

522 WIPO, *WIPO IP Handbook* (n 450) Page 41.

523 J Janewa Osei-Tutu, 'Harmonizing Cultural IP across Borders: Fashionable Bags & Ghanaian Adinkra Symbols' (2017) 51 Akron Law Review 1051, Page 1055.

524 *ibid* 1056.

525 Pires de Carvalho (n 158) 257.

526 Tom Greaves, *Intellectual Property Rights for Indigenous Peoples: A Source Book* (1st edn, Society for Applied Anthropology 1994) Page 7; Quoted in: Posey and Dutfield (n 180) Page 84.

527 Pires de Carvalho (n 158) Page 257.

One of the most famous cases, known as the 'carpet case,' is *Milpurrurru, G. & Ors v. Indofurn P/L & Ors*. In 1993, an Australian company called Beechrow (which later changed its name to Indofurn Pty Ltd) reproduced carpets in Vietnam and imported them to Australia. However, Indofurn used some Australian Aboriginal artists' designs on their carpets without the permission of indigenous artists. Those designs had been previously published as educational materials by the Australian National Gallery and in a calendar published by the Australian Information Service. "The reproduction of paintings which depict dreaming stories and designs of cultural significance has been a matter of great concern to the Aboriginal community. Pirating of Aboriginal designs and paintings for commercial use without the consent of the artist or the traditional owners was common for a long time." Judge Von Doussa believed that "in the present case the copyright infringement was plainly deliberate and calculated by Beechrow." Therefore, he ordered an injunction against further infringement of the artwork's copyright and compensation for cultural damage stemming from the unauthorized use of the Aboriginal designs.[528]

In the Australian Federal Court case of *John Bulun Bulun & Anor v R & T Textiles Pty Ltd.*, two leading Aboriginals artists successfully brought an action for damages against a textile company that infringed the copyright of their artistic work known as 'Magpie Geese and Water Lilies at the Waterhole' by the importation and sale of printed clothing fabric in Australia. The plaintiffs created their artwork with the permission of the Ganalbingu People. The Ganalbingu people's communal right over the artwork and traditional ritual knowledge is recognized and protected by the Australian legal system, and they have the right to control and corpus of their ritual knowledge. The plaintiffs attempted to maintain the copyright on their artistic work for the benefit of the Ganalbingu people. In due course the respondent acknowledged infringement of the claimant's copyright in their artistic work and acknowledged that they had breached the copyright.[529]

Mira Burri noted this discussion, and pointed out:

> One could argue that TCE and copyright are a good match because they are both about creative works.[530]

---

528 *Milpurrurru, G & Ors v Indofurn P/L & Ors* [1994] FCA 1082, DG4 of 1993.

529 *John Bulun Bulun & Anor v R & T Textiles Pty Ltd.* [1998] Federal Court of Australia FCA 0975, DG3 of 1996.

530 Mira Burri, 'Cultural Heritage and Intellectual Property' in Francesco Francioni and Ana Filipa Vrdoljak (eds), *The Oxford Handbook of International Cultural Heritage Law* (Oxford University Press 2020) Page 479.

The sentiment expressed in Burri's statement, embodies the view that the copyright regime has some advantages for providing the necessary mechanisms for protection of TCEs. However, this proposal is also the subject of a heated debate, because despite the potential of the copyright law for protecting the TCEs, there are considerable inconsistencies and certain deficiencies that limit the potential of using this regime to protect PCs and meet TKHs' expectations. The limitations identified can be summarized as follows:

First: copyright protection is available for all forms of literary and artistic works. As mentioned in the Berne Convention,[531] a wide range of literary, artistic, and scientific works fall within the scope of copyright protection. The Convention prohibits limitations because of the modes or form of expression of the works. In addition, the Convention enumerated a non-exclusive list of protected subject matters. Undoubtedly, TCEs are artistic and literary works of TKHs and include productions such as designs, patterns, handicrafts and carpets that as artistic works are eligible for protection under the rules of the Berne Convention.[532] According to the UNESCO Model Provisions:

> expressions of folklore means productions consisting of characteristic elements of the traditional artistic heritage developed and maintained by a community of [name of the country] or by individuals reflecting the traditional artistic expectations of such a community, in particular:
>
> (iv) tangible expressions, such as:
>
> (a) productions of folk art, in particular, drawings, paintings, …, carpets.[533]

In the same manner, it seems a convincing argument that copyright could be the most relevant regime for providing legal protection of PCs, because PCs are the tangible manifestations of TCEs, and the expressions of Iranians' national culture. It appears that Iranian legislators have also believed that copyright law can play an important role in the protection of PCs, whether as independent works or as a folklore works based on national cultural and artistic heritage:

> Works protected by copyright law are as follows:
>
> 9. Original articles of applied handicraft and industrial art, carpet and rug designs.

531 Berne Convention Article 2(1).

532 WIPO, *WIPO IP Handbook* (n 450) Page 59.

533 The Committee of Governmental Experts and WIPO (n 71) Section 2(iv)(a).

10. Original works based on folklore and national heritage of culture and arts.[534]

Therefore, due to the broad scope of subject matters protected by copyright, this system can encompass TCEs and PCs. However, it is important to acknowledge the limitations of copyright protection in covering all types of TCEs. As stipulated in the TRIPS Agreement and the WCT, "Copyright protection shall extend to expressions and not to ideas, procedures, methods of operation, or mathematical concepts as such."[535] It is crucial to note that copyright "protects expression of ideas but not knowledge itself."[536] Moreover, copyright law can potentially protect symbols of TCEs and PCs as works of writing or drawing.[537] However, it is crucial to bear in mind that the distinctive attributes and reputation associated with the styles of local and indigenous communities render them susceptible to misappropriation. While the copyright system may afford protection to specific elements of a style that satisfy the necessary criteria for originality, it falls short of adequately protecting the style itself. The PCs' styles, being an integral component of the historical, cultural, and artistic heritage of native and local communities, extend beyond the ambit of copyright protection. Consequently, the inherent limitations of the copyright system manifest when confronted with the task of effectively preserving and safeguarding the entirety of local and indigenous styles.[538] This restriction is explicitly delineated in Article 2(10) of Iran's copyright law. This provision unequivocally affirms that folklore, in and of itself, does not fall within the purview of copyright protection. Instead, the focus of copyright law lies on the original works that are derived from folklore. This legislative perspective reflects the distinct stance of the Iranian legislator, emphasizing the clear differentiation between the intangible cultural heritage of folklore and the creative expressions that stem from it, which are eligible for copyright protection. A good example that highlights the limitations of copyright for protection of TCEs is *ta moko*, a traditional form of tattooing that originated from the indigenous Māori people of New Zealand.[539] Frankel provides insights into these limitations through the illustrative example of *ta moko*. While copyright law may offer a certain level of protection to specific manifestations of *ta moko* due to their inherent

534 Iran – Act for Protection of Authors, Composers and Artists' Rights Article 2(9) & (10).

535 TRIPS Agreement Article 9(2); and WCT Article 2.

536 Posey and Dutfield (n 180) Page 90.

537 Berne Convention Article 2(1).

538 Burri (n 530) Pages 479–480.

539 For more information see: Ngahuia Te Awekotuku, 'Ta Moko: Maori Tattoo' in Roger Blackley (ed), *Goldie* (Auckland Art Gallery; David Bateman 1997).

uniqueness and personal nature, it falls short of encompassing the comprehensive protection of the associated knowledge, traditions, and rules that underpin diverse *ta moko* practices. Consequently, when entities such as the Ford Motor Company utilize *ta moko* designs on automobiles or Sony incorporates them into a video game, they effectively disengage *ta moko* from the very rules and traditions that provide the foundation for its sustenance and evolution.[540]

Second: copyright protection is not subject to registration by the government. Unlike for patents, the critical point in copyright is that the registration of literary and artistic works is not a prerequisite for protection.[541] Copyright protection begins at the time of the creation of the work, and, therefore, it is easy to obtain.[542] In this sense, as Burri points out, there is "a sort of automatism in the granting of copyright protection."[543] This automatic protection is known as the non-formality requirement. "The word 'formality' must be understood in the sense of a condition which is necessary for the right to exist – administrative obligations laid down by national laws, which, if not fulfilled, lead to loss of copyright."[544] The concept of the non-formality requirement was represented for the first time under Art. 4(2) of the 1908 Berlin Act of the Berne Convention, which stipulated that "the enjoyment and the exercise of these rights shall not be subject to any formality." Similarly, Art. 5(2) of the Paris Act of the Berne Convention reaffirms this commitment to the non-formality requirement. Thenceforth, the formality requirements as a condition for entitlement to copyright protection were lifted, and copyright protection became totally independent of the formality requirements applied by the countries of origin of the work.[545] Before this fundamental change, under the Act of 1886, the enjoyment of copyright protection was subject to the fulfillment of the applicable requirements and formalities by the works' country of origin. In other words, the entitlement to protection under the Convention depended

540 Susy Frankel, 'Using Intellectual Property Rules to Support the Self-Determination Goals of Indigenous Peoples,' *Research Handbook on Human Rights and Intellectual Property* (Edward Elgar Publishing 2015) Page 630; quoted in: Burri (n 530) Pages 479–480.

541 Deborah E Bouchoux, *Intellectual Property: The Law of Trademarks, Copyrights, Patents, and Trade Secrets* (4th edn, Cengage Learning 2012) Page 246.

542 Posey and Dutfield (n 180) Page 90.

543 Burri (n 530) Page 478.

544 WIPO, *Guide to the Berne Convention for the Protection of Literary and Artistic Works* (WIPO 1978) Page 33.

545 Ning Zhao, 'Choice-of-Law in Cross-Border Copyright and Related Rights Disputes: Comparative Inspiration for the PRC' (Doctor of Philosophy, Rijksuniversiteit Groningen 2012) Page 40.

on compliance with members' formality requirements. The non-formality requirement principle has been repeated in the TRIPS Agreement, the WCT, and the WPPT.[546]

It is important, however, not to assume the applicability of the non-formality requirement was initially accepted worldwide. For example, in the USA, works were required to be deposited and registered by related authorities to be protected under the Act of 1909. Therefore, in this case, American copyright law conflicted with the Berne Convention. However, the formality requirements under national law were canceled when the USA became a member of the Berne Convention on March 1, 1989. Still, it is important to note that in the USA, registration plays an essential role, as the registration of copyright is a prerequisite to the enjoyment of certain remedies:

> [n]o award of statutory damages or of attorney's fees, as provided by sections 504 and 505, shall be made for –
>
> (1) any infringement of copyright in an unpublished work commenced before the effective date of its registration; or
>
> (2) any infringement of copyright commenced after first publication of the work and before the effective date of its registration, unless such registration is made within three months after the first publication of the work.[547]

Iran's legal system took almost the same approach in which, although registration is merely a voluntary procedure, the registration will be a strong proof of ownership in case of any disputes.[548] As mentioned earlier, this characteristic of the copyright regime has distinguished it from patents and trademarks law, in which granting legal protection depends on registration with the authorities. From this point of view, the copyright system might seem suitable to protect TCEs by putting non-formality requirements in place and TKHs may benefit from the non-formality requirement of the copyright for protecting TCEs.[549] Nevertheless, it is crucial to understand that the act of registering a copyright is a precondition for accessing specific legal remedies.

546 TRIPS Agreement Article 9(1); and WCT Article 25(10); and WPPT Article 20.

547 The US – Copyright Act 1976 Section 412.

548 Iran – Act for Protection of Authors, Composers and Artists' Rights.

549 Zhao (n 545) Page 40.

Third: "The *sine qua non of* copyright is originality."[550] Every literary, scientific and artistic work regardless of its mode or form of expression must be an original creation to enjoy copyright protection.[551] Despite the fact that 'originality' plays a critical role in determining the copyrightability of work, international copyright treaties provide no definition of the term originality nor raise the originality requirement for the protection of works. There is, however, evidence that supports the concept of an originality requirement and that works must be original to be copyrightable. In the Berne Convention there are some indications that works must be intellectual creations.[552] The most compelling evidence is Article 2(5) which states that the works that "constitute intellectual creations shall be protected as such." Another key point in the Convention is a direct relationship between two concepts of 'author' and 'work.' In Article 1 of the Convention, the members of the Convention "constitute a Union for protection of the rights of authors in their literary and artistic works." The term 'work' itself is not defined by the Convention. However, Article 2(1) – which offers a non-exhaustive list of protectable works – stipulates that "literary and artistic works shall include every production in the literary, scientific and artistic domain." From a review of the discussions held in the revision conferences of the Berne Convention, it is evident that the participating delegations believed the condition that a work must be an intellectual creation means that the work must be original. Therefore, the concept of originality is totally different from the concept of novelty in industrial property rights, in which a work must be new to be protectable.[553] Also, during a WIPO Copyright Committee discussion, it was mentioned that "work could be defined as an intellectual creation consisting of an original structure of ideas or impressions."[554] The same committee pointed out that the originality "was an integral part of the definition of the concept of work."[555]

Some committee members emphasized that while they do not provide a specific definition for the concept of originality, they believe that it should be interpreted in accordance with the principles of the Berne Convention,

550 *Feist Publications, Inc, v Rural Tel Serv Co* [1991] Sup Ct 89–1909, 499 US 340; quoted in: Abbott, Cottier and Gurry (n 367) Page 484.

551 WIPO, *WIPO IP Handbook* (n 450) Page 42.

552 WIPO, *Guide to the Berne Convention for the Protection of Literary and Artistic Works* (n 544) Page 17.

553 Ficsor (n 428) Page 23.

554 WIPO, 'Copyright Monthly Review' (World Intellectual Property Organization 1990) 120-1990-09 Page 260.

555 Daniel J Gervais, 'Feist Goes Global: A Comparative Analysis of the Notion of Originality in Copyright Law' (2001) 49 Journal of the Copyright Society of the U.S.A. 949, Pages 971–972.

according to which, every intellectual creation in the literary and artistic domain should be protected, irrespective of its significance. Consequently, they argued that no test or higher standard for evaluating such works could be acceptable.[556] In the same manner, many countries have also interpreted the Berne Convention as meaning that the work must be 'original' to be protected by their copyright system.[557] It was left to national laws to decide whether and how to define the term 'originality.' Notwithstanding, only a few countries chose to define 'originality' in their national laws. According to the study conducted in 2002 by Gervais and his colleagues only three out of ninety-three countries, including Bulgaria, Burkina Faso and Malaysia, provided a definition of originality under their legal system.[558]

Legal systems do not have a homogeneous interpretation of the concept of originality. However, they establish a criterion known as the threshold of originality to determine the eligibility of a work for copyright protection. In other words, there is a threshold of originality that must be met in order for a work to qualify for copyright protection. For instance, within the common law system, countries such as Canada, the UK, and Australia adhere to the 'sweat of the brow' doctrine. This doctrine grants protection to literary or artistic works that result from the creator's 'skill and labor' or substantial individual effort. Consequently, copyright protection is extended to individuals who have invested their efforts in compiling, editing, or organizing existing information, even if their creations lack an underlying original work. However, according to the civil law system, in countries such as Switzerland, the concept of originality is a key requirement for copyright protection and a work is deemed original only if it is the author's own intellectual creation.[559] This means that the work must reflect the author's personal creative choices and must not be merely a copy or imitation of another work.

Despite the divergences among legal systems, a discernible trend towards a gradual convergence in the determination of the threshold of originality can be observed. Common law jurisdictions have progressively distanced themselves from the 'sweat of the brow' doctrine, exemplified by the landmark *Feist case* ruling in the United States in 1991, which unequivocally rejected this doctrine.[560] Conversely, civil law countries have embraced the notion that an

---

556 WIPO, 'Copyright Monthly Review' (n 554) Page 292.

557 WIPO, *Consolidated Analysis of the Legal Protection of Traditional Cultural Expressions/ Expressions of Folklore.* (n 393) Page 37.

558 Gervais, 'Feist Goes Global' (n 555) Page 970, Footnote 149.

559 Swiss – Federal Act on Copyright and Related Rights 1992 (231/1 (Status as of 1 January 2022)) Article 2.

560 *Feist Publications, Inc., v. Rural Tel. Serv. Co.* (n 550).

intellectual creation is the primary requisite for safeguarding a work. In these jurisdictions, originality is not contingent upon novelty, ingenuity, or aesthetic merit.[561] It is worth noting that the mere satisfaction of the 'sweat of the brow' condition alone does not suffice to render a creation eligible for protection; the work must also demonstrate a degree of creativity. However, it is pertinent to underscore that the level of creativity demanded does not necessitate a heightened or elevated standard, nor does it mandate the integration of the creator's persona into the work. This requirement transcends the confines of intellectual creation, as acknowledged within civil law frameworks.[562]

Given the discussions surrounding the concept and threshold of originality, it becomes apparent that at least two contentious issues hinder the feasibility of accommodating TCEs within the existing copyright protection framework:

a) The threshold of originality itself presents difficulties. TCEs are usually pre-existing and frequently passed down through generations, evolving and being shaped by the collective contribution of community members over time, and often lacking the level of originality required by copyright law.[563] The strict criteria for originality, which typically demand a certain level of individual creativity, may not adequately account for the cultural context and dynamic nature of TCEs. Despite efforts to diminish the threshold of originality in different jurisdictions, the requirement for originality remains fundamental in determining the eligibility of works for copyright protection. TCEs are works transmitted across generations, with deep historical and sacred importance to TKHs. From their standpoint, the modification of the TCEs is not permissible, and any reconfiguration within them is subject to restrictions and necessitates prior authorization.[564]

b) The utilization of TCEs for the creation of derivative works by third parties raises significant concerns within the realm of copyright law. It is noteworthy that novel expressions, arrangements, adaptations, collections, and even digitally enhanced packaging, derived from TCEs' materials that already reside in the public domain, may potentially qualify for copyright protection if they satisfy the criteria of originality. However, it is imperative to recognize that under the defensive protection system, the creation of derivative works

561 Burri (n 530) Page 478.

562 Ficsor (n 428) Page 23.

563 Sharon B Le Gall, 'Intellectual Property and Indigenous Arts and Cultural Expressions' (Virtual Seminar on Promoting and Protecting the Arts and Cultural Expressions of Indigenous Peoples: Perspectives on the Canadian Experience Organized by the World Intellectual Property Organization (WIPO), Geneva, Switzerland, 4 May 2022) Slide 16.

564 Christine Haight Farley, 'Protecting Folklore of Indigenous Peoples: Is Intellectual Property the Answer?' (1997) 30 Connecticut Law Review 1, Page 21.

based on TCEs necessitates prior informed consent from the TKHs. Failure to adhere to this fundamental principle may result in the misappropriation of TCEs. It is pertinent that, in numerous instances, creators of derivative works draw inspiration from TCEs without any direct engagement with TKHs, their cultural traditions, or heritage. This situation raises a critical question regarding the adequacy of the copyright legal system in protecting the rights of TKHs. Essentially, TKHs possess the potential to safeguard works derived from or inspired by TCEs, albeit within certain limitations.[565]

These controversies surrounding originality and the threshold of originality pose significant obstacles to effectively protecting TCEs within the existing copyright framework. While creations derived from TCEs could potentially rely on copyright protection, traditional designs and patterns of PCs may not meet the originality requirement.[566] Addressing these challenges necessitates careful consideration and potential adjustments to ensure the appropriate recognition and preservation of copyrights associated with cultural expressions and the communities that uphold them.

Fourth: the concept of originality, as defined in international copyright law, presents a significant challenge for protecting databases of TCEs. The most suitable method for documenting and formalizing the protection of TCEs is by utilizing collections and databases specifically dedicated to TCEs. A database of TCEs could encompass the compilation of information gathered through interviews conducted on specific subjects, along with the preparation of essential documents for the title application. These documents would include a map depicting significant cultural and physical elements, such as territorial boundaries, settlements, natural resources, sacred sites, ancestral areas, topographical features (rivers, rapids, mountains), and local place names. Additionally, it could encompass various aspects of the relationship between the communities and their land, including settlement patterns, practices related to the exploitation and management of natural resources, residential and life histories, kinship and ethnicity, notions of territoriality and property, ritual practices, environmental ethics, environmental terminology, and place names.[567] However, the originality requirement is an obstacle for protection

565 Burri (n 530) Page 479–480.

566 Masoud Taromsari, حمایت حقوقی بین المللی از طرح ها و نقش ها و سایر ویژگی های فرش دست باف ایرانی در مقابل تقلید خارجیان (*Legal Protection of Persian Carpets at National and International Levels Against Unauthorized Imitations: An Analytical Study*) (1st edn, Institute for Trade Studies and Research 2006) Page 86.

567 Stanford Zent and Egleé L Zent, 'On Biocultural Diversity from a Venezuelan Perspective: Tracing the Interrelationships among Biodiversity, Culture Change and Legal Reforms' in

of the databases of TCEs. In accordance with the international copyright law databases, by reason of the selection and arrangement of their contents, constitute intellectual creations and shall be protected as such.[568] In other words, the creator of a database must demonstrate an element of creativity, as a mere compilation or listing of works or extracts without any personal contribution would not suffice.[569] Thus, most databases of TCEs are not protectable by copyright law even if they are of a considerable size and have been expensive to prepare. For example, this is the case when a database is exhaustive, that is, it contains all the relevant data without any selection or omission, and the data is arranged according to basic, straightforward rules, such as alphabetically, or in numerical or chronological order.[570] Therefore, many databases of TCEs may not fulfill this requirement of originality. This is particularly challenging for databases of TCEs that are comprehensive by nature and are meant to be as complete as possible, capturing the cultural, environmental, and social nuances of a community. So, the concept of originality is a limiting factor when it comes to safeguarding TCEs databases under existing copyright law frameworks. Despite the amount of work and resources invested in creating these databases, the lack of 'originality' in the legal sense can render them vulnerable and unprotected.

Fifth: Another potential obstacle that arises in the protection of TCEs is the issue of fixation, according to which subject matter of copyright must exist in a tangible or physical form.[571] If non-material works are not fixed in some material form, they are excluded from protection.[572] Hofman defines 'fixation' as the act of "putting the work into some material form, for example, by writing it down or recording it."[573] The concept of fixation derives from the provisions of the Berne Convention and the WPPT. The definition of fixation provided in the WPPT refers to "the embodiment of sounds, or of the representations thereof, from which they can be perceived, reproduced or communicated through a device."[574] The Berne Convention grants member countries the flexibility to incorporate fixation as a requirement for copyright protection through their

---

Charles R McManis (ed), *Biodiversity and the Law – Intellectual Property, Biotechnology and Traditional Knowledge* (Earthscan 2007) Page 108.

568 Berne Convention Article 2(5); and TRIPS Agreement Article 10(2); and WCT Article 5.

569 WIPO, *Guide to the Berne Convention for the Protection of Literary and Artistic Works* (n 544) Page 20.

570 WIPO, *WIPO IP Handbook* (n 450) Page 441.

571 Posey and Dutfield (n 180) Page 90.

572 WIPO, *WIPO IP Handbook* (n 450) Page 50.

573 Hofman (n 335) Pages 30–31.

574 WPPT Article 2(c).

national legislation. It stipulates that countries have the authority to prescribe that works, either generally or specific categories of works, must be fixed in some material form to be eligible for protection.[575] Thus, in some countries, fixation in a tangible form is a fundamental requirement for copyright protection.[576] For instance, in the USA, a work is seen as 'created' only when it is fixed in a copy or phonorecord for the first time.[577] In Australia, copyright law provides protection for original works with identifiable authors provided that the works are expressed in a material form. It defines fixation as the act of embodying or capturing a work in a material form, whether by writing, recording, or any other method.[578]

Two critical components are essential for the effective protection of TK. The first component underscores the need for TK and TCEs to be engaged within their customary contexts, employing traditional methodologies for their development, transfer, and governance. The second component mandates the requirement for tangible fixation as a means of ensuring preservation. In adhering to this principle, TKHs strive to document their cultural expressions comprehensively, thereby satisfying the requirement of fixation. Such fixation is perceived as an essential strategy for the effective preservation and protection of TK.[579] There is also, however, a further point to be considered. In many local and indigenous communities, various forms of their cultural expressions are only transmitted orally across generations without being fixed in a tangible medium.[580] The fixation requirement present in various national copyright laws imposes limitations on the protection of intangible and oral expressions of culture. such as tales, dances, or songs, unless and until they are preserved or recorded in a tangible form or medium.[581] In the same manner, oral tradition plays a crucial role in the history of PCs, encapsulating myths, beliefs, legends, and hymns that accompany the weaving process.[582] Unfortunately, this lack of fixation often renders these expressions ineligible for copyright

575 Berne Convention Article 2(2).

576 Burri (n 530) Page 478.

577 The US – Copyright Act Section 101.

578 Australia – Copyright Act 1968 Section 22.

579 IGC-GRTKF Secretariat, 'Overview of Outcomes and Activities of the Intergovernmental Committee' (n 335) Page 7.

580 Posey and Dutfield (n 180) Page 84.

581 Burri (n 530) Page 481.

582 Shahdokht Rahimpour, 'سنت شفاهی وتوسعه مدیریت فرهنگی فرش (Oral Tradition and Development of Carpet Cultural Management),' *Contemporary Challenges and Needs in the Economics and Management of the Handwoven Carpets* (Islamic Art University of Tabriz 2018) Page 366–367.

protection.[583] These narratives, specific to ethnic and tribal communities, not only tell the story of the carpets but also serve as a vehicle for cultural transmission across generations. However, this invaluable oral tradition falls outside the purview of copyright protection due to the fixation requirements inherent in copyright laws. Furthermore, the rights pertaining to recordings and documentation of TCEs are vested in the individuals responsible for the acts of fixation, such as ethnomusicologists, folklorists, and other researchers, rather than in the bearers of the TCEs themselves.[584] Therefore, some scholars point out that protection of TK is not conditioned to fixation in a tangible form such as writing or drawing.[585] While the Tunis Model Law on Copyright for Developing Countries, adopted in 1976 through a collaborative effort between WIPO and UNESCO, made strides in establishing dedicated safeguards for the protection of works of national folklore – notably, without the requirement for tangible fixation – its effectiveness remains constrained due to its limited global acceptance.[586]

Sixth: Copyright protection is primarily tailored to identifiable authors, contrasting with the communal and collective nature of TCEs. These expressions often originate from a shared cultural heritage within a community, rather than being the result of individual authorship. The predominant focus of copyright law is on identifiable individual creators and their original works. This individualistic approach does not readily align with the communal aspect inherent to TCEs.

The Berne Convention, in its statutory provisions, does not categorically delineate the terms 'owner' or 'author' of a work, nor does it provide explicit guidance concerning the matter of authorship. It refrains from stipulating a definitive interpretation of these terminologies in relation to a work. Nevertheless, the Convention acknowledges that the rights delineated therein typically pertain to the author of the work. The Convention does provide an indication as to the identity of the author within the context of copyright law, and within this sphere, the author is commonly acknowledged as the initial proprietor of the work. In this regard, the Convention's provisions are often interpreted such that a real person is considered the creator of the work. This approach is evident in the legislative procedures of many countries, spanning both civil and common law traditions. Typically, these laws recognize

583 Posey and Dutfield (n 180) Page 84.
584 Burri (n 530) Page 481.
585 Munzer and Raustiala (n 5) Page 53.
586 The Committee of Governmental Experts, 'Tunis Model Law on Copyright for Developing Countries.'

a natural person as the original author of the work. While in many of these jurisdictions the authorship of a work is seldom attributed to anyone other than the natural creator, numerous countries acknowledge exceptions, allowing the ownership of the work to be assigned to legal entities and persons other than 'flesh-and-blood' creators.[587]

Pursuant to the above analysis, the system of copyright law presents two fundamental hurdles to the benefit of indigenous and local communities' intellectual creations.

Primarily, copyright law generally requires that the creator of a work be a natural person. Additionally, under certain conditions, copyright protection can extend to works produced by multiple authors, provided that these authors can be identified. This protection also applies when a company or an organization, as a legally recognized entity, owns the work.[588] This means the creator must have legal recognition as either an individual or a legally incorporated entity.[589] Consequently, the rights-holder can often be an individual other than the original TKHs.[590] TCEs originate from a community that could reasonably assert their collective rights over their cultural expressions. However, the current copyright system cannot protect the collective ownership of TKHs unless they are recognized as a legal entity. Indeed, one of the major criticisms of IPR systems, including copyright, is their individualistic approach to creators and their innovative works. Critics argue that these systems predominantly reflect Western values, thereby overlooking the communal and social values inherent in other societies. This can lead to neglect of these different values and, frequently, to conflicts. A glaring example of this deficiency is the oversight of the role that indigenous and local communities play in fostering creativity and cultural innovations.[591]

Secondarily, for the rights conferred by copyright law to be effective, the creator of the work must be identifiable. This requirement is essential in order to specify the right holders and to determine who precisely is a beneficiary of such rights. It is also needed to ensure the enforcement of the copyright and to facilitate communication between the copyright holder and any parties interested in seeking permission to use the copyrighted work. A particular

587 Paul Goldstein and P Bernt Hugenholtz, *International Copyright: Principles, Law, and Practice* (4th edn, Oxford University Press 2019) Pages 228–229.

588 Burri (n 530) Page 478.

589 Posey and Dutfield (n 180) Page 84.

590 Burri (n 530) Page 479.

591 Chidi Oguamanam, 'Localizing Intellectual Property in the Globalization Epoch the Integration of Indigenous Knowledge' (2004) 11 Indiana journal of global legal studies 135, Page 137.

limitation of copyright is its insistence on identifying the creator rather than acknowledging the community behind a cultural product, which is one of the critical challenges in protecting cultural IP.[592] Moreover, the creators of TCEs are mainly local communities. Pinpointing the originators of TCEs is challenging, if not unfeasible, due to their collective creation and maintenance.[593] Even if an individual member of a local and indigenous community creates or develops a tradition-based work, this is more a reflection of the common sense of their community than the individual. This marks the work as 'traditional.' While such works may have specific authors, they are often unknown or unlocatable, highlighting the collective nature of these creations. As asserted by the European Union and its Member States, copyright hinges on the ability to recognize the individual who created the work. In contrast, folklore is characterized either by the unknown identity of the originator of the tradition or by the understanding that the tradition is a collective attribute of a community.[594]

Then again, even in cases where creators could be identified, the creation is not solely 'owned' by the creator but falls under communal responsibility, reflecting shared identity and guardianship. In the Australian case of *John Bulun Bulun & Anor v R & T Textiles Pty Ltd*[595] the relationship between the Ganalbingu people and Mr. John Bulun Bulun serves as a clear example of this. The court ruled that the Ganalbingu people have communal title to their traditional ritual knowledge and can dictate that the use of this ritual knowledge and artwork by Mr. Bulun Bulun should comply with the community's customary requirements. As the creator of the artwork, he must take any necessary steps, in line with his fiduciary duties to the community, to prevent any misuse. The artist has an obligation to act in the interests of the Ganalbingu people with respect to the artwork in order to preserve the integrity of their culture and ritual knowledge. Such fiduciary obligations stem from a relationship of mutual trust and confidence between the artist and the community. Therefore, the community has the primary right to sue the artist in the event of a breach of his obligations in order to enforce his fiduciary duties. However, this does not mean that the artist should act entirely in the interests of the Ganalbingu people. Evidence indicates that an artist has the right to consider and pursue his own interests, for example, by selling the artwork. But the

---

592 Osei-Tutu (n 523) Page 1067.

593 WIPO, *Consolidated Analysis of the Legal Protection of Traditional Cultural Expressions/ Expressions of Folklore.* (n 393) Page 36.

594 IGC-GRTKF Secretariat, 'Draft Gap Analysis on the Protection of Traditional Cultural Expressions' (World Intellectual Property Organization 2008) WIPO Doc WIPO/GRTKF/ IC/13/4(b) Annex I Page 3.

595 *John Bulun Bulun & Anor v R & T Textiles Pty Ltd.* (n 529).

artist must not neglect his fundamental obligation to maintain the integrity of Ganalbingu culture.[596]

In conclusion, the current copyright law system poses significant challenges for indigenous and local communities seeking to protect their intellectual creations. The two primary hurdles are the system's insistence on legal recognition of the creator as a natural person or incorporated entity and its requirement of identifiable creators for rights to be effective. These conditions often overlook the collective ownership nature of TKHs and TCEs. The system's predominant reflection of Western, individualistic values leads to neglect of communal and societal values prevalent in other cultures. This often results in conflicts and overlooks the crucial role these communities play in fostering cultural innovations. Furthermore, identifying the creators of traditional works, which are typically a collective attribute of a community, is often challenging or unfeasible, further complicating the protection of cultural IP.

Seventh: Copyright protection is not infinite. Copyright encompasses two types of rights: moral and economic rights.[597] In certain jurisdictions, authors possess the right to be acknowledged as author of their works and to object to distortions of these works. The ultimate purpose of granting moral rights to the author is to protect the integrity of the work and the reputation of its creator. The moral rights remain with the author, even if the economic rights have been transferred to someone else. The recognition and duration of these moral rights, however, depend on national laws and may continue indefinitely. In contrast, the period of protection for economic rights is not unlimited.[598]

The minimum term of protection for economic rights, as stipulated by the Berne Convention and TRIPS Agreement and implemented in most countries, extends through the life of the authors and for at least 50 years after their death.[599] Recently, there has been a trend to further extend this period. In the case of sound recordings, the copyright generally lasts for 50 years and is held by the individual or company responsible for the recording.[600] However, it should be noted that in some circumstances, the duration can extend up to 70 years after the death of the creator of the sound recording.[601] Such extended protection

596 Burri (n 530) Pages 480–481.

597 See Chapter 2, Section 2.2.

598 Burri (n 530) Page 478.

599 Berne Convention Article 7(1); and TRIPS Agreement Article 12.

600 Posey and Dutfield (n 180) Page 83.

601 See for example: Directive 2011/77/EU of the European Parliament and of the Council of 27 September 2011 amending Directive 2006/116/EC on the term of protection of copyright and certain related rights 2011 (L 265/1) Article 1; and Australia – Copyright Act Section 33.

of the creator's work not only safeguards investments made in producing and distributing that work but also encourages creators and distributors. Knowing that their investment is protected for a substantial period, even many years after the creator's death, motivates them to continue investing time, effort, and resources into creating and disseminating new works.[602]

Although the protection period for economic rights is extensive, it is not infinite. Such a time constraint renders the current state of the copyright regime less suitable, or at least more challenging, for the protection of TCEs or other forms of cultural IP. The limited time frame for copyright protection raises at least two issues regarding the protection of TCEs: *Firstly*, after the expiry of economic rights protection, the TCEs will be placed in the public domain. Likewise, since copyright protection is time-limited, the protection for symbols may have already expired, leaving the symbols of PCs in the public domain.[603] And any third party may use traditional designs and patterns without permission from their original creators. While the original works of TKHs as part of their culture and heritage must be preserved and protected without any time limitation, placing them in the public domain would mean the destruction of this heritage.[604] Consequently, TKHs often want their cultural IP to be protected indefinitely or, at the very least, for the duration of their community's existence. *Secondly*, copyright protection begins from the time a work is created or published. However, the origins of cultural expressions are not always clear and may not have a specific starting point. These issues create difficulties in applying copyright rules to such expressions.[605]

These two issues could have profound implications for PCs, which stand as tangible representations of TCEs. The process of creation of these carpets is steeped in centuries-old heritage, knowledge, techniques, and storytelling. Determining the precise starting point for such deeply-entrenched cultural items is challenging. The concern is not just about pinpointing the date of creation for individual weavings, but understanding and acknowledging the ancient traditions they embody. Given the ambiguity surrounding their temporal origins and their immense cultural significance, the protection of such folklore artifacts should not be temporally constrained. Ideally, they warrant protection in perpetuity, ensuring that their cultural essence remains sacrosanct.

---

602 WIPO, *WIPO IP Handbook* (n 450) Page 50.

603 Osei-Tutu (n 523) Pages 1067–1068.

604 Taromsari (n 566) Page 86.

605 Burri (n 530) Page 481.

The challenging issue of limited copyright protection duration has not gone unnoticed by TKHs and policymakers. Various legal frameworks have been formulated to address this shortcoming. For example, the 'Tunis Model Law on Copyright for Developing Countries' includes an intriguing provision that does not set a specific time limit for the protection of national folklore, offering instead protection '*ad infinitum*.'[606] Similarly, the "Pacific Regional Framework for the Protection of Traditional Knowledge and Expressions of Culture"[607] aims to offer robust protection for TCEs in the Pacific region, including provisions for indefinite protection. Additionally, the 'Model Provisions for National Laws on the Protection of Expressions of Folklore Against Illicit Exploitation and other Prejudicial Actions,' jointly developed by UNESCO and WIPO, explicitly indicate in Note 65 of their commentary that the protection granted is not time-constrained.[608] However, it is crucial to acknowledge that these models are not universally implemented and are subject to territoriality principle variations depending on the individual country's legal systems.

Eighth: One of the key challenges in leveraging copyright laws to protect TCEs lies in navigating territorial complexities. The international exploitation of copyrighted cultural IP routinely gives rise to three questions about territoriality, national treatment, and choice of governing law.

1. Copyright laws are inherently territorial, meaning they have no jurisdiction beyond the borders of the enacting country. According to the principle of territoriality, a State generally lacks the authority to enact legal norms that would govern activities occurring outside its national territory.

2. National treatment is "the policy or practice of a country that accords the citizens of other countries the same intellectual property protection as it gives its own citizens, with no formal treaty of reciprocity required."[609] National treatment is a long-established standard in the industrial property and copyright conventions. Member States are required to extend the same level of protection to foreign works as they do to those created by their own citizens. According to Article 5(1) of the Berne Convention, a work copyrighted in one Member State generally receives equivalent protection in other Member States.

3. When it comes to determining the applicable law, the prevailing rule for resolving disputes in copyright infringement cases is to apply the law of the country where the unauthorized usage occurred. To illustrate this point,

606 The Committee of Governmental Experts (n 586) Section 6(2).

607 The Pacific Regional Framework for the Protection of Traditional Knowledge and Expressions of Culture 2002 Part 2(9).

608 The Committee of Governmental Experts and WIPO (n 71) Note 65.

609 Garner (n 19) Page 1125.

if a legal action is initiated in Country A for unauthorized usage taking place in Country B of a work originating from Country C, then the court in Country A would apply the law of Country B to ascertain whether infringement has occurred.

The principles of territoriality, national treatment, and choice of law are interrelated facets of copyright law. Generally, if a country's copyright law is confined to its own territory, it will be the exclusive law enforced within that territory – so long as other countries adhere to the same principle. Because the prevailing rule for determining copyright infringement involves applying the law of the country where the infringement transpired, territoriality essentially dictates that the governing law in most infringement cases will be that of the country where the infringement occurred. By the same token, although not explicitly defined as a choice-of-law rule, national treatment in copyright treaties often functions as such in practice, subjecting both foreign and domestic entities to the legal framework of the protecting country.[610] Nonetheless, in the realm of practical application, even if some jurisdictions could establish legislations for protecting TCEs under their copyright laws, and even if similarities exist among copyright statutes in different jurisdictions, works granted copyright protection in one jurisdiction may not necessarily enjoy similar protections internationally. For instance, if Ghanaian law identifies an author of TCEs and offers them copyright protection, that author could potentially seek similar protection in the USA. The USA would be obligated to treat this claim in the same manner as it would for its own nationals. However, USA law currently lacks provisions for protecting cultural IP.[611] Accordingly, even if we suppose that the Iranian copyrights law could provide strong protection for TCEs and PCs, such protection will be enforceable only in the territory of Iran. However, most cases of violation of TKHs' rights happen in other countries.[612]

To address the challenges posed by the principle of territoriality, some suggest that membership in international agreements can lessen the impact of these geographical limitations in practical terms.[613] This idea gains additional support from the 1982 Model Provisions, which delve into the concept of 'national treatment' as it relates to the protection of folklore expressions originating from foreign countries. According to these provisions, domestic laws on folklore protection could potentially serve as the groundwork for either regional or international protection of such expressions, through either

610 Goldstein and Hugenholtz (n 587) Pages 85–86.
611 Osei-Tutu (n 523) Page 1069.
612 Taromsari (n 566) Pages 68–69.
613 WIPO, *WIPO IP Handbook* (n 450) Pages 50 and 64.

reciprocal arrangements or international treaties.[614] Despite the optimism of experts who drafted the Model Provisions, advocating for an integrated approach that updates domestic laws to protect TCEs and utilizes reciprocal arrangements and regional and international agreements, these mechanisms appear to fall short of adequately protecting TCEs beyond national borders. Certainly, if copyright laws were standardized globally, there would be no need for distinct rules regarding territoriality, national treatment, and choice of law. Although, this may be true, efforts toward harmonization of copyright and related rights via international treaties should not be conflated with the establishment of a universal copyright system. The primary objectives of treaties like the Berne Convention, the TRIPS Agreement, the WCT, and the WPPT are simply to mandate member states to adhere to minimum protection standards for eligible foreign rights holders. Given that member states frequently exceed these minimum treaty requirements in their domestic laws, and that these minimum standards do not encompass critical issues such as copyright authorship and ownership, it is likely that rules on territoriality, national treatment, and conflicts will remain pertinent for the foreseeable future. Even the European Union's harmonization directives, aimed at achieving a comprehensive alignment of specific rules in the field of copyright and related rights, have fallen short of establishing a pan-European protective framework. This is largely because the harmonization efforts are still a work in progress, and copyright laws within Member States continue to be strictly territorial.[615]

In the final analysis, despite international treaties aiming to standardize minimum protections for creative works, the territorial nature of copyright laws remains a barrier, particularly for protecting TCEs. Although harmonization efforts are in progress, they have not yet eliminated the need for rules that consider geographic boundaries. Therefore, existing principles will likely continue to govern copyright matters for the foreseeable future, emphasizing the ongoing relevance of territorial issues in this domain, which make the copyright regime unable to provide protection for TKHs' cultural IP.

Ninth: Even if TCEs are eligible for copyright protection, the exceptions and limitations inherent in copyright laws can still compromise the rights of TKHs.[616] Copyright laws define authors' economic rights, but those rights are not absolute. Exceptions and limitations exist to enable public use of copyrighted works without requiring permission from authors or rights holders.

614 The Committee of Governmental Experts and WIPO (n 71) Section 14.

615 Goldstein and Hugenholtz (n 587) Pages 85–86.

616 WIPO, *Consolidated Analysis of the Legal Protection of Traditional Cultural Expressions/ Expressions of Folklore* (n 393) Page 42.

The primary aim of these exceptions is to balance the rights of copyright owners with public interests.[617] Moreover, proper limitations enable new authors to build on previous works, maximizing their beneficial use. Each country's system has limitations to accommodate cultural, social, technological, economic, and political objectives. The objectives that copyright limitations aim to achieve vary from nation to nation, depending on how they prioritize aspects like freedom of speech, research, education, public library and archive access, aid to disabled people, and market competition. Additionally, the economic justification for these limitations is subject to change, particularly as emerging technologies either reduce or raise associated transaction costs. In summary, change is a recurring theme in this particular area of copyright more than in any other. National laws impose varying kinds of limitations on copyright. Three primary frameworks govern copyright exceptions and limitations in national laws, ranging from the specific exceptions often seen in countries following the civil law system to the more flexible 'fair dealing' or 'fair use' clauses in common law countries. The more expansive and somewhat adaptable fair dealing rules predominate in many common law nations. Fair dealing serves as the central mechanism for copyright exceptions in both the UK and Australia, albeit with different scopes. In the UK, fair dealing is allowed for private study and non-commercial research, provided the author is acknowledged. In Australia, fair dealing extends to several categories such as research, criticism, parody, news reporting, and legal advice. Unlike the more flexible American 'fair use' doctrine, fair dealing in these common law countries is specific to its outlined categories. However, some judicial opinions have suggested a more generalized 'public interest' defense that resembles the American fair use concept. The fair use principle was initially exclusive to the USA but is now gaining traction in other common law jurisdictions.[618]

Fair use allows for the use of copyrighted material for specific purposes, such as criticism, comment, news reporting, teaching, scholarship, or research.[619] The key point about using copyright exceptions and limitations is that it is ultimately up to courts to determine whether a particular use qualifies under these legal provisions. Courts typically look at various factors, such as the type of work, why and how it has been used, the portion of the work used, and how this use affects the work's market value, to make their decision.[620]

617 WIPO, *WIPO IP Handbook* (n 450) Page 50.
618 Goldstein and Hugenholtz (n 587) Pages 349–351.
619 The US – Copyright Act Section 107.
620 Goldstein and Hugenholtz (n 587) Page 352.

Narrowly defined and specific exceptions are found in civil law countries. Some important limitations scenarios include: *Freedom of Panorama* which allows reproduction of creative crafts permanently shown in a public space in photos or drawings without permission.[621] Duplication of a work made only for the maker's own *personal and private usage*.[622] *Libraries and archives*' can apply specific exceptions which enable them to reproduce works for purposes such as preservation, research, and lending while maintaining public access.[623] *Quoting*, which is mentioned in Article 10(1) of the Berne Convention, is covered in almost every national law. According to the quotation right, using a protected work is permitted as long as the source is acknowledged, along with the author's identity, and the scope of the quote complies with fair practice.[624] Such use is also permitted in Iranian copyright law according to which published works can be quoted and referred to for various purposes, provided the sources are cited and limitations are observed, and monetary gain is not required for educational institutions.[625] As an example, the 1982 Model Provisions outline four scenarios in which the use of TCEs or folklore do not require authorization. First, TCEs can be employed for educational purposes, encompassing both tuition-based courses and the sale of textbooks. Second, the 'by way of illustration' provision permits the inclusion of TCEs in original works, provided it adheres to fair practice guidelines. Unlike standard copyright laws, this is not confined solely to educational contexts. Third, the provisions allow for the uninhibited creation of new, original works in fields like literature, music, and visual arts that are inspired by folklore. Fourth, 'incidental utilization' covers scenarios such as the use of folklore in public spaces and current event reporting. Although some experts suggested harmonizing these provisions with existing copyright laws, this approach was not adopted. Instead, the Model Provisions are designed to adapt relevant aspects of copyright laws specifically to protect TCEs.[626]

As discussed above, application of exceptions in copyright laws can vary widely depending on the jurisdiction and the specific case in question. While international treaties allow for these exceptions within certain boundaries, they do little to standardize them. The absence of internationally enforceable

621 For more information see: Bruce Kilpatrick, Pierre Kobel and Pranvera Këllezi (eds), *Antitrust Analysis of Online Sales Platforms & Copyright Limitations and Exceptions* (Springer 2018).

622 WIPO, *WIPO IP Handbook* (n 450) Page 50.

623 Burri (n 530) Page 481.

624 WIPO, *WIPO IP Handbook* (n 450) Page 50.

625 Iran – Act for Protection of Authors, Composers and Artists' Rights Article 7.

626 The Committee of Governmental Experts and WIPO (n 71) Section 4.

minimum standards makes it challenging to address concerns about the use of cultural symbols outside of their country of origin.[627]

In conclusion, the inherent variation and fluidity of exceptions and limitations in copyright laws make them an unsuitable framework for the protection of TCEs and folklore. While these laws aim to balance public interest with authors' economic rights, their objectives are not universally standardized and vary from country to country, subject to cultural, economic, and technological considerations. Such a diverse landscape of exceptions makes it challenging to protect the rights of TKHs, as the exceptions can easily compromise these rights under different legal systems. Furthermore, the absence of internationally enforceable minimum standards for copyright exceptions exacerbates these challenges, particularly when TCEs are used outside their country of origin. Therefore, relying solely on copyright laws for the protection of TCEs and folklore appears to be inadequate, and a more tailored approach is needed to address the specific concerns related to these unique forms of cultural expression.

Copyright law, despite its potential to protect certain facets of TCEs, exhibits substantial limitations in protecting cultural IP and PCs. First, it is primarily geared towards protecting the expression of ideas rather than protecting the holistic richness and diversity of TKHs including their products' styles, traditions and methods of production. Second, although the non-formality requirement of copyright law could potentially benefit TCEs, its universal applicability should not be assumed. Third, the current regime poses challenges in terms of originality criteria, making it difficult for customary designs and patterns to gain protection. Fourth, the fixation requirement often excludes non-material cultural expressions like oral stories, dances, and songs from copyright protection. Fifth, current copyright laws are ill-suited to recognize collective ownership, which is often the norm among TKHs. Sixth, time-bound limitations inherent in copyright laws lead to the eventual lapse of protection, putting TCEs in the public domain and at risk of unauthorized usage. Seventh, the territorial nature of copyright law complicates international protection, even in the face of international treaties aiming for standardization. Lastly, the lack of universally recognized exceptions and limitations renders copyright law inadequate for protecting TCEs across diverse jurisdictions. Therefore, alternative IP regimes offering lasting protection, such as trademarks and GIs, warrant closer attention for the effective safeguarding of TCEs.

627 Osei-Tutu (n 523) Page 1056.

6.2 *Preventing Unfair Competition against TKHs' Rights*

Counterfeits pose a significant challenge to the integrity and accurate representation of TKHs' cultural artifacts. By creating a distorted narrative of history, these fabrications not only misrepresent cultural identities but also obscure humanity's true legacy. While fakes and forgeries can be considered cultural items in their own regard, their primary function until their identification and proper categorization is to deceive. The intention behind these counterfeits is to mislead by promoting inaccuracies and misrepresentations, diverging from authentic cultural expressions.[628] In the context of Western IPRs and competition laws, the act of appropriating content, concealing its origins, and marketing the adulterated content to unsuspecting consumers is recognized as both unfair and dishonest. It undermines cultural authenticity and dilutes the value of genuine artifacts. Consequently, safeguarding cultural cohesiveness and protecting public welfare emerge as complementary objectives. The preservation and protection of TK and cultural IP not only honor and respect the source communities but also serve the broader interest of maintaining the fidelity of our shared cultural heritage.[629] When competition fails to regulate itself, leading to inadequate recovery of costs and fair profits, legal intervention becomes imperative to maintain necessary market incentives.[630] This is where the legal doctrine of UC plays a crucial role, and underscores the core principle that deceitful business practices are not only unethical but also illegal.[631] Given these considerations, UC laws, which traditionally aimed at protecting business interests against deceptive market practices, may provide innovative approaches to preventing and suppressing the misappropriation and misuse of TK and TCEs.[632] The concept of protection of TK is fundamentally rooted in and derived from the doctrine of misappropriation. Misappropriation is a category of UC that involves the unauthorized use or appropriation of another party's property or rights for one's own benefit. As a distinct branch of UC, the

628 John Henry Merryman, 'The Public Interest in Cultural Property' (1989) 77 California Law Review 339, Pages 359–360.

629 Danielle Conway-Jones, 'Safeguarding Hawaiian Traditional Knowledge and Cultural Heritage: Supporting the Right to Self-Determination and Preventing the Co-Modification of Culture' (2005) 48 Howard Law Journal 737, Page 752.

630 Reto Hilty, 'Rationales for the Legal Protection of Intangible Goods and Cultural Heritage' (Max Planck Institute for Intellectual Property, Competition & Tax Law 2009) Research Paper 9 Page 6 <http://papers.ssrn.com/abstract=1470602> accessed 1 November 2014.

631 Harry Dwight Nims, *The Law of Unfair Competition and Trade-Marks* (Baker, Voorhis 1917) 6; quoted in: Garner (n 19) Page 1667.

632 WIPO, *Intellectual Property and Traditional Knowledge* (World Intellectual Property Organization 2008) Page 25.

doctrine of misappropriation applies to various situations in which one person deals unfairly with another. This is particularly relevant when the interests of the TKHs are not covered by existing statutory systems of IP protection of copyright, patent and trademark, or against deception as to origin.[633] As Daes points out in paragraphs 26 and 27 of the 'Principles and Guidelines for the Protection of the Heritage of Indigenous Peoples:'

> National laws should deny to any person or corporation the right to obtain patent, copyright or other legal protection for any element of indigenous peoples' heritage without adequate documentation of the free and informed consent of the traditional owners to an arrangement for the sharing of ownership, control, use and benefits.
>
> National laws should ensure the labelling and correct attribution of indigenous peoples' artistic, literary and cultural works whenever they are offered for public display or sale. Attribution should be in the form of a trademark or an appellation of origin, authorized by the peoples or communities concerned.[634]

Echoing these principles, Dutfield emphasizes that a regime addressing misappropriation ought to incorporate, alongside other key aspects, the concept of UC, as a pivotal component.[635] In the common law system: "tort of using the non-copyrightable information or ideas that an organization collects and disseminates for a profit to compete unfairly against that organization or copying a work whose creator has not yet claimed or been granted exclusive rights in the work." In this system, the tort of misappropriation is subject matter of UC law according to which wrongful or dishonest use or borrowing of others' property is not itself an infringement of his or her property rights.[636]

As reflected and emphasized repeatedly in the WIPO IGC's draft Provisions for the Protection of TK, TKHs are entitled to be protected against

633 Garner (n 19) Page 1088.

634 These principles and guidelines was developed in 1995 by Erica-Irene Daes, who was the Special Rapporteur of the UN Sub-commission on Prevention of Discrimination and Protection of Minorities at the time. See: Erica-Irene Daes, 'Principles and Guidelines for the Protection of the Heritage of Indigenous People' (1995) UN ESCOR, 47th sess, Agenda Item 15, UN Doc E/CN.4/Sub.2/1995/26 Annex.

635 Dutfield, 'Legal and Economic Aspects of Traditional Knowledge' (n 271) Page 512.

636 IGC-GRTKF Secretariat, 'Glossary of Key Terms Related to Intellectual Property and Genetic Resources, Traditional Knowledge and Traditional Cultural Expressions' (n 161) Page 26.

misappropriation and misuse of their TK beyond its traditional context.[637] In same manner, the Swakopmund Protocol obliged its members to protect TK against misappropriation and misuse.[638] Also, TKHs have been taking necessary measures to deal with misappropriation and misuse of their TK.[639] In the 'Draft Provisions for the Protection of Traditional Knowledge,' misappropriation is defined as follows:

> Any acquisition, appropriation or utilization of traditional knowledge by unfair or illicit means constitutes an act of misappropriation. Misappropriation may also include deriving commercial benefit from the acquisition, appropriation or utilization of traditional knowledge when the person using that knowledge knows, or is negligent in failing to know, that it was acquired or appropriated by unfair means; and other commercial activities contrary to honest practices that gain inequitable benefit from traditional knowledge.[640]

Application of these norms under the broader concept of UC is used as a framework for establishing the general principle of protection against misappropriation of TK. For example, Sri Lanka's legal system introduced the concept of protection against misappropriation of TK in terms of the following categories:

> (i) acquisition, appropriation or use of traditional knowledge in violation of the provisions of this Act,
>
> (ii) deriving benefits from acquisition, appropriation or use of traditional knowledge where the person who acquires, appropriates or uses traditional knowledge is aware of, or could not have been unaware of, or is negligent to become aware of the fact that the traditional knowledge was acquired, appropriated or used by any unfair means; and
>
> (iii) any commercial activity contrary to honest practices that results in unfair or inequitable benefits from traditional knowledge.[641]

---

637 IGC-GRTKF Secretariat, 'Revised Draft Provisions for the Protection of Traditional Knowledge: Policy Objectives and Core Principles' (World Intellectual Property Organization 2005) WIPO Doc WIPO/GRTKF/IC/8/5 Annex Pages 20 and 49.

638 Swakopmund Protocol Section 21.

639 Posey and Dutfield (n 180) Page 130.

640 IGC-GRTKF Secretariat, 'Revised Draft Provisions for the Protection of Traditional Knowledge: Policy Objectives and Core Principles' (n 637) Article 1(2).

641 *Sri Lanka – A Legal Framework for the Protection of Traditional Knowledge 2009 Art 3.*

Misuse: Another form of illegal act against TK is misuse. In general, misuse is defined as: "improper use, in an unintended or unforeseeable manner."[642] In the context of the IGC's work, the term refers to "improper or excessive use, or to acts which change the inherent purpose or function of something."[643] Protection against misuse is one of the TKHs' obligations, because if the TK "is not properly guarded, the rights of those who are holding it may cease."[644] Thus, it would cause the loss of rights over TK. A well-known case regarding misuse of TK concerns Australian Aboriginal painting, which was misused by the tourism and textile industries in the production of carpets and clothes.[645] To prevent misuse of TK, in Indonesia, for instance, a design patent protection system has been developed by local authorities to prevent misappropriation and misuse of traditional designs of batik. Under this system thousands of motifs were to be registered at the local level and use of registered designs would need the permission from the government.[646]

Causing Confusion: Within the framework of UC laws, the range of actions that may lead to consumer confusion is widely recognized. Article 10bis(3)(1) specifically addresses this issue, prohibiting any acts capable of creating confusion, through any means, with a competitor's establishment, goods, or industrial or commercial activities. This encompasses actions that might generate uncertainty among consumers regarding the origin or source of goods or services, the association of a product or service with a competitor (confusion regarding source), the business connection between competitors (confusion regarding affiliation), or the endorsement of a product by a well-known figure (confusion regarding sponsorship). Confusion may arise from the use of logos, brand names, or other identifying elements that closely resemble those of a competitor, as well as from the visual presentation of goods and services, compromising the consumer's ability to make clear distinctions. Such acts, characterized as creating confusion, are prohibited because they dilute the distinctive character of a competitor's industrial or commercial activities. Moreover, UC laws offer a broader scope of protection against confusion than traditional trademark law, extending to unregistered trademarks, trade names, product shapes, and

642 Garner (n 19).

643 'Glossary of Key Terms Related to Intellectual Property and Genetic Resources, Traditional Knowledge and Traditional Cultural Expressions' (n 161) Pages 26–27.

644 Popova-Gosart (n 117) Page 98.

645 See: Terri Janke, *Minding Culture: Case Studies on Intellectual Property and Traditional Cultural Expressions* (World Intellectual Property Organization 2003).

646 See: Charles Knobloch and Dewi Savitri Reni, 'Using "Batikmark" as a First Step to Extend Protection of Indonesian Javanese-Batik Patterned Textile in Foreign Countries.' (5 February 2009) <https://www.usptclaw.com/pdfs/Batikmark_Article.pdf>.

other source indicators. To establish a successful UC claim based on confusion regarding marks, consideration is given to several factors, including:

- The distinctiveness of the indication (e.g., trademark, trade name, product shape),
- The degree of similarity between the indications,
- The similarity of the goods or services involved,
- The likelihood of consumer confusion.[647]

In the context of UC law as it applies to PCs, acts that create confusion could involve a manufacturer or seller using designs, patterns, or branding elements that closely mimic those of a renowned PC producer. For instance, if a carpet company adopts a design pattern or a branding strategy remarkably similar to those used by a well-established PCs weaver, it may lead consumers to believe that the carpets originate from the same source. Such deceptive practices could blur the distinction between the authentic, traditionally crafted PCs and those produced by the imitating entity, thereby infringing upon the unique cultural and commercial identity of the original creators. Section 43(a)(1) of the Lanham Act prohibits any false designations of origin or false descriptions. It is commonly recognized that this section covers not only explicitly false or misleading descriptions but also those that, while factually correct, are potentially confusing or give a false impression. The determination of whether the public is likely to be confused hinges on an analysis of all pertinent facts and circumstances.[648]

Misleading: Communities also express concerns about the misappropriation of their cultural items, particularly when these items are marketed with misleading and deceptive claims regarding their authenticity or origins. In this regard, States and communities have the right to stop uses that wrongly suggest that products are linked to a cultural group, are disrespectful, or involve sacred or secret knowledge.[649] Communities, particularly those known for their PCs, often face issues with the misappropriation of their cultural heritage through the use of false and misleading claims regarding the authenticity or origin of products.[650] For instance, an inferior quality carpet might be falsely marketed

---

647 WIPO, *Protection Against Unfair Competition: Analysis of the Present World Situation* (WIPO 1994) Pages 27–31.

648 Steven M Cordero, 'Cocaine-Cola, the Velvet Elvis, and Anti-Barbie: Defending the Trademark and Publicity Rights to Cultural Icons' (1998) 8 Fordham Intellectual Property, Media and Entertainment Law Journal 599, Page 615.

649 IGC-GRTKF Secretariat, 'Consolidated Analysis of the Legal Protection of Traditional Cultural Expressions' (World Intellectual Property Organization 2003) WIPO Doc WIPO/GRTKF/IC/5/3 Page 6.

650 WIPO, *Intellectual Property and Traditional Knowledge* (n 632) Page 18.

as an 'authentic' item originating from a renowned carpet-making community. Laws addressing UC and deceptive trade practices enable legal action against such fraudulent claims. These laws are designed to combat misrepresentations that a product, like a PC, is genuinely local, or has been produced, endorsed by, or is somehow affiliated with a specific community.[651]

Misleading practices in the context of UC represent a broad spectrum of deceptive tactics that can have a significant impact on both consumers and competitors. These practices are not limited to causing confusion through similarities in branding or marketing; they extend to a range of actions that deliberately provide false or deceptive information. This can include, but is not limited to, false advertising, misrepresenting product features or benefits, and providing incomplete or inaccurate product details. Misleading practices can also involve the manipulation of visuals, endorsements, or testimonials, creating false perceptions about a product's quality, performance, or value. Such deceptive actions have the potential to mislead consumers, influencing their purchasing decisions and adversely affecting fair market competition. Under Article 10bis(3)(3) of the Paris Convention "indications or allegations the use of which in the course of trade is *liable to mislead* the public as to the nature, the manufacturing process, the characteristics, the suitability for their purpose, or the quantity, of the goods" are prohibited. For example, it would be forbidden to employ indications suggesting that a product is authentically indigenous or created by a specific community, when in fact it is not genuinely indigenous or produced by the said community. These acts of misleading are seen as contrary to honest practices in industrial or commercial matters. As such, they fall within the ambit of UC, requiring Member States to provide remedies and enforcement mechanisms against these practices, thereby upholding the integrity of market competition and protecting consumer interests.

In Australia, pursuant to the Trade Practices Act of 1974 (Cth), corporations were legally prohibited from engaging in misleading or deceptive conduct within the realm of trade or commerce. This legislative framework was central to the adjudication in the carpet case of *George M*, Payunka, Marika & Others v Indofurn*. The case hinged on the application of the Act to the marketing and labeling practices for carpets, specifically addressing the legal prohibition against corporate conduct that misleads or deceives in trade or commerce. A pivotal aspect of the case was the examination of carpet labels claiming that 'Royalties are paid to Aboriginal Artists.' Justice Von Doussa found these labels to be misleading, particularly as they were also attached to carpets that had

651 WIPO, *Intellectual Property and Genetic Resources, Traditional Knowledge and Traditional Cultural Expressions* (n 231) Pages 32–33.

no Aboriginal association. Thus, consumers were misled into believing in a non-existent copyright affiliation, ownership, or approval by Aboriginal artists. The court's decision established that such practices by the carpet distributors amounted to false and misleading conduct, infringing sections 52 and 53 of the Trade Practices Act.[652] This judgment serves as a quintessential example of how UC laws can be utilized to protect the interests of TKHs and prevent consumer deception.[653]

In the USA, the interpretation of Section 43(a) of the Lanham Act was initially confined to encompass only passing off and trademark infringement. However, the scope of legal protections against UC has been gradually expanding, through legislative amendments by Congress and the evolution of judicial interpretation. These developments have broadened the Act's coverage, transforming it into an effective tool for combating infringements of common law trademarks, trade dress, false advertising and other UC-related activities.[654] The protection extends to prohibiting any false origins or descriptions. This section is broadly interpreted to include statements not only that are literally false but also those that, despite being factually accurate, are likely to mislead or create incorrect perceptions. The assessment of public deception is a factual matter, requiring a comprehensive review of all the relevant situations and contexts.[655] Consequently, it is reasonable to suggest that the legal protection against UC could potentially be extended to include TK and TCEs. Moreover, the Indian Arts and Crafts Act of 1990 serves to safeguard Native American artisans by guaranteeing the genuineness of Indian artifacts, overseen by the Indian Arts and Crafts Board. This legislation, functioning as a 'truth-in-marketing' measure, prohibits the sale of items falsely advertised as 'Indian made' if they are not created by individuals who qualify as Indians under the terms of the Act.[656] As the discussion shifts from the broader challenges of misleading practices within the realm of TK and TCEs to specific legal remedies, it is imperative to explore the doctrine of passing off. This legal principle offers a direct avenue for TKHs to assert their rights against the misrepresentation of their cultural products. The transition from addressing general UC issues to the specific application of passing off highlights the legal toolkit available for protecting

652 *George M*, Payunka, Marika & Others v Indofurn Pty Ltd* [1994] FCA 1215.

653 Janke (n 645) Pages 9–13.

654 Ethan Horwitz and Benjamin Levi, 'Fifty Years of the Lanham Act: A Retrospective of Section 43(a)' (1996) 7 Fordham Intellectual Property, Media & Entertainment Law Journal 59, Page 66.

655 Cordero (n 648) Page 615.

656 WIPO, *Intellectual Property and Traditional Cultural Expressions/Folklore-Booklet N°1* (World Intellectual Property Organization 2007) Page 17.

the authenticity and integrity of indigenous and local communities' contributions to cultural heritage.

Passing off is a doctrine under common law that protects a business's rights to its name and the associated goodwill, playing a pivotal role in the artisanal product market. This legal principle is instrumental in reinforcing cultural identity and enhancing cultural diversity by ensuring that artisanal products are accurately represented and protected.[657] As explained in Chapter 1, Section 5.1.2, merchants associated with TKHs and PCs are increasingly recognized as distinct producers within their geographical regions. They are often able to demonstrate that they have developed a favorable reputation for creating artifacts, such as handwoven carpets, that drive consumer interest and contribute to the IP cultural heritage.[658] Typically, passing off occurs when an individual implies an association between their products and those of another business, capitalizing on the latter's established goodwill and market reputation. This deceptive practice can lead to market confusion as well as harm to the original business's sales and reputation, particularly if the counterfeit products are of inferior quality. For instance, a merchant selling low-quality carpets may falsely advertise them as authentic PC from well-known carpet-producing regions like Tabriz or Kashan, misleading consumers and diluting the genuine products' market value. By leveraging the doctrine of passing off, communities can distinguish authentic artisanal goods such as PCs from counterfeit ones, preventing the misrepresentation of fake goods as 'authentic' and safeguarding their cultural significance and value.[659] This crucial aspect of IP law allows communities to control the use of TCEs and safeguard them against misuse or degradation. Through passing off, the integrity, cultural significance, and value of traditional works like PCs are preserved, ensuring respect for and protection of the rich cultural heritage they represent.[660]

Protection under the passing off doctrine also extends to unregistered trademarks in certain circumstances. To enforce this protection, the holder of an unregistered trademark must demonstrate in court their prior use of the mark and the development of significant goodwill and a positive reputation among consumers through its use and that the infringing use is likely to cause

657 *ibid Pages 6–7*; and WIPO, *Intellectual Property and Genetic Resources, Traditional Knowledge and Traditional Cultural Expressions* (n 231) Page 28.

658 Janke (n 645) Pages 37–38.

659 WIPO, *Intellectual Property and Genetic Resources, Traditional Knowledge and Traditional Cultural Expressions* (n 231) Page 28.

660 WIPO, *Intellectual Property and Traditional Cultural Expressions/Folklore-Booklet N°1* (n 656) Page 6.

confusion or deceive the public.[661] Distinctive patterns or specific weaving techniques unique to PCs' unregistered brands are good examples of development of significant goodwill and a positive reputation among consumers through its use.

Moreover, laws against passing off can offer protection for trade names. It is important to note that simply registering a business name does not confer the same proprietary rights as a trademark registration. Many indigenous individuals, under the misconception that registering a trade name grants them exclusive rights similar to a trademark, register such names with the intent to preclude other competing entities from using identical or similar names. However, unlike a trademark, a trade name registration does not inherently grant proprietary rights, leaving the name less protected against use by others. This distinction is particularly relevant as numerous companies today adopt TKHs' names and words for their business names. Additionally, a certification mark can be utilized even before registration, with its protection during this period deriving from copyright and the legal principle of passing off, rather than from infringement laws related to a registered trademark. This early use of a certification mark means that, while it is not yet formally recognized as a registered trademark, the owner can still enforce rights through copyright claims and by invoking passing off, which protects against the unauthorized use of the mark that could mislead consumers about the product's certification or origin. The use of passing off in this context serves to prevent others from falsely representing their products as meeting the standards or origins that the certification mark signifies.[662] Furthermore, the legal concept of the tort of passing off could be applicable as well. In several jurisdictions such as the UK and Australia, passing off is recognized as a form of UC.[663] Successful legal action against passing off may be possible if goods are falsely represented as being produced or endorsed by a specific community. To prevail in such a case, the plaintiff would need to demonstrate established goodwill and reputation and that a likely misrepresentation occurred.[664]

---

661 New Zealand Intellectual Property Office, *Protecting Intellectual Property with a Māori Cultural Element: User Guide* (Ministry of Business, Innovation & Employment 2016) Page 40.

662 Janke (n 645) Pages 30, 36–37 & 138.

663 See: Australia – Trade Practices Act 1974 (Cth) 1974; and Australia – Competition and Consumer Act 2010 (Cth) 2010. In Australia the Competition and Consumer Act 2010 largely replaced the Trade Practices Act 1974, while also expanding and refining it.

664 WIPO, *Protect and Promote Your Culture: A Practical Guide to Intellectual Property for Indigenous Peoples and Local Communities* (World Intellectual Property Organization 2017) Page 56.

TKHs of unregistered trademarks might utilize the legal doctrine of passing off as a form of protection if they can demonstrate adherence to its key principles, which include:

- Establishing that their business or products have garnered substantial goodwill and reputation;
- Providing evidence that the defendant's actions have led, or are likely to lead, consumers to mistakenly associate the defendant's goods with those of the plaintiff;
- Showing that this misrepresentation has resulted, or is likely to result, in damage or harm to the plaintiff's business or trade.

For example, products like postcards and CDs labeled as 'Aboriginal' and 'authentic' could potentially violate Section 52 of the Australian Trade Practices Act of 1974 (Cth) if such labels mislead the public into believing these products are authentically linked to indigenous communities or have genuine Aboriginal origins. Furthermore, representations or imagery on products that falsely imply an endorsement or affiliation with indigenous groups, such as the 'Wik' tribe dancers, that do not exist (as referred to in Section 53(d)) could also constitute a breach of the Trade Practices Act.[665] This legislation holds corporations accountable for inaccurately claiming endorsements, affiliations, or origins of their products, thereby safeguarding both consumers and the misrepresented parties.[666]

Arguments supporting the application of UC laws to TK and TCEs suggest they are well-suited to guard against the unauthorized use and commercialization of such knowledge, thus offering a legal basis for addressing these challenges. They highlight the strengths of UC law in offering protection against the misappropriation of TK as detailed below:

6.2.1 Potential of UC Law in Protecting TK

First: UC laws are instrumental in meeting the expectations of TKHs by offering protection against the misappropriation and commercial exploitation of TK.

665 Janke (n 645) Pages 37–38 and 92–93.

666 The Australian Consumer Law (ACL), encapsulated within Schedule 2 of the Competition and Consumer Act 2010, updates and supersedes provisions from the Trade Practices Act 1974 concerning consumer protection and fair trading. Notably, Section 18 of the ACL replaces Section 52, addressing misleading or deceptive conduct in trade or commerce. Additionally, the prohibitions against making false or misleading representations about sponsorship, approval, or other attributes, previously covered under Section 53(d) of the Trade Practices Act, are now encapsulated in Section 29(1)(h) of the ACL. This reorganization and updating of laws enhances clarity and effectiveness in safeguarding consumer rights against deceptive practices.

These laws can ensure that TKHs retain control over their knowledge and are duly recognized and compensated for its use.[667] In contrast to the more rigid structures of copyright and patent law, UC law provides a more user-friendly route for the legal protection of TK. Moreover, because UC law is generally applied in the context of commercial activities, issues related to the infringement of the right to free speech are not as acute. This makes it a more tailored fit for protecting the commercial aspects of TK without unnecessarily limiting the dissemination of cultural knowledge. Furthermore, implementing such UC rules for TK protection would exert a minimal impact on commercial morality norms, without causing significant disruption to existing business practices or ethical standards.[668]

Second: UC laws play a pivotal role in safeguarding the integrity of cultural expressions. They focus on preserving the established reputation, uniqueness, and goodwill typically linked to TKHs involved in creating handicrafts, art, and other customary products.[669] These significant yet intangible assets might be protected through a range of measures provided by UC law, which varies depending on the legal jurisdiction.[670] They prevent the distortion and dilution of cultural significance that often accompanies unauthorized commercial use, thereby maintaining the authenticity of traditional expressions.[671]

Third: UC laws serve as a deterrent to entities that might otherwise exploit TK for commercial gain. By imposing legal consequences for unauthorized use, UC laws discourage exploitation and encourage respectful and authorized use of TK.[672] In the context of the 1982 model provisions, any use of TCEs, whether willfully (or negligently), without acquiring consent from the relevant authorities or communities, falls under the category of offenses. One notable instance of offenses mentioned includes misleading the public regarding the origin of a folklore expression, wherein the offender falsely represents the expression as stemming from a specific community when it does not. Another offense is the distortion of the expression of folklore in any direct or indirect way that is deemed prejudicial to the cultural interests of the community concerned.[673]

667 Torsen and Anderson (n 440) Page 57.

668 Sean A Pager, 'Traditional Knowledge Rights and Wrongs' (2016) 20 Virginia Journal of Law & Technology 82, Page 116.

669 WIPO, *Intellectual Property and Genetic Resources, Traditional Knowledge and Traditional Cultural Expressions* (n 231) Page 32.

670 WIPO, *Protect and Promote Your Culture* (n 664) Page 56.

671 Dionyssia Kallinikou, 'Protection of Traditional Cultural Expressions or Expressions of Folklore' (International Council of Museums 2005) Page 4.

672 *ibid.*

673 The Committee of Governmental Experts and WIPO (n 71) Section 6(3),(4).

Fourth: A critical application of UC laws is in preventing the commercial misuse of folklore. This aspect is particularly relevant to entities that profit from folklore while neglecting its traditional and cultural significance.[674]

Fifth: UC law aligns well with the various facets of TK protection. The subject matter eligible for protection under UC law is incredibly expansive, offering a broader range of coverage.[675] Furthermore, UC laws extend beyond the unauthorized use of TK to cover a wide range of unjust practices. This includes deceptive marketing practices and misrepresentations that could harm the interests of both TKHs and consumers.[676] However, UC laws might not adequately address all forms of TK misappropriation, such as digital exploitation or cultural appropriation. Sari Sharoni describes cultural appropriation as "the taking-from a culture that is not one's own-of intellectual property, cultural expressions or artifacts, history and ways of knowledge." Drawing from various sources, she points out that while the broad scope of 'cultural appropriation' might make its definition seem elusive, instances of it are frequently observed. It usually involves the unauthorized use of various elements – such as 'words, names, designs, motifs, symbols, artworks, art styles, songs, musical genres, stories, or dances' forms – belonging to one cultural group (known as the source community) by another group in their artistic productions or commercial goods.[677]

Sixth: UC laws are particularly relevant in cases where products are falsely presented as 'authentic' or purported to be produced or endorsed by TKHs. This protection is crucial to prevent the dilution of cultural identity and ensure that consumers are not misled about the authenticity and origins of products linked to TK.[678] For instance, in the landmark Australian case of *Milpurrurru, G. & Ors v. Indofurn P/L & Ors*,[679] under trade practices law, Indofurn Pty Ltd was found to have misleadingly labeled its range of indigenous-oriented souvenirs as 'Aboriginal art' or 'authentic.' The case was brought against the company because it misrepresented that its hand-painted, Aboriginal-style souvenirs were authentic, when, in fact, most of the artists involved were not of Aboriginal descent. As a result, the company was prevented from using such descriptions

---

674 Kallinikou (n 671) Page 4.

675 Pager (n 668) Pages 115–116.

676 WIPO, *Intellectual Property and Genetic Resources, Traditional Knowledge and Traditional Cultural Expressions* (n 231) Page 26.

677 Sari Sharoni, 'The Mark of a Culture: The Efficacy and Propriety of Using Trademark Law to Deter Cultural Appropriation' (2016) 26 Federal Circuit Bar Journal 407, Page 410.

678 WIPO, *Intellectual Property and Genetic Resources, Traditional Knowledge and Traditional Cultural Expressions* (n 231) Page 32.

679 *Milpurrurru, G. & Ors v. Indofurn P/L & Ors* (n 528).

unless it could reasonably believe that the artwork or souvenir was created by a person of Aboriginal descent.[680] The Authenticity labeling system aims to provide indigenous communities with a competitive edge in a market flooded with items that seem 'indigenous' but are actually not of indigenous origin. The purpose of this system is to help consumers distinguish genuine cultural products, thereby enhancing the financial gains that Indigenous people can derive from the commercial exploitation of their cultures.[681]

Seventh: UC laws offer both direct and indirect protections for TK. Laws governing UC, along with consumer protection statutes related to marketing and labeling, can be especially pertinent and beneficial. This is particularly true given that issues of commercial exploitation of TCEs frequently stem from the notion that such expressions are being employed to falsely convey a product's 'authenticity' or its endorsement by a traditional community.[682] Moreover, consumers often lack the ability to autonomously identify counterfeit or imitated TCEs, let alone generate an effective countermeasure. Consumer awareness of TK and its cultural significance may be limited. Unscrupulous businesses can take advantage of this lack of awareness to engage in UC practices. It is important to recognize that the protection against UC serves not only to benefit TKHs but is also crucial for safeguarding the consumers of TCEs.

Eighth: Unlike copyright and patent law regimes, UC laws do not require elements of originality and novelty for protection, making these laws more accessible for the types of knowledge and practices that are often associated with TK.[683]

Ninth: Formal legal requirements for protecting TK through UC laws are generally minimal, which streamlines the safeguarding process.[684] UC law either complements industrial property statutes or offers forms of protection that these statutes do not provide. Notably, UC law does not grant exclusive rights, nor does it require registration, emphasizing its accessibility.[685] This area of law is designed to be versatile, adapting to emerging market practices without relying on formalities like registration. Such adaptability ensures

680 WIPO, *Consolidated Analysis of the Legal Protection of Traditional Cultural Expressions/Expressions of Folklore.* (n 393) Page 55.

681 Marianna Annas, 'The Label of Authenticity: A Certification Trade Mark for Goods and Services of Indigenous Origin' (1997) 3 Aboriginal Law Bulletin 4, Page 4.

682 WIPO, *WIPO IP Handbook* (n 450) Page 64.

683 Pager (n 668) Pages 115–116.

684 *ibid.*

685 WIPO, *Protect and Promote Your Culture* (n 664) Page 58.

that UC law can respond effectively to new challenges without leading to legal unpredictability.[686]

Tenth: Protection against UC practices has no time limit. Protection remains in place as long as the unfair practice could harm consumers or competitors.[687] Therefore, UC law aligns with the concept of indefinite duration for TK rights. This is particularly relevant because, unlike copyright and patent protections that have fixed time limits, UC norms can be applied indefinitely. This ensures that acts constituting UC can be legally contested at any point in time, without the limitations imposed by statutory duration on the applicability of protection. This is especially important for TK, which often has an ongoing, timeless cultural value.[688] However, if an aspect of TK becomes widely used and loses its association with a specific company or product, the likelihood of unfair advantage decreases, and protection may lessen accordingly.[689]

Eleventh: The principle of 'use it or lose it,' which forms the basis for the protection of trademarks and trade secrets, resonates well with the term provisions for TK and TCEs as proposed in the IGC's working documents. This principle ensures that rights are maintained only when the trademark or trade secret is actively being used, thus aligning closely with the sustainable and active utilization goals of TK and TCEs.[690] UC laws prevent the deceitful commercial exploitation of TK and TCEs, ensuring that these cultural assets are actively used and respected within their communities, thus avoiding dilution or misappropriation. By promoting sustainability, UC laws encourage communities to maintain and evolve their cultural practices, ensuring that these traditions thrive and remain commercially viable. The flexibility of UC laws allows them to protect diverse cultural identifiers that existing IP might not cover, adapting to protect the dynamic nature of TK and TCEs effectively. Moreover, UC laws align with international norms that advocate for the active preservation and respectful utilization of cultural knowledge, thus operationalizing these global principles at the national level and ensuring that cultural heritage is both legally recognized and practically protected. This holistic approach not only bridges traditional practices and modern legal frameworks but also enhances the cultural and economic sustainability of TK and TCEs in the global marketplace.

686 WIPO, *Consolidated Analysis of the Legal Protection of Traditional Cultural Expressions/ Expressions of Folklore.* (n 393) Page 55.

687 WIPO, *Protection Against Unfair Competition* (n 647) Page 28.

688 Pager (n 668) Pages 115–116.

689 WIPO, *Protection Against Unfair Competition* (n 647) Page 28.

690 Pager (n 668) Pages 115–116.

While the arguments presented above underscore the promise of leveraging UC regulations for safeguarding TK, it is imperative to acknowledge the complexities and challenges inherent in this approach. The endeavor to protect TK under the umbrella of UC laws faces numerous obstacles, which include:

6.2.2 Challenges of UC Law in Protecting TK

First: Integrating UC with established IP frameworks like patents and trademarks might lead to inconsistencies and complexities in enforcement. TK, enriched with cultural, historical, and social dimensions, frequently surpasses the conventional scope of IP categories. Moreover, TK often intersects with various IPRs, including patents and copyrights. However, not all aspects of IP protection focus exclusively on innovation and creativity. Trademark laws, GIs, and indications of source primarily safeguard established reputation, distinctiveness, and goodwill, which can be crucial for TKHs engaged in producing handicrafts, artworks, and other traditional products.[691] For instance, while elements like names, titles, and short phrases generally do not qualify for copyright protection, they may fall under trademark regulations or UC laws if they meet specific criteria. This is particularly relevant for elements like festival names or slogans, which, although not typically protected by copyright, may still receive legal protection under other IP frameworks.[692] In this regard, protection against UC can further enhance and complement the safeguards provided by conventional IP rights.[693] In the context of existing legal frameworks (*de lege lata*), utilizing UC law presents the sole international avenue for addressing misappropriation of TK. This approach is grounded in applying and interpreting the law as it currently stands, without proposing new legal amendments or hypothetical scenarios.[694] However, integrating protection under UC laws alongside these existing IP rights can present complexities. This is because UC law covers a broader range of issues, including deceptive practices and misrepresentation, which are not always directly addressed by standard IP rights. Therefore, while UC laws can bolster the overall protection of TK, carefully navigating their relationship with established IP rights is essential to ensure effective and comprehensive safeguarding of TK. On the other hand, adapting UC rules to the context of TK can be challenging if we consider TK as

691 WIPO, *Intellectual Property and Traditional Cultural Expressions/Folklore-Booklet N°1* (n 656) Page 10.

692 WIPO, *Intellectual Property and Folk, Arts and Cultural Festivals: Practical Guide* (World Intellectual Property Organization 2014) Page 18.

693 WIPO, *Protect and Promote Your Culture* (n 664) Page 57.

694 Riffel (n 3) Page 159.

a unique form of IP. Defining what constitutes UC when it comes to TK may require careful consideration and legal innovation.

Second: UC laws are characterized by inherent subjectivity and a certain lack of definitive clarity, which complicates their application to TK. The concept of 'unfairness' is particularly challenging, as it is highly interpretable and misappropriation within this realm is difficult to define clearly. Despite these challenges, it is important to recognize the broader utility of UC laws. These laws address a wide range of unfair acts, from misleading practices to violations of trade secrets, which are often beyond the scope of traditional industrial property laws. Therefore, UC laws are essential not only for augmenting these laws but also for offering protections that they fail to provide. To fulfill this role effectively, UC laws must maintain flexibility, enabling protection independent of formalities such as registration, and be adaptable to evolving market behaviors. This flexibility does not necessarily undermine predictability, but, rather, it ensures that UC laws can respond effectively to the dynamic nature of TK.[695]

Third: The defensive nature of UC laws, which often address misuse and misappropriation only after they have occurred, presents significant challenges in the context of TK, which may be irreversibly lost once exploited. Over the last two decades, negotiations under the IGC have focused on identifying and filling gaps in existing IP frameworks to strengthen the protection of TK and TCEs through both defensive and proactive measures.[696] However, scholars like Munzer and Raustiala argue for a predominance of defensive protection strategies to prevent misuse of TK in patents and copyrights, questioning the efficacy of more aggressive 'offensive' protection that would give TKHs broader control over their knowledge. They caution that strong TK protection might conflict with fundamental principles of the current IP system and could disproportionately favor indigenous groups without a clear justification for such distinction.[697] Meanwhile, Pager criticizes the IGC's broad approach, suggesting it risks unintended consequences by conflating TCEs with TK and blending cultural with technical innovation. He advocates for a more focused strategy that emphasizes benefit-sharing, cultural integrity, and preventing UC.[698]

Fourth: UC laws focus on commercialization. To categorize the misappropriation of TK as UC, the presence of competitive activity is crucial. This concept is derived from Article 10bis of the Paris Convention, which implies that a competitive relationship must exist between the TKHs and the unauthorized

695 WIPO, *Protection Against Unfair Competition* (n 647) Page 13.
696 Burri (n 530) Page 482.
697 Munzer and Raustiala (n 5) Pages 40 & 66.
698 Pager (n 668) Page 200.

user, where the unauthorized use results in a competitive advantage and loss of economic interests for TKHs. Consequently, this diminishes the likelihood of a direct competitive relationship with unauthorized users, particularly in instances where TK has not been commercialized, and, notably, "much TK has not been commercialized."[699] Therefore, no economic damage can be assumed for TKHs. Significant areas of TK, such as medicinal practices and herbal remedies – encompassing a broad understanding of medicinal plants and their uses for treating various health conditions – and agricultural practices, including techniques like crop rotation, natural pest control, and seed saving, illustrate segments of TK that are predominantly non-commercialized. This non-commercialization, as Riffel points out, does not preclude the possibility of TKHs entering into a competitive relationship in the future. Even in scenarios where TKHs do not immediately incur economic losses, the prospect of entering into a competitive relationship remains viable, as delineated by Article 10bis of the Paris Convention. This conjecture is based on the possibility that the exploitation of TK by external parties could, over time, reveal its economic potential, leading to its commercialization. Such a development would thrust the original TKHs into a competitive arena, making them active participants in the marketplace. Accordingly, the potential for such a competitive dynamic is deemed adequate for TKHs to legitimate their participation as competitors at any juncture.[700] The Hoodia case serves as a pivotal example, illustrating the legal and ethical challenges in exploiting non-commercialized TK in the commercial sector. This case underscores the imperative for just and equitable recognition and compensation for TKHs during the commercialization process.[701] Conversely, PCs' beneficiaries present a distinct scenario, characterized by the vigorous commercial activities of the participants, including producers, designers, and merchants. This domain is directly implicated in matters of UC, attributed to its stakeholders' active involvement in the marketplace. The contrasting scenarios underscore the diverse nature of TK, ranging from purely cultural to commercial applications, and the corresponding legal frameworks required to recognize TK's variations and protect them effectively. In sum, UC usually requires proof of commercial harm. TK's value might be cultural, spiritual, or ecological, and these attributes are hard to quantify in

---

699 IGC-GRTKF Secretariat, 'List and Brief Technical Explanation of Various Forms in Which Traditional Knowledge May Be Found' (n 187) Note 46.

700 Riffel (n 3) Page 178.

701 Sarah A Laird and Wynberg Rachel, 'Institutional Policies for Biodiversity Research' in Sarah A Laird (ed), *Biodiversity and Traditional Knowledge: Equitable Partnerships in Practice* (Earthscan Publications 2002) Page 62.

legal terms. However, while the application of UC laws to the protection of TK necessitates a nuanced understanding of the competitive dynamics at play, the commercial activities inherent in sectors such as those relevant to PCs underscore the relevance of legal protections against UC. The discourse underscores that even the lack of economic exploitation by TKHs does not negate their economic rights, particularly in contexts where commercial activities are prevalent.

Fifth: While many countries have pioneered national and regional legal frameworks to protect TK from misappropriation and misuse, these efforts alone are often insufficient in the face of globalization. As products and services that incorporate TK increasingly cross borders, tracking and preventing UC practices becomes a formidable challenge. The global nature of TK and TCEs necessitates that countries participating in their trade implement stringent protective measures. Without cohesive international standards and collaborative enforcement, the risk of continued misappropriation and misuse of TK remains high, underscoring the urgent need for a unified global response to safeguard these invaluable cultural assets effectively.

Sixth: TK commonly emerges from indigenous or local communities and can extend across national borders. The task of pinpointing the legitimate holder(s) can prove daunting, especially when the TK is distributed across one or several communities, which is often the norm.[702] Furthermore, protecting TK from UC practices on an international scale poses considerable challenges, given the variations in legal systems and jurisdictional differences. While commonalities in minimum standards of protection typically exist, including prohibitions against creating market confusion, discrediting competitors or their offerings, and employing misleading representations as outlined in Article 10bis,[703] protection against UC is addressed through diverse legal frameworks in different countries. Some nations have dedicated laws on UC, trade practices, or labeling, while others integrate this protection within their civil litigation system, allowing aggrieved parties to seek legal redress for perceived harm. The methods employed to guard against UC can significantly differ from one country to another. Additionally, the categorization of this case necessitates a comprehensive legal analysis, taking into account the specific laws and regulations of each pertinent jurisdiction. Furthermore, cultural and ethical considerations are critical in these situations, as well as the potential impact on the heritage and identity of the community involved.

702 IGC-GRTKF Secretariat, 'List and Brief Technical Explanation of Various Forms in Which Traditional Knowledge May Be Found' (n 187) Paragraph 43.

703 WIPO, *Protect and Promote Your Culture* (n 664) Page 56.

Seventh: The mandate to suppress UC, although included in the Paris Convention, remains the least defined and most ambiguous among the various forms of industrial property protection covered by the Convention. Notably, even though the Convention does not precisely define other more established forms of protection like patents, trademarks, designs, and trade names, these areas have well-established roles in national laws and clear, albeit sometimes controversial, reasons for their recognition. This clarity is not mirrored in the case of UC, which can have varying meanings and theoretical justifications in different jurisdictions. The boundaries of what constitutes UC are nebulous. Despite a general consensus that competition should be 'fair,' opinions may significantly diverge regarding the role of competition in distributing goods and services across societies. Given that competition inherently produces winners and losers, the challenge lies in determining what constitutes a fair competitive act versus an unfair one. This raises the fundamental question: what are the 'rules' of this competition, and how are they established and enforced?[704]

Eighth: As previously explained, the principle of extraterritoriality in IP regimes typically confines national laws within their territorial boundaries, a notion aligned with the respect for national sovereignty.[705] Osei-Tutu's exploration of the international protection of Ghanaian cultural IP raises fundamental queries: Can Ghanaian legal provisions be enforced in the USA against American entities that misappropriate Ghanaian cultural IP? Moreover, is it practical for Ghanaian TKHs to engage USA legal mechanisms to redress violations of their TK rights? In his discourse, Osei-Tutu references the *Belmora LLC v. Bayer Consumer Care AG*[706] and *Trader Joe's Company v. Hallat*[707] cases as illustrative of a trend in the USA courts toward an extraterritorial application of USA trademark law. The Belmora case saw Bayer successfully contest Belmora's use of a similar trademark in the absence of a USA trademark registration, citing consumer deception and potential harm to Bayer's interests. Likewise, the Trader Joe's case demonstrated the application of USA trademark law against a Canadian entity, emphasizing the infringement's impact on USA commerce and the plaintiff's recognizable injury under the Lanham Act. These cases, though grounded in USA law, initiate discourse on the extraterritorial application of trademark laws in contexts such as the misuse

704 Sam Ricketson, *The Paris Convention for the Protection of Industrial Property: A Commentary* (Oxford University Press 2015) Paragraph [13.34].

705 Graeme B Dinwoodie, 'Developing a Private International Intellectual Property Law: The Demise of Territoriality?' (2009) 51 William and Mary Law Review 711, Page 717.

706 *Belmora LLC v Bayer Consumer Care AG* [2016] 4th Cir 15-1335, 819 F3d 697.

707 *Trader Joe's Company v Hallat* [2016] 9th Cir 14-35035, 835 F3d 960.

of Ghanaian cultural IP in the USA. They imply that if cultural IP enters the global commerce arena, its influence on international trade and reputation might necessitate a reevaluation of the territoriality principle in IP law. However, these USA legal precedents do not directly pertain to Ghanaian law, nor do they advocate for other countries to emulate the USA stance. Instead, they raise a theoretical question: should USA commercial activities involving cultural IP, deemed to be infringements outside USA borders, be subject to regulation? This consideration challenges the conventional territoriality concept in IP, proposing the need for governance when the commercialization of goods, inclusive of cultural IP, exerts transnational impacts.[708]

Having explored the complexities and possibilities of utilizing UC laws to safeguard TK and TCEs, it becomes pertinent to examine another significant legal mechanism: Trade Secrets. This aspect of IP law offers a distinct approach, potentially complementing UC laws by providing a framework for protecting confidential business information. As we delve into the realm of trade secrets, it is essential to assess their suitability and effectiveness in protecting TK and TCEs, especially in cases where these cultural assets intersect with commercial values and practices.

6.3 *Protection of TK under Trade Secret Laws*

A trade secret is characterized as confidential business information that bestows a competitive edge upon an enterprise and can encompass a variety of secrets related to manufacturing, industrial, or commercial processes.[709] The term 'trade secret' "include[s] undisclosed valuable business, commercial, technical or other proprietary data as well as technical information."[710] The illicit use or revelation of such information by parties other than the legitimate holder is deemed a violation of the trade secret and is recognized as an unfair competitive practice. The concept of misappropriation pertains to the improper handling of trade secrets or sensitive information. It is frequently associated with activities such as the theft of business secrets or the unauthorized exposure of proprietary details. Such acts of misappropriation, which are viewed as infringements of trade secrets, are conventionally classified under the umbrella of UC.[711] In this regard, the most compelling evidence is the first paragraph of Article 39 of the TRIPS Agreement, which aligns the protection

708 Osei-Tutu (n 523) Pages 1064–1067.
709 WIPO, *Protect and Promote Your Culture* (n 664) Page 58.
710 WTO, 'Compilation of Written Submissions and Oral Statements' (World Trade Organization 1988) Special Distribution MTN.GNG/NGll/W/12/Rev.l Page 46.
711 WIPO, *Protect and Promote Your Culture* (n 664) Page 58.

of trade secrets within the framework of unfair competition, explicitly drawing from Article 10bis of the Paris Convention. This connection is highlighted in the mandate for Member States to protect undisclosed information, aligning the protection against UC with the standards set by Article 10bis. The provision stipulates:

> In the course of ensuring effective protection against unfair competition as provided in Article 10bis of the Paris Convention (1967), Members shall protect undisclosed information.[712]

Under Article 39(2), protecting trade secrets is confined to "the possibility of preventing information lawfully within their control from being disclosed to, acquired by, or used by others without their consent in a manner *contrary to honest commercial practices.*" The provision's footnote 10 further explicates the criteria for honest commercial practices, explicitly embedding breach of confidentiality as a benchmark for determining the misappropriation of trade secrets. It specifies:

> "a manner contrary to honest commercial practices" shall mean at least practices such as breach of contract, breach of confidence and inducement to breach, and includes the acquisition of undisclosed information by third parties who knew, or were grossly negligent in failing to know, that such practices were involved in the acquisition.

Protection of trade secrets is recognized as a viable alternative for securing confidential information that falls outside the purview of traditional IPRs. Even in instances where patent or copyright protection could theoretically apply, opting for trade secret protection may be more advantageous. A notable advantage of trade secret protection is its potential for indefinite duration, devoid of the need for formal registration with any governmental entity. Moreover, as Cottier points out, "Here, no requirement of novelty exists."[713] This form of protection is specifically geared towards safeguarding against illicit practices such as industrial espionage, contractual breaches, and violations of confidence. However, it is essential to note that trade secret protection does not extend to prohibiting independent discovery or the autonomous development of the information in question. The overarching importance of trade secret protection lies in its capacity to forestall the unauthorized exposure, acquisition,

---

712 TRIPS Agreement Article 39(1).

713 Cottier, 'The Protection of Genetic Resources and Traditional Knowledge' (n 179) Page 570.

or utilization of confidential information that is crucial for commercial success and competitiveness.[714] Furthermore, the provisions of competition law extend beyond the confines of traditional property rights analysis by incorporating considerations of competitive ethics, as underscored in Article 10bis. This principle of commercial honesty is seamlessly integrated into the international protection of trade secrets under Article 39 of the TRIPS Agreement. This methodological shift from a stringent property rights regime enables a more flexible application of trade secrecy, which is crucial for safeguarding indigenous forms of innovation. A rigidly defined property rights approach often delineates sharp boundaries for the public domain, potentially excluding TK from protection. Conversely, grounding trade secret protection in UC law aligns more closely with the objective of shielding indigenous innovations that may not meet conventional criteria of novelty or creativity, but nonetheless require defense against unauthorized competitive exploitation or cultural dilution. This perspective is particularly attuned to ethical considerations relevant to the protection of TK. Thus, the competition-based theory of protection encapsulated in Article 39 of the TRIPS Agreement holds significant promise for addressing the distinctive challenges related to the ownership and confidentiality of indigenous innovations.[715]

Trade secrets protection extends to a diverse range of knowledge and skills, including technical expertise such as formulas, manufacturing processes, and other intellectual abilities developed through experience, talent and innovation.[716] This protection extends to various forms of knowledge, particularly those manifested through skills, whether they are repetitive or involve significant judgmental skills that are often scarce and highly valued.[717] For instance, in the context of traditional arts and crafts like PCs, certain skills are critical. These include the ability to select quality materials, understanding the intricacies of dyeing processes, expertise in weaving techniques, and the capacity to judge the authenticity and quality of finished carpets. These skills are often learned and perfected over time and can become a significant source

714 WIPO, *Protect and Promote Your Culture* (n 664) Page 60.

715 Doris Estelle Long, 'Trade Secrets and Traditional Knowledge: Strengthening International Protection of Indigenous Innovation' in Rochelle C Dreyfuss and Katherine J Strandburg (eds), *The Law and Theory of Trade Secrecy: A Handbook of Contemporary Research* (Edward Elgar 2011) Page 519.

716 WIPO, *Protect and Promote Your Culture* (n 664) Page 60.

717 Gupta, *WIPO-UNEP Study on the Role of Intellectual Property Rights in the Sharing of Benefits Arising from the Use of Biological Resources and Associated Traditional Knowledge* (n 363) Page 36.

of employment and cultural preservation in communities in famous places known for their carpet weaving, such as Tabriz, Kashan and Isfahan.

Individuals possessing these skills can be recognized as local experts or masters in their field. While some of these skills can be codified into specific know-how for industrial applications, others remain as tacit knowledge, deeply embedded in the artisans themselves. The latter form of knowledge can be protected as a trade secret or as personalized expertise. While codified knowledge can benefit from broader IP applications, tacit knowledge is typically safeguarded through trade secret protection, ensuring the preservation of these unique and culturally significant skills.[718]

TK can originate from various sources, including individuals, groups, or local and indigenous communities. The confidentiality and dissemination of this knowledge vary significantly based on its nature and the cultural practices of its originators. Some TK remains confidential, accessible only to its creators and their descendants, often bound by restrictions. Other forms of TK might be locally disseminated but still subject to limitations in terms of scope and accessibility. In contrast, certain TK is shared broadly within a community and even with outsiders, leading to its classification as public domain knowledge.[719] For example, while basic weaving techniques might be common knowledge within a carpet-weaving community, intricate and unique designs or dyeing methods may be exclusive to certain artisans. These specialized skills, such as the precise method of creating a particular pattern or blending natural dyes to achieve a specific hue, are often the result of years of experience and experimentation. For instance, Mr. Akbar Mahdiei is a legendary figure in the contemporary PCs industry, renowned for his expertise in designing and painting Persian rug patterns. His specialty lies in narrative and floral patterns known as Golfarang. Mahdiei's rugs are distinguished by their vibrant depictions of red and pink roses, purple irises, and lilies.[720] Such artisans might choose to keep this detailed knowledge secret, adhering to cultural norms or beliefs that the uniqueness and spiritual value of these designs could diminish if shared widely. This selective sharing of knowledge ensures the preservation of unique cultural identity and value associated with PCs, but it also risks the loss of this specialized knowledge if not passed down effectively to the next generation of weavers.

---

718 *ibid.*

719 *ibid Page 11.*

720 'Akbar Mahdiei – The Creator of Colorful Gardens in Persian Rugs' (*Percarin – Persian Carpet Industry*, 2024) <https://percarin.com/bignames/akbar-mahdiei> accessed 24 April 2024.

In 1987, Dr. Pushpangadan and his team embarked on an ethnobotanical journey to the Western Ghats, where they collaborated with the 'Kani tribe.' This expedition led to the discovery of a distinctive herb, known as 'Arogyapaacha,' which the tribe had long considered a closely guarded secret, akin to a trade secret in its exclusivity. Initially reluctant to disclose its identity, the tribe eventually shared the knowledge of the herb with Dr. Pushpangadan's team. This revelation spurred a series of in-depth scientific analyses and research efforts. The research culminated in the development of 'Jeevani,' a drug formulated from the Arogyapaacha herb. The drug underwent rigorous clinical trials and demonstrated significant health benefits, capturing the attention of the global medical and scientific communities. The case of Arogyapaacha and the development of Jeevani is noteworthy for several reasons. It highlights the intersection of TK and modern scientific research. Initially a closely-guarded secret of the Kani tribe, the knowledge of Arogyapaacha's properties transformed it into a scientifically validated drug, transcending its origins as a tribal secret to become a product of global interest. Furthermore, this case underscores the importance of acknowledging and respecting the origins of TK. The transition of Arogyapaacha from a tribal secret to a key ingredient in a commercially successful drug raises questions about IPRS, benefit-sharing, and the ethical considerations of utilizing a closely-held trade secret of the Kani tribe in scientific research. The success of Jeevani also opened discussions about the need for equitable benefit-sharing frameworks. It brought to the forefront the need to ensure that communities, like the Kani tribe, which contribute their secret TK to scientific advancements, are duly recognized and compensated. This case serves as a pivotal example in the ongoing dialogue about the protection of TK and the rights of indigenous communities in the realm of IP law and bioprospecting.[721] Here the question arises of whether TK aligns with the protective measures outlined in Article 39.2 of the TRIPS Agreement.

6.3.1 Tripartite Criteria for Trade Secret Protection of TK

To determine whether Article 39 of the TRIPS Agreement offers a suitable protective framework for TK, a detailed analysis of the Article's requirements, often referred to as the tripartite test, is essential. This involves interpreting each condition carefully. When these conditions are consistently met, protection under Article 39 of the TRIPS Agreement is maintained indefinitely. According to Article 39(2):

---

721 Gupta, *WIPO-UNEP Study on the Role of Intellectual Property Rights in the Sharing of Benefits Arising from the Use of Biological Resources and Associated Traditional Knowledge* (n 363) Pages 111–112.

> Natural and legal persons shall have the possibility of preventing information lawfully within their control from being disclosed to, acquired by, or used by others without their consent in a manner contrary to honest commercial practices so long as such information:
>
> (a) is secret in the sense that it is not, as a body or in the precise configuration and assembly of its components, generally known among or readily accessible to persons within the circles that normally deal with the kind of information in question;
>
> (b) has commercial value because it is secret; and
>
> (c) has been subject to reasonable steps under the circumstances, by the person lawfully in control of the information, to keep it secret.

Having established the overarching framework of the tripartite criteria within Article 39 of the TRIPS Agreement for protecting TK, it becomes imperative to delve into the nuances of each stipulation. These three pillars – secrecy, commercial value, and protection efforts – collectively shape the robustness of trade secret protection. Let us unpack these components to discern how they interact with the unique attributes of TK, evaluating their applicability and addressing potential challenges in upholding them. We will embark on a comprehensive exploration of each criterion, commencing with the requirement of secrecy, followed by commercial value, and concluding with the measures taken to preserve confidentiality.

6.3.1.1 *Assessing Secrecy and Accessibility*

Clause (a) of Article 39(2) states that information is considered secret if it is not widely known or easily accessible to others within the circles that typically deal with the type of information in question, either as a whole or in the precise configuration and assembly of its components. This clause sets out an objective criterion for secrecy. To qualify for protection, it must be demonstrated that the pertinent information is neither widely known nor easily obtainable. The criterion for secrecy is comparatively flexible, acknowledging that protection does not hinge on exclusive control over the information by the claimant. It may be known to some competitors who also maintain its confidentiality, but crucially, it should not be common knowledge or easily accessible to the majority, or all, of the entities operating in the relevant business sector or field.[722] Protection under Articles 39(1) and (2) of the TRIPS Agreement ceases to apply if the information becomes either widely known or easily accessible

722 UNCTAD-ICTSD (n 492) Page 529.

to individuals routinely involved with such types of information. This loss of protection occurs regardless of whether the disclosure of the information was intentional or accidental.[723]

Given the nuanced criteria for secrecy detailed in Article 39(2) of the TRIPS Agreement, it becomes imperative to consider the varied landscapes of information accessibility within TKHs. These communities' engagement with TK, which may be pertinent to practices such as making PCs, illustrates the practical application of these legal protections. S. Biber-Klemm's insights further illuminate the distinctions in TK accessibility, crucial for understanding how trade secret protection under the TRIPS Agreement can be actualized in diverse community contexts:

a) *Specific Group TKHs:* This group consists of TKHs who belong to a specific, clearly defined subset of the community. They are the custodians and stewards of particular knowledge, like master weavers or artisans who possess specialized knowledge about creating intricate, high-quality hand-woven carpets. These individuals are often revered within their communities for their exceptional skills and knowledge, which may have been passed down through generations within their family or specific group.

b) *Regulated Access TKHs:* These TKHs possess knowledge that is specifically regulated or restricted within the community. This knowledge is confined to certain individuals or groups within the community who are permitted to access and use it. These TKHs might be specialists who work with specific types of hand-woven carpets used for sacred or ceremonial purposes. For example, a particular community might have specific patterns or weaving techniques reserved for religious or cultural ceremonies, and only specific, trained individuals within the community are permitted to create these carpets.

c) *Community-Wide TKHs:* These are TKHs whose knowledge is accessible to and shared by the entire community. To fit into this category, the knowledge of carpet-weaving techniques, patterns, and colour choices should be known and practiced by almost everyone in the community. For instance, in some areas of Iran, almost every household may have someone skilled in the basic techniques of carpet weaving, making this knowledge a common cultural heritage.

d) *Community as a Whole TKHs:* To fit into this category, the entire community needs to collectively hold and manage the TK. This knowledge is not

723 Riffel (n 3) Page 164.

a specific individual or group's possession but is the collective knowledge and shared heritage of the entire community. In this scenario, a particular design or style of hand-woven carpet might be a hallmark of an entire community. For example, the entire community of Qashqai nomads in Iran are known for their specific carpet-weaving style, representing their collective cultural identity.

e) *Societally Integrated TKHs:* These TKHs have knowledge that is ingrained in the broader culture of their society. The knowledge is not limited to a particular community or group but is widespread and practiced across various strata of society. In this case, the knowledge of carpet weaving is not confined to a specific community but is a widespread practice across various regions. For instance, the basic techniques and motifs of PC weaving might be common knowledge and practiced across different communities in Iran, making it an integral part of the broader Iranian cultural heritage.[724]

It seems that only the first two categories, namely, 'Specific Group TKHs' and 'Regulated Access TKHs' are likely to be reasonably protectable under Article 39 of the TRIPS Agreement while the protectability of TK as undisclosed information for other categories is more challenging. Regulated Access TK includes specialized knowledge closely guarded within the community and accessed only by certain individuals. The secrecy and restricted access inherent to this category align well with the requirements of Article 39, which necessitates that the information is not generally known or readily accessible. Similarly, Specific Group TK comprises individuals or sub-groups within a community with unique, specialized skills or knowledge, often passed down through generations. Due to its specialized nature and limited dissemination, this type of knowledge can also be considered a trade secret under Article 39. Unlike these two categories, the TK in the 'community-wide' and 'community as a whole' categories is widely known and practiced within the TKHs' communities. Besides, identifying the contractual counterparty can be challenging since TK is often held by one or more communities. Although trade secret law theoretically allows for several holders to independently claim ownership of the same secret, this complicates efforts to control its spread.[725] While a group may enforce internal restrictions on disclosure and a court may respect its customs,

---

724 Susette Biber-Klemm, 'Origin and Allocation of Traditional Knowledge and Landraces' in Susette Biber-Klemm and Thomas Cottier (eds), *Rights to Plant Genetic Resources and Traditional Knowledge: Basic Issues and Perspectives* (CABI 2006) Page 160.

725 Paul J Heald, 'The Rhetoric of Biopiracy' (2003) 11 Cardozo Journal of International and Comparative Law 519, Page 522.

it has no influence over another group's choice to divulge identical knowledge. Consequently, the broader the distribution of the same knowledge across diverse indigenous and local communities, the less likely it is that trade secret law will serve as an effective means of protection. This situation brings to the forefront the issue of the authority to dispose of such knowledge.[726] Likewise, with Societally integrated TK, the knowledge is integrated into the broader society and not confined to a community or group. It typically does not fulfill the criteria of being undisclosed or secret, which are essential for protection under Article 39. The broader and more openly shared the knowledge, the less likely it is to qualify for protection under the provisions related to trade secrets. Therefore, considering the special challenges related to TKHs' innovation, such as cultural foundations and the historical absence of dominion that many of these communities have held over their territories, cultural heritage, and self-definition, the effectiveness of trade secret systems hinges on their adaptable implementation.[727] The craft and knowledge associated with PCs exemplify the widespread distribution of traditional expertise. The artistry of PCs transcends local communities within Iran, resonating with similar weaving traditions across national borders, especially in areas where historical and cultural connections make national demarcations less distinct. The Turkmen Carpet of Golestan Province in Iran is a prime example, sharing a rich heritage with the carpet-making traditions of Turkmenistan. This commonality bears witness to the dynamic and fluid nature of these cultural practices, highlighting a complex network of influences and skills that have come to define carpet weaving in these regions. The similarities in design, technique, and motifs between nations speak to an enduring and interwoven history of craftsmanship, a legacy enriched by generations of exchange and geographical closeness. Such a legacy in carpet weaving is highly valued and honored by communities on both sides of the Iran-Turkmenistan border.[728]

Riffel examines three possible solutions to address the issue of information disclosure. He suggests three levels of TK exchanges:

- Between indigenous and local communities and the rest of the world.
- Among different indigenous or local communities.
- Within the same community.

He asserts that information crossing any of these demarcation lines is considered disclosed. Then, he discusses these solutions as follows:

---

726 Riffel (n 3) Page 160.

727 Long (n 715) Page 514.

728 Farkhondeh Nouraie, 'ریشه یابی وسبک شناسی طرح ونقشه د رقالی ترکمن (Origins and Stylistic Features of Designs and Motifs in Turkmen Carpets)' (Iran National Carpet Centre 2009).

First Solution: This approach allows TKHs to share their TK (which is not globally known or easily accessible online) with other communities without losing protection under Article 39. He points out that this idea is consistent with laws in Costa Rica, Peru, and Ethiopia. The solution supports the exchange of TK among different TKHs, fostering a sense of unity and sharing. However, despite arguments for a broad interpretation of 'secrecy' in a traditional context, this solution is not viable under Article 39(2)(a) of the TRIPS Agreement if the knowledge becomes known to multiple communities. Protection continues only if two communities independently develop and keep the same information secret or if the information is shared under a confidentiality agreement.

Second Solution: This solution allows TKHs to freely share their TK within the same community, treating the community as a single legal entity. If a community is recognized as a legal entity under Article 39(2) of TRIPS, information can be freely exchanged within it, similar to the sharing of trade secrets within a corporation. However, Riffel prefers a better suited approach that acknowledges that multiple individuals can hold the same secret under specific conditions, instead of drawing parallels between TK and corporate secrets. He points out that while communitarian rights are often seen as an exception within the current IP framework, Article 39(2) of the TRIPS Agreement seems to allow for the possibility of considering several custodians, as it refers to both 'natural and legal persons.' Such a group must be defined, akin to a community whose members recognize each other and live under their own customary law. As exemplified in the Australian case *Foster v Mountford*, indigenous and local community customary laws can create enforceable commitments to confidentiality, establishing a recognized system of secrecy among their community members. This implies that customary laws are decisive in determining the lawful control of information under Article 39.2(c) of the TRIPS Agreement, adhering to the doctrine of breach of confidence.

Third Solution: Confidentiality agreements, recognized as one of the strictest approaches for maintaining secrecy, assert that sharing information even within the same community constitutes disclosure under Article 39(2)(a) of the TRIPS Agreement. This perspective aligns with the requirements of the Agreement, ensuring protection for knowledge shared confidentially. Therefore, confidentiality agreements, along with indigenous customary laws regulating TK access, seem to be adequate for preserving confidentiality and are comparable in nature. The principle of implied confidentiality is exemplified within the employer–employee dynamic. Customary employment arrangements frequently embed contractual provisions intended to secure confidential business information. Nonetheless, even in the absence of such formal contracts, there is an inherent expectation for employees to safeguard their employer's proprietary methods and information. This tacit duty is reflective of the analogous expectations placed upon members of indigenous communities regarding the safeguarding of communal secrets, where individual liberties are counterbalanced by a commitment to the community. Within the context of TK, it is the unwritten customs and community norms that frequently govern confidentiality, substituting for the formal non-disclosure agreements typically found in commercial environments.[729] As such, it appears that the customary laws of TKHs are sufficiently robust to meet the stipulations of subparagraph 39(2)(c) of the TRIPS Agreement.

The Agreement's provision for 'reasonable steps' to maintain secrecy is designed to be practical and not overly demanding, for instance by requiring advanced security measures. This approach acknowledges that imposing excessively stringent requirements could inadvertently facilitate dishonest acquisition or use of information. Therefore, the applicability of Article 39 remains intact as long as the dissemination of the information is confined within a community that has a well-defined membership. This understanding is crucial in ensuring that shared knowledge within these defined communities continues to be safeguarded under the TRIPS Agreement. The discussion can now extend to subparagraph (b), which further elaborates on these principles.[730]

6.3.1.2 *The Commercial Value of Secrecy*

Information has commercial value because it is secret. The necessity for confidential information to possess genuine commercial value is a crucial criterion for its eligibility for protection. This broad stipulation suggests that any information pertinent to business falls within this scope. The commercial value of information as contemplated under Article 39 of the TRIPS Agreement is typically gauged by market forces. However, since the type of information protected by Article 39(2)(b) is not intended for market transactions, its commercial worth cannot be inferred from traditional market valuations. Therefore, the interpretation of subparagraph (b) should be such that any information, provided it remains confidential, is considered to have commercial value if it confers a competitive advantage.[731] The assessment of whether specific information has 'commercial value' is determined by national laws and judicial decisions. In several jurisdictions, the primary standard used is the degree to which the information offers a competitive edge over rivals who

729 Deepa Varadarajan, 'A Trade Secret Approach to Protecting Traditional Knowledge' (2011) 36, *Yale Journal of International Law* 371, Page 401.

730 Riffel (n 3) Pages 164–166.

731 *ibid Page 169.*

are unaware of or do not utilize it.[732] As Varadarajan suggests: "Under any version of the commercial use requirement, claimants would need to show that the information has more than just spiritual or other non-economic value – if not to themselves, then to the parties that misappropriated it."[733]

Long posits that the commercial value criterion within the trade secret protection framework may restrict its applicability for safeguarding TK on two main fronts: Firstly, the eligible scope of protectable information under trade secret law is confined. While numerous forms of TK hold significant spiritual and sacred value, they often do not possess inherent commercial value, thus potentially excluding them from trade secret protection. Secondly, the motivations for TKHs to maintain secrecy of their information are not necessarily based on commercial considerations. As noted by Mahdiei, a renowned designer and producer of PCs, these works are emblematic of a balance between commercial appeal and artistic merit. The PC stands as a testament to the ingenuity of Iranian artisanship, its historical fabric woven with distinctive attributes that distinguish it from any other global artistic creation throughout the ages. The weaves of yesteryear were composed with a keen eye for aesthetic allure, featuring patterns, designs, and hues that have perennially captivated history's discerning audience. These elements were not incorporated into the fabric by chance; each placement was deliberate, contributing to a unique style that resonates with the splendor of artistic mastery. This enchanting amalgam of art, innovation, and the intrinsic talent of Iranian artisans is magical. Delving into the rich tapestry of these elements, exploring their underlying concepts and narratives, reveals the critical role of colour as a dominant force in the tapestry's narrative.[734] Therefore, it would be an understatement to say that the cultural value of hand-woven PCs is merely commensurate with their commercial worth; indeed, it often surpasses it. In light of this discussion, it is pertinent to recognize that while trade secret law is intended to protect commercial value, TK is frequently viewed as a cultural asset meant for broader sharing and preservation. This means that there is often a tension between the goals of trade secret law and the goals of TKHs.

However, Long contends that such limitations do not altogether preclude the use of trade secrets for the protection of TK. She explains that while the commercial value prerequisite may limit the scope to only certain types of TK, those that meet this requirement can still be effectively shielded under the trade secret regime. This limitation on the scope of protection is not unique

732 UNCTAD-ICTSD (n 492) Page 529.

733 Varadarajan (n 729) Page 408.

734 'Interview with Mr. Mahdiei,' (3 February 2024).

to TK but is an intrinsic feature of trade secret laws across various jurisdictions. Only information that meets locally established legal criteria – typically that with commercial value – is eligible for protection as a trade secret. She provides examples from some jurisdictions. For instance, in the USA, the Uniform Trade Secrets Act protects information that provides economic value by not being publicly known or easily discovered, thus giving a competitive advantage.[735] German law only shields 'secret information' when the owner can justify a commercial need for confidentiality. Japan offers protection for technical information that has practical application in business activities. In the UK, protection is granted to information with business utility if its exposure would substantially harm the owner. Long goes on to refer to the challenges in protecting non-commercial TK within trade secret frameworks. In numerous cases, TK is preserved and closely held for reasons that extend beyond its economic significance. Often, the impetus for safeguarding this knowledge is rooted in its profound sacred or cultural importance rather than its market value. This emphasis on commercial utility poses challenges in protecting TK. Certain categories of TK, like spiritual teachings or scholarly content, might be systematically excluded if they do not fit into the category of 'commercial' assets. Therefore, the validity of the protection may be questioned if the community in possession of the knowledge does not attribute commercial value to it, or if it keeps the knowledge confidential for non-commercial reasons. Whether these considerations should undermine the protection afforded to such information is a matter of debate. In this regard, it should be noted that within the conventional realm of trade secret protection, recognizing information that provides a commercial edge – such as technical expertise, trade methods, or proprietary customer data – is straightforward. These elements are typically shielded from disclosure due to the competitive edge they provide if leaked to business rivals. Various security measures, including confidentiality contracts, encryption, access restrictions, and compartmentalization of knowledge within a company, are all implemented to ensure that potentially valuable information does not escape the bounds of authorized corporate stakeholders. In contrast, within the pragmatic realm of commerce, safeguarding information for its educational, spiritual, or cultural significance is frequently deemed beyond the purview of trade secret protection, largely due to its apparent lack of economic or commercial value. Consequently, if the aim of shielding TK is to spur innovation across generations, then the role of sacred knowledge in this context may be considered marginal. For example, in the case

735 The US – Uniform Trade Secrets Act 1985 (14 ULA 529) Section 1.

of *Religious Technology Center v. Wollersheim*, the USA Court of Appeals for the Ninth Circuit ruled against protecting the Church of Scientology's scriptural materials as trade secrets, as they did not offer any economic advantage, which is a prerequisite for trade secret status under California law.[736] This decision was based not on the sacred nature of the materials but on the lack of commercial harm claimed by the Church. Later rulings maintained that religious materials could not be categorically excluded from trade secret protection, yet emphasized the challenge of safeguarding sacred knowledge without proof of competitive harm. This suggests that while religious or sacred knowledge may be difficult to protect as a trade secret in the absence of a clear economic value, it is not entirely outside the scope of trade secret protection if an economic disadvantage to the holder can be demonstrated. Subsequent jurisprudence has not definitively precluded religious materials from trade secret protection but has underscored the complexity of defending sacred knowledge without demonstrable competitive harm. Therefore, while trade secret laws do not inherently exempt religious or sacred knowledge, establishing economic harm is pivotal for such knowledge to be legally protected, as unauthorized competitive use that undermines the holder's market position could constitute a qualifying harm. Moreover, Long points out the legal hurdles in safeguarding indigenous knowledge from deculturization under trade secret laws. The utilization of indigenous knowledge in ways that conflict with its traditional cultural context, known as deculturization, presents challenges for protection under trade secret law. Deculturization extends beyond the unauthorized use of sacred knowledge without proper attribution; it encompasses any use that distorts or misrepresents cultural practices. The legal framework, specifically Article 39 of the TRIPS Agreement, does not necessitate that the holders of such knowledge acknowledge its commercial value for it to qualify for trade secret protection. The criterion for protection is the information's commercial value, even if this is only recognized by those using it without authorization. Legally, efforts to keep information confidential need only aim at preserving its secrecy, irrespective of the original holder's perception of its commercial value. This interpretation underscores that trade secret protection can extend to indigenous knowledge if misappropriated for commercial gain, despite the cultural or sacred nature of the knowledge itself.[737]

Building on the discourse presented by Long, it is my contention that the commercial value criterion inherent in trade secret laws presents further complexities. Specifically, when holders of analogous knowledge choose to provide

---

736 *Religious Technology Center v Wollersheim* (1992) 971 F2d 364 (9th Cir).

737 Long (n 715) Pages 520–525.

it to third parties at lower costs or value non-monetary benefits more highly in their exchanges, it may undermine the core commercial value requirement that is foundational to the protection of trade secrets. This perspective offers an additional layer to the conversation on the applicability of trade secret protection to TK.

6.3.1.3 *Maintaining Confidentiality*

According to Article 39(2)(c), the persons who are lawfully in control of a trade secret need to take reasonable steps to preserve information secrecy. The protection of trade secrets is fundamentally dependent on the actions taken by their holders to maintain their secrecy or confidentiality, a concept influenced by USA law, like the other two prerequisites. This raises the question of what measures are considered legally sufficient to constitute reasonable steps to maintain confidentiality? The Article does not specify particular methods for ensuring secrecy, leaving open various possibilities like the use of encryption, secure storage, division of labor, or contractual limitations.[738] This concept can be extended to safeguard confidential TK as a trade secret, provided that similar measures to maintain secrecy are implemented. In instances of a breach of confidence involving a trade secret, the holder of the secret must demonstrate that the prerequisites for trade secret protection were fulfilled and that a breach of confidence occurred.[739] Nonetheless, the assessment of 'reasonable' measures taken to safeguard the secrecy of TK must consider the historical challenges faced by these knowledge holders. Often, due to various forms of historical oppression, including legal disenfranchisement, TKHS may not have had full autonomy over their cultural expressions. These past power imbalances could have hindered their ability to prevent the misappropriation and unauthorized dissemination of their knowledge. In applying trade secret laws, such historical factors should be taken into consideration, ensuring that standards for 'reasonable protection' are not inappropriately applied, ignoring the context of these communities' experiences.[740]

Long suggests that the "efforts to maintain the sacred nature of certain types of indigenous innovation, including its limitation to members of the tribe or of a particular segment of the tribe, such as a medical society, should easily meet the definition of reasonable efforts."[741] However, the establishment of trade secret rights typically occurs under three conditions: through explicit

738 UNCTAD-ICTSD (n 492) Page 530.
739 WIPO, *Protect and Promote Your Culture* (n 664) Page 60.
740 Long (n 715) Page 529.
741 *ibid Page 525.*

contractual terms, via an implied confidentiality agreement based on the relationship and conduct of the parties, or through the illicit acquisition of the information, known as 'competitive intelligence.' For TKHs, these scenarios present potential loopholes for safeguarding their knowledge within the trade secret framework.[742]

6.3.2 Potential Loopholes for Protection TK under Trade Secret Laws

6.3.2.1 *Imbalance in Parties' Bargaining Power*

Within the purview of contract law, arrangements that regulate access to TK can be effectively managed by the pertinent national legislation.[743] In such contractual agreements, TKHs, as proprietors of confidential information, customarily engage with recipients as the secondary party under explicit terms that dictate the conditions governing access to and use of this knowledge. These agreements often mandate compensation in the form of royalties or profit-sharing in favor of TKHs for the use of their undisclosed knowledge. Such contractual measures, provided TKHs undertake all reasonable steps to prevent unauthorized public disclosure, do not equate to making the information public. Moreover, pursuant to trade secret legislation, the secondary party is prohibited from disseminating the confidential information to tertiary entities without express consent from the TKHs. The TKHs retain the right to impose confidentiality and restricted use conditions from the original contract onto any third parties privy to the information via subsequent agreements. While some TKHs have successfully brokered such contracts, often with NGO support or governmental backing, others lack the essential capabilities for effective negotiation, drafting, and enforcement of such contracts. For these groups, reliance on statutory trade secret protection mechanisms may be more relevant.[744]

The contractual relationship is characterized by an imbalance in negotiating power, affecting the execution and enforcement of the finalized agreements,[745] in a situation in which the parties in a contract (who are in privity with each other) face an imbalance in their bargaining power. This imbalance affects not only the negotiation and formation of the contract but also extends to the enforcement of its terms. In other words, the party with more power may not only dictate the terms of the contract but also have the upper hand in how

742 Varadarajan (n 729) Page 399.

743 WTO, 'The Protection of Traditional Knowledge and Folklore: Summary of Issues Raised and Points Made' (2006) WTO Doc IP/C/W/370/Rev.1 Page 12.

744 Varadarajan (n 729) Page 399.

745 Riffel (n 3) Page 160.

the contract is enforced, potentially disadvantaging the weaker party. This scenario is commonly observed in contexts where there is a significant disparity in resources or knowledge between parties, such as in negotiations between large corporations and individual consumers, or between developed and developing countries.

6.3.2.2 *Third Parties' Role*

A significant challenge in incorporating the duty of non-disclosure of TK within contractual agreements between TKHs and users is the non-binding nature of these obligations on third parties. A contractual approach to protecting undisclosed TK differs from a proprietary one in that it does not offer universal protection. This means if the knowledge is somehow made public, there are no mechanisms in place to prohibit its use by uninformed third parties. While it is possible to hold the responsible party accountable for any damages to the community, such compensation does not fully address the community's loss.[746] Consequently, it is imperative for TKHs to take measures to ensure that the knowledge they share remains inaccessible to external entities. This necessity is exemplified in the Peruvian Law for 'Introducing the Protection Regime for the Collective Knowledge of Indigenous Peoples derived from Biological Resources':

> The contract may not be consulted by third parties except with the express permission of both parties.[747]

In legal contexts, the complexity of proving a breach of confidentiality in TK agreements increases significantly with the lengthening of the chain between the end user and the original source or holder of the TK. As the number of intermediaries or transactions involving the TK expands, the ability of the TKHs to effectively trace and demonstrate a direct breach of confidentiality becomes more challenging. This difficulty arises because each successive transfer or use of the TK can potentially obscure its original terms of use and the agreed-upon confidentiality obligations. This obscurity complicates the holder's ability to pinpoint where and how the breach occurred and who is responsible. Additionally, in such extended chains, the TK's nuances and specific cultural contexts may need to be clarified or understood, further

746 WTO, 'Review of Article 27.3(b)' (World Trade Organization 2000) WTO Doc IP/C/W/228 Paragraph 34.

747 Peru – Law Introducing a Protection Regime for the Collective Knowledge of Indigenous Peoples Derived from Biological Resources Article 28(2).

complicating the process of proving a breach. The situation underscores the need for clear, robust legal frameworks and documentation at every stage of TK transfer to ensure its protection and to uphold its original holders' rights. This is particularly crucial when TK moves beyond its traditional or local context into wider commercial or global spheres, where the risk of misappropriation or misuse can increase significantly.[748]

6.3.2.3 *Non-transparent Nature of Contractual Relations*

Another problem concerning the contract law regime is its non-transparency. This opacity can manifest in several ways, including a lack of clarity regarding the terms and conditions agreed upon, and potential obscurity in the negotiation processes. This lack of transparency can result in unequal power dynamics between parties, where TKHs may not have a full awareness or understanding of the implications of the agreements they enter into. Furthermore, the confidential nature of many contracts can impede broader community awareness and input, which is particularly crucial when dealing with communal or collectively-held TK. This non-transparency can lead to agreements that may not fully reflect the interests or the will of the entire community, potentially leading to exploitation or unfair terms that disadvantage TKHs.[749]

6.3.2.4 *Implied Confidentiality and Customary Law*

TKHs often lack hard evidence, such as contracts, to substantiate their endeavors to maintain the secrecy of their knowledge.[750] As such, reliance on non-disclosure agreements, despite their ubiquity, might not be feasible. Instead, protection may derive from the inherent expectations of secrecy within the relationships of the parties, obviating the need for formal agreements. Courts interpret the obligation to keep information confidential as adaptable, considering the specific context of each case. Evidence evaluated by courts includes a company's standard practices for maintaining secrecy, the employment of safeguards such as passwords or secure databases, and measures to inform employees about the confidentiality of information and restrictions on its external disclosure.[751] In the realm of TK, judicial bodies

748 Antony Taubman and Matthias Leistner, 'Traditional Knowledge' in Silke von Lewinski (ed), *Indigenous Heritage and Intellectual Property: Genetic Resources, Traditional Knowledge, and Folklore* (2nd edn, Kluwer Law International 2008) Page 178.

749 Riffel (n 3) Page 161.

750 Daniel J Gervais, 'The Internationalization of Intellectual Property: New Challenges From the Very Old and the Very New' (2002) 12 Fordham Intellectual Property, Media & Entertainment Law Journal 929, Page 968.

751 Varadarajan (n 729) Pages 404–405.

may consider a community's indigenous customary laws as an indication of the measures taken to restrict the dissemination of TK to external parties.[752] For example, when a TKH imparts confidential information to a company with a mutual understanding of limited use, an implicit obligation to maintain secrecy is created. This duty can extend to third parties if they are cognizant of the information's confidential nature. In practice, such as when a firm shares non-public data with a consultant without a written agreement, the consultant is expected not to further disclose the information. The USA case *Smith v. Dravo Corp.* illustrates that trade secret obligations can be implied from the interactions between negotiating parties.[753] Similarly, if an indigenous group shares TK under specific conditions, recipients are bound not to exploit the information beyond agreed purposes. Cases like *Foster v Mountford* in Australia have recognized implied confidentiality duties in the absence of written agreements, emphasizing the respect for indigenous knowledge shared during anthropological research.[754] In employment, even without absent explicit contracts, employees are expected to safeguard their employer's confidential practices, paralleling the duties within indigenous communities to protect communal secrets.[755] Customary laws within TKHs can inform such implicit obligations, as seen in *John Bulun Bulun & Anor v R & T Textiles Pty Ltd.*, where an Aboriginal artist's cultural duties to his community were acknowledged by the court.[756] Despite the protection offered, these cases also highlight the delicate balance between individual autonomy and collective rights, especially when cultural norms intersect with broader societal integration. Courts may use local customs to assess the implied duties of individuals towards their communities, integrating traditional practices into the legal understanding of trade secret protection.

While the aforementioned discussions are crucial, it is essential to bear in mind that, without explicit agreements, the boundaries of confidentiality and the extent of the obligation to preserve it are subject to varying interpretations. This ambiguity may lead to disputes over the existence of an implicit understanding of secrecy and the scope of the information it encompasses. Moreover, customary laws and practices may not be consistently recognized or enforced by judicial systems, particularly in regions unfamiliar with indigenous legal concepts. Additionally, TK that transcends national borders may

---

752 Taubman and Leistner (n 748) Page 133.

753 *Smith v Dravo Corp* (1953) 203 F2d 369 (Ct App 7th Cir).

754 *Foster v Mountford* (1976) 29 FLR 233 (Austl).

755 WIPO, *Protect and Promote Your Culture* (n 664) Page 60.

756 *John Bulun Bulun & Anor v R & T Textiles Pty Ltd.* (n 529).

not be protected uniformly, posing challenges for international enforcement of trade secret protections.

6.3.2.5 *Applying Suitable National Law*

The legal framework established by the TRIPS Agreement for the protection of trade secrets underlines a dualistic approach, situating it firmly within the realm of IPRs while also subjecting it to the principles of UC. This dualistic approach introduces a substantive level of flexibility, which proves to be indispensable when tailoring the scope of trade secret protection globally. Such malleability is particularly pertinent in affording TK the requisite safeguarding, taking into account the historical and cultural hurdles that are intrinsic to the enforcement of these protections in different territories.[757] As we consider the dualistic nature of the TRIPS Agreement's legal framework for trade secret protection, which blends IPRs with UC principles, we must also acknowledge the flexibility it imparts. This adaptability is essential for customizing trade secret safeguards on a global scale, especially when addressing the unique challenges of TK protection within various national contexts. Moving from this global perspective to a more localized interpretation, Article 39 of the TRIPS Agreement allows each member state the discretion to define UC and fair commercial practices according to its own legal and commercial environment. This flexibility is vital for nations to effectively integrate the protection of trade secrets into their respective legal systems, considering both local customs and international standards.

Article 39 of the TRIPS Agreement, drawing from Article 10bis of the Paris Convention, establishes that Member States must protect trade secrets as part of their commitment to prevent UC. While the Agreement emphasizes the importance of 'honest commercial practices,' it does not provide a strict definition, allowing for flexibility in its application. Article 10bis, although it specifies certain acts to be prohibited, leaves room for interpretation, enabling member states to define what constitutes fair competition and deceptive practices. This flexibility allows each nation to tailor the protection of trade secrets to their unique legal and commercial environment, ensuring consumer protection while adapting to local market regulations.[758] In this regard, Bodenhausen argues that the interpretation of 'competition' varies by country, with each nation defining UC according to its own standards. This means that the concept can be broadened beyond direct competition within the same industry to include acts that unjustly benefit from the reputation of a different industry,

757 Long (n 715) Page 518.

758 *ibid Page 514.*

thereby diluting that reputation. An act is deemed 'unfair' if it contravenes established principles of honesty in business and industry. The criterion for determining honesty is not confined to domestic practices but extends to those recognized in international commerce. Thus, national authorities must consider both local and global standards of fair business practices when addressing UC.[759] In this regard, numerous countries offer legal protection for confidential information, commonly grouped under the banner of trade secrets or undisclosed information laws in which protection of trade secrets occurs through various legal means, including general laws against UC, specific national legislative provisions, or through case law – where courts have established legal precedents for the protection of such confidential information.[760] Therefore, at its core, a thoughtfully constructed trade secret framework at the national level that considers the unique requirements of TKHs has the potential to be instrumental in protecting and fostering TK.[761]

Satisfying and applying national laws to protect the undisclosed knowledge of TKHs in other countries and in the absence of minimum standards recognized at the international level, of course, creates its own problems and limitations for the said communities. Even if trade secrets are deemed suitable for protecting confidential TK, the establishment of a comprehensive trade secret enforcement mechanism is beyond the means currently available in most developing nations, where this knowledge is predominantly held. The crux of the issue lies not only in enforcement but also in the adequacy of domestic trade secret laws to protect TK. Many developing nations currently lack robust legal frameworks in this area. While Article 41 of TRIPS mandates effective enforcement of IPRs, including trade secrets, the implementation remains scant. Furthermore, the enforcement of such laws, especially considering the unique characteristics of TK and the cultural ramifications of its misuse, necessitates a tailored approach that goes beyond standard legal applications and considers the cultural sensitivity of the matter.[762] What is more, TK frequently extends beyond the confines of a single jurisdiction, yet trade secret protections are typically constrained by national borders, complicating cross-border enforcement and undermining the cohesive safeguarding of TK.

---

759 Georg Hendrik Christiaan Bodenhausen, *Guide to the Application of the Paris Convention for the Protection of Industrial Property, as Revised at Stockholm in 1967* (WIPO 1968) Pages 144–145.

760 WIPO, *Protect and Promote Your Culture* (n 664) Page 60.

761 Long (n 715) Page 510.

762 *ibid Page 524.*

6.3.2.6 *The Impact of Improper Means of Undisclosed TK*

Trade secrets shall be protected from misappropriation by improper means.[763] The scope of what constitutes improper means is extensive and not exhaustively defined but includes activities like theft, bribery, misrepresentation, breach of confidence, and espionage. Even acts not independently illegal, such as searching through a company's waste (sometimes known as 'dumpster diving'), can be considered improper if used to gain a competitive edge.[764] Furthermore, even those who did not directly use improper means but knowingly received information obtained improperly can be held liable under trade secret laws.[765] In the realm of TK, claims of misappropriation might emerge if an entity, such as a company, acquires sensitive information from an indigenous or local group by deceit or bribery. In this regard, IGC has identified a non-exclusive series of actions that constitute misappropriation, providing context for what may be deemed improper use in the sphere of TK.[766] However, distinguishing between legitimate and illicit acquisition of trade secrets is often complex and can be particularly challenging in cases involving TK, where there might be a significant disparity in the negotiating power and cultural understanding of the parties involved.[767]

Unauthorized replication or utilization of a cultural product can potentially compromise or even obliterate its intangible elements. Such actions can dilute or eliminate the cultural significance or message inherent in the product. In extreme cases, this could result in the erasure of the product's association with its source community, leading to its genericization. Within its originating community, the cultural product may lose its efficacy or cease to represent collective values. Economic value is also at risk as unauthorized copies could saturate the market, undermining exclusivity and raising questions about quality and authenticity. Once a cultural product is reduced to a mere commodity due to the loss of its intangible value, it is challenging to restore it to its original state within the source community. This situation is akin to a misappropriated trade secret. It is like the genie that cannot be put back into the bottle, as once the secret is disclosed, it becomes known to competitors and cannot be

763 Bouchoux (n 541) Page 445.

764 Varadarajan (n 729) Page 403.

765 Winston Nagan and others, 'Misappropriation of Shuar Traditional Knowledge (TK) and Trade Secrets: A Case Study on Biopiracy in the Amazon' (2010) 15 UF Law Faculty Publication 9, Page 26.

766 IGC-GRTKF Secretariat, 'Draft Policy Objectives and Core Principles: Background Information and Discussion' (n 376) Page 21.

767 Varadarajan (n 729) Page 404.

reclaimed for exclusive use by its original owner.[768] The analogy of the genie is often used in UC law, exemplified in cases like *Phillip Morris Inc. v. Reilly*, where tobacco companies successfully contested state laws mandating the disclosure of their products' ingredients, citing the irreversible harm of such disclosure.[769] Thus, protection as a trade secret would only be effective for TK and TCEs that have not yet been disclosed to the public.[770]

After it is ascertained that TKHs have implemented the necessary precautions to guard their secrets, their usual legal redress involves monetary restitution. Nonetheless, when confidentiality is compromised, the very essence of a trade secret – its secrecy – is lost, as the information then becomes public knowledge.[771]

A notable example of this situation is the case involving the Pitjantjatjara Council of Australia and the book 'Nomads of the Desert,' authored by Charles Mountford. This publication contained extensive and confidential ceremonial information about the Pitjantjatjara people, including sensitive religious practices and sacred rites.[772] The Pitjantjatjara Council argued that Mountford had been entrusted with this information under the condition of confidence, which he subsequently breached by documenting it in various forms, including photographs, drawings, and descriptive texts. The case was brought to court, where the Pitjantjatjara Council's concerns were acknowledged. The court recognized the deep religious and cultural significance of the information detailed in Mountford's book to the Pitjantjatjara community as the plaintiffs. It was determined that the unauthorized disclosure of such sensitive information posed a serious risk to the social and religious fabric of the community. Recognizing the potential harm, the court ruled in favor of the Pitjantjatjara Council. An injunction was issued, effectively prohibiting the sale of 'Nomads of the Desert' in Western Australia.[773] This decision was pivotal in demonstrating the legal recognition of TK as a form of IP that warrants protection, similar to trade secrets. It also highlighted the importance of respecting the confidentiality agreements and the cultural sensitivities associated with TK, setting a

768 Susan Scafidi, 'Intellectual Property and Cultural Products' (2001) 81 Boston University Law Review 793, Page 829.

769 *Phillip Morris Inc v Reilly* [2000] F Supp 2d 142, 113 129.

770 Riffel (n 3) Page 161.

771 WIPO, *Protect and Promote Your Culture* (n 664) Page 60.

772 Jane Anderson, 'Indigenous/Traditional Knowledge & Intellectual Property' [2010] Center for the Study of the Public Domain, Duke University School of Law 82, Pages 21–22.

773 Sarah Holcombe, 'Confidential Information and Anthropology: The Politics of the Digital Knowledge Economy' in Matthew Rimmer (ed), *Indigenous Intellectual Property: A Handbook of Contemporary Research* (Edward Elgar Publishing 2015) Page 424.

precedent for future cases where indigenous or TK is at risk of unauthorized exploitation or exposure.[774]

6.3.2.7 *The Impact of Documentation in Weakening of Undisclosed TK*

TK may lack the conventional documentation expected by legal systems, making it difficult to prove and validate it as a trade secret. One of the main challenges is that TK is often not documented in a way that would allow it to be protected by trade secret law. While the internet has proven to be an effective platform for preserving cultural heritage, it concurrently jeopardizes the ability of indigenous groups to keep their customs and rituals confidential and culturally meaningful. A number of these communities have resorted to forming digital databases to record their ancestral knowledge.[775] If TKHs consciously and fully comprehend the implications of sharing their knowledge through a database, and decide to do so, acknowledging their right to keep certain information in these databases confidential becomes not just beneficial but essential to ensure proper protection of their innovations. Regrettably, the accessibility of these archives to the wider public can also be all too straightforward. Creating inventories or databases to document TK could inadvertently undermine its protection under trade secret laws, by exposing confidential aspects and creating uncertainty regarding use of TK. Additionally, developing regional and national legislation to protect TK may set up the regulatory frameworks that determine who has the right to benefit from and control TK. This could potentially include related trade secrets.[776] However, legal frameworks must acknowledge that the lack of formal documentation of long-standing customs and practices does not necessarily equate to a failure in preserving the secrecy of vital information. Many TKHs have successfully kept their oral traditions and ceremonies confidential, even without written evidence. In evaluating the adequacy of trade secret protection, it is essential to recognize and respect these age-old methods of information preservation.[777]

Despite the above-mentioned disparities, trade secret protection, when thoughtfully established and managed, can also offer economic empowerment to TKHs. Without valuing and protecting intergenerational innovation, economic advancement will continue to be controlled predominantly by the

---

774 WIPO, *Protect and Promote Your Culture* (n 664) Page 60.

775 WIPO, *Intellectual Property Needs and Expectations of Traditional Knowledge Holders* (n 166) Page 120.

776 Miranda Forsyth, 'Lifting the Lid on "The Community": Who Has the Right to Control Access to Traditional Knowledge and Expressions of Culture?' (2012) 19 International Journal of Cultural Property 1, Page 12.

777 Long (n 715) Page 529.

affluent, non-indigenous global sectors. Trade secrecy should constitute an essential, albeit limited, element within an expansive system aimed at safeguarding TK.[778] Specifically, in the context of PCs, it is observed that only a negligible fraction of the knowledge and information possessed by local communities remains undisclosed. Furthermore, the benefits accruing from such knowledge are restricted to an exceedingly small subset of the community members.

7 Summary

Returning to the diverse debates over TK, it seems to be widely accepted that there is an established need for protection of TK. In the same manner, as previously described, PCs as an expression of TK also deserve protection. Nevertheless, the question arises as to how the concept of protection can be applied to PCs. Several concepts have been proposed for the protection of TK. Regarding biodiversity, protection could mean conservation, preservation and safeguarding of TK. Also, TK has been created by the innovative and creative efforts of TKHs. Thus, TK could be counted as subject matter protectable under IPRs. Likewise, PCs manifest the creativity and innovation of the local and tribal communities. Therefore, protection of PCs is consistent with the goals of legal regimes on IP, which are designed to encourage innovation and creativity. Besides, IPRs are an integral part of world trade, and thus commercialization of PCs would require the appropriate application of IPRs. Moreover, proponents of protection of TK offer a list of reasons that IPRs could be a proper means for supporting TKHs and protecting their TK. Despite the arguments of those who favor protection of TK under IPRs and the strong links between them, some counter-arguments have been raised by those who are opposed to protection of TK under IPRs. Taking both arguments into consideration, it is necessary to study existing gaps in IPRs to find out how IPRs can be used as a tool for protection of PCs as TK. Such an examination would require recognising TKHs of PCs, their rights, including the scope of their moral and economic rights, and exceptions and limitations to those rights.

IPRs are supposed to prevent misappropriation and misuse of intellectual creativity and creations. Misappropriation and misuse are widely known to be illegal actions against PCs, which should be prevented. While such failures to

778 *ibid Page 500.*

provide protection must not be discounted, Cottier's TIP-rights theory fundamentally builds upon the concept of UC to fill the gaps and deal with those failures. This *sui generis* regime is expected to promote legal protection and security and to improve trade as well as leading to more certainty and a rebalancing of IPRs to meet the expectations of TKHs. However, the use of UC and its components, such as protection of names, marks and GIs is still untested and the potential consequences are unclear. Therefore, it is crucial to analyze defensive and positive protection in the context of PCs' trademarks and GIs.

Considering the distinctive nature of infringement of TKHs' rights through misappropriation and misuse, protection of TK might be sought through a wide spectrum of mechanisms, including defensive and positive protection of TK under existing IPRs. In the context of PCs, TKHs need defensive protection to be recognized with respect to preventing any use and avoiding any acquisition or exercise of IPRs which could wrongfully suggest a link between PCs and their reputation with competitors in the global markets. On the other hand, positive protection of PCs could lawfully grant exclusive rights to a recognized community and may prevent outsiders from making illegitimate use of TK. In this manner, the regime of TIP-rights is a proper answer to the requirement for defensive and positive protection of PCs.

Beneficiaries of PCs include an extensive list of communities, associations, companies and individuals. TIP-rights provide protection for all prospective beneficiaries, and cover TKHs, both as communities and individuals. This mechanism also addresses the legal difficulty with protection of TK as a private law entitlement vested in communities.

An important issue regarding any protection mechanism is the necessity for or lack of formality as a precondition of protection. While some types of IP like patents and trademark, are highly dependent on formalities to allow holders to enjoy effective protection; as a general and public concept, protection of PCs against misappropriation and misuse under TIP-rights shall not be subject to any formality.

Duration of protection and contradictions between TK and the public domain are two other challenges to the recognition of IPRs as a tool for protection of PCs. Considering the IPRs approach to protection duration raises the question of how long TKHs' rights over their TK should be protected. One view is that TKHs' rights should survive in perpetuity; but others hold the opinion that TK protection shall continue as long as certain criteria for protection are fulfilled. The TIP-rights support the latter viewpoint. In other words, protection of PCs shall be continued without limit as long as the specific criteria for their protection are met. Regarding the issue of public domain, it should be noted that public domain has different aspects in different regimes of IPRs, leading some scholars to argue that a new concept of public domain in relation to TK might be identified. TIP-rights provide a protection regime that covers data and information regardless of whether they are in the public domain or not.

Copyright law encounters significant challenges in effectively protecting TK and TCEs. This legal framework is primarily devised to shield the expression of ideas rather than the extensive cultural heritage, which includes traditional styles, methods of production, and cultural practices of TKHs. The non-formality requirement of copyright offers benefits but is not universally applicable and should not be assumed to cover all facets of TK comprehensively. Additionally, the originality criterion in copyright often prevent customary designs and patterns from gaining protection due to their communal origins. Moreover, the requirement for fixation typically excludes non-material cultural expressions such as oral traditions, dances, and songs, as these are not readily captured in a fixed medium. The prevalent notion of individual authorship within copyright law does not recognize the collective ownership common among TK communities. The temporal limitations of copyright cause TCEs to eventually enter the public domain, making them vulnerable to unauthorized commercial exploitation. The territorial nature of copyright impedes consistent international protection of TCEs, despite international treaties aimed at standardizing protections. Furthermore, the absence of universally recognized exceptions and limitations in copyright laws across various jurisdictions restricts the adaptability needed to effectively protect TCEs in diverse cultural contexts.

UC laws, traditionally focused on protecting businesses from deceptive market practices, present potential strategies for protecting TK and TCEs against misappropriation and misuse. UC laws can be particularly relevant in cases where other IP regimes fall short, providing robust protection against unauthorized commercialization and misuse of TK. These laws support TKHs by ensuring their control and fair compensation for the use of their knowledge, while also helping to maintain the integrity of cultural expressions. They also act as a deterrent against exploiting TK for commercial gain and effectively prevent the misrepresentation of products as 'authentic' TK products. Moreover, UC laws offer both direct protection of TK and indirect protection through the protection of consumers' interests. Unlike copyright and patent laws, they do not impose stringent requirements of originality and novelty, and they have no limitation period, enhancing their utility in protecting TK and TCEs indefinitely. Despite their advantages, applying UC laws to TK protection presents complexities. Potential conflicts with existing IP frameworks, the subjective nature of UC law interpretations, and challenges in enforcement across jurisdictions due to their inherently territorial nature. Additionally, the reactive nature of UC laws, which often address infringement only after it occurs, poses significant challenges, especially when dealing with the irreversible loss of TK once it is exploited.

The discussion on using UC laws for protecting TK has also expanded into considering trade secrets as a valuable legal mechanism. The application of trade secret protection to TK presents both opportunities and challenges. TK, which originates from various sources and may be held confidentially or disseminated within communities, can potentially be safeguarded under Article 39 of the TRIPS Agreement. However, meeting the tripartite test for trade secret protection – establishing secrecy, commercial value, and reasonable efforts to maintain confidentiality – can be problematic for TKHs. Several obstacles exist. Power imbalances in contractual negotiations, the non-binding nature of confidentiality obligations on third parties, and the lack of transparency in agreements can all undermine the protection of TK as a trade secret. Additionally, the reliance on implied confidentiality and customary law may be insufficient when clear documentation is lacking. The territorial nature of trade secret protection further complicates cross-border enforcement, while the definition of 'improper means' of misappropriation leaves room for interpretation. Furthermore, the disclosure or documentation of TK, often necessary for its utilization, can weaken its status as a trade secret. Despite these challenges, trade secret protection can offer economic empowerment to TKHs when implemented effectively. It is crucial to recognize that trade secret protection should be part of a broader, multi-faceted system for safeguarding TK, as it may not be suitable for all forms of TK, particularly those that are widely shared within communities.

Given the substantial limitations of copyright, UC, and trade secret laws, there is a pressing need for alternative regimes that can offer more enduring and culturally sensitive protection mechanisms. Against this background, the need to study and examine the protection of PCs from the perspective of trademarks and GIs, and the applicability of TIP-rights, is evident. Therefore, the next chapters of this study are devoted to testing the applicability of rules on trademarks and GIs, as a part of IPRs, to the protection of TK.

CHAPTER 3

Protection of Persian Carpets under Trademark Law

1 Introduction

In the debate on protection of TK under UC rules, it is worth considering how TK might be linked to trademark law. One answer might be implied in the conception of TK itself discussed above in Chapter 1 of this study.[779] TK as a broad description (TK in *lato sensu*) *inter alia* "embraces the distinctive signs and symbols associated with TK."[780] It refers to tradition-based designs, marks, names and symbols.[781] Hereinafter I use TK-related signs (TK-RS) to refer to TKHs' signs, marks, words, names, symbols, icons, motifs, designs and concepts.

Regarding traditional aspects of TK-RS, traders' use of marks on their works is a tradition in itself, dating back more than a thousand years, and some say it is as ancient as trade itself. "In the Arsacid era, Iranian colourful rugs used to be marketed very costly for decorating the Roman palaces."[782] There are examples of ancient marks which are still in use today. The Japanese inn, Hoshi Ryokan, has been in the business for 1,300 years, and one Japanese construction company has been in operation for 1,400 years. The famous European beers, Löwenbräu and Stella Artois, have been on the market since the 14th century.[783]

Also, protection of TK has close ties with protection of the reputation or distinctive character of TK.[784] In a nutshell, a trademark serves two main functions: first it protects the goodwill of producers and secondly it prevents confusion among consumers about what they are purchasing.[785] On the one hand, trademarks have been important for gaining a reputation in the market

---

779 Chapter 1, Section 2.2 of this work.

780 WIPO, *Intellectual Property, Traditional Knowledge and Traditional Cultural Expressions/ Folklore: A Guide for Countries in Transition* (n 327) Page 4.

781 See: IGC-GRTKF Secretariat, 'List and Brief Technical Explanation of Various Forms in Which Traditional Knowledge May Be Found' (n 187); and Also: IGC-GRTKF Secretariat, 'Revised Provisions for the Protection of Traditional Cultural Expressions/Expressions of Folklore – Policy Objectives and Core Principles' (World Intellectual Property Organization 2007) WIPO Doc WIPO/GRTKF/IC/12/4(c) Annex Article 1(a)(i) & (iv) In accordance with: names, symbols and words among others are accounted as verbal expression and designs, carpets and handicrafts are tangible expressions within TCEs.

782 Mojabi (n 237) Page 12.

783 Aaron Schwabach, *Intellectual Property: A Reference Handbook* (ABC-CLIO 2007) Page 8.

784 WIPO, *WIPO IP Handbook* (n 450) Page 57.

785 See Abbott, Cottier and Gurry (n 367) Page 9.

 | DOI:10.1163/9789004721364_005

for merchandise known for its high quality and value.[786] This helps customers in choosing and buying goods, because the trademark actually represents the characteristics of a product. On the other hand, more than a thousand years ago, craftsman marked their goods with TK-RS to distinguish themselves, their business and goods from those of like manufacturers, before selling them in the local and distant markets.[787] Thus, they could easily introduce their products to the public. Also, trademarks help the customer to choose easily between similar goods without needing comprehensive and detailed information about the manufacturer.

Having considered the ties mentioned above between TK and trademark law, it seems reasonable to ask whether and to what extent the existing trademark regime is a potential tool to protect TK; and if trademarks might be used for the protection of TK-RS.[788] Some scholars believe trademark law can help to differentiate authentic TKHs' artworks through a distinctive sign. In this regard, Downes and Laird argue that trademark law is able to meet some concerns of TKHs. Rights on trademarks can apply forever and limit the use of certain names and symbols. They state:

> [t]hat geographical indications and trademarks can be used by producers to differentiate their products, according to various criteria such as the sustainability or traditional nature of production, and thus create specific market niches and appeal to the consumers.[789]

Some authors go even further, suggesting goods created by and services offered by TKHs or by those who represent them may be distinguished from those of others by using a trademark and service mark, and that "the trademark is an essential element in the commercial promotion of goods and services both within the country and abroad."[790]

---

786 Dana Shilling, *Essentials of Trademarks and Unfair Competition* (John Wiley & Sons 2002) Page 1.

787 WIPO, *WIPO IP Handbook* (n 450) Page 67.

788 Susy Frankel, 'Trademarks and Traditional Knowledge and Cultural Property Rights' in Graeme B Dinwoodie and Mark D Janis (eds), *Trademark Law and Theory: A Handbook of Contemporary Research* (Edward Elgar Publishing 2008) Page 434.

789 See: David R Downes and Sarah A Laird, 'Community Registries of Biodiversity-Related Knowledge-The Role of Intellectual Property in Managing Access and Benefit Sharing' (UNCTAD Biotrade Initiative 1999); quoted in: Gupta, *WIPO-UNEP Study on the Role of Intellectual Property Rights in the Sharing of Benefits Arising from the Use of Biological Resources and Associated Traditional Knowledge* (n 363) Page 58.

790 See: GRULAC, 'Traditional Knowledge and the Need to Give It Adequate Intellectual Property Protection' (World Intellectual Property Organization 2001) WIPO Doc WIPO/GRTKF/IC/1/5 Annex II Page 3.

Similarly, many TKHs' businesses use the trademark law to promote their products often preferring the longer term of trademark and certification mark protection.[791] For instance, Chinese producers have used a trademark for protection of traditional Chinese foods for a very long time.[792] In Iran, hundreds of parties with an interest in PCs have registered their trademarks in different classes for goods and services involved in the production and commercialization of PCs and offering related services. Figure 1 illustrates a registered trademark in Iran, categorized under classes 7 and 27, specifically associated with goods such as carpet weaving and carpet workshops. Additionally, it covers a wide array of services under classes 35, 39, and 42, including bargaining, packaging, warehousing, transportation, preservation, and the design of carpets.

FIGURE 1
Registered trademark for the House of Artist Carpet Weavers

Trademark law cannot only help TKHs to commercialize certain elements of TK, but it can also provide protection against UC by competitors. Unfair acts by competitors can create confusion about their goods and services; mislead consumers as to their nature, features, quality, quantity and manufacturing process; or false allegations aimed to discredit the establishment, the goods and commercial activities of TKHs. "However, legal action on the basis of

791 Gupta, *WIPO-UNEP Study on the Role of Intellectual Property Rights in the Sharing of Benefits Arising from the Use of Biological Resources and Associated Traditional Knowledge* (n 363) Page 62.

792 See Chinese Delegation statement: IGC-GRTKF Secretariat, 'Report of Intergovernmental Committee on Intellectual Property and Genetic Resources, Traditional Knowledge and Folklore' (n 61) Page 20.

unfair competition does not require that goods be already protected by trademark or other forms of legal protection."[793]

In contrast, trademark law may serve as a vehicle for third parties to legally obtain exclusive rights over specific names of TKHs for their own commercial benefit.[794] An example of such use is the car producer Nissan, which branded one of its crossover models after the name of the Iranian Qashqai tribe (see Figure 2).[795]

#	Trademark	Image	Status	Origin	Holder	Int. Reg. No.	Reg. Date	Nice Cl.	Vienna Cl.
1	QASHQAI	QASHQAI	Active	JP	Nissan Jidosha Kabushiki Kaisha (also trading as NISSAN MOTOR Co., LTD.)	906254	2006-04-28	12	

FIGURE 2 International registration under the Madrid System[796]

The Qashqai is the name of a tribal confederacy of Iran. Its members are nomadic pastoralists who live and migrate with their flocks twice yearly between highland summer pastures in Iran's central and western provinces and lowland winter pastures near the Persian Gulf. The hand-woven carpets produced by Qashqai are well-known worldwide because of the beauty of the designs and quality of the products. In particular, the highly specialized techniques for producing high-quality crewel yarn, herbal colours and the weaving is incomparable.[797]

There are several more examples of trademark rights over TK being granted to third parties. For instance, 'Arte Seri' is a registered trademark for mass production of ironwood products, which have been traditionally produced from the *Olneya tesota* tree by the Seri people of Mexico.[798] Another example is the traditional medicine 'Truong Son Balsam' from Vietnam, which has been registered as a trademark by third parties.[799] There is also the case of Moana Maniapoto who is a New Zealand singer. As her name 'Moana' is protected by

793 Posey and Dutfield (n 180) Page 87.

794 Frankel (n 788) Pages 434–435.

795 See: Nissan, 'The Qashqai Story: Necessity Is The Mother of Innovation' (*NISSAN INSIDER*, 1 February 2017) <http://nissaninsider.co.uk/the-qashqai-story-necessity-is-the-mother-of-innovation/>.

796 'Madrid Monitor' (*WIPO*, 2006) <http://www.wipo.int/madrid/monitor/en/index.jsp?search=MARK_ALL,HOL:qashqai>

797 See: Julia Huang, *Tribeswomen of Iran: Weaving Memories among Qashqai Nomads* (IB Tauris 2014) Page 3; and Abolghasem Dadvar and Hamid Reza Momenian, 'عوامل موثر بر شکل گیری و پیدایش نقوش گلیم قشقایی (Factors Influencing the Formation and Development of Qashqai Kilim Motifs)' (2006) 2 Goljaam, Iranian Carpet Scientific Society Quarterly 47, Page 50.

798 WIPO, *Intellectual Property and Genetic Resources, Traditional Knowledge and Traditional Cultural Expressions* (n 231) Page 34.

799 Ryan Abbott, *Documenting Traditional Medical Knowledge* (WIPO 2014) Page 24.

a registered trademark in Germany, she was not able to use her own name on her CDs during her concert tour of Germany.[800]

Some believe that the IPR regimes in general, and trademarks law in particular, are not suitable for protecting the rights of TKHs. It has been said that: "One should not attempt to amend Western laws to cater for indigenous peoples. Attempts to do so will be doomed, because the IP system and the needs of indigenous peoples are too distinct."[801] Thus the use of trademarks to protect TK-RS, raises the concerns that the existing system of trademarks "is not their system."[802]

To avoid the trademark being a double-edged sword, some believe that trademarks and the registration system within existing IPRs could be amended and adapted to provide a proper protection mechanism for TK-RS.

Following the idea of amending trademark law to address TKHs' concerns regarding inappropriate registration of TK-RS, New Zealand created a community-centred system for protection of Māori trademarks through consultations with Māori representatives and amendment of the national trademarks act.[803] The Russian Law on Trademark, Service Marks and Appellation of Origin has established legal protection for goods with specific characteristics which reflects Russian culture and history.[804] Other countries like Canada, Australia and Portugal use their national trademark law to guarantee the quality and originality of their TKHs' arts and crafts.[805]

Having considered the various positions, it is reasonable to look at advantages and disadvantages of using trademarks for the protection of TK. It is important, however, to review the applicability of the trademark regime to the protection of TK. In this regard, and following the general approach of this research, the questions that will be asked are as follows:

---

800 IGC-GRTKF Secretariat, 'Consolidated Analysis of the Legal Protection of Traditional Cultural Expressions' (World Intellectual Property Organization 2003) WIPO Doc WIPO/GRTKF/IC/5/3 Annex Pages 33–34.

801 'Roundtable' (1998); quoted in: WIPO, *Intellectual Property Needs and Expectations of Traditional Knowledge Holders* (n 166) Page 72.

802 WIPO, *Intellectual Property Needs and Expectations of Traditional Knowledge Holders* (n 166) Page 72.

803 See the Delegation of New Zealand statement: IGC-GRTKF Secretariat, 'Report of Intergovernmental Committee on Intellectual Property and Genetic Resources, Traditional Knowledge and Folklore' (n 61) Page 47.

804 See the Delegation of the Russian Federation: IGC-GRTKF Secretariat, 'Report of Intergovernmental Committee on Intellectual Property and Genetic Resources, Traditional Knowledge and Folklore' (World Intellectual Property Organization 2001) WIPO Doc WIPO/GRTKF/IC/2/16 Pages 12–13.

805 WIPO, *WIPO IP Handbook* (n 450) Page 65.

- What do TKHs' expect from trademark law?
- What are the TKHs' approaches to the protection of TK-RS under trademark law?
- What are the challenges to the protection of the TK-RS under trademark law?
- Who are the beneficiaries of TK-RS?
- For how long should TKHs' rights over TK-RS be protected?

In order to answer these questions, international instruments that play a significant role in protection of trademarks need to be reviewed.

2 Brief Review of International Instruments regarding Trademark Law

There are three types of international legally binding instruments regarding protection of trademarks. The first type includes treaties that establish substantive regulations for protection of trademarks at the international level. The four main conventions in this regard are:

- The Paris Convention for the Protection of Industrial Property;
- The TRIPS Agreement;
- The Nairobi Treaty on the Protection of the Olympic Symbol;
- The Madrid Agreement for the Repression of False or Deceptive Indications of Source on Goods.

Instruments of the second type fall under the so-called Madrid System and are intended to facilitate international registration and protection of trademarks. The Madrid System consists of:

- The Madrid Agreement Concerning the International Registration of Marks; and
- The Protocol Relating to the Madrid Agreement Concerning the International Registration of Marks.

The third kind comprises treaties that establish classification systems and provide list of goods and services under that classification system. The system and the lists are subject to procedures for improvement by a group of experts. Two treaties under the industrial property regime deal with trademarks classification. They are:

- The Nice Agreement Concerning the International Classification of Goods and Services for the Purposes of the Registration of Marks;
- The Vienna Agreement Establishing an International Classification of the Figurative Elements of Marks.

All these three kinds of treaties are important for setting standards on worldwide protection of trademarks. Moreover, they have a significant impact on the level and scale of protection of TK-RS. Therefore, before considering the possibility of protection of TK under the trademark law regime, a brief review of these treaties is essential.

2.1 *Paris Convention*

The Paris Convention for the Protection of Industrial Property[806] with 178 members is one of the most widely ratified international treaties.[807] It establishes a union for protecting industrial properties and includes trademarks, service marks and trade names among other types of industrial property subject matters.[808] Besides the substantive principles of 'national treatment'[809] and the 'right of priority,' a considerable numbers of the Paris Convention articles are dedicated to common rules on trademarks. Key aspects also cover the use and non-use of marks, conditions for registration, and special provisions for well-known marks and collective marks. Additionally, the Convention addresses the assignment of marks, prohibits the registration of State emblems, and outlines the procedure for protection of marks registered in one Member States across other Union States. It also provides measures against unauthorized use, including the seizure of goods bearing marks unlawfully and legal remedies for infringement, and stipulates temporary protection for marks at certain international exhibitions. These comprehensive articles ensure robust protection and uniform standards for the registration and management of trademarks globally.

2.2 *TRIPS Agreement*

The TRIPS Agreement requires members of the WTO to protect trademarks in accordance with the provisions of the Paris Convention:

> Members shall comply with Articles 1 through 12, and Article 19, of the Paris Convention.[810]

806 See: Paris Convention.

807 See: WIPO, 'WIPO-Administered Treaties: Members of the Paris Convention for the Protection of Industrial Property, Stockholm Act (1967)' (*World Intellectual Property Organization*, January 2019) <https://www.wipo.int/export/sites/www/treaties/en/documents/pdf/paris.pdf> accessed 12 June 2018.

808 Paris Convention Article 1(1)–(2).

809 *ibid Article* 2.

810 TRIPS Agreement Article 2(1).

Furthermore, it contains a set of obligations that go beyond the provisions of the Paris Convention.[811] The TRIPS Agreement sets forth comprehensive rules for the protection of trademarks to ensure uniform standards across its Member States. Key provisions encompass the eligibility criteria for trademark registration, the grounds upon which registration may be denied, and the dependency of registration on the actual use of the mark. Additionally, the Agreement ensures that the rights of trademark owners are clearly defined, including special considerations for well-known trademarks and stipulated exceptions to these rights. The Agreement also mandates the publication of trademark registrations to allow for opposition, establishes the minimum term for trademark protection, and outlines requirements related to the use of trademarks. Furthermore, it specifies conditions under which trademarks may be licensed or assigned and provides extensive measures for enforcing trademark rights, including specific Articles dedicated to combating counterfeit goods. Service marks are afforded the same level of protection as marks distinguishing goods, emphasizing the Agreement's aim to facilitate a balanced and effective trademark protection system.

2.3 *Nairobi Treaty*

The Olympic Games, symbolized by five interlaced rings of blue, yellow, black, green, and red, are among the world's premier sporting events.[812] This symbol is protected under the Nairobi Treaty, which prevents its commercial use without the International Olympic Committee (IOC)'s approval.[813] Member States must deny or invalidate any mark containing the Olympic symbol and prevent its unauthorized commercial use. Moreover, if the IOC earns revenue from authorizing the symbol's use within a Member State, that nation's Olympic Committee receives a share of the profits.[814] Unauthorized use of the Olympic Symbol, such as in advertising or on goods, requires a licensing fee.[815]

2.4 *Madrid System for International Registration of Marks*

The Madrid System includes two treaties: namely 'The Madrid Agreement Concerning the International Registration of Marks'[816] and the 'Protocol

811 UNCTAD-ICTSD (n 492) Pages 214–248 and 575–623.

812 Ian S Blackshaw, *Sports Marketing Agreements: Legal, Fiscal and Practical Aspects* (Springer Science & Business Media 2012) Page 18.

813 Nairobi Treaty on the Protection of the Olympic Symbol 1981 (1863 UNTS 367 (entered into force 25 September 1982)).

814 *ibid Article 3.*

815 William J Miller, *Dictionary of International Commerce* (Chapman and Hall 1985) Page 179.

816 Madrid Agreement Concerning the International Registration of Marks 1979 (828 UNTS 389 (entered into force 23 October 1983)).

Relating to the Madrid Agreement Concerning the International Registration of Marks.'[817] The Madrid System deals with issues regarding international registration of marks, such as users of the system, international applications, procedures for registration, duration of procedures, and statements of grant or refusal of protection of marks. The owners of a trademark may enjoy several advantages of registering their trademarks in foreign territories.[818] By submitting a single international trademark application and paying a single set of fees, trademark holders can seek protection in as many as 130 countries. Additionally, they can modify, renew, or extend their trademark portfolio internationally through a single centralized system.[819]

2.5 *Nice Agreement*

The Nice Agreement Concerning the International Classification of Goods and Services for the Purposes of the Registration of Marks[820] "constitutes a Special Union and adopts a common classification of goods and services for the purposes of the registration of marks."[821] The purpose of the Agreement was to establish a coherent system and, in a way, to facilitate registration of trademarks for both trademark offices and applicants. By using the Nice Classification system, applicants may apply easily for registration of their marks in the trademark offices of other member states of the Agreement. In addition, this system allows trademark offices to ensure better organization and administration regarding registration of trademarks of foreign applicants.[822] The Nice Classification includes a list of 45 classes (consisting of 34 classes for goods and 11 classes for services) as well as an alphabetical list of goods which comprises 11,000 items.[823] According to Article 3 of the Nice Agreement, a committee of experts shall decide on changes in the classification. The committee may request the WIPO Director-General to invite experts from Member States of the WIPO or the Paris Convention. Class 27 includes carpets, rugs, mats and

817 Protocol Relating to the Madrid Agreement Concerning the International Registration of Marks 2007 ((entered into force 1 September 2008)).

818 WIPO, *Summaries of Conventions, Treaties and Agreements Administered by WIPO* (World Intellectual Property Organization 2013) Pages 13–14.

819 See: WIPO, *Guide to the Madrid System* (WIPO 2022).

820 See: Nice Agreement Concerning the International Classification of Goods and Services for the Purposes of the Registration of Marks 1977 (1154 UNTS 89 (entered into force 6 February 1979)).

821 *ibid Article 1(1)*.

822 Jessie N Roberts, *International Trademark Classification: A Guide to the Nice Agreement* (OUP USA 2012) Page xiii.

823 WIPO, *Summaries of Conventions, Treaties and Agreements Administered by WIPO* (n 818) Page 19.

matting, linoleum and other materials for covering existing floors as well as wall hangings (non-textile), which are the products that are intended to be added as furnishings to previously constructed floors and walls.[824] Applicants must indicate the number of classes under which their marks are intended to be registered by trademark offices. Also, trademark offices must indicate the number of classes in connection with each registration in the official documents for registration and publication.

2.6 *Vienna Agreement*

'The Vienna Agreement Establishing an International Classification of the Figurative Elements of Marks'[825] creates a specialized classification system for signs that contain or consist of figurative elements. The reason for establishing this type of classification was that a significant number of trademarks include such elements. "The Classification of Figurative Elements comprises a list of categories, divisions and sections in which the figurative elements of marks are classified, together with, as the case may be, explanatory notes."[826] The Agreement is consistent with the Nice Agreement. According to the Vienna Agreement, figurative elements of marks are classified under 29 categories, 145 divisions and 1700 sections.[827] Trademark offices of the Contracting Parties may use the Classification of Figurative Elements as either the principal or a subsidiary system of their national classification system, but are required to include the number of categories, divisions, and sections in the official documents and publications regarding the registration and renewal of the trademarks.[828]

2.7 *Trademark Law Treaty*

The Trademark Law Treaty (TLT)[829] is designed to facilitate and standardize the procedure for registration and protection of trademarks at the national and regional levels and make the procedure more user-friendly.[830] The treaty makes the registration procedure more predictable and less complex as it provides "a maximum level of information that national authorities may require from trademark applicants – seeking to reduce the burden on applicants from

824 Roberts (n 822) Page 171.

825 Vienna Agreement Establishing an International Classification of the Figurative Elements of Marks 1973 (1863 UNTS 317 (entered into force 9 August 1985)).

826 *ibid Article 2.*

827 WIPO, *Summaries of Conventions, Treaties and Agreements Administered by WIPO* (n 818) Page 27.

828 Vienna Agreement Article 4(2) & (3).

829 Trademark Law Treaty 1994 (2037 UNTS 196 (entered into force 1 August 1996)).

830 WIPO, *WIPO IP Handbook* (n 450) Page 297.

complying with differing requirements."[831] Therefore, it should be clear to the applicants what registration offices may or may not require from them. The TLT sets out an exhaustive list of requirements regarding application for registration, changes and amendments after registration, and duration and renewal of registration. Member States shall comply with the provisions of the Paris Convention[832] and must apply the Classification System under the Nice Agreement.[833]

2.8 *Singapore Treaty*

The Singapore Treaty on the Law of Trademarks[834] was established to resolve some restrictions of the TLT.[835] Technological advances and increasing requests for electronic registration of trademarks at the national and international levels have led the TLT's Member States to call for the TLT to be updated to meet these challenges and to harmonize related administrative procedures. Therefore, the Singapore Treaty has built on the TLT. While both treaties are applicable to trademarks and service marks,[836] neither the TLT nor the Singapore Treaty apply to collective marks, certification marks, or guarantee marks.[837] Unlike the TLT, which applies only to the marks consisting of visible signs,[838] the Singapore Treaty applies to marks of all natures consisting of signs and non-traditional visible marks such as holograms, movement marks, olfactory or sound and taste marks, provided that they are registrable under the national law of the Member State concerned.[839]

2.9 *Producers' and Consumers' Memberships in the International Treaties on Trademarks*

Iran, India, Pakistan, Türkiye, China, Afghanistan and Nepal are the world's main producers of handwoven carpets. In 2017, the principal importers of PCs were the USA, Germany, Lebanon, England, Japan, the UAE, Pakistan, South Africa, Italy, Australia, Canada, and Switzerland. Iran and all the countries that

831 Abbott, Cottier and Gurry (n 367) Page 434.
832 TLT Article 15.
833 *ibid Article 3(1)(a)(xv),(5) and Articles 6, 9, 13(1)(a)(vii) and 22(a)–(b).*
834 Singapore Treaty on the Law of Trademarks 2006 (2633 UNTC 3 (entered into force 16 March 2009)).
835 Abbott, Cottier and Gurry (n 367) Page 435.
836 TLT Article 2(2)(a); Singapore Treaty Article 2(2)(a).
837 TLT Article 2(2)(b); Singapore Treaty Article 2(2)(b).
838 TLT Article 2(1).
839 Singapore Treaty Article 2(1).

are the world's primary producers of handmade carpets in the world,[840] as well as all countries that are the primary market for PCs,[841] are parties to the Paris Convention. Tables 4 and 5 below delineate the status of membership in the Paris Convention, the TRIPS Agreement, and the Madrid System for the world's principal exporting and importing countries of handwoven carpets:

TABLE 4 Membership of key carpet producers in trademark treaties

Treaty \ Country	Iran	Afghanistan	China	India	Nepal	Pakistan	Türkiye
TRIPS Agreement	--	√	√	√	√	√	√
Paris Convention	√	√	√	√	√	√	√
Madrid System (Registration of Marks)	√	√	√	√	--	√	√

TABLE 5 Memberships of key PCs markets in trademark treaties

Treaty \ Country	The U.S.A	Germany	Lebanon	The UK	Japan	The UAE	Pakistan	South Africa	Italy	Australia	Canada	Switzerland
TRIPS Agreement	√	√	√	√	√	√	√	√	√	√	√	√
Paris Convention	√	√	√	√	√	√	√	√	√	√	√	√
Madrid System (Reg. of Marks)	√	√	--	√	√	√	√	--	√	√	√	√

840 Tehran Chamber, 'چرا فرش ایرانی آب رفته است؟ (The Shrinking Trade of Persian Carpets: What Went Wrong?)' *Fasleqtesad* (Tehran, Iran, 14 May 2018).

841 Iran National Carpet Centre, 'آمار صادرات فرش دست باف ایران در سال ۱۳۹۶ (Export Statistics of Iran Handmade Carpets in the year of 1396)' (*Data System of the Iran National Carpet Centre*, 2018) <http://www.incc.ir/آمار-و-اطلاعات>.

3 What Do TKHs Expect from the Trademark Legal Regime?

Although, trademark law is not inherently designed to protect TK, TKHs use it as a tool for protection of at least some elements of their TK including TK-RS. Trademark law is also expected to help TKHs to receive acknowledgement from their respective states of their moral rights as well as their rights to maintain, control and develop their TK under the protection of trademark law.[842] Frankel explains signs and symbols are not just simple art of indigenous peoples' culture. They carry and express the spirituality of them. This spirituality is "to a certain extent a similar theme is arguably behind moral claims in copyright law."[843] Furthermore, TKHs demand recognition of their rights to maintain, control, protect and develop their TK and its elements including TK-RS.[844] Moreover, TKHs will be able to appropriate their TK-RS for marketing their original and distinct products and gain commercial benefits from them.[845] These of course are not the ultimate goals of demanding protection of TK under trademark law. Trademark law has the capability to provide information on the originality of a product and its link to a specific community, which could lead to commercial benefits for TKHs; but the unauthorized use of words and symbols by parties other than TKHs can potentially cause confusion in the minds of consumers about the source of the products. The use of TK-RS as trademarks by non-native competitors may lead consumers to believe that particular products genuinely originated from the relevant community or that they have certain qualities and traits, which in reality they do not possess.[846] In fact, the reputation of TKHs products, which reflects their stylish distinctive products is often misappropriated and misrepresented by non-local and

842 'United Nations Declaration on the Rights of Indigenous Peoples' (n 48) Article 11(1) – "Indigenous peoples have the right to practice and revitalize their cultural traditions and customs. This includes the right to maintain, protect and develop the past, present and future manifestations of their cultures, such as ... artefacts, designs." Article 31(1) – "Indigenous peoples have the rights to maintain, control, protect and develop their cultural heritage, TK and TCEs as their intellectual property, as well as the manifestations of their cultures, including ... designs, ... visual and performing arts."

843 Frankel (n 788) Page 437.

844 See: 'United Nations Declaration on the Rights of Indigenous Peoples' (n 48) Article 31.

845 Felicia AB Sandler, 'Music of the Village in the Global Marketplace: Self-Expression, Inspiration, Appropriation, or Exploitation?' (PhD Dissertation, University of Michigan 2001) Page 39.

846 Simon Brascoupé and Karin Endemann, 'Intellectual Property and Aboriginal People: A Working Paper' (Research and Analysis Directorate, Department of Indian Affairs and Northern Development 1999) Page 22.

non-indigenous legal entities or individuals.[847] For instance, "scientific institutions use traditional cultural symbols and practices to generate an extra ounce of confidence or certainty."[848] Similarly, large pharmaceutical companies have been using the Inookshook rock formations as symbol of their products while these formations were used initially by Inuit to mark their land.[849] Symbols and words such as Ayurveda, Veda and Yoga, with immense value for India's local communities[850] and the word Ashanti in Ghana[851] are examples that have been registered as trademarks by people other than TKHs or by multinational companies. During the Vancouver Olympic Games of 2010, the trademarked logo of the games, which is a symbol used by the Inuit people, was used by non-indigenous people for commercial products such as clothing, alcohol labels, umbrellas and many others.[852] TKHs are also concerned about mass production of their products using new technologies. For example, hand-woven carpets take months to produce, but machine-made carpets may be manufactured in factories in just a few hours. These machine-made carpets, which use the TK-RS of original products, are available to consumers at lower prices. In Iran alone, between March 20, 2015 and March 20, 2016, more than 1000 manufactures were actively producing machine-made carpets and employed 35 thousand workers. They produced 80 million m^2 of machine-made carpet, of which 30 million m^2 were exported to foreign markets.[853] For instance, "Farrahi Carpet Group has started its activity since

847 IGC-GRTKF Secretariat, 'Draft Gap Analysis on the Protection of Traditional Cultural Expressions' (n 594) Page 20.

848 Gupta, *WIPO-UNEP Study on the Role of Intellectual Property Rights in the Sharing of Benefits Arising from the Use of Biological Resources and Associated Traditional Knowledge* (n 363) Page 28.

849 See the Representative of the Inuit Circumpolar Conference statement: IGC-GRTKF Secretariat, 'Report of Intergovernmental Committee on Intellectual Property and Genetic Resources, Traditional Knowledge and Folklore' (World Intellectual Property Organization 2003) WIPO Doc WIPO/GRTKF/IC/5/15 Page 66.

850 See Statement of the Indian Delegation: IGC-GRTKF Secretariat, 'Report of Intergovernmental Committee on Intellectual Property and Genetic Resources, Traditional Knowledge and Folklore' (n 68) Page 22.

851 See the Delegation of Ghana Statement: IGC-GRTKF Secretariat, 'Report of Intergovernmental Committee on Intellectual Property and Genetic Resources, Traditional Knowledge and Traditional Cultural Expressions' (n 355) Page 65 Paragraph 388.

852 See the Representative of the Indigenous Peoples Caucus of the Creators' Rights Alliance (CRA) Statement: IGC-GRTKF Secretariat, 'Second Draft Report of Intergovernmental Committee on Intellectual Property and Genetic Resources, Traditional Knowledge and Folklore' (World Intellectual Property Organization 2005) WIPO Doc WIPO/GRTKF/IC/8/15 Prov 2. Pages 55–56, Paragraph 103.

853 Ali Yazdani, 'عملکرد صنعت فرش ماشینی در سال ۱۳۹۵ (Performance of the Machine-Made Carpet Industry in 2015–16)' *Donya-e-Eqtesad* (Tehran, Iran, 5 September 2017).

1990. By producing different kind of *handmade look and silk look carpets* in wide variety of designs … has been succeeded to satisfy the customers but also this company has reached a proper place in machine made carpet industry in Iran."[854] Figures 3 and 4 illustrate the national and international registrations of the trademark for Farhi carpets.

FIGURE 3 National Trademark Registration for the Machine-Made Carpets Manufacturing Company of the Farrahi Group[855]

#	Trademark	Image	Status	Origin	Holder	Int. Reg. No.	Reg. Date	Nice Cl.	Vienna Cl.
1	Farrahi carpet	farrahi carpet	Active	IR	Farrokh Sepehr Kashan Textile Company	1323936	2016-07-02	27, 35, 39	05.03, 26.13, 27.05, 29.01

FIGURE 4 International Trademark Registration for the Machine-Made Manufacturing Company of the Farrahi Group[856]

TKHs perceive this activity as UC against their traditional methods, materials and techniques. Such inappropriate use not only may result in "financial loss but can cause considerable spiritual offence"[857] to the TKHs. The TKHs suffer misuse and misappropriation of their TK-RS by the private sector and even by public institutions, which amounts to a denial of the TKHs' dignity and integrity.[858]

854 'About Us | Farrahi' (*Farrahi Carpet Co. – Farrahi Group*, 2016) <http://farrahicarpet.com/EN/about_us/>.

855 Iran Intellectual Property Centre, 'جستجوی علامت فرش – فرش یعنی فرهی (Search for Carpet Trademark – Carpet Means Farrahi)' (*Trademark National Database*, 20 December 2016) <http://ip.ssaa.ir/BSigns/SearchResult.aspx?DecNo=139350140001036412&RN=227565>

856 WIPO, 'Madrid Monitor' (*WIPO Madrid System*, 2 July 2016) <http://www.wipo.int/madrid/monitor/en/#>

857 WIPO, *Intellectual Property and Genetic Resources, Traditional Knowledge and Traditional Cultural Expressions* (n 231) Page 46.

858 See the representative of Foundation for Aboriginal and Islander Research Action (FAIRA) Statement: IGC-GRTKF Secretariat, 'Draft Report of Intergovernmental Committee on Intellectual Property and Genetic Resources, Traditional Knowledge and Folklore' (World

Another significant concern of TKHs is the lack of appropriate recognition of local artists and designers who form part of TK.[859] This is a crucial issue that has been raised in almost every discourse on the protection of TK. TKHs demand recognition to able them to continue to control, preserve, develop and exploit their TK-RS.[860] Moreover, many communities believe that local artists and their products are not recognized properly. In addition, in the process of marketing TKHs' products in the national, regional and international markets, no credit is given either to these communities as holder and provider of TK-based commodities or to the traditions, stories and information which is relevant to communities. This refusal to recognize TKHs and their artists and designers creates a real problem for these communities because it does not take into consideration the distinctive character and status of local artists and designers. In consequence, their products cannot be distinguished, and the TK-RS of these communities and artists can be easily registered by others. Particularly the traditional weavers' cooperatives are faced with different types of registered marks and brands in the market, which prevent them from marketing their handcrafted products in local, regional and national markets. Acknowledgement of TKHs will also help raise awareness among people and markets about the living source of TK and will benefit both communities and consumers.[861]

To address the above-mentioned concerns, TKHs try to gain acknowledgement and exclusive rights over their TK-RS. They also attempt to impede misuse and misappropriation of TK either by controlling the trademark registration system to prevent third parties' claims over identical and similar marks with the TK-RS or by invalidating trademark rights which were granted to third parties in ignorance. In this regard, trademark law might assist TKHs to achieve those goals through providing a legal ground for positive and defensive protection of TKHs' trademarks. As its ultimate goal this approach may help TKHs to restore and maintain TK-RS which have been destroyed or are feared to be almost extinct and preserve them as elements of their culture.[862] In fact, the appropriate exploitation of TK-RS could assist in preserving and promoting TKHs cultures too.[863] TKHs are also interested in looking into how the

Intellectual Property Organization 2004) WIPO Doc WIPO/GRTKF/IC/7/15 Prov. Page 46 Paragraph 92.

859 Popova-Gosart (n 117) Page 92.

860 Frankel (n 788) Page 438.

861 A Håkansson and K Deer. "Indigenous Ethics: Practicing Cultural Diversity in the Information Society." quoted in: Popova-Gosart (n 117) Pages 61–62 and 92.

862 Frankel (n 788) Page 438.

863 IGC-GRTKF Secretariat, 'Draft Gap Analysis on the Protection of Traditional Cultural Expressions' (n 594) Page 22.

international IPRs system within WIPO could address the extensive concerns of TKHs about the theft of their cultural identities embodied in their TK-RS.[864] Therefore, it is necessary to understand how TKHs could exploit the trademark regime for registration of their marks. Another question is how trademark law could prevent culturally offensive marks from being registered and whether it is possible to avoid TK-RSs being misappropriated. These questions might be answered while looking into the approaches for protection of TK-RS.

4 Approach for Protection of TK-Related Signs

Trademark law in its current state is simultaneously an instrument for protecting the rights of TKHs on the one hand and for facilitating the abuse of their TK-RS on the other. TKHs have found that, in some circumstances, the legal regime of trademarks can be used as a means of protecting their culture and traditions. Meanwhile, third parties misuse the trademark system to register trademarks and exploit TK-RS that are inherently owned by TKHs, to achieve their own business goals. Therefore, this system can work against TKHs because they lose their rights and control over their heritage and TK-RS in favor of the trademark owner, at least for certain classes of goods and services. Here two approaches for protection of TK-RS could be taken into consideration: (a) positive protection: to grant exclusive rights on TK-RS as trademarks to TKHs; (b) defensive protection: to prevent unauthorized registration of TK-RS as trademark by companies and persons other than TKHs.[865]

4.1 *Positive Protection*

Products of TK might be branded and protected using trademark legal regimes at the national and international levels. Various advantages of registration of TK-RS for TKHs have been noted. Using trademarks could be a mechanism for identifying the original TKHs' products and artworks. Distinctive signs in relation to TKHs' products indicate how these products are made, based on their knowhow, knowledge and practices. Likewise, relying on trademarked TK-RS, TKHs could establish a system under which their goods and services that adhere to specific standards and methods might be traded. For example, the

864 Aroha Te Pareake Mead, 'Intellectual Property, Genetic Resources and Associated Traditional Knowledge: Sharing Indigenous and Local Community Experiences' (Intergovernmental Committee on Intellectual Property and Genetic Resources, Traditional Knowledge and Folklore, Thirtieth Session, Geneva, Switzerland, 30 May 2018) Page 1 <www.iucn.org/ceesp>.

865 WIPO, *Intellectual Property Needs and Expectations of Traditional Knowledge Holders* (n 166) Page 224.

Māori Community Mark is intended to indicate to consumers that quality of goods and products is certified by Māori descent. This positive protection was intended to address the concerns of misuse and abuse of Māori imagery, styles and concepts by non-Māoris and to provide, even if limited, protection for the original community.[866] Also, by registration of their marks, these communities could prevent third parties from using signs that may lead to confusion of consumers and the public.[867] In this regard, in Canada, the petroglyph has a significant religious value for the 'Snuneymuxw First Nation.' Therefore, they have registered ten petroglyphs to halt the commercial use of their sacred images on items such as postcards and T-shirts.[868] Moreover, TKHs seem to be required to register their trademark before marketing and commercialization of their products. If the registration office finds their marks are not registrable, all their investments and expenses are wasted.[869] On the other hand, in cases where the law of UC is not enforceable, the registration of the TK-RS at the national level, and even the international level, can be used as a means of preventing the abuse of TKHs' cultural symbols. Another advantage of trademark registration is that it can help TKHs to focus on those signs that are vital for their communities. Precision and reliability of trademark law for TKHs is another important feature not found in other legal systems, such as contract law or customary law.[870] In addition, traditional designers and artists from local and indigenous communities can apply for registration of new products which are made based on the TKHs' cultural heritage.[871] An example is the registered trademark for Australian indigenous peoples' products "in respect of cultural festivals, soaps, perfumery, essential oils, body lotions and other natural resource products, arts centres, clothing and textiles, music, film and broadcasting, publications, and Internet-related services."[872]

Panama, trying to provide a system for protection of TK-RS, established a registration system through special legislation, with an approach similar to the

866 IGC-GRTKF Secretariat, 'Report of Intergovernmental Committee on Intellectual Property and Genetic Resources, Traditional Knowledge and Folklore' (n 804) Page 56.

867 WIPO and UNEP, 'The Role of Intellectual Property Rights in the Sharing of Benefits Arising from the Use of Biological Resources and Associated Traditional Knowledge: Selected Case Studies' (WIPO 2001) Pages 80–81.

868 Pires de Carvalho (n 158) Page 271.

869 ITC and WIPO, *Marketing Crafts and Visual Arts: The Role of Intellectual Property – a Practical Guide* (World Intellectual Property Organization 2003) Page 74.

870 IGC-GRTKF Secretariat, 'Consolidated Analysis of the Legal Protection of Traditional Cultural Expressions' (n 800) Page 20.

871 WIPO, *Intellectual Property and Traditional Cultural Expressions/Folklore-Booklet N°1* (n 656) Page 16.

872 Janke (n 645); quoted in: IGC-GRTKF Secretariat, 'Consolidated Analysis of the Legal Protection of Traditional Cultural Expressions' (n 800) Page 49.

Pacific Regional Framework for the Protection of TK and EoF, which recognizes for the 'traditional Owners' the right to prevent or authorize use and exploitation of a trademark.[873] However, to understand such a system, it is necessary to understand the trademark law. Besides, protection may be applied to different types of marks including trademarks, service marks and collective marks, and may include certification marks too. Therefore, a brief introduction to the different faces of trademarks seems essential.

4.1.1 Types of Trademarks

4.1.1.1 *Trademarks and Service Marks*

4.1.1.1.1 Trademarks

A trademark is a *sign or any combination of signs*[874] that distinguishes and separates goods and services of an institution or producer from the goods and services of its associates and competitors. The sign may consist of "words including personal names, letters, numerals, figurative elements and combinations of colours as well as any combination of such signs."[875] Also, it may consist of drawings, devices and shapes of product.[876] Under Iranian law "mark means any *visible sign* …"[877]

The Paris Convention, despite addressing trademarks in a few of its articles, does not provide a definition, but the TRIPS Agreement describes what could comprise a trademark:

> Any sign, or any combination of signs, capable of distinguishing the goods or services of one undertaking from those of other undertakings, shall be capable of constituting a trademark.[878]

This definition emphasizes the two features of 'ability to distinguish' and 'one undertaking from … other undertakings.' These two features were also used in the North American Free Trade Agreement:

873 IGC-GRTKF Secretariat, 'Survey of Existing Forms of Intellectual Property Protection for Traditional Knowledge' (n 361) Page 11.

874 TRIPS Agreement Article 15(1); and Regulation (EU) 2017/1001 of the European Parliament and of the Council of 14 June 2017 on the European Union Trade Mark 2017 (OJ L 154/1) Article 4; and The North American Free Trade Agreement 1992 (32 ILM 289 (entered into force 01 January 1994)) Article 1708(1).

875 TRIPS Agreement Article 15(1).

876 IGC-GRTKF Secretariat, 'Consolidated Analysis of the Legal Protection of Traditional Cultural Expressions' (n 800) Page 45.

877 Iran – Patents, Industrial Designs and Trademarks Registration Law 2007 Article 30(a).

878 TRIPS Agreement Article 15.

> trademark consists of any sign, or any combination of signs, capable of distinguishing the goods or services of one person from those of another, including personal names, designs, letters, numerals, colours, figurative elements, or the shape of goods or of their packaging.[879]

The trademark laws in Iran also mention the distinctive feature in the definition of a trademark:

> "Mark" means any visible sign capable of distinguishing the goods or services of legal entities or of natural persons.[880]

According to this definition, the mark must be *visible* to be registered. Therefore, invisible marks, such as acoustic marks, olfactory marks, taste marks, etc. are excluded from the above definition. With respect to visually understandable marks, the TRIPS Agreement stipulates that members as a condition of registration may request that a mark be visually perceptible.[881] The Paris Convention does not include any limitation in this regard. The TLT stipulates that the provisions of the treaty "shall not apply to hologram marks and to marks not consisting of visible signs, in particular, sound marks and olfactory marks."[882] Since carpets are considered as handicrafts and the industry is generally characterized by visible marks, this definition appears to exhibit the characteristics necessary to protect the trademarks of carpet manufacturers, whether they are individual producers or workshops. Therefore, natural and legal parties involved in the production and trade of handmade carpets might market their goods or services using the mark through the trademark system. In this regard, some PC producers and beneficiaries have registered and have been using their exclusive trademarks. Figure 5 presents two instances of trademarks registered in Iran: one associated with Tabriz Shafaghi Carpets and the other with Iran Carpet Co.

FIGURE 5 Two examples of registered trademarks in the PC industry

879 NAFTA Agreement Article 1708(1).
880 Iran – Patents, Industrial Designs and Trademarks Registration Law Article 30(a).
881 TRIPS Agreement Article 15(1).
882 TLT Article 2(1).

Although the Paris Convention offers no definition of a trademark, it stipulates that Member States may not deny an application for registration of industrial or commercial marks unless the marks are devoid of any *distinctive* character.[883] The TRIPS Agreement refers to the function of the trademark, which is distinguishing goods and services in trade. Through this function trademarks provide protection of the reputation, quality and economic value of products and their producer. This function also assists consumers to distinguish between products on the market, as trademarks offer them enhanced information on products and markets.[884] It seems that having distinctive attributes is a necessary feature of a sign to constitute a trademark; otherwise it might not help the customer in choosing the desired product.[885] In other words, the trademark must have the ability to make the goods and services recognizable.

Under Iran's trademark law, in the absence of a distinctive character, the mark might not be registered.[886] The capability of distinguishing a trademark, may arise because of distinctiveness acquired through use.[887] The Paris Convention also called on Member States to consider all actual circumstances in addition to the attributes as distinctive features, especially for how long the mark has been used, to determine whether the mark is eligible for registration:

> In determining whether a mark is eligible for protection, all the factual circumstances must be taken into consideration, particularly the length of time the mark has been in use.[888]

883 Paris Convention Article 6^{quinquies}(B)(2).

884 Thomas Cottier and Christophe Germann, 'Agreement on Trade-Related Aspects of Intellectual Property Rights: Part I. General Provisions and Basic Principles' in Thomas Cottier and Pierre Véron (eds), *Concise International and European IP Law: TRIPS, Paris Convention, European Enforcement and Transfer of Technology*, vol 4 (2nd edn, Kluwer Law International 2008) Page 52.

885 "Distinctive signs refer to the reputation and the certain qualities of the product and it is a shorthand way of passing information to consumers on specific aspects of a product. It helps consumers to differentiate products and services of competitors." See: Mariano Riccheri, 'The Importance of "Distinctive Signs" for the Handmade Carpet Sector: Trade Marks, Collective Marks and Certification Marks (Main Features)' (Seminar on 'The Use of Industrial Property for the Protection of Iranian Handmade Carpets,' Tehran, Iran, 26 April 2011) Page 7.

886 Iran – Patents, Industrial Designs and Trademarks Registration Law Article 32.

887 TRIPS Agreement Article 15(1).

888 Paris Convention Article 6^{quinquies}(C)(1).

Being distinctive is one of the main features of TKHs and their culture, habits, ceremonies and products. Accordingly, TK-RS are distinctive signs, which are able to distinguish communities and their products from others. Therefore, trademark law may provide protection for their signs and grant exclusive rights to TKHs for registration of their trademarks and using their signs in the process of marketing their products.[889]

The Maqui trademark is a good example of TK-RS of Ecuadorian hand-woven straw producers. The mark Maqui means 'hand' in the local language. This high-quality hat, known worldwide as the 'Panama hat,' is produced using the TK of Ecuadorian weavers. Over the course of more than 20 years, this mark has become well-known in global markets. This mark represents the quality and style of Ecuadorian hand-woven hats. Consumers can identify their branded hats from a wide range of hats and be assured about their quality and originality. Consumers can also be sure that each hat is made in Ecuador and is completely unique. The mark has been increasingly recognized and its value has been rising steadily.[890]

4.1.1.1.2 Service Marks

Service marks are like trademarks, with the same functions, only they apply to services rather than goods. Enterprises use service marks to offer consumers a way to distinguish their services in sectors such as food, finance, tourism, transport and repairs, from those of other enterprises. Therefore, the service mark must also distinguish the services of a company from other services of other companies. The Paris Convention provides for the support of service marks:

> The countries of the Union undertake to protect service marks. They shall not be required to provide for the registration of such marks.[891]

In the Madrid Protocol, any references to 'marks' refers to both trademarks and service marks:

> any reference in this Protocol to "marks" shall be construed as a reference to trademarks and service marks.[892]

889 GRULAC, 'Traditional Knowledge and the Need to Give It Adequate Intellectual Property Protection' (World Intellectual Property Organization 2001) WIPO Doc WIPO/GRTKF/IC/1/5 Annex I Page 6, Paragraph 3.

890 ITC and WIPO (n 869) Pages 118–119.

891 Paris Convention Article 6sexies.

892 Madrid Protocol Article 2(3).

In accordance with this Article, Member States are committed to protect service marks, but they are not obliged to provide special legislation or registration for such marks. Still, states may grant protection for service marks by other means, such as a law against UC.[893] According to Iranian trademark law, mark means:

> [a]ny visible sign capable of distinguishing the goods or services of legal entities or of natural persons.[894]

Therefore, service marks for PCs are registerable at the Iranian Intellectual Property Centre. Figure 6 refers to a service mark for the association of carpet cleaning services, registered under registration no. 261196.

FIGURE 6
Registered mark for the Association of Carpet Cleaning, Carpet Weavers and Carpet Services

4.1.1.2 *Trade Names*

Examples of abuse of PCs include the exploitation of the names of well-known designers, producers and merchants; using their designs or works and sailing the fake products under third parties' names in domestic and international markets. The question is, whether the legal regime on trade names provides the necessary framework to prevent such abuses? In order to understand how important the trade name could be in the production and trade of PCs, one only has to consider the number of exhibitors participating in Iran's yearly international exhibition of handmade carpets. In terms of quantity, quality and

893 WIPO, *WIPO IP Handbook* (n 450) Page 255.
894 Iran – Patents, Industrial Designs and Trademarks Registration Law Article 30(a).

production, this is the largest exhibition of PCs in the world. For example, at the 27th Iran Handmade Carpet Exhibition which ran from 25–31 August 2018, more than 670 manufactures, merchants and exporters, companies, and craftspeople of the country participated, and showed a treasure trove of handmade carpets and rare works of Iranian weavers and artists.[895]

Although no internationally agreed definition of 'trade names' has been agreed, by and large it is accepted that "a trade name is a name or designation distinguishing the enterprise of a natural or legal person from that of others."[896] Trade names are also known as commercial names and designations[897] and any "corporate names; fictitious business names; assumed names; partnership names; the names of non-profit, charitable, religious, and educational institutions; and the names of sole proprietorships," which could single out a business or person may create a trade name.[898] Therefore, producers, artists, professionals or traders in local and indigenous communities, as well as the groups which are formed by them and represent them (cooperation, institutions etc.) may use trade names by which they are recognized as true TKHs or their affiliated institutions.

Without providing any definition of a trade name or of what constitutes a trade name, Articles 1(2), 8, 9 and 10ter of the Paris Convention deal with trade names. While Article 1(2) designate the trade name as the protectable object of the industrial properties, Article 8 requires that "a trade name shall be protected in all the countries of the Union without the obligation of filing or registration, whether or not it forms part of a trademark."[899] Article 9 includes rules on seizure of the goods that bear unlawful trade names, and Article 10ter deals with the right to sue and to compensation in the event of a violation of the rights relating to trade names, among other things, The TRIPS Agreement makes no mention of 'trade name,' but in accordance with the WTO Appellate Body decision regarding the Havana Club case the TRIPS Agreement refers to

895 See: 'Iran Handmade Carpet Exhibition Kicks Off in Tehran' (*Islamic Republic News Agency*, 25 August 2018) <http://www.irna.ir/en/News/83011584/> accessed 17 January 2019.

896 Martin Pflüger, 'Paris Convention for the Protection of Industrial Property' in Thomas Cottier and Pierre Véron (eds), *Concise International and European IP Law: TRIPS, Paris Convention, European Enforcement and Transfer of Technology*, vol 4 (2nd edn, Kluwer Law International 2008) Page 203.

897 WIPO Convention Article 2(viii).

898 Stephen Elias and Richard Stim, *Trademark: Legal Care for Your Business & Product Name* (9th edn, Nolo 2010) Page 37.

899 Paris Convention Article 8.

trade name as an IP category.[900] Therefore, the members of the WTO have the same commitment to protect trade names by way of Article 2(1) TRIPS.[901]

In order to allow national legislators to determine the objectives and methods of legal protection; the Paris Convention left the issue of defining trade names and the manner of their protection to national laws. Therefore, it is entirely conceivable that protection might be enforced through specific rules regarding trade names or by general laws, such as UC rules or personality rights to the names. In most cases, countries provide a mixed legal protection of trade names in their territories. For instance, Swiss Civil Code, and Swiss Federal Law on UC provide a legal basis for protection of trade names.[902] Also, Iranian law in the commercial code, the tort law, the act on the registration of companies, and in the law of industrial property, provided detailed rules on the definition[903] and protection of trade names.

Protection of trade names shall not be conditional on their being registered; however, if the protection of a trade name in a country is conditioned on use, or if a trade name is a basis for confusing or damaging another trade name, countries can impose such a requirement.[904] Registration of trade names in Iran is optional and trade names shall enjoy protection against illegal activities of other persons even without registration[905] unless registration of a trade name is required according to other laws and under certain regulations.[906] For example, prior approval of the Iranian Ministry of Health, Treatment and Medical Education is necessary for registration of trade names of any medicine or pharmaceutical and of medical institutes and pharmacists.[907] The registered trade name cannot be used by any other person.[908] Regarding use requirements of trade names, many states protect trade names upon their

900 See: UNCTAD-ICTSD (n 492) Page 53.

901 TRIPS Agreement Article 2(1) – 'In respect of Parts II, III and IV of this Agreement, Members shall comply with Articles 1 through 12, and Article 19, of the Paris Convention (1967).'

902 See: Swiss – Civil Code 1907 (210 (entered into force 10 December 1907)) Article 29; and Swiss – Federal Law on Unfair Competition 1986 ((entered into force 01 March 1988)) Principle 3.

903 In Iranian Industrial Property Law, the 'trade name' means "the name or designation identifying and distinguishing a natural person or a legal entity." See: Iran – Patents, Industrial Designs and Trademarks Registration Law Art 30(c).

904 WIPO, *WIPO IP Handbook* (n 450) Page 257.

905 Iran – Patents, Industrial Designs and Trademarks Registration Law Art 47.

906 Iran – Commercial Code 1932 Art 576.

907 Iran – Law on the Rules of Medical and Pharmaceutical Affairs and Eatable and Drinkable Materials 1955 Art 13(note 1).

908 Iran – Commercial Code Art 578.

use. For example, in accordance with Finnish law "the exclusive right to use a trade name is acquired either by registering that name or by establishing it through use." And "a trade name is regarded as having been established by use where it is generally well known by the public targeted by the activity of the economic operator." "However, according to that case-law, protection of such foreign trade names is subject to the condition that the 'effective' element of that trade name be, at least to some extent, well known in the relevant Finnish trade circles."[909] In other words, Finnish law protects trade names only if they are well known at a specified level by the interested parties in the relevant business circle in Finland. The ECJ in the *Anheuser-Busch v. Budějovický Budvar* case ruled that such a requirement is not contrary to either the Paris Convention or the TRIPS Agreement.[910]

Despite the importance of a trade names mechanism to protect the names of TKHs, it should be noted that there often is a misconception about trade names. Many traders and manufacturers mistakenly believe that if their business is registered in the national business registry, their trade name is eligible to be protected automatically as a trademark. In fact, registration in a national business registry is completely different from registration of a trademark, even if the subject of both registrations is a unique trade name. Although a trade name can function as a trademark if it is used or registered as a trademark, it is important to apprehend the difference between trade names and trademarks. A trade name is the name of a business and often includes the legal character of the business such as 'Ltd' or 'GmbH.' A trademark is the name of a product or a service of a business. An individual or an enterprise only possesses one trade name while they may possess different trademarks for their different products or services.[911] In this regard, even a registered trademark may not prevent a person the *bona fide* practicing of their name as trade name,[912] unless the use of a trade name is "made for the purposes of distinguishing goods or services."[913]

As explained earlier in the first chapter of this study, the PCs' TKHs include cities, rural and nomadic communities. Members of these communities incorporate a wide range of individuals and legal entities who play a critical role

909 Finland Toiminimilaki 1979 (128) Paragraphs 2(1) & (3); quoted in: *Anheuser-Busch Inc v Budějovický Budvar, národní podnik* [2004] ECJ C-245/02, 2004 I-10989 Paragraphs 21–23.

910 *Anheuser-Busch Inc v Budějovický Budvar, národní podnik* (n 909) Paragraph 97.

911 ITC and WIPO (n 869) Page 75.

912 John S McKeown, *Canadian Intellectual Property Law and Strategy: Trademarks, Copyright and Industrial Designs* (Oxford University Press 2010) Page 36.

913 Directive 2015/2436 of the European Parliament and of the Council of 16 December 2015 to Approximate the Laws of the Member States Relating to Trade Marks 2015 (OJ L 336/1) Preamble, Note (19).

in the PC production chain. Also, associations and merchants and, in some cases, public institutions play the role of representatives of these communities. Except in limited cases, merchants and independent retailers are widely active in the target markets. Therefore, even if trade names of the TKHs from the cities and rural and nomadic communities are legally acknowledged, it is merely the trade name of the merchants and retailers that are used in target markets and might be protected. Consequently, TKHs may have their unique trade names for the community, but they would need to have different trademarks for their TK-RS. However, the TKHs can apply for protection of their names as trademarks.

Another critical issue is the impact of freedom of expression (also known as freedom of speech) on the protection of TKHs' trademarks in general and trade names in particular. Freedom of expression is one of the most fundamental human rights[914] and it is guaranteed globally by international human rights instruments[915] and by countries' constitutional law.[916] Although, freedom of expression is a fundamental right that should not be restricted in any way, in certain circumstances it is limited by other rights *inter alia* the IPRs. For example, in the USA, the First Amendment of the Constitution protects rights to free speech in general and commercial speech (including use of trade names); nevertheless, individuals and legal entities cannot expect to enjoy full protection for every commercial expression they make. The commercial expressions are legally protected only to the degree that they are not misleading or false.[917] Therefore, the use of trade names in commercial speech, such as advertisements for products which do not come from certain geographical origins, are not eligible to be protected under the freedom of speech principle of the First Amendment of the USA Constitution.[918] In this context, in the case of *Piazza's Seafood World LLC v Bob Odom*, the Court ruled that consumers

914 H Victor Condä, *A Handbook of International Human Rights Terminology* (University of Nebraska Press 2004) Pages 23, 92 and 93.

915 'Everyone has the right to freedom of opinion and expression; this right includes freedom to hold opinions without interference and to seek, receive and impart information and ideas through any media and regardless of frontiers.' See: United Nations (n 366) Article 19; and also 'Everyone shall have the right to freedom of expression; this right shall include freedom to seek, receive and impart information and ideas of all kinds, regardless of frontiers, either orally, in writing or in print, in the form of art, or through any other media of his choice.' See: ICCPR Article 19(2).

916 See: Iran – The Constitution of the Islamic Republic of Iran Principles 23 and 24.

917 Stephanie Marcantonio, 'What Is Commercial Speech? An Analysis in Light of Kasky v. Nike' (2003) 24 Pace Law Review 357, Page 359.

918 *Piazza's Seafood World LLC v Bob Odom* [2006] USA Court of Appeals, 5 Circuit 448 F. 3d 744, 448 Federal Reporter 744.

must be protected from actually or inherently misleading and deceptive use of trade names; thus one cannot use trade names for products which do not come from specific geographical origins. It seems in this case that a trademark should be treated as a trade name, as their functions and application are not different in respect of trademark law.[919] It appears that there is a possibility to demand protection of PCs' trade names with reference to this case, as PCs originate from a specific geographical source and also consumers of PCs shall be protected against use of trade names in commercial expressions that are deceptive and may mislead them.

4.1.1.3 *Collective Marks*

TKHs consider the collective marks mechanism as an appropriate tool for protection of their communities' TK-RS as they are able to protect shared interests of producers in associations. TK is often considered to be the collective knowledge of traditional communities. Therefore, the collective ownership by these associations shall be recognized and protected under the notion of the collective mark in a such a way as to accommodate the interests and profits of TKHs.[920] Besides, TK includes communities' TK-RS, encompassing designs, images, figures, symbols, models and other cultural elements.[921] The concept of the collective mark is potentially useful to provide partial protection for TK-RS. To understand whether the collective mark can truly meet the expectations of TKHs, the elements of the collective marks protection system and its functions need to be studied. Although there has been no formal and generally accepted definition of collective mark, it may be defined as a "sign to distinguish the origins or other common characteristics of goods or services of different enterprises, and different enterprises are controlled by the owner of the registered trademarks when using such a trademark."[922]

919 Burkhart Goebel, 'Trademarks as Fundamental Rights – Europe' (2009) 99 The Trademark Reporter 931, Pages 931–932.

920 WIPO, *Intellectual Property and Genetic Resources, Traditional Knowledge and Traditional Cultural Expressions* (n 231) Page 35.

921 Panama – Special System for the Collective Intellectual Property Rights of Indigenous Peoples 2000 (Act No 20, Published in Gaceta Oficial (Official Gazette) No 24,083 of June 27, 2000); and Panama – Regulating Law No. 20 of June 26, 2000, on the Special Intellectual Property Regime Governing the Collective Rights of Indigenous Peoples for the Protection and Defence of their Cultural Identity and their Traditional Knowledge, and Enacting Other Provisions 2001 (Executive Decree No 12) Article 1.

922 BIRPI, *Model Law for Developing Countries on Marks, Trade Names, and Acts of Unfair Competition* (BIRPI Publication 1967) Art 1(c).

The Paris Convention does not define collective marks, but it deals with these types of marks in Article 7bis.

> The countries of the Union undertake to accept for filing and to protect collective marks belonging to associations the existence of which is not contrary to the law of the country of origin, even if such associations do not possess an industrial or commercial establishment.[923]

The TRIPS Agreement by virtue of Article 2 has incorporated such marks.

The Paris Convention obliges Member States to register and protect collective marks belonging to unions or associations including producers, designers, craftsmen, etc., either operating in a particular region or country or sharing other common features. Secondly, the existence and activities of such unions must not be in conflict with the laws of the country of origin. Otherwise, registration and protection of their marks will be refused. Thirdly, applicants for registration are not required to have an industrial or commercial establishment.[924] Therefore, if TKHs constitute legally legitimate associations or unions in the country where they are domiciled, they will be able to apply for and acquire collective marks for their distinctive signs.[925] They are not required to establish a business directly in the target markets.

Collective marks are established either by meeting certain criteria and standards or are only based on an individual criterion which stipulates a given community or a certain place as the origin of products or services. Thus, the function of the collective mark is to inform the general public about certain aspects of the product for which the mark is used. For this reason, in most IP offices, applicants are required to submit the regulations based on which use of collective marks are permitted. The rules for using the collective mark must be attached to the application for registration, and any changes thereto must also be notified to the IP offices. Typically, these regulations include the conditions for using collective marks and membership requirements.[926] If such a mark is used in a manner contrary to the terms of the above-mentioned regulations or in a way which would lead to misleading the public, the mark will be cancelled. That is why the collective mark plays a vital role in protecting

923 Paris Convention Article $7^{bis}(1)$.

924 WIPO, *WIPO IP Handbook* (n 450) Page 256.

925 John Mugabe, 'Intellectual Property Protection and Traditional Knowledge, an Exploration in International Policy Disclosure,' *Intellectual Property and Human Rights* (World Intellectual Property Organization 1999) Page 107.

926 ITC and WIPO (n 869) Page 83.

consumers against misleading practices. In this regard, collective marked TK-RS can represent a specific quality standard for traditional commodities or their geographical origins. For instance, this would apply to handicrafts that are produced according to traditional production methods by TKHs.[927] Produced and processed products of stylish, typical and characteristic TK in a given region can be identified and recognized through their specific and distinctive collective marks. These signs can be utilized as collective marks of these communities and their associated unions, such as farmers; cotton, wool, silk and herbal colours producers; designers, weavers, traders, and other individuals affiliated with these communities, to serve as a guarantee of credibility and quality of their products. It is not an easy task for TKHs to attract consumers' recognition and loyalty. It is even more difficult to keep them attracted. Moreover, access to markets, wholesale and retail of local products and dealing with the distribution system require considerable investment that usually goes beyond the financial and knowledge resources of TKHs.[928] Therefore, collective marks may help TKHs to improve marketing and increase profits from their traditional activities.[929]

The other advantage of the collective mark is its link with individual trademarks of members of traditional communities. In principle, a collective mark may be owned by group of people or their representatives, such as associations, unions, cooperatives of producers or traders, or even a public body,[930] which does not use a collective mark itself, but the members benefit from the mark. However, a business that allows the use of a collective mark could at the same time have its own trademark. As communities include individual producers of goods and services, those individuals may together establish community collective marks using TK-RS. As members of a community, they will be able to use a collective mark for marketing and protecting their traditional products and related services,[931] which in turn can decrease their marketing expenses.[932] But, community members can still use their own individual trademarks along with the community's collective mark. The main difference between a trademark and a collective mark is that a trademark can only be used to distinguish the products or services of a person or company, whereas similar products and

927 WIPO, *Protect and Promote Your Culture* (n 664) Page 42.

928 ITC and WIPO (n 869) Page 82.

929 Gupta, *WIPO-UNEP Study on the Role of Intellectual Property Rights in the Sharing of Benefits Arising from the Use of Biological Resources and Associated Traditional Knowledge* (n 363) Page 159.

930 WIPO, *WIPO IP Handbook* (n 450) Page 256, Paragraph 5.119.

931 WIPO, *Protect and Promote Your Culture* (n 664) Page 42.

932 *ibid.*

services of members (whether individuals or enterprises) of a community are allowed to use a collective mark.[933]

This offers some advantages for members of the local community. They can benefit from the trust of consumers in the products and services supplied under the community collective mark and, at the same time, they are allowed to distinguish their own products and services from those of their fellow members in a given community. Sometimes this permission is limited as specific conditions apply to concurrent use of individual trademarks with a certification mark.[934] This is very significant for TKHs in general and for PCs in particular. Although PCs' reputation is strongly associated with different regions in Iran, hundreds of thousands of designers, producers and service providers within these communities are working to improve the quality and beauty of their products and services, and they are well-known even worldwide.[935]

A good example of a collective mark for traditional art is the 'Taita Basket,' which has been produced by local women in Kenya for generations (see Figure 7 below). The Taita Basket Association is the owner of the collective mark. Members are allowed to use it under regulations established by the association and they have to adopt the quality standards set under those regulations.[936]

FIGURE 7
Taita Basket collective mark (Kenya IP Office Registration no. 94134)

933 *ibid.*

934 ITC and WIPO (n 869) Page 83.

935 In the second chapter of this work, the most important name of these designers, producers and service providers are mentioned.

936 WIPO, 'WIPO Project: Collective Mark for Kenyan Basket Weavers' (2017) <http://www.wipo.int/cooperation/en/funds_in_trust/japan_fitip/news/2017/news_0001.html>.

In accordance with Iranian industrial property law, a collective mark is defined as:

> any visible sign designated as such in the application for registration and capable of distinguishing the origin or any other characteristics, including the quality, of goods or services of natural persons or of legal entities which use the sign under the control of the registered owner of the Collective Mark.[937]

Use of collective marks is allowed for producers, traders or other related parties, subject to the terms of the contract in which quality controls are imposed on the products by the licensor and must effectively control the perceived quality of the goods and services. Otherwise, if the control is not effective, the contract will be invalidated:

> Any License Contract concerning the use of registration of a Mark, or an application thereof, must provide for effective control by the licensor of the quality of goods or services of the licensee. Otherwise, or if such control is not effectively carried out, the License Contract shall not be valid.[938]

A very important aspect that becomes apparent through the careful examination of the above-mentioned articles is that the PCs' unions, which are located and active in the production and distribution areas of PCs all over the country, can design their collective marks. This would include a description of the specific features of PCs associated with the mark, such as knot types, traditional and herbal colours, original designs and drawings of their PCs. Then they could register the mark for the production of carpets by their real and legal members. For example, the Isfahan carpet weavers' association could register its collective mark with the intellectual property centre by choosing a famous and historic symbol of that region, such as 'Si-O-Se-Pol' Bridge or 'Aaliqapou' and incorporating the name 'Isfahan Carpet' into the symbol. It could then, apply for international registration of the mark based on the mechanisms under the Madrid System. Thus, consumers buying PCs would be able to distinguish original Isfahan carpets from fake carpets marketed under the name 'Isfahan carpet' by unauthorized manufacturers and other commercial rivals. This would also enable them to achieve the predicted national and international performances to prevent fraudulent actions by competitors.

---

937 Iran – Patents, Industrial Designs and Trademarks Registration Law Article 30(b).

938 *ibid Article 44.*

4.1.1.4 *Certification Marks*

Certification marks might be considered a special type of collective mark that are used only when based on a specific standard such as GIs, substances, production methods, method of services' performances, quality and accuracy of products or services.[939] In this manner, both collective mark and certification mark goals are informing consumers that the products or services possess assured characteristics.[940] Collective marks are used only by certain companies that are members of an association or a union that owns the collective mark. In other words, the collective mark concentrates on membership while the certification marks may be used by anyone who can ensure that their goods and services comply with the corresponding standards which have already been defined by the owner.[941] Therefore, certification marks are not expected to imply production of products in a specific geographical area: there is no dependence on the land or climate in this type of mark.

FIGURE 8 Two examples of registered certification marks

The Paris Convention does not explicitly refer to this category of trademarks, but the nature of certification marks is not essentially different from that of collective marks. The main purpose of both marks is to support the specific characteristics of a product or service. Therefore, it might be concluded that the provisions of the Paris Convention for collective marks apply to the certification marks as well.[942]

A major problem faced by TKHs concerns false and misleading signs that are alleged to be origin and authentic. TK-RS are often copied and attached to

939 ITC and WIPO (n 869) Page 84.

940 WIPO, 'Intellectual Property & Traditional Handicrafts' (World Intellectual Property Organization) Background Brief No 5 Page 2.

941 WIPO, *Making a Mark – An Introduction to Trademarks for Small and Medium-Sized Enterprises* (WIPO 2006) Page 16.

942 Paris Convention Article 7bis.

fake products and fake traditional creative arts (sometimes called 'fakelore'[943]) to make consumers believe they are original or of the same quality. This problem is very common in the area of PCs.

To avoid such confusing and misleading practices by competitors, certification marks for protection of TK-RS have been gradually developed by TKHs. They use certification marks for goods or services with distinctive and specific qualities and standards to protect the originality and authenticity of their arts.[944] In Nigeria, the Bioresources Development and Conservation Program[945] brand, as shown in Figure 9, has been used as an assurance of traditional drug quality.[946]

FIGURE 9
A brand for traditional herbal drugs[947]

In Australia, the National Indigenous Arts Advocacy Association uses certification marks for guaranteeing the authenticity of indigenous people's products and to prevent fake commodities.[948]

---

943 Torsen and Anderson (n 440) Page 16.

944 WIPO, *Intellectual Property and Genetic Resources, Traditional Knowledge and Traditional Cultural Expressions* (n 231) Page 32.

945 'BDCP is a globally recognized not-for-profit organization established in 1992 that promotes the sustainable utilization of natural products. BDCP and its affiliates promote high quality scientific research on sustainable utilization of biological resources for health, economic development and conservation of the environment; create knowledge in the application of technology and global commerce for poverty alleviation; and develop partnerships with agencies, communities and governments for sustainable development.' See: Isa Bashir, 'About Us | Bioresources' (*Bioresources Development and Conservation Program*, 2014) <http://bioresources.org/about/> accessed 24 May 2018.

946 See: WIPO, 'Traditional Medicine as a Tonic for Development' (World Intellectual Property Organization and Bioresources Development and Conservation Programme 2015) Project Report.

947 See: InterCEDD Health Products, 'About Us|Intercedd Health Products' (*Intercedd Health Products*, 2007) <http://intercedd.com.ng/about-us/> accessed 24 May 2018

948 Gupta, *WIPO-UNEP Study on the Role of Intellectual Property Rights in the Sharing of Benefits Arising from the Use of Biological Resources and Associated Traditional Knowledge* (n 363) Page 63.

FIGURE 10
The Label of Authenticity Trade Mark Project

Another example is the 'COWICHAN' certification mark of the Cowichan Tribes in British Colombia in Canada. The Cowichan tribes include seven traditional villages and, with more than 4900 members, are the largest First Nation Band in the state of British Colombia. They are also famous for their blankets and knitted clothes, which withstand the cold and are known as Cowichan Sweaters.[949] In September 1995, the Cowichan Band Council applied for registration of the COWICHAN certification mark by the Canadian Intellectual Property Office. The certification mark was granted in 1996 and in accordance with the Canadian Trademark Details webpage, it "to be used by persons authorized by the certifier, will certify that the wares have been hand-knit in one piece in accordance with traditional tribal methods by members of the Coast Salish Nation using raw, unprocessed, undyed, hand-spun wool made and prepared in accordance with traditional tribal methods." The COWICHAN mark distinguishes "clothing, namely sweaters, vests, ponchos, hats, toques, mittens, scarves, socks and slippers."[950]

Harris Tweed is another good example of a certification mark for traditional hand-woven cloths made by the islanders of Lewis, Harris, Uist and Barra in Scotland (see Figure 11 below). The mark was registered as a certification mark in 1910[951] and later in 1911 it was stamped on the local products of "hand-woven cloths made from yarn spun and dyed in the Outer Hebrides."[952] Use of the Harris Tweed brand is subject to conformity with the 'Brand Use Rules.' These

949 See: 'About Cowichan Tribes' (*Cowichan Tribes*, 1995) <https://ised-isde.canada.ca/cipo/trademark-search/pdf/0792173?lang=eng>.

950 Canada Trademark Office, 'COWICHAN Certificate Mark' (*Canadian Trademarks Detail*, 6 November 1996) <https://ised-isde.canada.ca/cipo/trademark-search/pdf/0792173?lang=eng>.

951 'Trade Mark Number UK00000319214' (*Intellectual Property Office of UK*) <https://trademarks.ipo.gov.uk/ipo-tmcase/page/Results/1/UK00000319214> accessed 25 May 2018.

952 ITC and WIPO (n 869) Pages 119–120.

rules are approved by the Harris Tweed Authority and certify that "the brand is used appropriately to preserve its integrity for generation to come." The rules include:

- Introduction of the brand, and the objectives of the rules;
- Key elements of the brand itself;
- Conditions for using the brand;
- Labels and swing tags;
- Naming and describing products containing Harris Tweed;
- Example of products suitable for use of the accessory or seam label.[953]

FIGURE 11 Harris Tweed hand-woven certification mark

In New Zealand, the 'Māori Arts Board' known as 'Te Waka Toi' developed and used a certification mark to authenticate their handicrafts.[954] 'Toi Iho' was registered in 2001.[955] Their mark as a mark of authenticity was intended to guarantee the quality of products made by Māori tribes to consumers. It was also created and registered to tackle the increasing concerns about misuse and misappropriation of Māori TK-RS and to provide commercial advantages for the Māori people. Four categories of the toi iho™ marks were designed and registered:

---

953 Harris Tweed Authority (HTA), 'Brand Use Rules' (Harris Tweed Authority 2017) Version 2.

954 'Report of the UNCTAD-Commonwealth Secretariat Workshop on Elements of National Sui Generis Systems for the Preservation, Protection and Promotion of Traditional Knowledge, Innovations and Practices and Options for an International Framework, Geneva, 4–6 February 2004.' (United Nations 2005) UNCTAD/DITC/TED/2005/18 4.

955 See: New Zealand Intellectual Property Office, 'Search Trade Mark Case(s)' (2018) <https://app.iponz.govt.nz/app/Extra/IP/TM/Qbe.aspx?sid=636629099839050546>.

- Māori Made Mark, which only artists of Māori descent are allowed to use. The use of this kind of sign has enabled Māori artists to be identified as authentic artists and allows consumers to purchase their products with full knowledge of their authenticity (see Figure 12).
- Mainly Māori Mark, which is allowed to be used by groups of artists of Māori descent to create, offer, perform and sell Māori art-works. The purpose of this trademark is to promote Māori arts in global markets. In this way, Māori artists are supposed to be more motivated to produce high-quality works and to maintain the integrity of the TKHs' culture. The sign also means that customers can be confident that when they buy a product with this mark, it is actually a real product of Māori tribes and it is not a mass-produced product imported from another country (see Figure 12).
- Māori Co-production Mark, which was designed to be used by Māori and non-Māori artists and businesses working together to create, present and perform art works. This type of Māori mark recognizes the need for cooperation between different stakeholders for protection of TK and to promote marketing for TK-RS. The benefits of this method are substantial. For example, the collaboration between a traditional artist and a large clothing manufacturer can help to maintain the originality and quality of products while increasing production and sales (see Figure 12).
- Licensed Stockist Mark, which was designed to be used by craft retailers and galleries under Māori licenses. This mark allows Māori to determine an appropriate price for their products, which assures the protection of their own interests as well as those of their consumers. Also, it allows them to control the supply of their goods and services. Moreover, they can exploit the excellent standards, experience and knowledge of galleries, retailers and art dealers in order to promote their marketing and sales of their products and services.[956]

FIGURE 12 The Toi Iho's registered trademarks[957]

956 See: IGC-GRTKF Secretariat, 'Consolidated Analysis of the Legal Protection of Traditional Cultural Expressions' (n 800) Page 48; also: ITC and WIPO (n 869) Pages 120–121.

957 See: 'What Is the Attitude the Use of Māori Images for Artistic or Commercial Purposes?' (*Māori Information Sources*) <http://oil.otago.ac.nz/oil/module11/Scenarios/Maori-images.html>

Iran's abolished 'Trademark and Patent Registration Law of 1931,' which has been replaced with the 'Patents, Industrial Designs and Trademarks Registration Law of 2007,' stated that trademarks may be used to distinguish the products of a group of farmers, traders or craftsmen, or to identify a product of one area of the country.[958] The registration of such marks required certification by the competent authority to allow the use of these marks by the manufacturers of the products, which included the trade unions, chamber of commerce, municipality or governors.[959] The new rules on trademarks in Iran have been developed in such a way that collective marks in the general sense and confirmatory marks in the specific sense are also included within the scope of this definition.[960] In other words, the legislator has referred to the general concept of this clause in the general sense of collective marks (*any visible sign designated as such in the application for registration …*) while some certification marks are mentioned as examples of collective marks (*… capable of distinguishing the origin or any other characteristics, including the quality, of goods or services of natural persons or of legal entities which use the sign under the control of the registered owner of the Collective Mark*). In general, there is a considerable potential in Iran's Industrial Property Law to provide a registration system for certification marks in the context of PCs. To exploit this law, PC producers and their representatives may use certification marks to notify their consumers about the standards of PCs and their originality and authenticity. For example, standards such as:

- PCs are hand-made products;
- Certain biological resources have been exploited to produce PCs;
- PCs are made purely from natural local materials, such as herbal colours;
- Certain TK-RS are used for production of PCs;
- Certain quality controls are applied to the process of PC production;
- The role of women in production of PCs and/or no children were engaged in the production process;
- PCs are made by known local and tribal communities.

In brief, positive protection of TK-RS under trademark law, especially the use of collective marks and certification marks will help TKHs to:

- decrease and discourage the imitation of TKHs' products in the market through distinct and original traditional crafts;
- increase public awareness;

958 Iran – Law on Registration of Marks and Inventions 1931 Article 1.

959 *ibid Article* 2(5).

960 Iran – Patents, Industrial Designs and Trademarks Registration Law Article 30(b).

- provide reassurance to consumers as to the authenticity of the goods they are buying;
- help TKHs to distinguish their products and crafts from those made by non-local suppliers;
- assist them to promote the reputation of the local artists and producers nationally and internationally;
- increase TKHs' fair and equitable economic benefits.

Despite the advantages of positive protection of TK-RS, it is, however, important to note the challenges regarding this type of protection.

4.1.2 Challenges of Positive Protection of TK-RS

4.1.2.1 *Challenge of Descriptive Characteristics of TK-RS*

Descriptive marks usually describe significant features of a product or a service.[961] Trademarks are 'descriptive' mainly when consumers make a connection between the marks and the goods or services they are assigned to.[962] Terms such as 'bicycle for make of bicycles' is an example of marks that are descriptive.[963] In the same manner, incorporating the term 'carpet' or 'rug' in the trademarks for PCs might construct a descriptive mark. Almost all traders and manufacturers providing goods and services are interested in offering their products with a type of mark that includes a descriptive feature, which could immediately convey information on their products to customers. This might put mark holders at serious risk, because even if they succeed in registering their marks at the trademark offices, they may have to abandon their marks because there is a considerable possibility that they could have to face litigation from competitors. The grounds for refusal or invalidation of the descriptive marks are mentioned in the diverse instruments. In accordance with the Paris Convention descriptive signs may be denied registration or invalidated if they are "devoid of any distinctive character, or to designate the kind, quality, quantity, intended purpose, value, place of origin, of the goods, or the time of production."[964] EU legislation on trademarks follows the same approach as the Paris Convention. According to the EU law, trademarks which "are devoid of any distinctive character" or "consist exclusively of signs or indications which may serve, in trade, to designate the kind, quality, quantity,

961 ITC and WIPO (n 869) Page 77.

962 Abbott, Cottier and Gurry (n 367) Page 318.

963 Adam Jolly and Jeremy Philpott, *The Handbook of European Intellectual Property Management: Developing, Managing and Protecting Your Company's Intellectual Property* (2nd edn, Kogan Page 2009) Page 526.

964 Paris Convention Article $6^{quinquies}$(B)(2).

intended purpose, value, geographical origin, or the time of production of the goods or of rendering of the service, or other characteristics of the goods or services" either are not registrable or shall be invalidated even after registration.[965] Article 15(1) of the TRIPS Agreement stipulates that trademarks are not eligible for registration "where signs are not inherently capable of distinguishing the relevant goods or services." Although the TRIPS Agreement has not provided details of descriptive marks, it can be concluded that according to the agreement descriptive marks are not registrable as they fail to distinguish goods and services. Besides, Article 15(2) of the TRIPS Agreement obliges its Member States not to derogate from the provisions of the Paris Convention.

The Iranian industrial property law approach is like that of the TRIPS Agreement. According to this law, a trademark is not registrable if it "is not capable of distinguishing the goods or service of one enterprise from those belonging to another enterprise."[966] The general practice of the Iranian Intellectual Property Centre – which is to deny registration of descriptive marks – supports such an interpretation of the Article 15(1) of the TRIPS Agreement. For instance, applications for 'New Design Carpet' and 'Anti-Blot Carpet' were denied as they were descriptive in nature.[967]

Although TK-RS are distinctive as they have been used to refer to signs and symbols of given TKHs' communities, tribes, families and their products or their religious rituals and ceremonies,[968] they are nevertheless descriptive in nature. Therefore, in many cases, TKHs' applications for registration of their TK-RS have been unsuccessful.[969] Moreover, if TKHs want to register their marks in a foreign territory, the designated trademark office may ask for the translation of the mark. The officials will examine the mark in the local language and if they conclude it is descriptive in the local language they will probably reject the application. In this regard, in Australia "approximately 90 applications have been lodged for trademarks including the word 'Dreamtime' 15 have been registered and nine are pending."[970]

To deal with this challenge, TKHs are recommended to use collective marks and certification marks. Whereas a trademark should not be descriptive,

965 See: Directive 2015/2436 Article 4(1)(b) & (C); and EU Trademark Regulation Article 7(1)(b) & (c).

966 Iran – Patents, Industrial Designs and Trademarks Registration Law Article 32(a).

967 Interview with Gholamreza Bayat, 'Interview with Mr. Gholamreza Bayat, Head of Trademarks division of the Iranian Intellectual Property Centre' (2 September 2018).

968 GRULAC (n 889) Page 6, Paragraph 3.

969 IGC-GRTKF Secretariat, 'Consolidated Analysis of the Legal Protection of Traditional Cultural Expressions' (n 800) Page 49.

970 Janke (n 645) Pages 32–33 and 38.

collective and certification marks might be distinguished through describing geographical location or standards of the goods or services. As already mentioned, a significant distinction between them is that trademarks are used to identify just one individual enterprise that provides products or services while collective and certification marks describe and assure some characteristics of the products or services of different individuals or entities which are members of associations.[971] It is, however, important to note the limitations of collective marks and certification marks. According to WIPO, many countries protect collective and certification marks at the national and regional levels.[972] Nevertheless, "collective marks are not defined in the same way by the various national legislations."[973] Moreover, no standard procedure for registration and protection of such marks is established at the international level. In this regard, neither the TLT nor the Singapore Treaty apply to collective marks and certification marks:

> [Kind of Marks] This Treaty shall not apply to collective marks, certification marks and guarantee marks.[974]

While, as explained before, collective and certification marks are the most promising tools for providing positive protection of TK-RS in national legislations, existing international instruments have failed to take them into consideration.

4.1.2.2 *Challenge of Use Requirement*

It is important to TKHS to continue to use their marks; because registration is not sufficient for providing constant protection of a trademark. In a completely different approach from the copyright regime, right holders of trademarks must exercise and actively defend their exclusive rights to use their trademarks. Otherwise, their exclusive rights over their trademarks may be lost if they fail to actively use their trademarks or do not fight against any

---

971 ITC and WIPO (n 869) Pages 82 and 84.

972 SCT Secretariat, 'Summary of Replies to the Questionnaire on Trademark Law and Practice (SCT/11/6)' (World Intellectual Property Organization 2005) WIPO Doc SCT/14/5 Pages 33–35.

973 SCT Secretariat, 'Technical and Procedural Aspects Relating to the Registration of Certification and Collective Marks' (World Intellectual Property Organization 2010) WIPO Doc WIPO/STrad/INF/6 Page 3.

974 TLT Article 2(2)(b); and Singapore Treaty Article 2(2)(b).

infringements. The philosophy of the 'Use Requirement' rule is to reduce the numbers of trademarks and avoid conflict between trademarks.[975]

The requirements of use to maintain protection of IPRs are also known as local working requirements. Those requirements and the limitation on them are spread throughout the Paris Convention and the TRIPS Agreement.[976] Although, neither the Paris Convention nor the TRIPS Agreement has required the termination of a trademark in the case of non-use,[977] they do not prevent their Member States from setting local use requirements and cancelling registrations in the case of non-use. In accordance with the Paris Convention, cancellation is permitted only after a certain period of non-use:

> If, in any country, use of the registered mark is compulsory, the registration may be cancelled only after a reasonable period, and then only if the person concerned does not justify his inaction.[978]

The TRIPS Agreement stipulates a three-year period to allow right holders to use their trademarks.

> an application shall not be refused solely on the ground that intended use has not taken place before the expiry of a period of three years from the date of application.[979]
>
> If use is required to maintain a registration, the registration may be cancelled only after an uninterrupted period of at least three years of non-use.[980]

975 Robin Jacob, Daniel Alexander and Matthew Fisher, *Guidebook to Intellectual Property* (A&C Black 2014) Page 111.

976 Thomas Cottier, Shaheeza Lalani and Michelangelo Temmerman, 'Use It or Lose It: Assessing the Compatibility of the Paris Convention and TRIPS Agreement with Respect to Local Working Requirements' (2014) 17 Journal of International Economic Law 437, Page 442.

977 Jürg Simon, 'Agreement on Trade-Related Aspects of Intellectual Property Rights: Section 2: Trademarks' in Thomas Cottier and Pierre Véron (eds), *Concise International and European IP Law: TRIPS, Paris Convention, European Enforcement and Transfer of Technology*, vol 4 (2nd edn, Kluwer Law International 2008) Page 59.

978 Paris Convention Article 5(C)(1).

979 TRIPS Agreement Article 15(3).

980 *ibid Article 19(1).*

Also, according to the TLT "any Contracting Party may require that an application contain … a declaration of intention to use the mark."[981] Similarly, the EU Directive on protection of trademarks states that trademarks may fulfill their purpose only when they are used on the market:

> It is therefore essential to require that registered trade marks actually be used in connection with the goods or services for which they are registered, or, if not used in that connection within five years of the date of the completion of the registration procedure, be liable to be revoked.[982]

Most countries assign a fixed period of time (usually a three- or five-year period)[983] within which a trademark shall be used. Otherwise, the rights will be assumed abandoned and the registration might be cancelled.

Regarding the concept of 'use of a trademark,' the approach varies considerably between countries, but the general rule is that the use of the sign is related to a specific product or service in the context of business. Procedures such as binding marks on product packaging or on containers and labels, as well as trademark advertisements, can be considered instances of the notion of 'use of a trademark.'[984] In this regard, for instance, in the United States trademark act of 1946 'use in commerce' is a fundamental issue for protection of trademarks.[985] In this context "use in commerce means the bona fide use of a mark in the ordinary course of trade," which include placing a mark on the goods, on their containers, on the tags or labels affixed to the goods, or on the documents associated with the goods or sale of goods, and also in the sale or advertising of service marks.[986] According to the EU trademarks law, 'genuine use' in connection with the goods or services in respect of which a trade mark is registered is necessary to prevent revocation of marks on the ground of non-use.[987] The concept of 'genuine use' is interpreted in *Ansul v Ajax* case by the European

981 TLT Article 3(1)(a)(xvii).

982 Directive 2015/2436 Preamble note 31.

983 This period is 5 years in the member states of the EU, see: Directive 2015/2436; also 5 years in Switzerland, see: Swiss – Federal Act on the Protection of Trade Marks and Indications of Source 1992 (232/11 (entered into force 1 April 1993)); and 3 years in Iran, see: Iran – Patents, Industrial Designs and Trademarks Registration Law.

984 SCT Secretariat, 'Summary of Replies to the Questionnaire on Trademark Law and Practice' (n 972) Pages 139–143.

985 Arnold Lutzker, *Content Rights for Creative Professionals: Copyrights and Trademarks in a Digital Age* (Focal Press 2003) Page 97.

986 The US – Trademark Act 1946 (Pub L No 79-489, 60 Stat 427,) § 45.

987 See: Directive 2015/2436 Articles 18(1), 47(2), 58(1)(a) and 64(2).

Court of Justice (ECJ) in which "there is 'genuine use' of a trade mark where the mark is used in accordance with its essential function." In evaluating the genuine use of a trademark, the following facts must be examined:

> whether the commercial exploitation of mark is real,
> whether such use is viewed as warranted in the economic sector concerned to maintain or create a share in the market for the goods or services,
> the nature of the goods or services at issue,
> the characteristics of the market and the scale and frequency of use of the mark.[988]

Therefore, TKHs' intention to maintain the registration of their registered TK-RS through use would not be enough. Effective use is required.[989]

In the same manner, Iranian industrial property law takes revocation of a registered trademark as the consequence of non-use, while it stipulates:

> Any interested person may request the court to invalidate the registration, if he establishes that, the owner of a registered Mark, or a person authorized by him, has not used the said Mark for a period of at least three full years running from the date of registration up to one month prior to filing the request.[990]

Yet it provides no definition of use of a trademark or any criteria to identify non-use conditions. Therefore, it is up to the courts to decide case by case if the requirement for use of a mark has been met.[991] Iranian jurisprudence on the context of the use requirement is sparse. Yet in the cases that have been brought, courts ordered proprietors of the disputed trademarks to offer evidence of their use as the defendant without making it clear what kinds of use are acceptable to prevent revocation of the marks.[992] Despite the court practice, in Iran's industrial property law, it is stipulated that the burden is on the

---

988 See: *Ansul BV v Ajax Brandbeveiliging BV* [2003] ECJ C-40/01, ECR I-2439; quoted in: Annette Kur and Thomas Dreier, *European Intellectual Property Law: Text, Cases and Materials* (Edward Elgar 2013) Page 231.

989 Jacob, Alexander and Fisher (n 975) Page 112.

990 Iran – Patents, Industrial Designs and Trademarks Registration Law Article 41.

991 Seyed Hassan Mirhosseini, حقوق علائم تجاری (*The Law of Trademarks*) (4th edn, Mizan Legal Foundation 2016) Page 420.

992 *Hamid v Arman Co* [2014] Tehran Civil Inferior Court 9209980226300930; and *Mehrdad & Reza v Saeed* [2016] Tehran Civil Court of Appeal 93099802263916.

plaintiff to show that disputed trademark has not really been used.[993] This goes completely against the current procedure in the EU, WTO and national laws of many other countries. For instance, in the EU, the proprietor of the trade mark shall furnish proof that the trade mark has been put to genuine use.[994] Therefore, when a trademark is "challenged for non-use, the burden is on the trademark owner to show that the mark has been used."[995] In the WTO judicial precedent, in the *US – Wool Shirt and Blouses* case, the Appellate Body states that "the party who asserts a fact, whether claimant or respondent, is responsible for providing proof thereof" and that the "burden of proof rests upon the party, whether complaining or defending, who asserts the affirmative of a particular claim or defence."[996] Also, according to Swiss Trade Mark Law "evidence of use is required to be provided by the proprietor of the trade mark."[997]

Iranian scholar Mirhosseini suggests that the approach of the Iranian trademark law follows the general principle of *actori incumbit onus probandi*[998] where the burden of proof will be on the plaintiff who claims that a trademark owner has not been using their trademark in the given period.[999] It seems that the approach of Iran trademark law is not supported by the principle of *negativa non sunt probanda* and by the Iranian Civil Code. According to the principle of *negativa non sunt probanda* it is "virtually impossible to prove a negative since proof requires some concrete evidence and a negative does not readily offer that possibility."[1000] The 'non-use requirement' is a missing circumstance or negative fact which cannot be proved or at least is very hard for a plaintiff to prove. Therefore, the trademark owner must provide positive evidence that they have been using the marks in the given period.[1001] Also, the most recent part of Article 1257 of the Iranian Civil Code stipulates that respondent is responsible for providing proof if they claim something which needs evidence:

---

993 Iran – Patents, Industrial Designs and Trademarks Registration Law Article 41.

994 Directive 2015/2436 Article 17.

995 Jacob, Alexander and Fisher (n 975) Page 111.

996 *United States – Measure Affecting Imports of Woven Wool Shirts and Blouses from India* [1997] World Trade Organization (Appellate Body); quoted in: Andrew D Mitchell, *Legal Principles in WTO Disputes* (Cambridge University Press 2008) Page 101.

997 Swiss – Federal Act on the Protection of Trade Marks and Indications of Source Article 12(3).

998 This Latin term means: 'the burden of proof rests with the claimant.'

999 Mirhosseini (n 991) Page 420.

1000 James T Bretzke, *Consecrated Phrases: A Latin Theological Dictionary; Latin Expressions Commonly Found in Theological Writings* (3rd edn, Liturgical Press 2013) Page 111.

1001 See: Abdolkarim Lahiji, 'دعوی عدم استفاده از علامت تجاری (Trademark Non-Use Litigation)' (1973) 124 Iranian Central Bar Association Law Review 80, Page 82.

> Anyone who claims a right has to establish the same and if the defendant, wishing to defend himself, claims something which may require evidence, it is he who must prove it.[1002]

Hence, in the context of the use requirement of trademarks, if the proprietor of a trade mark alleges constant use of their mark, they are required to provide evidence of that use. As mentioned before, such an argument has been used in courts' verdicts as they required the owner to provide the evidence that they were using their marks.[1003]

It seems that the local use requirement will raise real concerns for TKHs who are required not only to register their TK-RS as trademarks but also to use them actively in the course of trade. Moreover, TKHs or their representatives are required to provide the evidence of constant and genuine use of their registered trademarks. In many cases, this does not help TKHs whose wish is to protect TK-RS against third parties' exploitation,[1004] but in the case of PCs, the use requirement does seem have a less negative impact on protection of TK-RS abroad. The reason for such a conclusion is the vast dimensions of the PCs' market and the number of territories that are PCs consumers. In only one year, between 2017 and 2018, more than 71 countries were among the PCs' target markets.[1005] Nevertheless, the PCs would lack protection in more than half of the world's countries.

To overcome the challenge of the use requirement, it seems that the concept of genuine use or use in commerce must be developed in a way to include the cultural and social characteristics of TK-RS.

In this regard, the theory of TIP-rights shall be considered as a solution to promote the concept of use. According to Cottier and Panizzon: "Active use of TK should constitute the required limit of protection. Rights to TK should only arise so long as the process or information exists within, and is being used by, a particular community."[1006] It seems that their theory is compatible with the TK criteria. Because, TKHs argue TK an essential element of their cultural life; and if TKHs cease using their TK-RS, the traditional character of the given TK would not be relevant and qualify for protection.[1007] Moreover, by using TIP-rights theory, active use and activities and applications by given communities could possibly be expanded as the use concept under trademark law.

1002 Iran – Civil Code 1928 Article 1257.

1003 *Hamid v Arman Co.* (n 992); and *Mehrdad & Reza v Saeed* (n 992).

1004 IGC-GRTKF Secretariat, 'Consolidated Analysis of the Legal Protection of Traditional Cultural Expressions' (n 800) Pages 48–49.

1005 Iran National Carpet Centre (n 841).

1006 Cottier and Panizzon, 'Legal Perspectives on Traditional Knowledge' (n 359) Page 393.

1007 Riffel (n 3) Pages 184–185.

This in turn requires that the geographical scope of use must also be transposed from the national level to include the regional and international level.

4.1.2.3 *Challenge of the Classification System*

One of the characteristics of the trademark regime is the creation of a classification system for goods and services. According to this system, any goods or services are placed in one or more categories. The principle purpose of establishing a classification system under the Nice and Vienna Agreements was to facilitate searching, registration, documentation and publication of trademarks. Therefore, the classification was not intended to affect the scope of protection afforded to a mark. But, in practice, acceptance of an application for the registration of a trademark is subject to providing a list of goods and services to which that sign is attributed. In some countries, applicants are asked to submit a separate application for every class. For others, several classes could be applied for the same application.[1008] However, protection of registered TK-RS is linked to specific categories and thus positive protection of the trademark is only available for designated categories. Therefore, others are not prevented from registering the mark for other categories.[1009] "While trademarks can help distinguish authentic goods, they do not prohibit third parties from using traditional knowledge"[1010] and they do not avoid misuse of TK-RS or impede the sale of imitations.[1011] To prevent such a scenario, some TKHs have registered their TK-RS in all categories under the Nice and Vienna classification systems. For example, in the Nice Agreement, PCs are categorized under class 27 (Basic No. 270011) for goods, and for services regarding PCs under classes 35 (for export), 37 (for repair including cleansing), 39 (packaging of goods and distribution), 40 (for treatment of materials) and 42 (for designing carpets).[1012] But some well-known PC producers like Seirafian have registered their mark even for clothes and shoes (class 25), for laces and embroidery, ribbons and braid; buttons, hooks and eyes, pins and needles; artificial flowers (class 26), for games and playthings (class 28) and for foods and vegetables (class 29),[1013] which are not related to the PCs or TK-RS or even TKHs. Choosing an appropriate strategy to determine the class of goods and services is considered to

1008 WIPO, *WIPO IP Handbook* (n 450) Page 80.

1009 WIPO, *Intellectual Property, Traditional Knowledge and Traditional Cultural Expressions / Folklore: A Guide for Countries in Transition* (n 327) Page 15.

1010 Abbott (n 799) Page 24.

1011 WIPO, 'Intellectual Property & Traditional Handicrafts' (n 940) Page 2.

1012 See: Roberts (n 822).

1013 Iran Intellectual Property Centre, 'جستجوی علامت فرش - صیرفیان (Search for Carpet Trademark – SEIRAFIAN)' (*Trademark National Database*, 18 November 2002) <http://ip.ssaa.ir/BSigns/SearchResult.aspx?DecNo=108618&RN=105642>.

be very consequential, because if the number of classes is too high, this will increase the likelihood of a refusal or opposition to the application, and if it is too limited then it will limit the scope of protection of the mark. Besides, in practice, TKHs could not afford to maintain the use of their registered marks in commerce (as the trademark law of the USA requires), to practice the genuine use of their marks (as the EU trademark regime implies) or to provide the evidence of use (as national laws in Switzerland and Iran demand) in all categories of the international classification system and they would lose their rights over their TK-RS at least in some classes in the target markets.

One solution to the problem of classification could be approval of a new class for the TK-RS through the WIPO Preparatory Working Group and Committee of Experts for the Nice Agreement.[1014] In accordance with the Nice Agreement:

> "Amendment" shall mean any transfer of goods or services from one class to another or the creation of any new class.[1015]

Therefore, the creation of new classes is entirely possible. At first, the Nice Classification only involved 34 classes of goods, and 11 more classes relating to services. More classes were gradually added to the classification system. For example, in 2000, Class 43 "services for providing food and drink; temporary accommodation," Class 44 "Medical services; veterinary services; hygienic and beauty care for human beings or animals; agriculture, horticulture and forestry services" and Class 45 "personal and social services rendered by others to meet the needs of individuals; security services for the protection of property and individuals" were created and added to the Nice Classification system.[1016] Moreover, the group of experts made numerous essential amendments to the international trademark classification of the Nice Agreement.[1017]

4.1.2.4 *Challenge of Cost of Positive Protection*

The protection of a trademark through registration is always subject to payment of related fees. Normally paying for registration of trademarks, especially

---

1014 Since the first meeting from 1961 and during their discussions the group of experts has been revising the Nice Classification continuously, and their most recent meeting (the 35th meeting) was held from April 28 to May 2, 2025. See: 'Committee of Experts of the Nice Union' (*World Intellectual Property Organization*, May 2025) <https://www.wipo.int/meetings/en/details.jsp?meeting_id=46428>.

1015 Nice Agreement Article 3(7)(b).

1016 *International Classification of Goods and Services for the Purposes of the Registration of Marks (Nice Classification)*, vol II (8th edn, World Intellectual Property Organization 2001) Page v.

1017 Roberts (n 822) Introduction.

at the international level, goes far beyond the financial resources of TKHs. The principle costs could include fees for:

- filing the application,
- applying for additional classes (beyond principle classes),
- registration or publication of registered marks,
- payment of renewal fees.[1018]

Also, there are diverse additional fees which are applicable in different trademark offices, such as:

- statement of use,
- amendment to allege use,
- examination,
- dividing an application,
- amending a deficiency in an application,
- objections or reply to objections,
- new certificate of registration,
- certificate of correction,
- application for collective marks.

These costs are even higher if the applicant seeks international registration, which would add more expense for:

- International registration fees based on the Madrid System which vary depending on the number of classes and the countries in which the protection is sought;
- Hiring a professional trademark lawyer or agent to assist with filing an application or to help with the registration process;
- Costs associated with continued use of a trademark in goods and services, such as use of marks in advertising, labels, packaging, brochures and displays, etc.;
- Renewal fees for international registration.

Some argue that although the costs of positive protection may appear to be high, but one should take into consideration that applicants often have limited numbers of marks to be registered. Also, once a mark is registered, it could be used for a wide range of products and services. Furthermore, the costs could be shared among members of community or association if the mark is registered as collective mark or certification mark.[1019]

To work out the possible minimum costs for registration of a TK-RS, some examples of registrations fees charged by trademark offices of Iran,[1020]

1018 WIPO, *WIPO IP Handbook* (n 450) Pages 80–83.

1019 ITC and WIPO (n 869) Pages 77–78.

1020 Iran – Executive Regulation of Patents, Industrial Designs and Trademarks Registration Law 2009 Annex 1.

Switzerland,[1021] the USA,[1022] the EU[1023] and the WIPO Madrid System are presented in Table 6:[1024]

TABLE 6 Trademark registration fees in Iran, Switzerland, USA, EU and WIPO

Office/Rate \ Fee Titles	Iran IPC/Rials		Swiss IGE|IPI/CHF	USA USPTO/ $		European Union EUIPO/ €		WIPO Madrid System/CHF
	Individuals	Entities		E-Filing	on Paper	E-Filing	on Paper	
Application	200.000 First Class	400.000 First Class	450 for 3 First Classes	500 First Class	750 First Class	850 First Class	1000 First Class	653 Not Coloured 903 Coloured Marks for 3 First Classes
Fee for Additional Classes or Designated Countries	20.000 Per Class as of the 2nd Class	40.000 Per Class as of the 2nd Class	100 Per Class as of the 4th Class	100 Per Class	200 Per Class	50 for 2nd Class 150 Per Class as 3rd Class		100 Per Class for Designated Country[1025] 100 for Each Designated Country
Registration	1.200.000 First Class	2.400.000 First Class	—	—	—	—		—
Additional Fee for Registration	100.000 Per Class as of the 2nd Class	200.000 Per Class as of the 2nd Class	—	—	—	—		—

1021 Swiss Federal Institute of Intellectual Property, 'How Much Does It Cost to Protect a Trade Mark in Switzerland? Costs and Fees' (*IGE / IPI*) <https://www.ige.ch/en/protecting-your-ip/trade-marks/national-applications/costs-and-fees.html> accessed 16 October 2018.

1022 Office of the Chief Financial Officer, 'USPTO Fee Schedule' (*The USPTO*) Trademark Fees </learning-and-resources/fees-and-payment/uspto-fee-schedule> accessed 22 October 2018.

1023 EU Trademark Regulation Annex 1.

1024 See Articles 8(2) and 8(7) of both: Madrid Agreement; Madrid Protocol.

1025 Except to those Member States of Madrid Protocol which require individual fees including: Antigua and Barbuda, Australia, Bahrain, BES Islands, Brunei Darussalam, Cambodia, Columbia, Curaçao, Denmark, European Union, Estonia, Finland, Gambia, Georgia, Ghana, Greece, Iceland, India, Indonesia, Ireland, Israel, Japan, Laos, Mexico, New Zealand, Norway, OAPI, Oman, Philippines, Republic of Korea (South Korea), Singapore, St-Martin, Syrian Arab Republic, Sweden, Thailand, Tunisia, Türkiye, Turkmenistan, United Kingdom, United States of America, Uzbekistan, Zambia, Zimbabwe. Individual fees may be subject to change regularly.

TABLE 6 Trademark registration fees in Iran, Switzerland, USA, EU and WIPO (*cont.*)

Office/Rate / Fee Titles	Iran IPC/Rials		Swiss IGE|IPI/CHF	USA USPTO/ $		European Union EUIPO/ €		WIPO Madrid System/CHF
	Individuals	**Entities**		**E-Filing**	**on Paper**	**E-Filing**	**on Paper**	
Renewal	Equal to Registration Fee		550	300 Per Class	500 Per Class	Equal to Registration Fee		653 as Basic Fee 100 Per Class & 100 for Each Designated Country
Late Renewal	Half of Registration Fee		50	100 Per Class	200 Per Class	25% of the belated renewal fee, up to 1500		
International Application	200.000	400.000	100	—		300		

These costs appear to be too high for TKHs and PC producers to afford for positive protection of their TK-RS in their target markets. For instance, if a community or its members decide to register their mark in colour under the Madrid System in just 6 classes: 27 (for PCs), 35 (for export), 37 (for repair including cleansing), 39 (packaging of goods and distribution), 40 (for treatment of materials) and 42 (for designing carpets) with the 9 trademark offices of the countries – the USA, Germany, United Kingdom, Japan, Italy, Australia, Switzerland, Denmark and Sweden – which were among the main importers of PCs during the twelve months between 21 March 2017 and 20 March 2018,[1026] it would cost as much as 8810 Swiss Francs.[1027] In fact, PCs were exported to more than 71 countries during the same time period, which shows how expensive the process for positive protection in the target markets could be. In this regard, as Popova-Gosart points out:

> Many of the smaller producers cannot afford this initial fee, nor the accompanying fee for using the registered design. These smaller producers are

1026 See: Iran National Carpet Centre (n 841).

1027 Extracted from: 'International Registration of Marks – Fee Calculation' (*World Intellectual Property Organization*, 2018) <https://madrid.wipo.int/feecalcapp/> accessed 22 October 2018.

> usually the families or communities who employ the traditional process and designs. But with this registration process, they are being further marginalized from the industry that enables their livelihood.[1028]

In the light of the above, the positive protection of TK-RS is possible through the legal regime of trademarks. But, even if the TKHs could overcome the legal and technical complexities of the registration process, the fees for registration of TK-RS would have to be paid. Only those who have sufficient financial resources to go through with the registration process will be able to afford the expenses; and, unfortunately, TKHs or most of them are not a part of this group.

Cottier, however, notes that, in the case of collective and certification marks, the challenge of the high cost might be overcome by sharing the fees among the TKHs. His comment seems well-founded. Firstly, the cost for registration of collective or certification marks is almost as much as the registration fees for individual trademarks. For example, the registration fee for a collective mark under the Madrid System in the nine main PC-importing countries is about 8810 Swiss Francs. Secondly, as Gangjee points out, collective and certification marks are of "particular interest because the parties involved have voluntarily agreed to share the name in question"[1029] Therefore, they must share the cost of registration their collective and certification marks. For instance, 5200 members of the 16 apple-producing cooperatives working in Valle di Non and Valle di Sole (Italy) use the collective mark MELINDA.[1030] Clearly, if each of those members were to pay their share for registration of their collective mark, the registration fee would be greatly decreased.

To overcome the challenge of high fees for registration of trademarks, countries may offer specific mechanisms or financial packages to help TKHs. For example, they may:

- reduce the costs associated with the registration of trademarks,
- establish a special fund, grants or loans to TKHs to register their TK-RS,
- appoint professional trademark lawyers to provide free legal services to TKHs,
- reform tax laws so that TKHs could generate revenue from their trademarks,
- reduce taxes on TKHs' trademarked commercial products or services.[1031]

1028 Popova-Gosart (n 117) Pages 62 and 63.

1029 Fhima Ilanah Simon, 'Introduction' in Fhima Ilanah Simon (ed), *Trade Mark Law and Sharing Names: Exploring Use of the Same Mark by Multiple Undertakings* (Edward Elgar 2009) Page 6.

1030 WIPO, *Making a Mark – An Introduction to Trademarks for Small and Medium-Sized Enterprises* (n 941) Page 18.

1031 WIPO, *WIPO IP Handbook* (n 450) Page 167.

Although these solutions might help TKHs; but one should recall that the most TKHs are located in the developing and least-developed countries which have inadequate financial resources to provide the above-mentioned services to their TKHs.

Finally, positive protection might have a contrary effect on TK-RS. As already explained, most of the payments are related to registration fees, but the consequences of failure to pay the renewal fee are severe. Avoiding payment of a renewal fee will be deemed abandonment of the trademark. When a mark is abandoned by its owner "it may be adopted and used by another entity, who in doing so gains rights that are enforceable against others."[1032] In such a case third parties may adopt abandoned TK-RS. Also, they could prevent TKHs from using their own TK-RS.

4.1.2.5 *Outcome of Challenges*

Many TKHs have registered their TK-RS, but the number of unregistered marks of TKHs is considerably higher than the number that is registered.[1033] Besides, in the face of the above-mentioned challenges, positive protection offered by trademark law seems to be inadequate to provide full protection of TK-RS. As Frankel states, the trademark registration system has not been designed to protect TK-RS. This system is problematic in its entirety and cannot meet the TKHs' expectations for protection of TK. TKHs are only able to exploit this system occasionally when they see it as useful and convenient.[1034] In the meantime, failures must be noted and solved – there is a need for mechanisms to prevent trademarks being granted if they confer unfair and unjustified rights over TKHs' marks and signs "through efforts to 'exclude' certain material from trade mark registration."[1035] For instance the Andean Community, in Decision 486, stipulates that those sign may not be registered as marks which consists of:

> the names of indigenous Afro-American or local communities, or the names, words, letters, characters or signs used to distinguish their goods or services or the manner of their processing, or which constitute an

1032 David A Burge, *Patent and Trademark Tactics and Practice* (John Wiley & Sons 1999) Page 150.

1033 Pires de Carvalho (n 158) Page 258.

1034 Frankel (n 788) Pages 442–443.

1035 Johanna Gibson, 'Knowledge and Other Values – Intellectual Property and the Limitations for Traditional Knowledge' in Guido Westkamp (ed), *Emerging Issues in Intellectual Property: Trade, Technology and Market Freedom: Essays in Honour of Herchel Smith* (Edward Elgar Publishing 2007) Page 318.

> expression of their culture or practice, except where the application is filed by the community itself or with its express consent.[1036]

Therefore, defensive protection needs to be exploited as much as possible for supplementary protection of TK-RS at the national and international levels as discussed in the following section.

4.2 *Defensive Protection*

As already explained, TKHs are concerned about unauthorized commercial use and registration of the TK-RS as trademarks by parties other than themselves. Although some Aboriginal businesses and organizations have registered trademarks relating to traditional symbols and names, the number of unregistered trademarks used by Aboriginal businesses and organizations is considerably greater than those that are registered.

Therefore, in the context of trademark law, defensive protection must aim to prevent people other than TKHs from being granted IPRS over TK-RS. In other words, the defensive protection mechanism must be employed as a tool to reject applications of non-TKHs regarding registration of elements of TK-RS and to refuse to register them as trademarks. In principle, the mark applied for international registration can only be rejected for reasons justifiable under the Paris Convention. This has been emphasized in the Madrid System, which stipulates that "any such refusal can be based only on the grounds which would apply, under the Paris Convention."[1037] Here the question that emerges is whether these grounds under the Paris Convention are capable of providing a defensible basis for refusing an application for registration of a TK-RS as trademark. To answer this question, the applicability of these grounds is surveyed as bellow.

4.2.1 Defensive Protection Regarding Certain Signs and Symbols

Symbolism in the PCs has been passed down from generation to generation. The PCs' symbols also used to be considered as distinctive marks of the PCs in the course of trade. Examples of these symbols include the resting eagle as the sign for high-mindedness of the spirit; the paradise bird as the sign for heaven; the cypress tree as the sign for life after death; the iris as the sign for religious

---

1036 The Andean Community, 'Decision 486 – Common Intellectual Property Regime' (World Intellectual Property Organization 2001) WIPO Doc WIPO/GRTKF/IC/1/11 Annex IV Chapter I(136)(g).

1037 Madrid Agreement Article 5(1).

freedom; the *mihrab* as the sign for the gateway to paradise; the hyacinth as the sign for regeneration; and the comb as the sign for cleanliness.[1038]

The Paris Convention, in Article 6ter, mandates that Member States refuse or invalidate 'registration' or 'use' of some specific signs and symbols as marks or elements of marks. These specific signs and symbols include "armorial bearings, flags, and other State emblems, of the countries of the Union, official signs and hallmarks indicating control and warranty adopted by them, and any imitation from a heraldic point of view."[1039] For instance, application for registration of the Vietnamese flag for marketing Vietnamese silk weave shall be refused.[1040] Also, "armorial bearings, flags, other emblems, abbreviations, and names, of international intergovernmental organizations of which one or more countries of the Union are members."[1041] However, the signs and symbols that are already the subject of other international agreements in force are exempt from this Article.[1042] For example, The Nairobi Treaty obliges its Member States to refuse or invalidate the registration of any marks that contain Olympic symbols and prevent the unauthorized use of the symbol for commercial purposes.[1043]

It seems that the purpose of Article 6ter is not to create a right to claim industrial property in favor of a country or an intergovernmental organization in relation to distinctive marks, but rather to prevent the use of those marks as trademarks in industrial and commercial activities.[1044] Such an exclusion was maintained because it would affect that state's rights to control the use of symbols and signs of their identity and sovereignty.[1045] This type of prohibition might be considered as a defensive protection that could prevent registration and use of TK-RS.

For the implementation of the provisions of Article 6ter, a process has been established. According to this process, official signs, symbols, emblems, abbreviations and names for which protection is sought must to be communicated to the other States party to the Paris Convention through the International

1038 Ali Esmaili, 'Understanding Symbolism in Persian & Other Antique Rugs' (*Esmaili Rugs and Antiques*, 14 October 2016) <https://www.esmailirugs.com/index.php?dispatch=pages.view&product_id=75> accessed 17 November 2018.

1039 Paris Convention Article 6ter(1)(a).

1040 ITC and WIPO (n 869) Page 76.

1041 Paris Convention Article 6ter(1)(b).

1042 *ibid.*

1043 Nairobi Treaty Article 3.

1044 WIPO, *WIPO IP Handbook* (n 450) Page 253.

1045 SCT Secretariat, 'Article 6ter of the Paris Convention: Legal and Administrative Aspects' (World Intellectual Property Organization 2005) WIPO Doc SCT/15/3 Page 4.

Bureau of WIPO.[1046] This process of Article 6ter is also incorporated into the TRIPS Agreement by Article 2(1), which requires WTO members to "comply with Articles 1 through 12, and Article 19, of the Paris Convention (1967)." Besides, Article 63(2) of the TRIPS Agreement directly refers to Article 6ter of the Paris Convention:

> The Council shall also consider in this connection any action required regarding notifications pursuant to the obligations under this Agreement stemming from the provisions of Article 6ter of the Paris Convention (1967).

In this regard, Article 3 of the WTO-WIPO Cooperation Agreement stipulates that the International Bureau of WIPO should administer the procedures regarding Article 6ter of the Paris Convention:

> The procedures relating to communication of emblems and transmittal of objections under the TRIPS Agreement shall be administered by the International Bureau in accordance with the procedures applicable under Article 6ter of the Paris Convention (1967).[1047]

In accordance with the Madrid Agreement and its protocol, documentary evidence which approved the use of certain elements such as armorial bearings incorporated in marks, are legitimate shall be exempted from any reclamation or certification.[1048] In other words, in first place, use of such elements shall be legitimate.

At the national level, according to the abolished "law of the registration of marks and inventions" of Iran, "the flag of Iran, and any other flag that the Iranian Government prohibits its use as a trademark, the mark, …, badges, and symbols of the Iranian government" and "the marks of official institutions such as … Red Cross, and so on" were not registrable.[1049] This rule was later repeated in the industrial property law of 2007, in which marks are not registerable if:

> [i]t is identical with, or is an imitation of or contains as an element, an armorial bearing, flag or other emblem, a name or abbreviation or

1046 Paris Convention Article 6ter(3)(a).

1047 Agreement Between the World Intellectual Property Organization and the World Trade Organization 1995 (35 ILM 754 (entered into force 1 January 1996)) Article 3(1)(a).

1048 Madrid Agreement Article 5bis; and Madrid Protocol article 5bis.

1049 Iran – Law on Registration of Marks and Inventions Article 5(d).

> initials of the name of, or official sign or hallmark adopted by, any State, intergovernmental organization created under an international convention, unless authorized by the competent authority of that State or organization.[1050]

Although it seems that defensive mechanisms could be exploited to protect TK-RS, there are problems in relying on exclusions of TK-RS from the registration system under the prohibition laid down in Article 6ter. Firstly, this prohibition does not apply to the rights which had already been acquired over signs in good faith in a Member State of the Paris Convention.[1051] This means the TK-RS which have already been misused may no longer be the subject of protection. Secondly, prohibition under Article 6ter could only be applied when the mark in question is going to be registered and used on goods and services of the same kind as the signs and hallmarks indicating control and warranty are used for.[1052] In other words, even if TK-RS could be communicated to WIPO and other Member States of the Paris Convention, they might only prevent similar marks in the same class. Thirdly, the official signs and hallmarks indicating control and warranty under Article 6ter(1)(a) might be protected only if the states themselves adopt them. The adoption by the lower public bodies, institutions and organizations or public non-governmental bodies would be inadequate to protect those signs and symbols.[1053] Consequently, TK-RS which are adopted by the TKHs could not be covered by this Article. Fourthly, Article 6ter includes a mechanism according to which Member States of the Paris Convention may object to such prohibition.[1054]

Despite the above-mentioned obstacles to the defensive protection of TK-RS at the international level under Article 6ter, some national laws exploit such prohibition either through a *sui-generis* law or within their trademark law. For instance, the Swiss Federal Act on the Protection of the Swiss Coat of Arms and Other Public Signs is specifically dedicated to protecting the Swiss cross, coat of arms, flag, emblems and Swiss national figurative or word signs including national symbols such as Swiss landmarks, heroic figures, sites or monuments at the federal, cantonal and communal levels.[1055] And, according to the United

1050 Iran – Patents, Industrial Designs and Trademarks Registration Law Article 32(d).

1051 Paris Convention Article 6ter(1)(c).

1052 *ibid Article 6ter(2).*

1053 Bodenhausen (n 759) Pages 96–97; and SCT Secretariat, 'Article 6ter of the Paris Convention: Legal and Administrative Aspects' (n 1045) Page 4.

1054 Paris Convention Article 6ter(4).

1055 Swiss – Federal Act on the Protection of the Swiss Coat of Arms and Other Public Signs 2013 (232/21 (entered into force 1 January 2017)) Section 1.

States Trademark Act, the USPTO may refuse registration or cancel the registration of a mark if it is confusingly identical to Native Americans' flags, coat of arms, emblems, or devices of Native American tribes who are officially recognized federally or by any states. This prohibition does not include words:[1056]

> (b) Consists of or comprises the flag or coat of arms or other insignia of the United States, or of any State or municipality, or of any foreign nation, or any simulation thereof.[1057]

Unlike the Swiss Federal Act, which is solely focused on national protection of Swiss nationals' signs and symbols, the United States approach extends protection not only to American Indians and tribes but also to TKHs worldwide. Therefore, a useful strategy for protection of the PCs could be a bilateral agreement between Iran and the USA for protection of TK-RS to prevent registration of PCs' marks in the USA.

4.2.2 Defensive Protection against Deceptive Marks

As a principle, marks must not be misleading to the public[1058] and the most fundamentals goal of trademark law is to protect consumers' rights by preventing the supply of deceptive or misleading goods and services on the market.[1059] The Fair Trading Act of 1986 in New Zealand,[1060] for example, provides important protections for trademark owners, especially against misleading or deceptive conduct related to the use and application of trademarks. This includes penalties for forgery of trademarks or false application or use that could mislead or deceive consumers. The application of these provisions varies depending on the specific circumstances of each case, making the law flexible enough to address a range of situations concerning counterfeit goods. Despite this critical role of the legal regime concerning trademarks, challenges persist regarding the use of similar marks that may leverage the reputation or distinctive characteristics of these carpets. Such practices may result in consumer confusion regarding the authenticity, origin, production methods, or stylistic features of the goods. PCs along with a few other products such as Persian Caviar are the most important brands of Iranian products that have found a

1056 USPTO, 'Report on the Official Insignia of Native American Tribes' (United States Patent and Trademark Office 1999) Pages 24–26.
1057 The US – Trademark Act Section 2(b).
1058 WIPO, *WIPO IP Handbook* (n 450) Page 111.
1059 Popova-Gosart (n 117) Page 41.
1060 New Zealand – Fair Trading Act 1986.

place in the world markets. This reputation has led competitors to sell their carpets under the PCs brands.[1061]

Separately, the terms 'Persian Carpet' and 'Persian Rug' have been observed in trademark registrations or commercial use by certain private entities (see Figure 13 and Figure 14) that are not recognized as TKHs. The use of the term 'Persian' in these contexts may influence consumer perceptions concerning the authenticity and traditional characteristics of carpets that are not produced in Iran.

Image	Name	Class	Current status	Number	Owners	Filing date
Persian carpet	PERSIAN CARPET	27	Not update yet	22769860	苏州波联商贸有限公司	2017-02-07
波斯居鲁士地毯 Cyrus Persian Carpet	波斯居鲁士地毯 CYRUS PERSIAN CARPET	27	Waiting for registration certificate	17937880	杭州居鲁士地毯有限公司	2015-09-21

FIGURE 13 Example of Persian carpet trademarks filed in China

FIGURE 14 Example of Persian rug manufacturers produced in India

Therefore, some measures must be taken to prohibit producers from copying and making carpets and selling them using marks labelled as PCs.

Deceptive marks have harmful effects on fair competition and on consumer' rights, and it is a requirement that a sign must not deceive the public and it must not possess a misleading character.[1062] In this regard, according to the Paris Convention, when a trademark is likely to deceive the public it may be denied registration or invalidated.[1063] Also, in accordance with the TRIPS Agreement its Member States "shall refuse or invalidate the registration of trademarks which contain or consist of a geographical indication with respect to goods not originating in the territory indicated," if such use of the indication

1061 Esmail Ghaderi, 'فروش فرش چینی و هندی به نام فرش ایرانی (Selling Chinese and Indian Carpets under the name of Persian carpets)' *Iranian Students' News Agency* (7 July 2016).

1062 WIPO, *WIPO IP Handbook* (n 450) Page 71.

1063 Paris Convention Article 6^{quinquies}(B)(3).

would mislead the public as to the true place of origin.[1064] This provision was incorporated into the European Union Community Trademark law in which "trade marks which are of such a nature as to deceive the public, for instance as to the nature, quality or geographical origin of the goods or services," "shall not be registered or, if registered, shall be liable to be declared invalid."[1065] Iran's Trademark law follows the same wording. In accordance with this law, a trademark which is "likely to mislead the public or trade centres, in particular as regards the geographical origin of the goods or services concerned or their nature or characteristics" is not registerable.[1066]

Regarding the use of PCs' marks by foreign competitors, although these competitors correctly declare the place of carpet production, it seems that they attempt to mislead the consumer by attribution to their products of PCs' nature and quality, which is clearly against the international trademark law. To avoid such misappropriation the USA law has established a specific Act. The Indian Arts and Crafts Act of 1990 (IACA)[1067] updated the original 1935 Act to enhance the Indian Arts and Crafts Board's authority to protect Indian artists against UC arising from misrepresented arts and crafts claiming to be Native-made. This law includes more stringent criminal penalties and new civil remedies. The IACA's purpose is to protect and promote authentic Indian arts and crafts, support Indian American self-sufficiency, and safeguard consumers by ensuring the authenticity of goods marketed as Native-made.[1068] The 2000 amendment to the IACA, known as the Indian Arts and Crafts Enforcement Act, improved its enforcement by allowing Indian tribes, organizations, and individuals to initiate civil actions. It broadened the scope of liability to include manufacturers and wholesalers along with retailers, further protecting the economic and cultural integrity of Indian arts and crafts. The IACA thus serves to protect and promote Indian arts and crafts, promote Indian self-sufficiency, protect Native American culture and know how, and protect consumers. The original law of 1935 only allowed criminal penalties for false advertising of Native American crafts, but no one was ever charged. The 1990 update allowed the government and even individuals to sue violators, in addition to enabling criminal charges to be pressed. Since then, there have been a couple of federal criminal cases and a handful of lawsuits, most of which never went beyond

1064 TRIPS Agreement Article 22(3).

1065 See: Directive 2015/2436 Article 4(1)(g); and EU Trademark Regulation Article 7(1)(g).

1066 Iran – Patents, Industrial Designs and Trademarks Registration Law Article 32(c).

1067 The US – Indian Arts and Crafts Act of 1990 as amended as at September 2003 1990 (PL 101-644).

1068 Daphne Zografos, *Intellectual Property and Traditional Cultural Expressions* (Edward Elgar Publishing 2010) Pages 201–203.

a district court, with only one reaching a higher court.[1069] *The Navajo Nation v. Urban Outfitters*[1070] case was a landmark legal battle centered around IPRs and cultural appropriation. The Navajo Nation, the largest federally recognized Native American tribe, sued the popular retail chain Urban Outfitters and its subsidiaries in 2012. The case involves a trademark infringement and dilution claim filed by the Navajo Nation against Urban Outfitters. The lawsuit was initiated because Urban Outfitters used the 'Navajo' name and patterns associated with the Navajo culture in their clothing and accessory products without permission. The basis of this lawsuit was the company's extensive use of the term 'Navajo' to market and sell various products, including clothing, jewellery, and flasks, which often bore no connection to authentic Navajo designs or craftsmanship. The Navajo Nation, which holds trademarks for the 'Navajo' name, argued that Urban Outfitters' actions violated the Indian Arts and Crafts Act of 1990, under which it is illegal to offer or display for sale products in manner that falsely suggests they are Indian products:

> It is unlawful to offer or display for sale or sell any good, with or without a Government trademark, in a manner that falsely suggests it is Indian produced, an Indian product, or the product of a particular Indian or Indian tribe or Indian arts and crafts organization, resident within the United States.[1071]

This usage misled consumers about the origin of the products, which could potentially harm the reputation of Navajo arts and crafts. The case highlighted issues surrounding cultural appropriation and the commercial use of indigenous cultural elements in fashion. Additionally, the Navajo Nation claimed trademark infringement and dilution, asserting that the company's use of the 'Navajo' name damaged the reputation and value of authentic Navajo-made goods. The case dragged on for years, with legal arguments about fair use, abandonment of trademark rights, and the scope of protection for tribal names. Ultimately, in 2016, the two parties reached a confidential settlement, the details of which were not disclosed to the public.[1072] As a complementary step "U.S. law prevents the registration of a mark that is confusingly similar to

1069 *ibid Page 211.*

1070 *Navajo Nation v Urban Outfitters, Inc* (2019) 379 F Supp 3d 783.

1071 The US – Indian Arts and Crafts Act of 1990 as amended as at September 2003 Sec 1159(a).

1072 Semina Choi, 'Indigenous Intellectual Property and the Law: Navajo Nation v. Urban Outfitters' (2018) 1 Culture 91.

official insignia of any Native American tribe."[1073] Databases are extremely useful in these situations, aiding trademark offices in their evaluations. For example, the USPTO maintains a specific database for Native American tribal insignias. This database is used by examiners to ensure that any trademark application that falsely implies an association with a person or group is rejected on a case-by-case basis.[1074] Moreover, the USPTO may refuse or cancel at any time registration of a mark which may consist of a false suggestion of a connection between the mark and persons, institutions, beliefs or symbols.[1075]

4.2.3 Marks Contrary to Public Order or Morality

In some scenarios, governments may revoke trademarks due to concerns about or violations of public morality. In 2002, New Zealand introduced the Trade Marks Act, which disallows the registration of trademarks that could offend significant community sections, including the Māori. The legislation enables individuals who are 'culturally aggrieved' to seek invalidation of registered marks. Additionally, it established the Māori Trade Marks Advisory Committee to guide the trademarks commissioner on potential offense caused by trademarks featuring Māori symbols and language. Committee members are required to possess expertise in Māori culture and protocols.[1076] In Europe, both Article 7(1)(f) of the EU Trade Mark Regulation[1077] and Article 4(1)(f) of the EU Trade Marks Directive[1078] prohibit the registration of trademarks that conflict with public policy or accepted principles of morality. However, court practices have varied, often allowing or denying registration of cultural heritage items based mainly on their distinctiveness.[1079] The EFTA Court's ruling in the *Vigeland* case[1080] is a significant marker for the interpretation

1073 Coenraad J Visser, 'Making Intellectual Property Laws Work for Traditional Knowledge' in J Michael Finger and Philip Schuler (eds), *Poor People's Knowledge, Promoting Intellectual Property in Developing Countries* (The World Bank and Oxford University Press 2004) Page 217.

1074 Justin Hughes, 'Traditional Knowledge, Cultural Expression, and the Siren's Call of Property' (2012) 49 San Diego Law Review 1215, Page 1233.

1075 The US – Trademark Act Section 2(a).

1076 James AR Nafziger, Robert Kirkwood Paterson and Alison Dundes Renteln, *Cultural Law: International, Comparative, and Indigenous* (Cambridge University Press 2010) Pages 650–651.

1077 EU Trademark Regulation.

1078 Directive 2015/2436.

1079 Mira Burri, 'The Protection of Cultural Heritage by Trademarks' in Irini Stamatoudi (ed), *Research Handbook on Intellectual Property and Cultural Heritage* (Edward Elgar Publishing 2022) Page 66.

1080 *Municipality of Oslo ("Vigeland")* [2017] EFTA Court Case E-5/16.

of public order and morality in trademark law, especially concerning cultural heritage material. In this case, the court evaluated whether artworks by Gustav Vigeland, which had entered the public domain, could be registered as trademarks by the Municipality of Oslo. The court determined that such registration could contravene public order or accepted principles of morality under certain conditions. It emphasized that while trademark law typically provides exclusive rights, these should not impede public access to significant cultural works. The court opined that the safeguarding of the public domain represents a fundamental societal interest. It argued that the exclusivity granted by trademark law should not be used to unduly extend control over cultural expressions that have lapsed into the public domain. This stance introduces a nuanced approach to trademark law, aligning it with broader societal interests and acknowledging the intrinsic value of cultural and historical works. Moreover, the court clarified the application of public order and morality in rejecting trademark applications for cultural signs. It set a precedent that only under circumstances posing a genuine and serious threat to fundamental societal values, such as protecting the public domain, should such works be denied trademark registration. This decision marks a shift towards incorporating public policy considerations into the trademark registration process, potentially influencing future applications involving culturally significant symbols.[1081] Another example is recent disputes in the United States, which have underscored the conflict between trademark protection, individual or group identity, and the concept of freedom of expression. Unlike patent and copyright laws, Section 2(a) of Lanham Act prohibits the registration of trademarks that are deemed "immoral, deceptive, or scandalous matter; or matter which may disparage or falsely suggest a connection with persons, living or dead, institutions, beliefs, or national symbols, or bring them into contempt, or disrepute;" In 1992, Native American leaders challenged the sport team 'Redskins' trademark registration at the USPTO, arguing it was derogatory, supported by evidence of its usage as an ethnic slur, and condemnation by Native groups. By 1999, the USPTO had canceled the trademarks, but the team successfully appealed in the D.C. federal court, citing decades of use and registration prior to the complaint, which led to the dismissal of the case due to significant delay. However, in 2014, the issue resurfaced when another group of Native petitioners succeeded in having the trademarks canceled under the Lanham Act. The team challenged the decision again, arguing that the disparagement

1081 Martin Senftleben, 'No Trademark Protection for Artworks in the Public Domain – A Practical Guide to the Application of Public Order and Morality as Grounds for Refusal' (2021) 71 Journal of European and International Law 3, Pages 3–6.

clause violated the First Amendment, a claim upheld by the Supreme Court. As a result, the 'Redskins' trademark registrations were ultimately reinstated, despite ongoing controversy over the term's offensiveness.[1082]

As explained in Chapter 2 of this study, TK has various faces. It might be tangible or intangible and is mostly a combination of the two. In fact, the tangible and intangible characters of the TK are so entwined that they cannot be separated.[1083] A good example of tangible expression of TK is hand-woven rugs in which intangible characters are deeply incorporated. Rugs in Iran as an original and rich art have been one of the manifestations of the use of signs and symbols. It can be said that the PC is a symbol of itself, which has deep meanings behind its beautiful appearance.[1084] The PC designers, while paying attention to the appearances, size and forms of the hand-woven carpets, influenced by their religious beliefs have been attempting to enrich the content of the designs and praise the Iranian and Islamic principles.[1085] Symbols such as the Tree of Life of Persians and the Persian myth of Ahuramazda,[1086] or Hand for prayer and *mihrab* for the gateway to Paradise are some examples of sign of beliefs incorporated into the PCs.[1087] In this regard, "defensive strategies might also be used to protect sacred cultural manifestations, such as sacred symbols or words, from being registered as trademarks."[1088] The term 'sacred' in this context means "any expression of TK that symbolizes or pertains to religious and spiritual beliefs, practices or customs."[1089] Although it is up to the TKHs to decide whether their TK is sacred or not, the sacred signs and symbols might

1082 Fandiño Mariana Bernal, 'Controversial Trademarks: A Comparative Analysis' in Jamar Steven D. and Lateef Mtima (eds), *The Cambridge Handbook of Intellectual Property and Social Justice* (Cambridge University Press & Assessment 2024) Page 455.

1083 WIPO, *Intellectual Property and Genetic Resources, Traditional Knowledge and Traditional Cultural Expressions* (n 231) Page 15.

1084 Mohammad Afrough, 'نمادگرایی ونشانه شناسی در فرش ایرانی (Symbolism and Semiotics in Persian Carpets)' (2011) 10 Journal of The Iranian Studies 13, Page 15.

1085 Amirhossein Chitsazan and Mohammad Reza Pour Jafar, 'تاثیرپذیری طراحی فرش کاشان از نمادها (The Influence of Symbols on the Design of Kashan Carpet)' (2004) 40 & 41 *Tandis*; quoted in: Afrough (n 1084) Page 21.

1086 JE Cirlot, 'Dictionary of Symbols' 451 Pages 189 and 356.

1087 Esmaili (n 1038).

1088 WIPO, *Intellectual Property and Genetic Resources, Traditional Knowledge and Traditional Cultural Expressions* (n 231) Page 22.

1089 Doris Estelle Long, 'The Impact of Foreign Investment on Indigenous Culture: An Intellectual Property Perspective' (1997) 23 North Carolina Journal of International Law and Commercial Regulation 229; quoted in: Daniel J Gervais, 'Spiritual but Not Intellectual? The Protection of Sacred Intangible Traditional Knowledge' (2003) 11 Cardozo Journal of International and Comparative Law 467, Page 469.

be commercialized by the TKHs themselves or by third parties.[1090] The TKHs have a right to expect their religious and spiritual values and practices to be respected.[1091] To avoid commercialization of sacred trademarks by third parties, TKHs may use trademark law, which provides the grounds for refusal of registration, or invalidation of the registration of marks that are contrary to morality or public order[1092] while religious orientation is also concerned with morality.[1093] In this regard, according to the Paris Convention, marks that are "contrary to morality or public order" may be denied from registration.[1094] This provision is incorporated in the European trademark law in accordance with "trade marks which are contrary to public policy or to accepted principles of morality."[1095] In many countries, national laws include comparable rules.[1096] For instance, in Iran, a mark is not registerable If "it is contrary to Rules of Sharia, public order or morality."[1097] In Switzerland, signs contrary to public policy and morality are excluded from protection under trademark law.[1098]

The marks containing TKHs' religious symbols are examples of a mark contrary to public order[1099] that "would cause offence or offensive behaviour;"[1100] and 'culturally offensive' marks could be prevented from unauthorized registration because of being contrary to public order and morality.[1101] In this regard, the New Zealand legislation, addresses Māori concerns over the possibility of registration of trademarks which consist of Māori signs or those that are offensive to Māori. In accordance with the Act 'the Commissioner of Trade Marks'

1090 IGC-GRTKF Secretariat, 'List and Brief Technical Explanation of Various Forms in Which Traditional Knowledge May Be Found' (n 187) Pages 10–11.
1091 Indigenous and Tribal Peoples Convention Article 5(a).
1092 IGC-GRTKF Secretariat, 'Draft Gap Analysis on the Protection of Traditional Cultural Expressions' (n 594) Page 23.
1093 Ursula Goodenough, 'Naturalizing Morality' in Charles R McManis (ed), *Biodiversity and the Law: Intellectual Property, Biotechnology and Traditional Knowledge* (Earthscan 2007) Page 35.
1094 Paris Convention Article 6quinquies(B).
1095 Directive 2015/2436 Article 4(1)(f).; EU Trademark Regulation Article 7(1)(f). This provision was incorporated on the older version of European trademark law in the Article 3(1)(f) and (g) Directive 2008/95/EC and Article 7(f) and (g) Council Regulation (EC) No. 40/94.
1096 IGC-GRTKF Secretariat, 'Draft Gap Analysis on the Protection of Traditional Cultural Expressions' (n 594) Pages 18–19.
1097 Iran – Patents, Industrial Designs and Trademarks Registration Law Article 32(b).
1098 Swiss – Federal Act on the Protection of Trade Marks and Indications of Source Article 2(d).
1099 Bodenhausen (n 759) Page 116.
1100 Jacob, Alexander and Fisher (n 975) Page 84.
1101 WIPO, *Intellectual Property Needs and Expectations of Traditional Knowledge Holders* (n 166) Page 224.

is allowed to consider whether registration or use of a mark is probably offensive to a significant section of the community, including Māori. To execute this function, the Commissioner takes the advice of the advisory committee whose members must be qualified persons with knowledge of *te ao* Māori (Māori worldview) and *tikanga* Māori (Māori protocol and culture).[1102] For example, any mark including the word '*Papatūānuku*' which is an important element of Māori culture as *atua* or *tipuna* (god or spiritual ancestor) could be counted as offensive to New Zealand's indigenous peoples.[1103]

Experience in countries such as New Zealand may show that the defensive protection of sacred marks could be considered as appropriate and adequate to meet TKHs' expectations. However, it would seem that such a conclusion is not accurate. At present, the notion of what is contrary to morality or public order is strongly dependent on the domestic laws and regulations of the countries. As Gupta suggests, names and signs associated with religious beliefs should be respected not only domestically, but also a strong international agreement must establish means to prevent them from being used in a disrespectful manner.[1104] To consolidate his claims, he also cites Michael Blakeney's initiative. Blakeney suggests "perhaps as we have trademarks and service marks we may create a bunch of holy signs that are restricted to use by particular communities or their representatives, or those that are permitted by them." According to Blakeney, such a provision will lead to a remarkable mental and spiritual relaxation for TKHs who feels aggrieved because of unauthorized exploitation of their sacred signs and symbols.[1105] Therefore, both Blakeney and Gupta believe that as well as domestic defensive protection an international defensive protection system could be used to prevent registration of offensive marks.

Despite the above-mentioned approach, it should be noted that even such an international instrument does not seem sufficient to protect sacred marks beyond national borders. In this regard, the most compelling evidence is the domestic character of public order and morality. It is not easy to include examples of public order and morality in the international trademarks law. As Pflüger points out "public order means those provisions that

1102 New Zealand – Trade Marks Act 2002 Parts 1(3)(c), 2(17)(c), 5(178) and 5(179)(2).

1103 New Zealand Intellectual Property Office (n 661) Page 11.

1104 IGC-GRTKF Secretariat, 'Draft Gap Analysis on the Protection of Traditional Cultural Expressions' (n 594) Page 23.

1105 Michael Blakeney, *Intellectual Property Aspects of Ethnobiology* (Sweet & Maxwell 1999); quoted in: Gupta, *WIPO-UNEP Study on the Role of Intellectual Property Rights in the Sharing of Benefits Arising from the Use of Biological Resources and Associated Traditional Knowledge* (n 363) Page 70, Footnote 40.

are not mere 'rules of national trademark law,' but are essential principles of domestic legislation."[1106] On the other hand, the way in which these rules are interpreted and read is dependent on the judgement and experience of the employees of the Intellectual Property Offices and the judges of the courts.[1107] While such failures must not be discounted, defensive protection of sacred marks such as Māori in foreign territories seems almost impossible. It is up to the foreign trademark offices to decide based on their respective countries' national policy if they will expand defensive protection to TK-RS and refuse registration of offensive marks on the grounds of public order or morality of the designated countries. Different legal systems refuse trademark registration on specific accounts. In the European Union and the EFTA, trademarks can be refused registration on the grounds of public policy and accepted principles of morality, which are considered absolute reasons for refusal. The United States, under the Lanham Act, traditionally prohibited the registration of scandalous and disparaging trademarks. However, landmark decisions the United States Supreme Court deemed such restrictions unconstitutional, asserting that they infringed upon freedom of speech rights protected by the First Amendment. Consequently, from 2017 onwards, even offensive trademarks are protected under the First Amendment in the U.S.[1108]

4.2.4 Defensive Protection of the PCs' Well-Known Marks

For a professional expert, distinguishing PCs from other oriental rugs[1109] is easy. They use two lines of detailed surveys. Firstly, they examine the colours and designs, and then they review the technical details of weave and of finish.[1110] But, for the public, knowing whether they are really buying the noble and original PCs depends on the trust in the well-known brand of PCs on the carpet. As mentioned in the first chapter of this study, for many centuries, PCs have been well-known worldwide for their unique quality and beauty. As a French

1106 Pflüger (n 896) Page 263.

1107 IGC-GRTKF Secretariat, 'Draft Gap Analysis on the Protection of Traditional Cultural Expressions' (n 594) Page 23.

1108 Jeremy N Sheff, 'Misappropriation-Based Trademark Liability in Comparative Perspective' in Irene Calboli and Jane C Ginsburg (eds), *The Cambridge Handbook of International and Comparative Trademark Law* (Cambridge University Press 2020) Page 459.

1109 Oriental Carpets are the carpets and rugs which are from anywhere in Asia. See: KK Goswami, 'Developments in Handmade Carpets: Design and Manufacture' in KK Goswami (ed), *Advances in Carpet Manufacture* (Woodhead Publishing Limited 2009) Page 193.

1110 'The Eastern rug world of to-day is conveniently regarded as consisting of six main groups or divisions, as follows: Persia, China, Central Asia, Caucasia, Türkiye and India.' See: CJ Delabère May, *How to Identify Persian Rugs and Other Oriental Rugs: A Text Book for Collectors and Students* (Bell 1952) Pages 13 and 15.

officer writes in his report of 1845 "the reputation of the Persian carpets is not only due to the design's beauty but also the elegance of the wool and the good quality of the herbal colours."[1111] Undoubtedly, PCs and their related marks are very famous, but the question is if PCs and their affiliated signs are eligible to enjoy protection under well-known (famous) marks regulations.

Article 6bis of the Paris Convention requires its Member States to protect well-known marks without defining what well-known marks are. But it does outline the rules intended to protect these well-known trademarks. According to the Paris Convention, if a trademark causes confusion with a well-known mark, countries may refuse or cancel the registration of that mark if it is used for identical or similar goods.[1112] Or, they might even prevent use of the conflicting trademark. It seems that the main purpose of this provision is to allow the well-known marks to enjoy the legal protection of trademarks law in the territory of other Member States of the convention, merely due to the reputation of well-known marks and regardless of the registration or use of a disputed mark in the given territories. The protection of well-known trademarks is based on the fact that a trademark which has a good reputation in a Member State would merit protection in the other Member States. The registration or use of a similar trademark – which in most cases turns into UC – may prejudice the public interests, because they could potentially mislead consumers in connection with the well-known trademarks.[1113]

The Paris Convention refers to well-known trademarks but nothing more. Accordingly, its Member States have the liberty to apply the provisions of Article 6bis to service marks. But those member states who are members of the WTO have no such freedom. Because the TRIPS Agreement – again without defining a well-known mark – stipulates "Article 6bis of the Paris Convention shall apply, mutatis mutandis, to services" and "to goods or services which are

1111 JP Ferrier, *Voyages et Aventures en Perse* (Dentu 1870) Pages 46–49; quoted in: Homa Nategh, ایران درراهیابی فرهنگی (*La Perse tiraillée entre deux cultures 1834–1848*) (2nd edn, Khavaran 2001) Page 226.

1112 Paris Convention Article 6bis(1): "The countries of the Union undertake, ex officio if their legislation so permits, or at the request of an interested party, to refuse or to cancel the registration, and to prohibit the use, of a trademark which constitutes a reproduction, an imitation, or a translation, liable to create confusion, of a mark considered by the competent authority of the country of registration or use to be well known in that country as being already the mark of a person entitled to the benefits of this Convention and used for identical or similar goods. These provisions shall also apply when the essential part of the mark constitutes a reproduction of any such well-known mark or an imitation liable to create confusion therewith."

1113 WIPO, *WIPO IP Handbook* (n 450) Page 256.

not similar to those in respect of which a trademark is registered."[1114] Thus, the TRIPS Agreement acknowledges application of the well-known marks' regulations on service marks and in the same manner, the TLT applies to marks relating to goods (trademarks) or services (service marks) or to both goods and services.[1115] As Cottier points out as an outcome of the TRIPS Agreement "the protection of well-known trademarks and of internationally well-known trademarks is enhanced."[1116]

Protection of well-known marks is also incorporated in the regional instruments. For instance, in accordance with the Andean Community Decision No. 486, "A well-known distinctive sign shall be protected from use or registration that is not authorized."[1117] Moreover, use of all or a part of a well-known distinctive sign or the reproduction, imitation, translation, or transliteration thereof, that may create confusion in respect of identical or similar businesses, activities, products or services to those to which it is applied, shall constitute unauthorized use of that distinctive sign.[1118] Also, in the EU, a trademark shall not be registered or, even after registration, shall be liable to be invalidated, if it is identical to a well-known mark, or because of its identity with, or similarity to a well-known mark in the concerned Member States. In the EU trademark regime, the concept of well-known marks is aligned with Article 6bis of the Paris Convention.[1119]

Member states of the Paris Convention undertake to legislate on well-known marks. In this regard, the Switzerland's trademark law follows the same approach as the EU trade marks law with respect to protection of well-known marks. Thus, a trade mark is excluded from protection if it is identical to "a trade mark that is well known in Switzerland within the meaning of Article 6bis of the Paris Convention."[1120] Under the Iranian trademark law, a mark is not registerable if under certain conditions it is identical with or confusingly similar to a well-known mark regardless of the goods and services they are associated with.[1121]

1114 TRIPS Agreement Article 16(2) & (3).

1115 TLT Article 2(2)(a).

1116 Thomas Cottier, 'Trade and Intellectual Property: Background Paper' in Thomas Cottier, Matthias Oesch and Thomas M Fischer (eds), *International Trade Regulation: Law and Policy in the WTO, the European Union and Switzerland: Cases, Materials and Comments* (Staempfli Publishers 2005) Page 926.

1117 The Andean Community (n 1036) Article 225.

1118 *ibid Article 226.*

1119 Directive 2015/2436 Article 5(2)(d); and EU Trademark Regulation Article 8(2)(c).

1120 Swiss – Federal Act on the Protection of Trade Marks and Indications of Source Article 3.

1121 Iran – Patents, Industrial Designs and Trademarks Registration Law Article 32(e) & (f).

The protection of well-known marks is justified due to the significant investments and efforts of the marks' proprietor for maintaining their goodwill and reputation, which are achieved over time regarding their distinctive and attractive goods and services in a given territory. Such an achievement should not be allowed to be at risk of misappropriation by competitors through the registration or use of a similar trademark and unfair competitive practices. At the same time, maintaining public interest and the need to avoid misleading the consumers requires stronger support for well-known marks.[1122] In particular, in the era of globalization, use of similar or identical marks for similar and identical goods and services will increase the risk of misleading the public as to the origin of the goods and services.[1123] Therefore, the main idea of such strong protection of the famous marks is preventing competitors from "unfair exploitation of the sign's prestige or fame."[1124] In practice, the protection provided for the well-known marks stretches beyond the regular protection of other marks. In this regard, firstly, well-known marks enjoy protection even if they are not registered with competent authorities or even if they have not been used in the territory of a given country.[1125] In fact, well-known marks doctrine as an exception to the territoriality principle, expands protection to the foreign marks.[1126] Secondly, despite other trademarks, even if the goods or services connected to a well-known mark are not sold or marketed in a country, that mark still can be considered and recognized as a well-known mark in that country due to its reputation and public knowledge.[1127] Thirdly, the protection of well-known marks applies not only to preventing the registration and use of trademarks which are confusingly associated with similar goods and services but also to those which are associated to non-identical or dissimilar goods and services.[1128] Thus, no one is allowed to use the well-known mark, if such use indicates some

1122 Abbott, Cottier and Gurry (n 367) Page 356.

1123 Pflüger (n 896) Page 243.

1124 The Andean Community (n 1036) Article 226(c).

1125 Abbott, Cottier and Gurry (n 367) Page 356.

1126 Graeme B Dinwoodie, 'Trademarks and Territory: Detaching Trademark Law from the Nation-State' (2004) 41 Houston Law Review 885, Page 888.

1127 WIPO, *WIPO IP Handbook* (n 450) Page 252.

1128 See: TRIPS Agreement Article 16(3): "Article 6bis of the Paris Convention (1967) shall apply, mutatis mutandis, to goods or services which are not similar to those in respect of which a trademark is registered."; Andean Decision No. 344 – Common Regime on Industrial Property 1993 (entered into force 1 January 1994) Article 226: 'Also constituting unauthorized use of a well-known distinctive sign is the use of all or of an essential part of that sign, or the reproduction, imitation, translation, or transliteration thereof, even if in respect of businesses, activities, goods, or services other than those to which that well-known distinctive sign is applied.'

kind of connection between the famous mark's owner and causes damage to their reputation.[1129]

It seems that the trademarks and in particular collective and certification marks of the PCs and affiliated TK-RS would have the opportunity to be recognized as famous marks due to the well-known marks doctrine, which in turn prevents the registration or use of misleading trademarks. There are many examples in this regard. For example, Handwoven Carpets of Tabriz, Isfahan, Bijar, Naein, Senneh, Kashan and the like are famous signs that could enjoy the benefits of the famous marks mechanism. Despite the above-mentioned advantages of the famous marks doctrine, there are barriers to relying on this mechanism for providing protection of PCs.

Article 6bis of the Paris Convention and Article 16 of the TRIPS Agreement neither provide a formal, clear or uniform definition of well-known marks nor set out standards to determine what constitutes a well-known mark.[1130] The Paris Convention stipulates that recognition of the well-known marks is subject to the approval of the authorities of the country of registration or use.[1131] This ambiguous notion of well-known marks as well as the role of diverse decision-making authorities worldwide leads to different interpretation and implementation by the competent authorities in different member states. For example, In *Wagner Asia Equipment LLC v. Borogchin LLC*, with respect to the fact that the Mongolian IP law lacks the legal mechanisms for determining a well-known mark, the court decided to invoke Article 16(2) of the TRIPS Agreement to determine if the trademark claimed by Wagner is famous. For satisfying the court, Wagner made a survey among the mining industry of Mongolia and beyond, which proved that its mark was well-known to them due to the aggressive marketing and advertising. Accordingly, the court decided to sustain the plaintiff's claim and to cancel the Borogchin trademark's registration.[1132] In a completely opposite approach, the USA courts, revoking constitutional doctrine, believe that U.S. national law takes precedence over the USA's international obligations for protection of the well-known

---

1129 Cottier, 'Chapter 22 – The Agreement on Trade-Related Aspects of Intellectual Property Rights' (n 397) Page 1087.

1130 In this regard, Swiss Federal Court in its decision discusses in details the different possible notions of well-known marks. See: *Federal Court Case 4C229/2003/lma*; quoted in: Pflüger (n 896) Page 244.

1131 Paris Convention Article 6bis(1).

1132 See: *Wagner Asia Equipment LLC v Borogchin LLC* [2001] The Sukhbaatar District Court Decision No. 452; quoted in: Tsogtbaatar Damdin, 'Chapter 75 – Mongolia' in Patrick FJ Macrory, Arthur E Appleton and Michael G Plummer (eds), *The World Trade Organization: Legal, Economic and Political Analysis*, vol 3 (Springer 2005) Pages 264–5.

marks under Article 6bis of the Paris Convention. The USA has imposed a long-established embargo against Cuban companies and their businesses and assets in the USA. 'Cubatabaco' is a Cuban producer of a widely known cigar product 'Cohiba' worldwide. 'General Cigar' is a USA-based cigar company which has registered the trademark 'Cohiba' at the USPTO. 'Cubatabaco' filed a case against 'General Cigar' based on its rights over the well-known mark of 'Cohiba.' Cubatabaco demanded the Court to cancel the registration of the trademark 'Cohiba' as well as a Court injunction to prevent 'General Cigar' from marketing cigars under the mark 'Cohiba.' In *Empresa Cubana del Tabaco v. General Cigar Co.* the USA Court of Appeal (2nd Circuit) decided to reject the plaintiff's claim for protection of its well-known mark. The Court justified its decision because such protection was prohibited by the embargo regulations against Cuban nationals and entities.[1133] These examples show how the well-known marks doctrine of the Paris Convention is treated differently by the national laws and authorities.

In 1999, a 'Joint Recommendation Concerning Provisions on the Protection of Well-Known Marks' was adopted by the General Assembly of WIPO. The Joint Recommendation suggests a non-exhaustive list of elements that might be used by authorities to determine if a mark can be established as a well-known mark. The main goal of the recommendation was consolidating and clarifying an international mechanism for protection of well-known marks based on the Paris Convention and the TRIPS Agreement.[1134] In practice, some countries have brought the rules of the Joint Recommendation into their own national legislation. For example, the Republic of India refers to the Joint Recommendation provisions explicitly to regulate its national provisions regarding protection of well-known marks.[1135] Also, the factors mentioned in the Joint Recommendation for determining whether a mark is well-known have been recognized by Switzerland's Judiciary System. The Swiss Federal Court in decision No. 4C.229/2003 states that the notion of well-known marks is to be interpreted uniformly in the light of Article 6bis of the Paris Convention and Article 16(2) and (3) of the TRIPS Agreement having regard to the WIPO Recommendation.[1136]

The joint recommendation consists of rules and procedures on:

1133 Abbott, Cottier and Gurry (n 367) Pages 364–5.

1134 Paris Convention Article 6bis; TRIPS Agreement Article 16(2) & (3).

1135 India – Trade Marks Act 1999 (Act No 47 of 1999 (entered into force on 15 September 2003)) Chapter II, 11(6) to (10).

1136 *Federal Court Case 4C.229/2003/lma* (n 1130); quoted in: Pflüger (n 896) Page 245.

- definitions including the definition of 'competent authority' whose duty is to determine whether a mark is a well-known mark, or for enforcing the protection of well-known marks;
- determination of whether a mark is a well-known mark in a Member State;
- scope of protection of well-known marks;
- conflict between marks and well-known marks;
- conflict between business identifiers;
- conflict between domain names.[1137]

As mentioned earlier, the Joint Recommendation provides a non-exhaustive list of factors for determination of well-known marks. In brief, these factors, which competent authorities shall take into consideration, include:

- "the degree of knowledge or recognition of the mark in the relevant sector of the public;
- the duration, extent and geographical area of any use of the mark;
- the duration, extent and geographical area of any promotion of the mark;
- including advertising or publicity and the presentation, at fairs or exhibitions, of the goods and/or services to which the mark applies;
- the duration and geographical area of any registrations, and/or any applications for registration, of the mark, to the extent that they reflect use or recognition of the mark;
- the record of successful enforcement of rights in the mark, in particular, the extent to which the mark was recognized as well known by competent authorities;"[1138]

In the same manner, Decision No. 344 of the Andean Community introduces some criteria for recognizing well-known marks:

- "(a) the extent to which it is known to the consuming public as the distinguishing mark of the goods or services for which it was granted registration;
- (b) the scale and scope of the dissemination and advertising or promotion of the mark;
- (c) the age of the mark and the constancy of its use;
- (d) analysis of the production and marketing of the goods identified by the mark."[1139]

Despite their different wording, both documents suggest similar criteria for recognizing well-known marks, which include the knowledge and awareness of the public about distinguishing characteristics of the given mark; the

---

1137 WIPO, 'Joint Recommendation Concerning Provisions on the Protection of Well-Known Marks' (World Intellectual Property Organization 2000) 833(E). See articles 1–5.

1138 *ibid Article 2(1)(b)*.

1139 Andean Decision No. 344 Chapter V, Section 1(84).

extent, scale, scope and geographical distribution of associated goods and services; duration of exploitation of the given mark; and marketing activities like advertising, dissemination, publications and presentation in the market or at exhibitions and fairs for related goods and services. It seems that PCs can meet the above-mentioned criteria for enjoying protection under the well-known marks legal system. Yet, although these factors are recognized by some national authorities and courts as a tool for determining whether a mark is a famous mark, it should be noted that the WIPO Recommendation is not an internationally binding instrument and it is also not even accepted as a guidance document to be integrated into the national laws of all Member States of the Paris Convention.[1140]

5 Beneficiaries of TK-RS

In Chapter 1, Sections 3 and 4 of this study I discussed the general concept of the 'beneficiaries' in the context of TK and 'beneficiaries' regarding PCs. The beneficiaries of PCs are either individuals, such as producers, designers and members of 26 other related professions, or communities including nomadic peoples, rural communities and cities. I also explained that although the TKHs are the owners of rights, they are not the sole beneficiaries of the PCs. The merchants of the PCs are one of the most important links in the PCs marketing chain. Besides them, national and local authorities play a very critical role in protecting PCs. Therefore, not only owners but also beneficiaries of the PCs shall be acknowledged and have the power to exercise and enforce their rights. This approach is compatible with the TIP-rights theory which suggests:

> TIP right should be inclusive, rather than exclusive, with respect to prospective beneficiaries of protection. It should encompass the spectrum of all relevant persons touched by such a law, ranging from individuals to communities, from associations to cooperatives.[1141]

International trademark law appears to acknowledge the same concept of beneficiaries as it recognizes a wide range of individuals and groups as 'beneficiaries' of trademark law, and, therefore, it provides the necessary platform for protection of TK-RS of the PCs. Owners/proprietors, interested parties,

1140 Pflüger (n 896) Page 245.

1141 Cottier and Panizzon, 'Legal Perspectives on Traditional Knowledge: The Case for Intellectual Property Protection' (n 178) Page 583.

agents/representatives, producers/manufacturers and merchants and their federations or associations are subject to the protection of trademark law.

Article 6ter of the Paris Convention recognizes and acknowledges 'the owners of rights' (who acquired their rights in good faith).[1142] Also, the concept of ownership of the mark has been reflected in the term 'proprietor' in the various rules of the Paris Convention including:

- Use of trademark by the proprietor;
- Use of the same mark by co-proprietor;
- The assignment of the mark together with business or goodwill to the assignee;
- The action of the agent or representative of the proprietor to apply for the registration of the mark without proprietor's authorization;
- The right of the proprietor to oppose the use of their mark by their agent or representative;
- The period of time in which the proprietor of a mark may exercise their rights.[1143]

Also, in the context of the assignment of marks and collective marks, the Paris Convention acknowledges the concept of ownership while it stipulates that the mark belongs to associations, the businesses or goodwill:

> [t]he assignment of a mark is valid only if it takes place at the same time as the transfer of the business or goodwill to which the mark belongs ...[1144]
>
> The countries of the Union undertake to accept for filing and to protect collective marks belonging to associations ...[1145]

The TRIPS Agreement, like the Paris Convention, uses the term owner of trademarks regarding owners' exclusive rights over trademarks, owners' consent, interests of trademark owners, requirement of use by trademark owners, and owners' rights to assign or license trademarks to third parties.[1146] The Madrid agreement follows the procedure of the Paris Convention and refers several times to the term proprietor (of the mark) in its provisions.[1147] The Madrid Protocol, in an entirely different approach, refers to the notion of ownership, although only once.[1148] The Iranian legislator in a similar manner has

1142 Paris Convention Article 6ter(1)(c).

1143 *ibid Articles 5(C)(2) & (3) and* 6^{septis}.

1144 *ibid Article* 6^{quater}*(1).*

1145 *ibid Article* 7bis*(1).*

1146 TRIPS Agreement Articles 16, 17, 19 and 21.

1147 See: Madrid Agreement Articles 3bis(1), 4bis(1), 5(3) & (6), 7(4), 8(1), 9bis(1) & (3) and 9ter(3).

1148 Madrid Protocol Article 9.

considered the concept of the 'owner of the mark' as it recognizes the ownership relationship between the mark and its owner.[1149] According to this approach, a trademark is a mark which must in any case be owned by a person or group of persons, but their ownership over the trademark will be recognized if the trademark is registered. "The exclusive right to use a Mark shall belong to the person who registers his Mark."[1150] The Law also acknowledges the registered owner of the collective mark and its power to control the use of the mark.[1151] As described in Chapter 1, Section 3 of this study, the same relation between TKHs and TK is assumed. TKHs like trademarks' holders are owners of the TK whether communities or individuals. In summary, TKHs are owners of rights and therefore beneficiaries of TK and shall have the right to attain, exercise and enforce their rights.

Besides the concept of the owner of the trademark, the Paris Convention also refers to the interested party of the trademarks who might be:

> Any producer, manufacturer, or merchant, whether a natural person or a legal entity, engaged in the production or manufacture of or trade in such goods and established either in the locality falsely indicated as the source, or in the region where such locality is situated, or in the country falsely indicated, or in the country where the false indication of source is used ...[1152]

An interested party may request competent authorities to refuse, cancel or prohibit the registration of a trademark[1153] or to seize all goods unlawfully bearing a trademark or trade name which are entitled to protection on importation.[1154] Moreover, Member States of the Paris Convention shall allow representatives of interested parties, including federations and associations of industrialists, producers and merchants, to represent them and take action on their behalf before the courts or before executive authorities.[1155] Moreover, as mentioned earlier in Chapter 1, Section 5 of this study, TKHs' commercial representatives of PCs include associations and merchants. While efforts by associations and unions are focused on protecting the interests of their guild

1149 See: Iran – Patents, Industrial Designs and Trademarks Registration Law Articles 30(b), 31, 40(a) & (b), 42.
1150 *ibid Article 31.*
1151 *ibid Article 30(b).*
1152 Paris Convention Article 10(2).
1153 *ibid Article 6bis(1).*
1154 *ibid Article 9(3).*
1155 *ibid Article 10ter(2).*

members, merchants play a vital role in the PCs' life and trade. Trademark law may help to determine the most appropriate commercial relationship between TKHs and merchants in such a way that TKHs could benefit from their ownership PIC rights over TK-RS, and merchants could benefit from their licensed trade practices in the markets.

The Paris Convention provides no role for local or national institutions as an interested party to trademarks. However, these institutions act in accordance with the laws of some countries as the competent authority for verifying the registration or use of the mark by interested parties. According to the national laws and regulations of these countries, the registration of the marks is subject to obtaining the necessary approvals from the local and national authorities. Marks that do not have such approvals will not be registered. For instance, in the New Zealand trademarks law, an advisory committee is established to "advise the Commissioner whether the proposed use or registration of a trade mark that is, or appears to be, derivative of a Māori sign, including text and imagery, is, or is likely to be, offensive to Māori."[1156] In Malta, one of the duties of the 'Office of the Registrar of Crafts, Craftspersons and Craft Entrepreneurs' is to "establish and maintain a voluntary certification system of craft products which are in compliance with the definition of craft provided in this Act."[1157] In the USA, the Indian Arts and Crafts Board, has the authority "to create trademarks of genuineness and quality for Indian products and the products of" American Indians; "to establish standards and regulations for the use of Government-owned trademarks; to register any such trademark owned by the Government" in the USPTO.[1158] In Iran, as previously described, among the tasks of the National Carpet Centre is determining the provision of technical requirements for production and export of PCs, as well as the organization of the issues related to the provision of high-quality raw materials for the production and trade of PCs. But verifying the registration and use of trademarks is not included. Among other national and local authorities, other institutions like Iran High Council of Nomads, Provincial Councils for Planning and Development, village councils or city councils have no official function to approve the use of trademarks.

Existing trademark law, recognize fully and comprehensively the different beneficiaries under the TIP-rights theory. Moreover, it provides the opportunity for TKHs and their members – as beneficiaries of TK-RS – to resort to

1156 New Zealand – Trade Marks Act Note 178.
1157 Malta – Crafts Council Act 2020 Note 5(c).
1158 The US – Indian Arts and Crafts Act of 1990 as amended as at September 2003 Section 102(2).

trademark law for protecting their rights within the framework and concept of the beneficiaries under trademark law. However, there are issues which the trademarks law in its existing form is not able to resolve. In practice, the final benefits will be obtained only by the merchants of PCs; and other beneficiaries including TKHs as owners of TK-RS would not receive the final benefits of trademark law. Even if associations and unions act as representatives of TKHs, it is unknown how they could distribute the benefits of protecting TK-RS among different beneficiaries. Therefore, it is necessary to add new regulations to existing national trademark law in order to clarify the relationships among different beneficiaries and the method of benefit sharing among them.

6 Duration of Protection of TK-RS

As explained in Chapter 2, Section 4 of this study, there are two prevailing theories regarding the period of protection for TK. One view argues that TKHs' rights should apply in perpetuity without limitation. Munzer and Raustiala support this view.[1159] In contrast, the second theory, known as TIP-rights – which has been developed by Thomas Cottier and Marion Panizzon – suggests that TK protection shall continue as long as TKHs actively use TK and TK meets the criteria on eligibility for protection. To understand which of these two theories is most suitable for the protection of PCs' marks, it is necessary to examine the compatibility of the trademark protection duration with these theories. At first blush, the second theory seems likely to be applicable in trademark law as the protection period of a trademark is limited, but it is renewable periodically provided that the use of the registered marks continues.[1160]

The Paris Convention is silent about the duration of trademark protection. At the same time, it allows countries to renew the registration of the marks for unlimited times. While the Paris Convention has no fixed period for protection of trademark, the Nice Agreement Concerning the International Classification of Goods and Services for the Purposes of the Registration of Marks demands that "the same duration as the Paris Convention for the Protection of Industrial Property" should apply.[1161] Under the terms of the TRIPS Agreement "initial registration, and each renewal of registration, of a trademark shall be for a term of no less than seven years. The registration of a trademark shall be renewable

1159 Munzer and Raustiala (n 5) 55.

1160 WIPO, *Intellectual Property Needs and Expectations of Traditional Knowledge Holders* (n 166) Page 38.

1161 Nice Agreement Article 10.

indefinitely."[1162] According to the Madrid Agreement, the mark is protectable for more than twenty years with the possibility of unrestricted extension for 20-year periods from the expiration of the preceding period.[1163] The Madrid Protocol reduced this period to ten years with the extension possibility for periods of ten years without a time limit from the expiry of the prior period.[1164] Likewise, under the TLT the term of protection is up to ten years.[1165] Likewise, in the EU Directive, the registration period is for ten years from the application date, and it may be renewed for further periods of ten years' duration.[1166]

Typically, registration of a trademark will remain in force for a specific term of ten years from the date of application for registration. In Switzerland, trademark protection is valid for ten years from the date of the application, and there is the possibility of extending the term of protection for further ten years.[1167] In the Iranian law, the marks that are registered will be protected from the date of submission of the application for ten years. The owner of the mark can apply for a renewal, and, if granted, the owner's right will be extended for ten more years. The term of validity of the protection will be extendable for consecutive periods based on the mark owner's request.[1168] Conversely, in Canada, a trademark is registered initially for ten years starting from the registration date.[1169]

Although in principle, trademark law allows trademark owners to extend their exclusive rights indefinitely, the exercise of this right is subject to certain conditions. These conditions include compliance with the deadlines for the renewal of trademark registration, payment of the trademark renewal fees, and continuous use of the trademark. Regarding the first and second requirements, the owner of the trademark must request renewal of trademark registration and pay the renewal fees before the expiration date of the trademark registration. If the owner fails to pay the renewal fees before the expiration date, a period of grace of no less than six months shall be allowed for the late payment of renewal fees[1170] during which the owner's right will remain in force.

1162 TRIPS Agreement Article 18.
1163 Madrid Agreement Article 6 and 7(1).
1164 Madrid Protocol Article 6(1) and 7(1).
1165 TLT Article 13(7).
1166 Directive 2015/2436 Articles 48 and 49.
1167 Swiss – Federal Act on the Protection of Trade Marks and Indications of Source Article 10(1),(2).
1168 Iran – Patents, Industrial Designs and Trademarks Registration Law Article 40(d).
1169 Canada – Trademarks Act 1985 (RSC, 1985, c T-13) Subsection 46(1).
1170 See: Paris Convention Article 5bis(1); The request for renewal of a mark shall be given to trademark offices within 6 months promptly after the original expiration date. For example: Madrid Agreement Article 7(5); Madrid Protocol Article 7(4); The US – Trademark Act § 1058(a)(3); Swiss – Federal Act on the Protection of Trade Marks and Indications of

However, if they do not pay the renewal fees during the grace period, the termination of the registration will come into force from the original date of expiration.[1171] Concerning the third requirement, although trademarks are renewable for unlimited periods, merely paying the extension fees will not be enough to maintain trademark rights.[1172] According to the Paris Convention, if use of a trademark is required "the registration may be cancelled only after a reasonable period" and "if the person concerned does not justify his inaction."[1173] Previously in this chapter, the justification for non-use was discussed. Therefore, they are not repeated here. In brief, according to that discussion, if the trademark has not been used for a specific period of time, it might be cancelled.[1174] Likewise, TK-RS may receive indefinite protection as long as they are used actively by the TKHs. In this regard, Scafidi argues as long as the expressions of culture continues to be maintained and used by the relevant community, the protection would be continued. In her view, the protection of TK would lapse as soon as the TK ceases to be used. This is a trademark-like regime in its current use.[1175] Therefore, it seems that the theory of TIP-rights developed by Thomas Cottier and Marion Panizzon would provide a base for the needs for protection of TK-RS of TKHs based on trademarks rights.

7 Summary and Recommendations

Broadly speaking, TK refers among others to TKHs' signs, marks, words, names, symbols, icons, motifs, designs and concepts. These aspects of TK are tied to reputation and the distinctive character of TK. Trademark law's function is to distinguish goods and services of one entrepreneur from competitors' goods and services, to protect the goodwill and reputation of producers and to prevent confusion among consumers. TK is capable of distinguishing a local community from other communities. TKHs throughout the ages have distinguished their products with TK-RS and in modern times they seek to use

Source Article 10(3); Iran – Patents, Industrial Designs and Trademarks Registration Law Article 40(d).

1171 Abbott, Cottier and Gurry (n 367) Page 355.

1172 UNCTAD-ICTSD (n 492) Page 244.

1173 Paris Convention Article 5(C)(1).

1174 ITC and WIPO (n 869) Page 77.

1175 See: Scafidi (n 768); quoted in: Secretariat of the Pacific Community, *Guidelines for Developing National Legislation for the Protection of Traditional Knowledge and Expressions of Culture Based on the Pacific Model Law 2002* (Secretariat of the Pacific Community 2006) Page 47.

modern trademark law as a tool to differentiate goods created by and services offered by them or by those who represent them. TKHs seek acknowledgement and exclusive rights over their TK-RS. Trademark law may serve TKHs to recover and sustain TK-RS which have been demolished or are set to become extinct and preserve them as components of TKHs' culture. The appropriate use of TK-RS could serve in preserving and strengthening TKHs' cultures too. They also strive to prevent misuse and misappropriation of TK either by registration of their TK-RS under trademark law or through stopping third parties' claims for marks which are identical or similar to their TK-RS. In this regard, trademark law cannot only help TKHs to commercialize certain elements of TK, but it can also provide protection against UC by competitors. Trademark law might support TKHs to achieve those objects by presenting legal grounds for positive and defensive protection of TKHs' TK-RS.

Regarding positive protection, multiple benefits of registration of TK-RS for TKHs are evident, such as:

- identifying the original PCs' goods and artworks which can help customers to recognize genuine products and their commercial value;
- helping TKHs to raise the national and international reputation of their local artists and producers;
- preventing third parties from using marks identical or similar to TK-RS that may drive consumers and the public to make mistakes about products and services of PCs;
- applying for registration of TK-RS could help TKHs to understand if the designated office finds their marks registrable and help the TKHs to avoid wasting their investments on marketing and commercialization of their products and services;
- in the absence of protection against UC, registration of trademarks could prevent abuse of PCs' cultural symbols;
- precision and reliability of trademark law is useful for TKHs to protect TK-RS of PCs;
- different types of trademarks, including service marks, collective marks, certification marks and trade names provide a comprehensive platform for protection of different beneficiaries of the PCs including individuals and groups;
- develop fair and equitable economic benefits for TKHs.

Notwithstanding, the benefits of positive protection and registration of TK-RS, a number of challenges remain.

The first challenge, descriptive characteristics of TK-RS and especially PCs' marks might put mark owners at serious risk of litigation with their competitors. While TKHs may use collective marks and certification marks to deal with this challenge, these mechanisms are not protected under existing international trademark law, which does not provide a harmonized registration system for collective and certification marks. Therefore, first the national legislators must recognize such character of TK-RS, and second, recognition must take place at the international level, States needs to take the necessary steps to harmonize the international instruments to cover registration of collective marks and certification marks of TKHs. As long as recognition of the descriptive nature of TK-RS is not officially provided, the TKHs should use collective and certification marks mechanisms for registration of their PCs. Also, members and individual representatives of TKHs should not only use the collective and certification marks of the PCs but also their distinctive and non-descriptive marks for their products and related services. At the same time, they should use the trade name protection to introduce themselves as recognized activists for PCs.

The second challenge of positive protection is the requirement of active use of the trademark in the market. This condition is of concern to TKHs because it means that registration of TK-RS will not provide enough protection. Still, TKHs or their representatives need to maintain their ownership of their registered marks through constant use of their trademarks. Although, in many instances, this does not help TKHs whose wish is to protect TK-RS against third parties' exploitation, in the case of PCs, the use requirement does seem to have a less negative influence on the protection of TK-RS abroad. The reason for such a conclusion is the wide scope of the PCs' market and the number of territories that are consumers of PCs. However, PCs would suffer from lack of protection in more than half of the world's countries. To face this challenge, national legislators must expand the concept of use beyond the existing notions of genuine use or use in commerce to cover the cultural and social features of TK-RS. Moreover, national laws and international instruments should recognise cultural activities and applications as the proper means to meet the use requirement. Besides, they must also extend the geographic range of use from the local level to the international one. To overcome the challenge of the use requirement under existing trademark law, TKHs or their representatives and in particular merchants of the PCs must actively use TK-RS. As the concept of use varies between territories, the TKHs have to understand the concept of use in designated markets and met the requirements. If TKHs have no intention to be present in or supply their products and offer their services some markets, it is strongly recommended not to register their TK-RS in those markets.

The third challenge of positive protection of trademarks is the limitation of protection to those classes of goods and services that trademarks are registered for. Hence, third parties will be able to use similar or identical marks for other classes and related goods and services. Therefore, TKHs also face the challenge of deciding on a proper approach to determining the class of goods and services for the protection of their PCs. If they attribute their TK-RS to too many classes, the risk of refusal or opposition to their application will significantly increase. Moreover, even if TKHs can successfully register their TK-RS in a maximum number of classes, they will not be able to maintain genuine use of their registered marks or to provide evidence of the use of their marks in all these classes. On the other hand, if their application includes too few classes, then they only will enjoy a limited scope of protection for their TK-RS, and they will lose their rights over TK-RS at least in some classes in the destination markets. One possible solution could be the creation of a whole new class for TK-RS or to make the necessary amendments in the international trademark classification of the Nice Agreement to cover TK-RS. In the absence of such a modification in the Nice Agreement Classification regime, it is strongly recommended that TKHs avoid applying for registration of their marks for those goods and services which are beyond their abilities to supply in the targeted territorial markets.

The fourth challenge for positive protection of PCs' marks is the costs of registration of the trademarks at national and international levels, which is typically beyond the financial capacity of TKHs. However, the TKHs may overcome such a challenge by sharing the registration fees for their collective mark. Even more important, if the TKHs fail to pay renewal fees for their registration, the administrative and legal authorities in designated countries assume that the owners have legally abandoned their trademarks, and thus third parties will be allowed to use the abandoned marks. To overcome this challenge, countries may offer specific mechanisms or financial packages to help TKHs. Measures such as decreasing the fees for the registration of TK-RS, setting up a funding system to help TKHs with registration their marks, assignation of a pro-bono trademark lawyer or experts to assist TKHs with free legal services, reforming the tax law and reducing taxes on TK-RS products and services may help TKHs to overcome the expenses associated with the trademark registration system.

Need for defensive protection: It seems that positive protection of trademarks, despite its benefits for the protection of TK-RS, poses challenges for TKHs. On the other hand, registered TK-RS, represent only a small fraction of the whole TK-RS. In consequence, a large number of TK-RS do not receive any protection. Thus, positive protection alone would not be strong enough to meet the needs of TKHs to protect their TK-RS adequately. Besides, TKHs complain of misuse and misappropriation of their TK-RS by persons (either companies or individuals) and registration of them as their own trademarks. Nevertheless, it is necessary to use a preventive mechanism able to avoid third parties to being granted unfair and unjustified protection over registration of trademarks that are similar or identical to TK-RS. Therefore, in addition to the positive protection, it is necessary to use defensive protection at the national and international levels. In this regard, existing trademark law includes grounds for refusal of registration for some types of trademarks and applicability of these grounds as a defensible basis for rejecting applications for registration of TK-RS demanded by persons other than TKHs. Such defensive protection mechanisms include:

Defensive protection regarding certain signs and symbols: Under existing trademark law, some specific signs and symbols might not be registered as trademarks or elements of trademarks. For instance, armorial bearings, flags and State emblems, official signs and hallmarks, international organizations names and abbreviations, and Olympic symbols are not allowed to be registered as trademarks. Although, this type of prohibition is not designed as defensive protection for TK-RS, some national laws have incorporated such prohibitions to protect TK-RS at the national and international level. Still, prohibition of registration of certain signs and symbols of PCs faces some challenges. The marks which have already been misused and registered as trademarks can no longer be subject to such prohibition. Moreover, the prohibition applies only to those trademarks that are going to be registered on goods and services of the same class of PCs. Besides, only official State institutions might adopt signs and symbols and exclude them from registration, and TKHs have no role determining such prohibition. Finally, the officials in the designated office may object to and reject such prohibition and there is no means for TKHs to question such a decision. To overcome this challenge, the States should try to establish an internationally binding instrument which recognizes TK-RS as non-registrable signs and symbols. Regarding PCs, Iranian officials involved in negotiations on trade agreements should try to add a list of non-registrable PCs sings and symbols as trademarks in the designated trademarks office.

Defensive protection against deceptive marks: Preventing supply and marketing of goods and services with deceptive or misleading marks is one of the most fundamental aims of trademark law. One of the typical methods of misuse of PCs is the appropriation of their famous marks to mislead consumers about the authenticity, origin, manufacturing method or style of a product or regarding services. Deceptive marks on PCs will mislead the public in a way which has harmful effects on fair competition and on consumers' rights. Thus, registration and usage of such marks is clearly against international trademark law. National laws may avoid registration of marks which are confusingly similar to signs and symbols of PCs and falsely suggest that there is a connection between the goods and services they provide and those of the TKHs.

Defensive protection against marks which could be contrary to the public order or morality: PCs include many symbols or signs which represent religion and beliefs of TKHs. Although it is up to them to decide what part of their TK expressions are sacred and what part of sacred TK is suitable for commercialization, the sacred signs and symbols are at risk of being marketed by third parties. Therefore, TKHs should demand defensive protection to prevent registration or use of their sacred TK-RS as trademarks by third parties. Under existing trademark law competent national authorities may refuse or cancel the registration or use of marks which they recognize as incompatible with the given societies' public order, morality or religious rules. In some national laws, authorities identify trademarks containing sacred elements of TK-RS of their TKHs as culturally offensive and avoid registration of them. However, it seems that such a strategy only provides domestic protection of the sacred TK-RS; and to be effective the prohibition of registration and use of sacred TK-RS must be expanded to the international level through international agreements. Although establishing an internationally binding instrument has defenders among TKHs and some scholars, even such a binding agreement would not provide adequate protection of sacred marks beyond national borders, because the notion of morality and public order depends strongly on a society's norms, values and domestic laws and the opinions of its national authorities. Therefore, TKHs and the States must list their sacred TK-RS as certain signs which they want to be excluded from registrable marks not just because they are sacred but because they are a part of TKHs' signs and symbols.

Defensive protection of the well-known marks: PCs are well-known globally for their unparalleled excellence and elegance. They have obtained their great reputation through the ages by merit. Consumers and the public opinion trust the originality and distinguishing features of PCs' brand on the carpets. The registration or use of similar or identical trademarks could on one hand lead to UC against TKHs; and on the other hand, it could mislead customers about the connection between the trademark and PCs and lead customers to mistakenly trust in the quality of the fake products and services. Therefore, TKHs may demand PCs and PCs affiliated signs to be protected under the well-known marks regime! In particular, they believe the advantages of well-known marks will help them to protect their TK-RS. These benefits include:

- TKHs can demand the protection for their famous marks even if the marks have not been registered or used in the given foreign markets,
- TK-RS might be recognized as well-known marks in the given foreign markets due to their reputation and public knowledge,
- Well-known marks not only impede the registration and use of trademarks which are confusingly associated with similar goods and services but also to those which are associated to non-identical or dissimilar goods and services.

Notwithstanding the benefits of protection of well-known marks, protection of the PCs under the regime of well-known marks would face some impediments. Lack of uniform definitions, lack of harmonized standards, diverse decision-making authorities, different interpretation and implementation of well-known marks are some barriers to the effective protection of well-known marks. To overcome these hurdles and in order to avoid fragmentation among its members, WIPO provided a recommendation document on non-exhaustive list of elements that might be used by national authorities for protection of well-known marks. However, the recommendation is not an internationally binding instrument and therefore it has value only as a guidance document and countries have no obligation to accept the harmonization of the rules.

Beneficiaries of protection of PCs – matching with the TIP-rights approach – include an inclusive list of communities, associations, companies and individuals. Trademark law in its different types (trademarks, service marks, trade name, collective marks and certification marks) recognizes the concept of beneficiaries as it provides the necessary grounds for protection a wide range of PCs' beneficiaries under the concept of owners, interested parties, agents and representatives, producers, manufacturers and merchants and their federations or associations are subject to protection of trademark law. Moreover, trademark law may help to determine the most appropriate commercial relationship between TKHs and merchants in a way that TKHs could benefit from their ownership PIC rights over TK-RS, and merchants could benefit from their licensed trade practices in the markets. Besides role of local or national authorities for verifying and approval of registration or use of the mark by interested parties is recognized and accepted by trademark law; and marks that do not have such approvals will not be registered. Still States and TKHs must consider the difficulties of applying trademark law to the concept of beneficiaries under the TIP-rights. It seems that even if the trademark legal system could be used to protect TK-RS, in reality, the benefits will be gained only by the PCs merchants, and the real owners of these signs; that is, TKHs, cannot enjoy such benefits completely. Even if associations and unions act as representatives of TKHs and register TK-RS, it is unknown how they could distribute the benefits of protecting these marks among different beneficiaries.

Duration of Protection: According to the existing trademark law, registration of the marks may last for specified periods, and the registration and protection can potentially be renewed indefinitely without limitation. Although trademark law allows owners to renew the registration of their marks and extend their exclusive rights indefinitely, the exercise of this right is subject to constant use of the trademark. Likewise, the theory of TIP-rights suggests TK-RS may receive indefinite protection, as long as they are used actively by the TKHs. In this regard, the protection of TK would lapse as soon as TK ceases to be used. Therefore, it seems that the theory of TIP-rights will provide a base for the needs for protection of TK-RS of TKHs based on trademarks rights.

Conclusion: Among different legal regimes that might be capable of protecting TK, trademark law possesses the potential features to prevent use of misleading or deceptive marks that are falsely claiming to be TK-RS or have a connection with TKHs. Although TKHs and individuals have tried to use trademark law to obtain protection for their TK, they only achieved limited success. Besides, trademark law can be a double-edged sword rule leading to increased misappropriation of TK-RS, especially through the registration system. Therefore, specific revisions or adjustments to trademark law may be needed to meet the interests of TKHs better and to prevent misappropriation of their TK-RS. Some States are redesigning their national legal system to provide protection for TK and to avert misappropriation of TK-RS. Yet, as these efforts have not been supported by international trademark law, it is necessary to amend and establish norms and rules to meet the specific needs for protection of TK-RS based on the TIP-rights Principle.

CHAPTER 4

Protection of Persian Carpets under Geographical Indications

1 Introduction

The historical relationship between GIs and TK is almost as ancient as the historical links between trademarks and TK, which were mentioned in the introduction to Chapter 3 of this study. Since the emergence of trade, merchants and consumers have not only paid attention to the marks of the products but also to the quality characteristics of the goods in relation to the geographical location of their production.[1176] Therefore, using GIs is as much a tradition as TK itself.

TK, as explained in Chapter 1 of this study, refers to the knowledge that formed and has been managed through the centuries by TKHs. TKHs use the community's know-how and production techniques as the essential manner of producing traditional goods. The reputation of the TKHs' products often originates from the knowledge and know-how of their communities (known as human elements). TKHs also use and process local natural and biological resources from a given geographical region.[1177] Many TKHs distinguish their local products by using their well-known indications, signs and symbols.[1178] With this in mind, the IGC secretariat, as a working concept, refers among others to the names, GIs and symbols as categories of TK.[1179] In this regard, GIs may protect those categories of TK, including TK-related indications (TK-RI), which refer to the geographic locations as the true origin of TK products.[1180]

1176 Vadim Mantrov, *EU Law on Indications of Geographical Origin: Theory and Practice* (Springer 2014) Page 32.

1177 See the Delegation of Portugal statement on behalf of the European Communities and their Member States: IGC-GRTKF Secretariat, 'Revised Draft Report of Intergovernmental Committee on Intellectual Property and Genetic Resources, Traditional Knowledge and Folklore' (n 151) Paragraph 429.

1178 Frankel (n 788) Page 451.

1179 IGC-GRTKF Secretariat, 'Traditional Knowledge – Operational Terms and Definitions' (n 142) Paragraph 25.

1180 IGC-GRTKF Secretariat, 'Consolidated Analysis of the Legal Protection of Traditional Cultural Expressions' (n 800) Pages 33–34.

TK also embodies the lifestyle and culture of the TKHs, and the GIs regime might be used not only as a tool for protecting TKHs' distinctive signs but also to make "links between natural elements and traditional cultures"[1181] and safeguard TKHs' cultural heritage.[1182]

Of central concern therefore is the fundamental inconsistency between current IP regimes and TK. Downes and Laird explain how GIs show promise for meeting some concerns of TKHs that cannot easily be met by other IPRs. They point out that within the GIs regime TKHs would be the only group who are allowed to use TK-RS. Moreover, TKHs could maintain such a use of GIs perpetually. Besides, they would be able to discriminate their goods based on their distinct procedures and characteristics, such as the traditional essence of the production.[1183]

Cottier and Müller enumerate different advantages of protection of TK under GIs. According to them, the protection of TK under GIs which is a predictable systematic protection regime, is less risky than demanding protection under UC which includes a case-by-case procedural pursuit of protection. In their view, the GIs regime is an appropriate tool for marketing locally produced products. Thus, TKHs may use it for protection of their traditional products derived from their TK. Also, the GIs regime applies to bio-products derived from biological resources. Therefore, it may help TKHs to exploit the benefits, such as increasing production of TK-based goods and applying "special rates, lower than those applied to products that are not based on TK."[1184] Furthermore, the GIs protection may promote the demand for biological and natural-based products and crafts; and encourage TKHs to preserve and commercialise those products actively.[1185]

Alongside the benefit of a GIs protection regime for TKHs, such a regime would promote the protection of consumers' rights too. Consumers are

1181 See the Delegation of France statement: IGC-GRTKF Secretariat, 'Report of Intergovernmental Committee on Intellectual Property and Genetic Resources, Traditional Knowledge and Folklore' (n 849) Page 6.

1182 Gupta, *WIPO-UNEP Study on the Role of Intellectual Property Rights in the Sharing of Benefits Arising from the Use of Biological Resources and Associated Traditional Knowledge* (n 363) Page 159.

1183 See: Downes and Laird (n 789); quoted in: Gupta, *WIPO-UNEP Study on the Role of Intellectual Property Rights in the Sharing of Benefits Arising from the Use of Biological Resources and Associated Traditional Knowledge* (n 363).

1184 Cottier and Müller (n 140); in Cottier, *Trade and Intellectual Property Protection in WTO Law: Collected Essays* (n 140) Page 442.

1185 See the statement of South Africa Delegation: IGC-GRTKF Secretariat, 'Report of Intergovernmental Committee on Intellectual Property and Genetic Resources, Traditional Knowledge and Folklore' (n 61) Paragraph 52.

increasingly interested in choosing products based on their quality and origin[1186] and GIs provide a tool to prevent confusion for consumers by clearly indicating the goods' origins. The GIs regime protects the legitimate interests of consumers, prevents third parties from using false appellations and indications, and from misleading consumers about the authenticity, quality and characteristics of their worthless counterfeit products.[1187] Correspondingly, consumers are also aware of the global benefit of using these products to help preserve biodiversity, and therefore, they are willing to pay higher prices of such products.[1188] From the economic point of view, supporting and liberalising markets for these products of TKHs and reducing tariffs on them can help to integrate TKHs into the economy and re-evaluate their products.[1189] In this regard, the rural population is the principal beneficiary of the GIs regime, which would help them to generate employment and increase their income. Furthermore, effective protection for GIs would increase economic activities in rural regions "not only by the growth of GI production but also by developments in the other sectors as well."[1190]

The EU "which is the spiritual home of GIs"[1191] shares the belief with the TKHs recalling that GIs might be a readily accessible tool for the protection of the TCEs. The EU also suggests that countries should take measures to raise awareness among beneficiaries and encourage them to use the GIs legal framework.[1192] This approach seems to be in line with the WTO Ministerial Declaration. In the Declaration the TRIPS Council is required to note the

1186 Cottier and Müller (n 140); in Cottier, *Trade and Intellectual Property Protection in WTO Law: Collected Essays* (n 140) Page 435.

1187 ITC and WIPO (n 869) Page 86.

1188 Cottier and Müller (n 140); in Cottier, *Trade and Intellectual Property Protection in WTO Law: Collected Essays* (n 140) Page 435.

1189 David Vivas-Eugui, 'Negotiations on Geographical Indications in the TRIPS Council and Their Effect on the WTO Agricultural Negotiations-Implications for Developing Countries and the Case of Venezuela' (2001) 4 The Journal of World Intellectual Property 703, Page 718.

1190 Bilge Dogan and Ummuhan Gokovali, 'Geographical Indications: The Aspects of Rural Development and Marketing Through the Traditional Products' (2012) 62 Procedia – Social and Behavioral Sciences 761, Pages 764–765.

1191 Brad Sherman and Leanne Wiseman, 'From Terroir to Pangkarra: Geographical Indications of Origin and Indigenous Knowledge' in Dev S Gangjee (ed), *Research handbook on intellectual property and geographical indications* (Edward Elgar Publishing 2016) Page 486.

1192 IGC-GRTKF Secretariat, 'Report of Intergovernmental Committee on Intellectual Property and Genetic Resources, Traditional Knowledge and Traditional Cultural Expressions' (World Intellectual Property Organization 2018) WIPO Doc WIPO/GRTKF/IC/34/14 Page 8.

issues related to the extension of the protection of GIs[1193] and "to examine, among other things, the relationship between the TRIPS Agreement and the Convention on Biological Diversity, the protection of traditional knowledge and folklore, and other relevant new developments."[1194] In this regard, Cottier suggests:

> In the context of this mandate, geographical indications may be one of the forms of protection suitable to enhance development in accordance with these objectives.[1195]

Although, Switzerland and many other countries support the policy for extension of protection of GIs,[1196] other countries still do not agree with such a policy. The latter believe that such a proposal try to make artificial parallelism between two different issues with different and specific terms of reference and subject matters which "had nothing to do with each other."[1197] Countries with a colonial post and thus using traditional European brands, such as Australia or the USA, refuse the concept and work instead on the basis of certified and collective marks instead.

In particular, PCs – the subject of this study – are a commodity that has a clear and distinct connection with the geographical region and the community in which it is produced. Such an association is very well known and recognized by carpet specialists. In Chapter 1, Section 4 of this study, the author mentioned the well-known communities in the rural areas and cities, and nomadic people whose products are famous and recognized worldwide by the name of their regions and the names of communities. For instance, among others, Tabriz Carpet, Isfahan Carpet and Qum Carpet are some famous names of PCs, which are known by the region and reputation of Tabriz, Isfahan and Qum.[1198] Also, they are registered under the Lisbon Agreement.[1199] Unquestionably, the INCC

1193 WTO, 'Doha Ministerial Declaration' (n 110) Paragraph 18.

1194 *ibid Paragraph 19.*

1195 Cottier, 'Chapter 22 – The Agreement on Trade-Related Aspects of Intellectual Property Rights' (n 397) Page 1090.

1196 WTO, 'The Extension of the Additional Protection for Geographical Indications to Products Other than Wines and Spirits' WTO Doc IP/C/W/353.

1197 IGC-GRTKF Secretariat, 'Report of Intergovernmental Committee on Intellectual Property and Genetic Resources, Traditional Knowledge and Folklore' (World Intellectual Property Organization 2009) WIPO Doc WIPO/GRTKF/IC/13/11 Paragraph 156.

1198 By January 2019, 62 national GIs of the PCs have been registered by Iran Intellectual Property Centre. For more information see Table 10.

1199 By April 2024, 36 international AO of the PCs have been registered under Lisbon System. For more information see: WIPO, 'WIPO Lisbon Express Search' (*World Intellectual*

and the IPC in Iran have made considerable efforts to increase the capabilities of TKHs and convince them to register the nomadic, rural and urban carpets in the form of GIs and Appellations of Origin (AO). Unfortunately, despite the efforts made, these actions have not prevented the abuse and misappropriation of TK-RI of PCs at the international and even the national levels.

To understand the challenges and difficulties regarding protection of PCs under the GIs regime, this Chapter examines whether and to what extent GIs provide a suitable and forceful means for protecting TK-RI. In particular, it focuses on answering the following questions:

- What do TKHs expect from a GIs regime?
- What are the TKHs' approaches to the protection of TK under the law of GIs?
- What are the challenges to the protection of the TKHs' TK-RI?
- Who are the beneficiaries of TK-RI?
- How long should TKHs' rights over TK-RI be protected?

In order to answer the questions mentioned above, firstly various international IP instruments which play a significant role in the protection of origin or source need to be addressed:

2 Brief Review of International Instruments regarding Protection of GIs

2.1 *Paris Convention*

The Paris Convention is the first international treaty to mention 'indications of source' and 'appellations of origin' as protectable independent issues under the industrial property regime:

> The protection of industrial property has as its object patents, utility models, industrial designs, trademarks, service marks, trade names, indications of source or appellations of origin, and the repression of unfair competition.[1200]

Moreover, Article 10(1) of the Paris Convention extends the remedies of Article 9 – regarding the seizure of goods which illegally bear a mark or trade name – to the "direct or indirect use of a false indication of the source of the

---

Property Organization, 20 April 2024) <https://www.wipo.int/cgi-lis/bool_srch5?ENG+17> accessed 20 April 2024.

1200 Paris Convention Article 1(2).

goods." Also, Article 10(2), in trying to identify the interested party regarding remedies, refers to the false indication of source:

> Any producer, manufacturer, or merchant, whether a natural person or a legal entity, engaged in the production or manufacture of or trade in such goods and established either in the locality falsely indicated as the source, or in the region where such locality is situated, or in the country falsely indicated, or in the country where the false indication of source is used, shall in any case be deemed an interested party.[1201]

Article 10 does not refer to 'appellations of origin' and it only mentions the indications of source. However, Article 1(2) of the Convention contains the term indications of source alongside the appellations of origin, which are protectable in the form of industrial property.[1202]

Furthermore, the Paris Convention contains provisions regarding protection against UC. It provides a non-exclusive list of acts which Member States are obliged to provide effective protection against:

> 1. all acts of such a nature as to create confusion by any means whatever with the establishment, the goods, or the industrial or commercial activities, of a competitor;
> 2. false allegations in the course of trade of such a nature as to discredit the establishment, the goods, or the industrial or commercial activities, of a competitor;
> 3. indications or allegations the use of which in the course of trade is liable to mislead the public as to the nature, the manufacturing process, the characteristics, the suitability for their purpose, or the quantity, of the goods.[1203]

2.2 *Madrid Agreement*

The goal of the Madrid Agreement for the Repression of False or Deceptive Indications of Source on Goods is preventing the importation of all goods bearing a false or deceptive indication of source through seizure of importation prohibiting the importation of such goods, or taking necessary actions

---

1201 *ibid Article 10(2).*

1202 O'Connor, *The Law of Geographical Indications* (n 373) Page 29.

1203 Paris Convention Article $10^{bis}(3)$.

and sanctions against such importations.[1204] It also has provision regarding the way seizure could be requested and effected.[1205] Moreover, the agreement forbids the display, sale or offering for sale of all goods which deceive the public about the source of the goods.[1206] Finally, national courts have the competency to determine whether an indication in their respective country counts as an indication of source protected by the Madrid Agreement. If the court decides that indication is a generic appellation, then the provision of the agreement would not be applied to that appellation. Exceptionally, the jurisdiction of the national court would not apply to the regional appellations regarding the source of goods of the vine.[1207]

It seems that the Agreement has not been successful in preventing the use of false or deceptive indications of source. One reason could be the structure of the Agreement. The Agreement does not have institutions such as a union or governing body, or even a budget for monitoring the implementation of its provisions by its members. Moreover, as Conrad points out, only a small group of countries are members of this agreement; and they have divergent views regarding its provisions.[1208]

2.3 *Lisbon Agreement*

The 'Lisbon Agreement for the Protection of Appellations of Origin and their International Registration' was concluded on 31 October 1958 and was revised at Stockholm on 14 July 1967.[1209] The subject matter of the Lisbon Agreement is the registration and protection of the AO.[1210] According to the Lisbon Agreement, AO means "the geographical name of a country, region or locality, which serves to designate a product originating therein, the quality and characteristics of which are due exclusively or essentially to geographical environment, including natural and human factors."[1211] The provisions of the Agreement regarding protection of the AO includes notion of country of origin, content of protection, the procedure of international registration, duration of

1204 Madrid Agreement for the Repression of False or Deceptive Indications of Source on Goods 1958 (828 UNTS 165 (entered into force 1 June 1963)) Article 1.

1205 *ibid Articles 2 and 3.*

1206 *ibid Article 3bis.*

1207 *ibid Article 4.*

1208 Albrecht Conrad, 'The Protection of Geographical Indications in the TRIPS Agreement' (1996) 86 The Trademark Reporter 11, Page 25.

1209 Lisbon Agreement for the Protection of Appellations of Origin and their International Registration. 1967 (923 UNTS 205 (entered into force 31 October 1973)).

1210 *ibid Article 1.*

1211 *ibid Article 2(1).*

registration validity. As indicated in Table 7, by the end of 2023, 36 AO for PCs have been registered under the Lisbon Agreement,[1212] highlighting its pivotal role in internationally recognizing and protecting traditional products:

TABLE 7 International registrations of PCs under Lisbon System

	No.	Appellation / Translation	Holder	Region
1.	910	Heris/Heriz Handmade Carpet	1- Township of Heris Handmade Carpet Producers and Weavers Association 2- Heris Rural Handmade Carpet Cooperative Company 3- Heris Urban Handmade Carpet Cooperative Company	Heris and its regions (Bakhshayesh, Guravan, Khajeh)
2.	911	Isfahan/ Esfahan Handmade Carpet	1- Isfahan Township Handmade Carpet Producers Guild Association 2- Isfahan Province Carpet Exporters Association 3- Isfahan Township Carpet Sellers Association 4- Isfahan Province Rural Carpet Cooperative Association 5- Isfahan Province Civil Carpet Cooperative Association	Isfahan or Esfahan
3.	912	Khoy Fish Design Handmade Carpet	1- Rural Handmade Carpet Producers Cooperatives Association of West Azarbaijan Province 2- Khoy Handmade Carpet Weavers Guild Association 3- Khoy Rural Handmade Carpet Cooperative Company	Khoy

1212 WIPO, 'WIPO Lisbon Express Search' (n 1199).

TABLE 7 International registrations of PCs under Lisbon System (*cont.*)

	No.	Appellation / Translation	Holder	Region
4.	913	Qom/Qum/ Ghom Handmade Carpet	1- Qum Province Carpet Producing, Selling and Related Guilds Association 2- Qum Province Rural Carpet Cooperative Association 3- Qum Province Carpet Exporters Association 4- Qum Province Carpet Designers and Painters Artists Society	Qum Province consisting of the township of Qum, villages of Qum (Kahak, Ghanavat), Shahre Jafarieh, Shahre Khalajestan, Shahre Dastjerd, Shahre Salafchegan
5.	914	Tabriz Handmade Carpet	1- East Azerbaijan Rural Handmade Carpets Cooperative Association 2- The Province of Civil Handmade Carpets Cooperative Association 3- Tabriz Handmade Carpet Weavers and Producers Guild Association 4- Tabriz Carpet Sellers Guild Association 5- Tabriz Handmade Carpet Exporters Association	City of Tabriz, Markazi county and six rural districts: East Bedoustan, Khanmaroud, Barough, North and East Mavaze Khan, West Bedoustan
6.	948	Ardabil/ Ardebil Handmade Carpet	Producer or groups of producers benefiting from the appellation of origin concerned: I. Designers and Painters Association of Ardabil Province Handmade Carpet II. Guild Union of Ardabil Handmade Carpet Weavers III. Cooperatives Union of Ardabil Province Handmade Carpet Producers IV. Iran Carpet Company – Ardabil Branch	Ardabil or Ardebil

TABLE 7 International registrations of PCs under Lisbon System (*cont.*)

	No.	Appellation / Translation	Holder	Region
7.	949	Handmade carpet Handmade rug	Producer or groups of producers benefiting from the appellation of origin concerned: I. Cooperative Union for Rural Handmade Carpet of Golestan Province II. Guild Union for Handmade Carpet of Gonbad Township III. Cooperatives Union for Handmade Carpet Producers of Golestan Province	Torkman or Turkmen
8.	950	Hamedan Handmade Carpet	Producer or groups of producers benefiting from the appellation of origin concerned: I. Cooperatives Union of Hamedan Province Rural Handmade Carpet II. Guild Union of Hamedan City Handmade Carpet Sellers III. Guild Union of Hamedan City Handmade Carpet Weavers	Hamedan
9.	951	Kashan Handmade Carpet	Producer or groups of producers benefiting from the appellation of origin concerned: I. Cooperatives Company of Kashan Rural Handmade Carpet Producers II. Guild Union of Kashan Handmade Carpet Sellers III. Guild Union of Kashan Handmade Carpet Producers	Kashan

TABLE 7 International registrations of PCs under Lisbon System (*cont.*)

	No.	Appellation / Translation	Holder	Region
10.	952	Kashmar Handmade Carpet	Producer or groups of producers benefiting from the appellation of origin concerned: I. Ahmad Shjiee – Producer of carpets in non-centralized workshops II. Seyed Mehdi Hashemi – Producer of carpets in non-centralized workshops III. Abdolla Mostafavi – Producer of carpets in non-centralized workshops IV. Ali Asghar Mosafr – Producer of carpets in non-centralized workshops V. Cooperatives Company of Kashmar City Rural Handmade Carpet VI. Guild Union of Kashmar Handmade Carpet Sellers and related materials	Kashmar
11.	953	Kerman Handmade Carpet	Producer or groups of producers benefiting from the appellation of origin concerned: I. Guild Union for producers and Weavers of Kerman Handmade Carpets II. Cooperatives Union of Kerman Province Rural Handmade Carpets	Kerman

TABLE 7 International registrations of PCs under Lisbon System (*cont.*)

	No.	Appellation / Translation	Holder	Region
12.	954	Mashad/ Mashhad Handmade Carpet	Producer or groups of producers benefiting from the appellation of origin concerned: I. Guild Union of Mashad Handmade Carpet Weavers II. Export Union of Khorasan Province Handmade Carpet III. Guild Union for Sellers of Mashad Handmade Carpet and Related Materials IV. Cooperatives Union for Rural Handmade Carpet Producers of Khorasan Province V. Astan-e-ghods-e-Razavi Carpet Co.	Mashad or Mashhad
13.	955	Naein Handmade Carpet	Producer or groups of producers benefiting from the appellation of origin concerned: I. Guild Union of Naein Handmade Carpet Weavers II. Cooperative Company of Naein Rural Handmade Carpet Producers III. Iran Carpet Company – Naein Branch.	Naein
14.	956	Sarough Handmade Carpet	Producer or groups of producers benefiting from the appellation of origin concerned: I. Hossein Jiriaee sherahi – Producer of carpets in non-centralized workshops II. Hasan Jiriaee sherahi – Producer of carpets in non-centralized workshops III. Iran Carpet Company – Markazi Province Branch IV. Cooperatives Union of Markazi Province Rural Handmade Carpet	Sarough / Saruk

TABLE 7 International registrations of PCs under Lisbon System (*cont.*)

	No.	Appellation / Translation	Holder	Region
15.	957	Yazd Handmade Carpet	Producer or groups of producers benefiting from the appellation of origin concerned: I. Mahmod Ali Mandgari – Producer of carpets in non-centralized workshops II. Mohmmad Shekarideg – Producer of carpets in non-centralized workshops III. Ahmad Zare'khormizi – Producer of carpets in non-centralized workshops IV. Mohmmad Golkarieh – Producer of carpets in non-centralized workshops V. Cooperatives Union of Yazd Province Rural Handmade Carpets VI. Cooperative Company of Yazd Rural Handmade Carpets VII. Guild Union of Yazd Handmade Carpet Sellers VIII. Shahab Baft-e-Yazd Cooperative Company IX. Guild Union of Yazd Handmade Carpet Weavers X. Iran Carpet Company – Yazd Branch	Yazd

TABLE 7 International registrations of PCs under Lisbon System (*cont.*)

	No.	Appellation / Translation	Holder	Region
16.	1023	Kermanshah Songhor and Koleyaye Handmade Carpet	Producer or groups of producers benefiting from the appellation of origin concerned: 1. Mrs. Reihaneh Nazeri 2. Handmade Carpet Cooperative No. 4401 of Mr. Mohammad Nader Heydarian Koleyaye 3. Goldoz Koleyaye Handmade Carpet Cooperative No. 4295 4. Guild Union of Songhor Handmade Carpet	City of Songhor and Koleyaye located in the province of Kermanshah
17.	1024	Ghohestan Handmade Carpet	Producer or groups of producers benefiting from the appellation of origin concerned: 1. Mohammad Hassan Kamyabi Mesk 2. Guild Union of Birjand Handmade Carpet Weavers 3. Cooperative of Birjand Handmade Carpet Producers	City of Ghohestan (Regions of Derakhsh and Asyaban) located in the province of South Khorasan
18.	1025	Sardroud Pictorial Handmade Carpet	Producer or groups of producers benefiting from the appellation of origin concerned: 1. Kazem Sehat 2. Union of Pictorial Carpet producers and Homogeneous Guilds of the city of Sardroud	City of Sardroud
19.	1026	Ardakan Handmade Carpet	Producer or groups of producers benefiting from the appellation of origin concerned: 1. Fajr Cooperative Production for Handmade Carpet of the city of Ardakan 2. Guild Union of Ardakan Handmade Carpet Weavers	City of Ardakan

TABLE 7 International registrations of PCs under Lisbon System (*cont.*)

	No.	Appellation / Translation	Holder	Region
20.	1027	Birjand Mood Handmade Carpet	Producer or groups of producers benefiting from the appellation of origin concerned: 1. Guild Union of Birjand Handmade Carpet Weavers 2. Cooperative of Birjand Handmade Carpet Producers 3. Iran Carpet Company – Region of South Khorasan	Cities of Birjand, Sarbisheh, Khoosf, Nehbandan located in the province of South Khorasan
21.	1028	Chaharmahal and Bakhtiari Handmade Carpet	Producer or groups of producers benefiting from the appellation of origin concerned: 1. Cooperative of Shahrekord Rural Handmade Carpet 2. Cooperatives Union for Rural Handmade Carpet of the Province of Chaharmahal and Bakhtiari 3. Guild Union of Shahrekord Handmade Carpet 4. Cooperative of Shahrekord Carpet Weavers 5. Iran Carpet Company – Shahrekord Branch 6. Kiar Cooperative of Rural Handmade Carpet Producers of Chaharmahal and Bakhtiari 7. Zayandehrud Cooperative of Rural Handmade Carpet Producers of Chaharmahal and Bakhtiari	Cities of Shahrekord, Saman, Kiar located in the Province of Chaharmahal and Bakhtiari

TABLE 7 International registrations of PCs under Lisbon System (*cont.*)

	No.	Appellation / Translation	Holder	Region
22.	1029	Handmade Gabbeh of Fars	Producer or groups of producers benefiting from the appellation of origin concerned: 1. Union for Handmade Carpet Producers and Exporters of the Province of Fars 2. Cooperatives Union for Rural Handmade Carpet Producers of the Province of Fars 3. Guild Union of Shiraz Handmade Carpet Weavers and Producers	Regions of Shiraz, Firouzabad, Abadeh, Ghir and Karzin, Darab, Jahrom, Fasa, Kazeroun, Marvdasht, Mamassani, Khorram Bid, Eghlid, Neyriz, Estehban, Bovanat, Lar, Khonj, Lamrod, Zarindasht, Sarvestan, Koar, Khorrameh, Zarghan, Rostam located in the Province of Fars
23.	1030	Qashqaie Handmade Carpet of Fars	Producer or groups of producers benefiting from the appellation of origin concerned: 1. Union for Handmade Carpet Producers and Exporters of the Province of Fars 2. Cooperatives Union for Rural Handmade Carpet Producers of the Province of Fars 3. Guild Union of Shiraz Handmade Carpet Weavers and Producers	Shiraz, Firouzabad, Abadeh, Ghir and Karzin, Darab, Jahrom, Fasa, Kazeroun, Marvdasht, Mamassani, Khorram Bid, Eghlid, Neyriz, Estehban, Bovanat, Lar, Khonj, Lamrod, Zarindasht, Sarvestan, Koar, Khorrameh, Zarghan, Rostam located in the Province of Fars

TABLE 7 International registrations of PCs under Lisbon System (*cont.*)

	No.	Appellation / Translation	Holder	Region
24.	1031	Ilam Handmade Carpet	Producer or groups of producers benefiting from the appellation of origin concerned: 1. Guild Union of Ilam Handmade Carpet 2. Cooperatives Union for Production of Rural Handmade Carpet of the province of Ilam 3. Iran Carpet Company – Ilam Branch	The province of Ilam
25.	1032	Sistan Handmade Carpet	Producer or groups of producers benefiting from the appellation of origin concerned: 1. Mandegar Sculptors Cooperative No 1550 of Sistan and Balochistan 2. Carpet and Handicrafts Design and Production Cooperative No 4139 of Sistan and Balochistan 3. Cooperative for Production of Rural Handmade Carpet of the region of Sistan 4. Iran Carpet Company – Zabol Branch 5. Khoshnegar Carpet Company of Sistan	Cities of Zabol, Zahak, Hirmand, Nimrouz, Hamoun, Zahedan located in the province of Sistan and Balochistan

TABLE 7 International registrations of PCs under Lisbon System (*cont.*)

	No.	Appellation / Translation	Holder	Region
26.	1033	Lorestan Handmade Carpet	Producer or groups of producers benefiting from the appellation of origin concerned: 1. Cooperatives Union for Rural Handmade Carpet of the province of Lorestan 2. Guild Union of Khorram Abad Handmade Carpet Weavers 3. Union for Carpet Sellers of the city of Khorram Abad 4. Cooperative for Rural Handmade Carpet of the city of Delfan 5. Cooperative for Rural Handmade Carpet of the city of Doroud 6. Iran Carpet Company – Khorram Abad Branch	Cities of Khorram Abad, Kouhdasht, Azna, Aligoudarz, Boroujerd, Aleshtar, Nour Abad, Doroud, Poldokhtar located in the province of Lorestan
27.	1034	Kordi Handmade Carpet of north Khorasan	Producer or groups of producers benefiting from the appellation of origin concerned: 1. Guild Union of Bojnourd Handmade Carpet Weavers 2. Guild Union of Shirvan Handmade Carpet Weavers	Cities of Bojnourd, Shirvan located in the province of north Khorasan
28.	1035	Varamin Handmade Carpet	Producer or groups of producers benefiting from the appellation of origin concerned: 1. Cooperative of Varamin Carpet Weavers 2. Shahid Beheshti Cooperative of Rural Carpet of Varamin 3. Guild Union of Varamin Handmade Carpet Weavers	City of Varamin located in the province of Tehran

TABLE 7 International registrations of PCs under Lisbon System (*cont.*)

	No.	Appellation / Translation	Holder	Region
29.	1036	Torkman Handmade Carpet of Jarglan and Bojnord	Producer or groups of producers benefiting from the appellation of origin concerned: Guild Union of Bojnord Handmade Carpet Weavers	Cities of Jarglan, Bojnord located in the province of north Khorasan
30.	1124	Sirjan's Shirakipich Kilim	Producer or groups of producers benefiting from the appellation of origin concerned Cooperative of Firouzeh handmade carpet of Samangan of Sirjan	Sirjan
31.	1130	Harsin Kilim	Producer or groups of producers benefiting from the appellation of origin concerned Cooperative of Kilim weaving of Harsin	Harsin
32.	1140	Bijar Handmade Carpet		Bijar Region
33.	1141	Kelardasht Handmade Carpet	West of Mazandaran Handwoven Carpet Cooperative Company, Kelardasht Mazandaran Province Rural Handwoven Carpet Cooperative Companies Union Kelardasht County Guildhall Abbas Abad Handwoven Carpet Union Noshahr Rural Handwoven Carpet Cooperative Company Noor Handwoven Carpet Union Noshahr Handwoven Carpet Union Babolsar Handwoven Carpet Weavers Union Ramsar County Handwoven Carpet Weavers Union Chalus County Handwoven Carpet Union	Kelardasht

TABLE 7 International registrations of PCs under Lisbon System (*cont.*)

	No.	Appellation / Translation	Holder	Region
34.	1148	Tekab Afshar Handmade Carpet	West Azerbaijan Province Rural Handwoven Carpet Cooperative Companies Union Tekab Handwoven Carpet Weavers Union Tekab Rural Handwoven Carpet Cooperative Company Tekab Urban Handwoven Carpet Cooperative Company	Tekab Region
35.	1279	Josheghan Handmade Carpet	Kashan Rural Handmade Carpet Manufacturers Cooperative Kashan Handmade Carpet Sellers Union Kashan Handmade Carpet Weavers Union Iran Carpet Company	Josheghan county, Kashan city, Isfahan province, Iran
36.	1282	Senneh Handmade Carpet	Union of Rural Handwoven Carpet Cooperatives of Kurdistan Province Union of Sanandaj Handwoven Carpet Weavers Union of Kurdistan Handwoven Carpet Cooperatives Iran Carpet Company, Sanandaj Branch Union of Carpet Sellers and Carpet Weavers of Bijar City Iran Carpet Company, Bijar Branch Cooperative Company 3580 supplying the needs of Bijar Slim Carpets	The cities of Sanandaj, Bijar, Qorveh, Saqez, Kamyaran, Dehgolan, Marivan, Divandareh, located in Kurdistan Province, Iran.

On May 20, 2015, the 'Geneva Act of the Lisbon Agreement on Appellations of Origin and Geographical Indications'[1213] was adopted by the Diplomatic Conference of the WIPO. The Act updates the Lisbon Agreement, broadening its scope to include not only AO but also GIs, and allows international organizations to join as contracting parties. It also covers the expectations of those countries that protect GIs through the trademark system. Beyond signaling the geographic origin of a product, GIs also serve to highlight and enhance cultural contributions and the ingenuity of genuine expertise. Each contracting party must ensure the protection within its own territory, according to its legal norms and practices, of the AO and GIs of products originating from other member countries that it has agreed to protect.

TABLE 8 Membership of key carpet producers in AO and GIs treaties

Treaty \ Country	Iran	Afghanistan	China	India	Nepal	Pakistan	Türkiye
Lisbon Agreement (AO)	√	–	–	–	–	–	–
Geneva Act (AO & GIs)	–	–	–	–	–	–	–
Madrid Agreement (Indications of Source)	√	–	–	–	–	–	√

1213 Geneva Act of the Lisbon Agreement on Appellations of Origin and Geographical Indications 2015 (3384 UNTS (entered into force 26 February 2020)).

TABLE 9 Memberships of key PCs markets in AO and GIs treaties

Treaty \ Country	The U.S.A	Germany	Lebanon	The UK	Japan	The UAE	Pakistan	South Africa	Italy	Australia	Canada	Switzerland
Lisbon Agreement (AO)	–	–	–	–	–	–	–	–	√	–	–	–
Geneva Act (AO and GIs)	–	–	–	–	–	–	–	–	–	–	–	√
Madrid Agreement (Indications of Source)	–	√	√	√	√	–	–	–	√	–	–	√

2.4 *Madrid Agreement and Madrid Protocol*

As explained in Chapter 3, Section 2.4, the Madrid Agreement and its Protocol, known as the Madrid System are designed for international registration of marks. However, the Madrid System could also serve as a tool for international registration and protection of GIs. This, of course, is subject to two conditions: First, GIs must be applied for registration as collective or certification marks; and second, "this system could only be used by those countries that protect GIs via a certification trademark regime and have no specific rules on the protection of GIs."[1214]

2.5 *WIPO Model Law for Developing Countries on Appellations of Origin and Indications of Source*

The Model Law is a non-binding standard model text that was drafted by a group of developing country members of WIPO in 1975. National authorities may use the Model Law to adjust or adopt their national law and regulations for protection of AO and indications of source.[1215] This text was the main source for drafting Iran's Act for protection of GIs.[1216] The model law deals with various issues in five parts:

1214 O'Connor, *The Law of Geographical Indications* (n 373) Pages 32–33.

1215 David Thual and others, 'Study on the Protection of Geographical Indications for Products Other Than Wines, Spirits and Agricultural Products or Foodstuffs' (Insight Consulting, Origin, Agridea 2009) Page 12.

1216 Iran – Act for Protection of Geographical Indications.

- Part I on general provisions including definitions of AO, indications of source, products, producer; applicability of relevant provisions of international treaties; and provisions on foreigners' rights and position in the absence of international treaties;
- Part II on provisions concerning AO and relevant governing rules including requirement for and exclusion from protection; registration procedures; cancellation and rectification of registration; and rights and sanctions regarding registered AO;
- Part III on provisions concerning indications of source in which "direct or indirect use of an indication of source which is false or which is likely to mislead the public shall be unlawful;"
- Part IV on the courts' competency and applicable rules;
- Part V on final and transitional provisions which comprise adjective rules;
- An annex which comprises two further alternatives on provisions for the protection of AO.[1217]

2.6 *TRIPS Agreement*

Articles 22 to 24 of the TRIPS Agreement relate to the protection of GIs. The primary efforts to embed GIs in the final text of the Agreement were made by the EC and Switzerland,[1218] and despite little consensus among countries, they reached an agreement to support stronger protection of GIs in comparison with the Paris Convention.[1219] Article 22 defines GIs as "indications which identify a good originating in the territory of a Member, or a region or locality in that territory, where a given quality, reputation or other characteristic of the goods is essentially attributable to its geographic origin."[1220] Article 22 also provides a general set of standards which Member States have to comply with for protection of GIs in their territory, and Article 23 covers the additional protection for wines and spirits.

2.7 *Regional Agreements*

The International Convention for the Use of Appellations of Origin and Denominations of Cheeses, known as the Stresa Convention was signed

1217 WIPO, *Model Law for Developing Countries on Appellations of Origin and Indications of Source* (WIPO 1975).

1218 Conrad (n 1208) Pages 29–30.

1219 Jim Keon, 'Intellectual Property Rules for Trademarks and Geographical Indications: Important Parts of the New World Trade Order' in Carlos María Correa and Abdulqawi Yusuf (eds), *Intellectual Property and International Trade: The TRIPS Agreement* (2nd edn, Kluwer Law International 2008) Page 174.

1220 TRIPS Agreement Article 22(1).

on 1 June 1951 at Stresa, Italy.[1221] The Government of Italy is the depository of the Convention and acts as the secretariat of the Convention.[1222] The Stresa Convention was the first regional agreement in Europe establishing positive protection of GIs with both features of AO and indications of source regarding a specific type of product (i.e. cheeses).[1223] Later, the principle of the Stresa Convention regarding the protection and use of AO was reproduced in the Lisbon Agreement.[1224] According to the Convention, parties to the Convention "pledge themselves to take all the necessary measures, in accordance with their respective, internal legislation, to ensure the application of the principles as stated in art. 2 to 9 inclusive." They are committed "to prohibit and repress within their territories, in the languages of the State or in a foreign language, the use of the appellations d'origine, denominations and designations of cheeses contrary to the provisions of the Convention."[1225] Substantive Articles of the Convention deal with:

- Definition of the term 'cheese,'
- Protection of AO for cheeses that are manufactured or matured in traditional regions,
- Protection of denominations of cheese,
- The possibility to insert an appellation of origin or denomination of cheese or to add new annex to the Convention,
- Dispute settlement mechanisms concerning the interpretation of the Convention clauses, or difficulties with applications.[1226]

Protection of GIs is also addressed in some regional agreements. The Bangui Agreement Relating to the Creation of an African Intellectual Property Organization (OAPI),[1227] and Andean decision concerning a common regime on industrial property[1228] are two regional treaties in which protection of GIs was mentioned. Annex VI of the Bangui Agreement covers the issue of AO, including definitions, conditions for protection, the registration procedure, and rights and sanctions. Also, Chapter VII of the Andean decision No. 344 includes provisions regarding AO.

1221 The International Convention for the use of appellations d'origine and denominations of cheeses 1951 (entered into force on 12 July 1953).

1222 *ibid Article 5.*

1223 O'Connor, *The Law of Geographical Indications* (n 373) Page 34.

1224 Thual and others (n 1215) Page 12.

1225 The Stresa Convention Article 1.

1226 *ibid Articles 2–5 and 9.*

1227 Bangui Agreement Relating to the Creation of an African Intellectual Property Organization, Constituting a Revision of the Agreement Relating to the Creation of an African and Malagasy Office of Industrial Property 1977 (entered into force on 8 February 1982).

1228 Andean Decision No. 344.

As explained in Chapter 1, Section 1.2.2, along with TK, GIs are among the IPRs' subjects for which members of the ECOTA are committed to granting protection. The ECOTA does not define what the GIs or the scope of protection are, but those ECOTA Members who are members of the WTO are committed to extending to any other Contracting Parties, which are not members of WTO, treatment no less favorable than that extended to the WTO member concerning the protection of IPRs.[1229] Therefore, Iran could expect to enjoy the same level of protection of GIs in the territory of the ECOTA Members which are members of the WTO. It should be noted that in many cases when goods are produced in or derived from a region divided into different countries the only possible solution to protect the GIs of such a region would be to enter into regional agreements for their protection.[1230]

2.8 *Bilateral Agreements*

The intention of countries protecting GIs in their bilateral relations has historical antecedents. There are several examples of such bilateral agreements. Agreements between Switzerland with Spain,[1231] Germany with Switzerland[1232] and France[1233] (Germany concluded several agreements with a similar structure with other countries),[1234] Austria and France,[1235] Spain and Portugal,[1236]

1229 ECOTA Article 4(3).

1230 WIPO, *Intellectual Property Needs and Expectations of Traditional Knowledge Holders* (n 166) Page 92.

1231 Treaty between the Swiss Confederation and the Spanish State on the Protection of Indications of Source, Appellations of Origin and Similar Designations 1974 (entered into force on 10 March 1976).

1232 Treaty between the Swiss Confederation and the Federal Republic of Germany on the Protection of Indications of Source and Other Geographical Designations 1967 (entered into force on 30 August 1969).

1233 Agreement between the Federal Republic of Germany and France on the Protection of Indications of Source, Appellations of Origin and Other Geographical Denominations (entered into force on 7 May 1960; amendments entered into force on 1 November 1969).

1234 These agreements which are yet in force are concluded between Germany and Cuba (1954), France (1960), Italy (1963), Greece (1964), Switzerland (1967) and Spain (1970). See: The German customs, 'Customs Online – Bilateral Agreements and Treaties' (*Zoll*) <https://www.zoll.de/EN/Businesses/Movement-of-goods/Import/Restrictions/Goods/Protection-of-industrial-property/Indications-of-geographical-source/Protected-rights/Bilateral-agreements-and-treaties/bilateral-agreements-and-treaties_node.html> accessed 19 March 2019.

1235 Agreement between Austria and France on the Protection of Indications of Source, Appellations of Origin and Denominations of Products of Agriculture and Industry 1974 (entered into force on 24 September 1975).

1236 Agreement between Spain and Portugal on the Protection of Indications of Source, Appellations of Origin and the Denominations of Certain Products 1970 (entered into force on 23 August 1972).

Costa Rica and France,[1237] El Salvador and France,[1238] France and Italy,[1239] and the Czechoslovak and Austria are some examples of bilateral agreements whose subject matters are protection of GIs.[1240] Besides those bilateral agreements which are directly related to the protection of GIs, there are some other bilateral treaties in which protection of GIs is among other matters addressed. The Comprehensive Economic and Trade Agreement (CETA) between Canada and the EU in which for the first time a north American country recognizes protection of the GIs;[1241] Trade Agreement between Spain and Cuba; and Iran and Cuba[1242] are examples of such agreements.

Iranian policymakers consider bilateral agreements as an effective legal instrument in the trade, economic and investment relation with other States. However, Iran has not concluded any agreement with other States regarding the protection of GIs. As explained in Chapter 1, Section 1.3 of this study, none of the Iranian bilateral agreements is focused on GIs. They include amity, trade, customs, economic and industrial cooperation, investments, cultural and artistic affairs, scientific and technological cooperation, which directly or indirectly refer to protection of IPRs between parties. Of all those agreements, only the trade agreement between Iran and Cuba of 2008 refers directly to the Parties' intention regarding protection of AO and it does not provide any details of the elements of such protection.

Although such protection will be limited to the territory of the two contracting parties, it is an appropriate legal instrument for the protection of the GIs. Therefore, the TKHs may seek such protection for the GIs and TK-RI beyond national borders through bilateral agreements, especially with those countries that are the most important markets for the PCs.

1237 Agreement between Costa Rica and France on the Reciprocal Protection of Industrial Property and Appellations of Origin 1933 (entered into force on 23 July 1935).

1238 *Convention between El Salvador and France of concerning the Protection of Appellations of Origin 1932.*

1239 Convention between France and Italy on the Protection of Appellations of Origin, Indications of Source and Denominations of Certain Products 1964 (entered into force on 24 April 1969; additions and modifications agreed through an exchange of letters of 6 May 1969 and 13 February 1970).

1240 Agreement between the Czechoslovak Socialist Republic and the Republic of Austria on the Protection of Indications of Source, Appellations of Origin and Other Geographical Denominations (entered into force on 26 February 1981).

1241 The Comprehensive Economic and Trade Agreement (CETA) between Canada, of the one part, and the European Union and its Member States, of the other part 2016 (OJ L 11/1).

1242 *Trade Agreement between the government of the Islamic Republic of Iran and the government of the Republic of Cuba 2008 Article 10.*

3 What Do TKHs Expect from GIs Legal Regime?

Goods and services qualifying for GIs generally are precious and profitable assets. Therefore, they are always at risk of use by competitors. PCs provide a prominent example of such unauthorized use. At present, PCs face the active presence of many rivals who have supplied their products under the name of PCs GIs. These rivals have lowered their prices by leveraging their abundant, cheap human resources, and non-original designs. These rivals' activities have been somewhat reducing the final price of the products and are even affecting the sensitivity of the markets concerning the quality and beauty of PCs. These competitors use a variety of methods to benefit from PCs GIs.[1243]

The first type of exploitation occurs when producers use the famous name of geographical locations known for PCs on their products, but they do not hide the real place of production. An excellent example of such method is Bijar Carpets. "Bidjar is a town of northwest Iran surrounded by many rug-weaving villages whose output is also labelled Bijâr. The area is inhabited by Kurds. Rugs of Bijâr and its immediate area, are woven in a wide variety of patterns."[1244] (See: Figure 15)

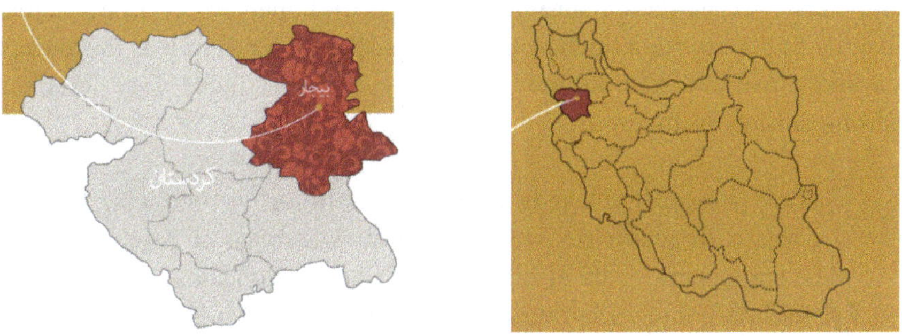

FIGURE 15 Geographical location of Bijar Region in Iran[1245]

The most important and most accomplished artistic achievement of Bijar villagers are their carpets. In Iran, people know it as 'iron carpet': this designation means high quality. Bijâr Carpet is excellent in terms of texture and colour too,

1243 Saeed Sehat and Mahsa Farajlou Motlagh, 'بررسی و آسیب شناسی صادرات فرش دستباف ایران (An Analysis and Critical Assessment of Persian Carpet Exports)' Allameh Tabataba'i University 23, Page 17.

1244 See: Stone (n 214).

1245 See: Abdolhossein Ghasem Nejhad, 'قالی بیجار (Bijar Rugs)' (*Iran National Carpet Centre*, 1 December 2018) <https://www.incc.ir/knowing/فرش-بیجار>

and it is distinctive among PCs because it is full of motifs and designs.[1246] Despite the reputation and quality of the Bijâr carpet, it has not been secured from exploitation by the third parties. The following is as an example of such appropriation (Figure 16):

FIGURE 16 Indo Bidjar carpet

As one can see in the advertisement, the producer has been using the GIs of Bijar for its product. They mix the Bijâr indication with the prefix 'Indo' and claim "Persian design faithfully replicated and finely woven in India. Just like the Bidjar but for a fraction of the price." Another example is the Sarouk Carpets. Goswami from the Indian Institute of Carpet Technology describes Sarouk Carpets as follows:

> Sarouk is a small village in central Iran famous for producing knotted carpets with geometric patterns known as Sarough or Sarouk carpets. The carpets are made of high-quality wool in workshops as well as on household looms. The traditional rug has Herati and Boteh patterns all over it or in a medallion layout of almost any geometric shape, the most common of which is a medallion and corner layout. After World War I, a branching type of medallion was introduced with the American markets specifically in mind. Customary colours are red, blue, burnt orange, ocher and champagne, with rich red and blue colours common in Saroughs destined for America. Lighter shades of red, yellow and turquoise are used for outlines. The carpets are made using the best quality lustrous

1246 *ibid.*

> wool and are woven with a Turkish knot density from 120 to 500 kpsi. Originally the piles were cut very short but now they are preferred long.[1247]

Sarouk Carpets are very expensive and some of them even hit "$45,000 to $60,000 for a great 9′ by 12′." However, Sarouk Carpets are also woven in the USA and India.[1248]

TKHs are seeking protection of the significant indications of those geographical locations. They believe their TK has unique communication with those specific places, especially in the case of tangible forms of TK products such as handicrafts, many of which are produced from local materials such as *in-situ* genetic resources. Therefore, the TKHs expect the GIs regime to adequately protect TK.[1249] They think of PCs as goods,[1250] which have a relationship to the true indication of the given places.

Another popular way to utilize PCs is to by employing Persian GIs for the products without mentioning the original GIs. For example, Haris, or Heris or Heriz, is the name of a city in the Iranian province of East Azerbaijan. The handwoven carpets made in Haris and the nearby villages are known as 'Hariz,' 'Bakhshayesh,' 'Mehrabân,' 'Serapi,' or 'Guravan.' "These are trade designations of general quality rather than specific geographic attributions."[1251] In the application for registration of the Haris Carpet under the Lisbon Agreement, a full description of the product, raw materials, the method of weaving, design and colours is provided.[1252] Still, an Indian producer uses Haris as a mark for its goods.[1253]

Therefore, TKHs demand the protection of designations even if they are not directly attributed to a geographic name. The GIs regime not only protects the geographic names directly, but also the signs and indications that are not geographical names but are names indirectly related to a geographic location

1247 Goswami (n 1109) Page 194.

1248 For examples, see the collections available at: 'Karastan Rugs – Vintage & Antique Wool Carpets for Sale Online' (*Jewel Rugs*) <https://jewelrugs.com/collections/karastan-rugs> accessed 12 December 2024.

1249 WIPO, *Intellectual Property and Traditional Cultural Expressions/Folklore-Booklet N°1* (n 656) Page 18.

1250 Good means any natural or agricultural product, or any product of handicraft and industry. See: Iran – Act for Protection of Geographical Indications Article 1(b).

1251 Stone (n 214).

1252 See: WIPO, 'WIPO Lisbon Express Search' (n 1199).

1253 'HARIS ORIENT TEPPICHE in New Delhi, Delhi, India – Company Profile' (*Tradeindia*, 16 March 2005) <https://www.tradeindia.com/Seller-1030976-HARIS-ORIENT-TEPPICHE/> accessed 23 March 2019.

such as TK-RI.[1254] GIs may protect TK-RI as a specific type of indications and symbols attributed to the PCs,[1255] and are specific to a region.[1256]

Another commonly observed practice is using GIs as trademarks for third-party products. An example of this is the use of Qum GIs, which may lead to unfair commercial practices. Qum is a delicate silk handwoven carpet well-known in Iran and worldwide. "The innovation of Qum carpet designers caused different designs in carpet weaving by using from the original motifs and establishing harmonies between elements and the methods of carpet designing. Wool, cotton, silk and mohair are the materials for carpet weaving in Qum."[1257] However, a machine-made carpet made of 100% pure silk was observed bearing the label "Qum" and marked as "Made in Belgium." This example reflects the ongoing use of geographical names – including those protected as AO under the Lisbon System – in commercial labeling outside the country of origin.

Therefore, TKHs also call the protection of the reputation of PCs. As already explained in Chapter 3 of this study about protection of the TK-RS as trademarks. TKHs expect the GIs protection mechanism to prevent the unauthorized use of their indications by third parties and to guarantee their rights to use their indications.[1258] In this regard, TKHs claim protection against "any false, confusing or misleading indications which in relation to goods or services, suggest any endorsement by or linkage with" such TKHs concerning the TK or TK-RI.[1259] This language is similar to the text of the Swakopmund Protocol, which stipulates:

> any false, confusing or misleading indications or allegations which, in relation to goods or services that refer to, draw upon or evoke the expressions of folklore of a community or suggest any endorsement by or linkage with that community, can be prevented and/or is subject to civil or criminal sanctions.[1260]

1254 WIPO, *Intellectual Property and Traditional Cultural Expressions/Folklore-Booklet N°1* (n 656) Page 18.
1255 IGC-GRTKF Secretariat, 'Consolidated Analysis of the Legal Protection of Traditional Cultural Expressions' (n 800) Page 50.
1256 Torsen and Anderson (n 440) Page 61.
1257 See: WIPO, 'WIPO Lisbon Express Search' (n 1199).
1258 Frankel (n 788) Page 452.
1259 See draft articles of the open-ended informal drafting group of IGC 17: IGC-GRTKF Secretariat, 'Draft Report of Intergovernmental Committee on Intellectual Property and Genetic Resources, Traditional Knowledge and Folklore' (n 241) Annex II, Article C.
1260 Swakopmund Protocol Section 19(3).

Cottier and Müller support TKHs' demands and point out that TKHs expect the GIs law to prevent undue free-riding and UC from competitors.[1261] In principle, third parties are not allowed to use the GIs in a manner that misleads consumers about the origin of the good.[1262]

Finally, TKHs expect GIs to help with identifying their communities and individuals, protecting their practices and the authenticity of their cultural products.[1263] They seek the protection of their culture through the GIs regime, and they expect such protection to help and encourage them to promote the creativity and innovation of their culture. Some IP scholars argue that because the GIs regime recognizes fundamental values and collective rights. Thus, it could be a model for a *sui generis* regime for the protection of the cultural property of TKHs.[1264]

Having considered TKHs' expectations from the GIs regime concerning the protection of their TK-RI, it is also pertinent to look at the possibility of protecting PCs as the subject matter of the GIs law.

4 The Possibility of Protection for PCs as Subject Matter of GIs Law

4.1 *Required Elements for Protection of PCs under GIs Law*

GIs could be a useful tool for the marketing and commercialization of TK, as well as for the promotion of the economic value of local products such as handmade carpets. However, the question arises as to whether PCs could be protected effectively within the framework of the GIs legal regime. To answer this question, PCs must meet the protection criteria under GIs laws. In accordance with the Iranian Act for Protection of GIs:

> "Geographical Indication" means an indication that identifies a good as originating in the territory, a region or locality of the country, provided that the quality, reputation or other characteristics of the good is essentially attributable to its geographical origin.

1261 Cottier and Müller (n 140); in Cottier, *Trade and Intellectual Property Protection in WTO Law: Collected Essays* (n 140) Page 437.

1262 ITC and WIPO (n 869) Page 86.

1263 Kal Raustiala and Stephen R Munzer, 'The Global Struggle Over Geographic Indications' (2007) 18 European Journal of International Law 337, Pages 345–346.

1264 Susan Frankel refers to the comments from Bently, Sherman and Wiseman. See: Frankel (n 788) Pages 452–453.

It seems that the definition presented by the Act has been inspired by the definition of GIs provided by the TRIPS Agreement:

> Geographical indications are, for the purposes of this Agreement, indications which identify a good as originating in the territory of a Member, or a region or locality in that territory, where a given quality, reputation or other characteristic of the good is essentially attributable to its geographical origin.[1265]

In both definitions, if the elements of 'quality,' 'reputation' and 'other characteristics' of goods are attributable to a geographical origin, then those goods are the subject matter of the definition provided by the Iranian law and the TRIPS Agreement.[1266] Different approaches to the protecting GIs and the variety of terms used in various laws, as well as the differences in the national regulations and procedures, have made it very difficult to analyze the scope and the extent of these elements. Notwithstanding the lack of global consensus concerning the interpretation of these elements,[1267] the following issues concerning the protection of PCs as the subject matter of GIs can be addressed:

First: Protection of PCs' Quality: Concerning the quality criterion referred to in the definition of GIs, there are no coherent or comprehensive criteria or any single interpretation. The interpretation of this criterion is solely the responsibility of the competent national authorities, and the culture and practices of the societies will differ in how effectively they provide such an interpretation. Hence, national authorities use different ways to attain the concept of qualified quality and use different words to refer to it. Terminologies such as 'established quality,' 'particular quality,' 'given quality,' 'specific quality,' 'special quality characteristics,' 'special outstanding quality distinguishing the product from generic products' and so on are used by different national laws.[1268]

Moreover, the assessment of the qualitative connection between a product and a geographic area is a challenging task. On the one hand, it requires the accurate determination of the factors affecting quality, such as the raw

1265 TRIPS Agreement Article 22(1).

1266 These elements are also referred in some other documents. See: Geneva Act of the Lisbon Agreement Article 2(1)(ii); and Glossary in the WIPO, *Intellectual Property and Folk, Arts and Cultural Festivals* (n 692) Page 54.

1267 SCT Secretariat, 'Geographical Indications' (World Intellectual Property Organization 2003) WIPO Doc SCT/10/4 Paragraph 16.

1268 See: WTO, 'Review under Article 24.2 of the Application of the Provisions of the Section of the TRIPS AGREEMENT on Geographical Indications' (2001) WTO Doc IP/C/W/253 Paragraphs 40 and 41.

materials and their processing methods; and, on the other hand, it will be necessary to determine how those factors and the geographic area are linked.[1269]

Overall, it seems that the requirement for the existence of a qualitative relationship between a specific geographical area and production would weaken those communities whose geographical locations are not related to their industrial products.[1270] Therefore, using GIs to protecting Persian machine-made carpets or even for those handwoven carpets whose quality has no specific relation with a geographical area would not be likely to work.

Second: Protection of the PCs' Reputation: There are two legal models concerning the element of reputation within the GIs regimes: the TRIPS model and the Lisbon model. Commonly, the national laws that are harmonized with the first model systematically use and apply 'reputation' either separately or in combination with a qualifier such as 'general reputation,' 'given reputation,' or 'specific reputation.'[1271] "The reputation of products of a designated origin would generally have been acquired over a lengthy period of time by the products' own merits rather than clever public relations and advertising."[1272] In a different approach from the TRIPS model, the Lisbon model does not consider 'reputation':

> [t]he geographical denomination of a country, region or locality, which serves to designate a product originating therein, the quality and characteristics of which are due exclusively or essentially to the geographical environment, including natural and human factors.[1273]

Similarly, the domestic laws which abide by the Lisbon Agreement do not attribute the reputation as an element related to the geographical origin of a good. Rather, the Lisbon model focuses on two other elements of the quality and characteristics of the products.[1274] However, the Geneva Act of the

1269 SCT Secretariat, 'Geographical Indications' (n 1267) Paragraph 12.

1270 *ibid Paragraph 13.*

1271 WTO, 'Review under Article 24.2 of the Application of the Provisions of the Section of the TRIPS AGREEMENT on Geographical Indications' (n 1268) Paragraph 42.

1272 Felix Addor and Alexandra Grazioli, 'Agreement on Trade-Related Aspects of Intellectual Property Rights: Section 3: Geographical Indications' in Thomas Cottier and Pierre Véron (eds), *Concise International and European IP Law: TRIPS, Paris Convention, European Enforcement and Transfer of Technology*, vol 4 (2nd edn, Kluwer Law International 2008) Pages 64–65.

1273 Lisbon Agreement Article 2(1).

1274 WTO, 'Review under Article 24.2 of the Application of the Provisions of the Section of the TRIPS AGREEMENT on Geographical Indications' (n 1268) Paragraph 42.

Lisbon Agreement refers to the reputation of goods "where the quality or characteristics of the good are due exclusively or essentially to the geographical environment, including natural and human factors, and which has given the good its reputation."[1275]

Third: Protection of Other Characteristics of PCs: Consideration of the use of the phrase 'other characteristics' in the definitions given in the TRIPS Agreement and the Iranian Act, leads to the conclusion that the characteristics of quality and reputation are not exclusive. In other words, if there are other characteristics which are attributable to the geographical origin of the good, that good would qualify to be regarded as a subject matter of the definition of GIs. Such characteristics may include human professional skills and natural elements, such as environment, natural resources and climates of the given geographical locations.[1276] Moreover, it should be noted that the existence of any of these three factors of quality, reputation and other characteristics alone or in combination may be subject to the definition of the TRIPS Agreement and the subject of the protection of the GIs regime under the TRIPS Agreement.[1277]

Concerning human factors, the protection of GIs does not rely merely on geographical places.[1278] In the current age of globalization, skilled artisans who use traditional methods for producing traditional goods do not have much to do with a specific geographical area; because they could readily move from their original geographic locations to other places within professional mobility programs.[1279] Thus, 'distinctive human factors' must be developed and combined with other elements of quality, reputation or other attributes of local products.[1280]

It seems that under the TRIPS Agreement the quality and other characteristics elements are more natural than the reputation factor, and therefore have a special relationship with their place of origin meaning that they could not be attributed to other geographic locations.[1281]

1275 Geneva Act of the Lisbon Agreement Articles 2(1)(i).

1276 SCT Secretariat, 'Geographical Indications' (n 1267) Paragraph 15.

1277 Addor and Grazioli (n 1272) Pages 64–65.

1278 IGC-GRTKF Secretariat, 'Review of Existing Intellectual Property Protection of Traditional Knowledge' (World Intellectual Property Organization 2002) WIPO Doc WIPO/GRTKF/IC/3/7 Page 13; and ITC and WIPO (n 869) Page 86.

1279 SCT Secretariat, 'Geographical Indications' (n 1267) Paragraph 13.

1280 IGC-GRTKF Secretariat, 'Review of Existing Intellectual Property Protection of Traditional Knowledge' (n 1278) Page 13; and ITC and WIPO (n 869) Page 86.

1281 Addor and Grazioli (n 1272) Pages 64–65.

Fourth: Protection of Geographical Origins of PCs: GIs could help to advise consumers about the source of the goods[1282] as they inform the consumers that a product with a specific quality has been produced and originated from a specific location. The "term GIs must be interpreted broadly," and may include the name of a country, or an area within a country, a geographical name, or a name of a town (Qum Carpet), a traditional area (Sarouk), a place which is divided among official subdivisions of a country (Torkman Carpet). GIs could also refer to "a traditional denomination, which is not a geographical place name as such, but which nevertheless designates a product as coming from a particular place."[1283] For example, when we talk about a 'Persian' carpet, it refers to an identity of people who have been living in the same geographic place. It is the old name of what is known nowadays as Iran. Moreover, the terms 'Persian carpets' and 'Persian rugs' refer to carpets that are produced in the geographic region, which the world knows as Iran.

The essential role of a given place has been in the core of debates concerning the protection of GIs. In this regard, Addor and Grazioli argue that under the TRIPS Agreement all elements whether "known or unknown, natural or human, may underpin a 'quality,' 'reputation' or 'other characteristics' of a product" must be identified as originating from a specific place.[1284] According to the Lisbon Agreement "specific qualities or characteristics need to be expressed in the product itself and that the names directly relates to a particular geographical name of a country, region or locality."[1285] In order to be protected under the Lisbon Agreement, there should be a strong link between the product and the geographical area in which that product originates.[1286]

Still, there are some difficulties concerning the protection of PCs with GIs. As Addor and Grazioli point out, to determine and evaluate the association between a product and its geographical origin is one of the most complex elements of the definition used in the TRIPS Agreement. According to the principle of territoriality of the protection of IPRs, the protection of GIs is governed by the law of the country in which the protection is sought, and not according to the laws of the country of origin. Therefore, the determination of the elements of the quality, reputation and other characteristics should be based on the perspective of the designated country of the protection. However,

1282 Abbott (n 799) Page 24.

1283 Addor and Grazioli (n 1272) Pages 64–65.

1284 *ibid.*

1285 Cottier and Müller (n 140); in Cottier, *Trade and Intellectual Property Protection in WTO Law: Collected Essays* (n 140) Page 436.

1286 WIPO, *Protect and Promote Your Culture* (n 664) Page 48.

it is better to make such an examination under the law and the statutes of the country of origin because, only in such situation, the laws, regulations and practices of the country of origin shall be necessarily examined to determine the connection between a product and its geographical origin. This approach would avoid the various laws and decisions of the countries in which the protection are sought to be applied to TK subject matters such as PCs.[1287]

Moreover, although GIs can identify and protect PCs through their places, it fails to prevent the use of PCs' names when the actual locations of manufacturing are indicated.[1288] For example, the GIs regime cannot prevent misappropriation, as discussed above, by Indian producers who have been using the GI Bijar for their product under the name *Indo Bijar*. However, the GIs regime under the TRIPS Agreement did make an exception concerning wines and spirits and provided additional protection for them. The TRIPS Agreement prohibits the use of the geographical names of wines and spirits for other products even if the true place of origin is indicated.[1289] For instance, using the GI Champagne for wine made in California or the GI Bordeaux for cookies produced in the Netherlands is prohibited. Therefore, in order to avoid such misappropriation, there is a need to extend similar additional protection to TK products.

4.2 *Using Trademark Law as Protection Regime of GIs*

As mentioned in Chapter 3 of this study, some TKHs around the world have been using trademarks for protection of their TK-RS.[1290] Like trademarks, GIs carry a message. Both are able to convince the potential consumers that specific characteristics may be found in a product from a particular source. In the same fashion, TKHs "seek to protect the goodwill of the product as it relates to its origin."[1291] Torsen and Anderson suggest that "Just like trademarks, the protection of geographical indications is aimed at the protection of the goodwill and reputation of indigenous and traditional communities."[1292] The GIs system allows TK with exclusive qualities and reputation to be protected in

1287 Addor and Grazioli (n 1272) Pages 64–65.
1288 Abbott (n 799) Page 24.
1289 TRIPS Agreement Article 23.
1290 IGC-GRTKF Secretariat, 'Report of Intergovernmental Committee on Intellectual Property and Genetic Resources, Traditional Knowledge and Folklore' (World Intellectual Property Organization 2008) WIPO Doc WIPO/GRTKF/IC/12/9 Paragraph 150.
1291 Cottier and Müller (n 140); in Cottier, *Trade and Intellectual Property Protection in WTO Law: Collected Essays* (n 140) Page 436.
1292 Torsen and Anderson (n 440) Page 59.

the market at a premium.[1293] Notwithstanding, the question as to what the differences are between GIs and trademarks, and which may provide a more effective legal mechanism for protecting TK-RI, is always a significant one.

As Abbott, Cottier and Gurry have noted a trademark aims firstly to protect the goodwill of producers and secondly to prevents confusion among consumers about what they are purchasing.[1294] Thus, the subject matter of trademark law protection is the producers of the goods and services that could help customers to choose the right products and services by knowing the producers. Contrary to the system of trademarks, the GIs regime does not protect the goodwill and reputation of the producers. It protects indications and symbols which refer to the geographical areas "where a given quality, reputation or other characteristics of the good is essentially attributable to its geographical origin."[1295] In brief, trademark protection is about distinguishing and protecting one enterprise from others, while protection of GIs is about distinguishing the products. Of course, the result of such a protection regime would be to prevent mistakes by consumers when choosing the goods they buy. There are also, however, further dissimilarities between the GIs and trademarks regimes to be considered.

Sometimes it is indeed challenging to protect TK-RI as GIs as it does not match the concept of GIs. For example, protecting 'Cupuaçu,' which is a spirit made from fermented sugarcane juice in Brazil, could be an issue because Cupuaçu is not an indication that is associated to a region.[1296]

GIs are also protectable under the concept of collective and certificate marks,[1297] which might be used to protect "the reputation and special qualities of traditional products."[1298] The primary use of the collective mark is to show specific characteristics, such as nature, properties or quality of the products.[1299] Similarly, in the certification marks system, the main feature is the technical content of the knowledge used to produce the goods, regardless

1293 Agaba Gilbert, 'Intellectual Property & Traditional Knowledge and Traditional Cultural Expressions' (Workshop on Intellectual Property and Traditional Knowledge for Economic Development: Empowering Local Communities of Uganda, Kampala, Uganda, 4 July 2017).

1294 See Abbott, Cottier and Gurry (n 367) Page 9.

1295 See subject matter of protection: Geneva Act of the Lisbon Agreement Article 2(1)(ii).

1296 Cottier and Müller (n 140); in Cottier, *Trade and Intellectual Property Protection in WTO Law: Collected Essays* (n 140) Page 444.

1297 ITC and WIPO (n 869) Page 86.

1298 WIPO, *Documenting Traditional Knowledge – A Toolkit* (World Intellectual Property Organization 2017) Page 13.

1299 See the Delegation of Portugal statement on behalf of the European Communities and their Member States: IGC-GRTKF Secretariat, 'Revised Draft Report of Intergovernmental

of the geographical link of the products to a particular location. The most striking example of such a certification mark is the TK-RS of the Māori that is mentioned in the Chapter 3 of this study. In this regard, this system has a fundamental difference from the GIs system in which a link to a geographic location is essential.[1300] When a GI is registered as a certification or collective mark, any natural person or legal entity whose products meet the requirements of the relevant mark has the right to use it. However, the owner of the mark would have the right to prevent such use if the user is no longer meeting those requirements. In contrast, GIs have no specific owner, and all persons located in the given geographic location are allowed to use the GIs.

One of the main reasons for opposing the extension of the GIs protection is that, contrary to the trademark law, GIs prevent or at least detract from the subject matters being generic or in the public domain[1301] while the innate nature of collective and certification marks cannot prevent their subject matters from becoming generic. For instance, if the owner fails to renew the registration of marks every ten years,[1302] or if the mark becomes subject to revocation because of the non-use condition, the mark would become generic and free to use by the public. Under the GIs system, protection is not limited to a period of time,[1303] registration is not a precondition for protection of subject matters,[1304] and there are "no sanctions for non-use or insufficient use."[1305] Besides, according to the GIs regime, TKHs could maintain the distinctiveness of their goods. This principle has been recognized under the Lisbon Agreement in which the validity of the registration of the AO is not limited. Moreover, the Lisbon system makes no exception for the appellations that have already become generic in the territory of the contracting parties. However, if the protection of the name in the country of origin stops, other Member States of the Lisbon Agreement will be able to consider it as a generic name. Also, Parties to the agreement, within one year of international registration, are allowed to

---

Committee on Intellectual Property and Genetic Resources, Traditional Knowledge and Folklore' (n 151) Paragraph 429.

1300 IGC-GRTKF Secretariat, 'Review of Existing Intellectual Property Protection of Traditional Knowledge' (n 1278) Page 14.

1301 Frankel (n 788) Page 453.

1302 Pardis Moslemzadeh Tehrani and Nazura Abdul Manap, 'Urgency and Benefits of Protecting Iranian Carpets Using Geographical Indications' (2013) 18 Journal of Intellectual Property Law 72, Page 73.

1303 See the discussion on 'duration of protection' on section 7 of this chapter.

1304 See the discussion on 'registration of GIs as positive protection for TK-RI' at the end of this section.

1305 Mantrov (n 1176) Page 269.

decide to reject the registration of a name, if they consider the name has previously been used as a generic name or as a trademark. Then, within two years, they may take the necessary measures to halt the use of the name.

It can be seen from the above analysis that, as Cottier and Müller state "there is a need to increase the practice of applying geographical indication and also to assess which are the products that could be protected."[1306] However, there is also the point that in order to support the interests of developing countries, it is necessary to use all existing IPRs to protect TK. Thereupon, the collective marks and certification marks may also be used to protect TKHs who produce traditional products whose quality and reputation depend on TK.[1307]

4.3 *Registration of GIs as Positive Protection for TK-RI*

As explained in Chapter 2, Section 3.1 of this study, the protection of TK shall not be conditioned on registration of TK or any other formalities. The registration requirement "in some cases may run counter to the very objectives of the protection" of the TK.[1308] Therefore, one may ask what the GIs law does require concerning the registration of TK-RI.

There are two different approaches concerning the registration of the GIs. The proponents of the registration of GIs point out that registration is the prerequisite for the protection of GIs. Some argue that the goal of establishing a registration system for TK is to find the beneficiaries of TK-RI.[1309] Other consider that the option for use of GIs by individuals or legal entities is provided to comply with the criteria and specific terms and conditions in the relevant context. As a result, only those users who are located in the given geographical area and meet those criteria in the given context may use the GIs. Therefore, there is a need for registration of these criteria and relevant contexts to examine users' compliance with them.[1310] Gangjee mentions the link between the registration process and the place. He notes that "since the link to place is

1306 Cottier and Müller (n 140); in Cottier, *Trade and Intellectual Property Protection in WTO Law: Collected Essays* (n 140) Page 444.

1307 See the Delegation of France statement: IGC-GRTKF Secretariat, 'Report of Intergovernmental Committee on Intellectual Property and Genetic Resources, Traditional Knowledge and Folklore' (n 849) Page 6.

1308 See the statement of the Brazil delegation: IGC-GRTKF Secretariat, 'Report of Intergovernmental Committee on Intellectual Property and Genetic Resources, Traditional Knowledge and Folklore' (n 68) Paragraph 69.

1309 IGC-GRTKF Secretariat, 'Draft Articles on the Protection of Traditional Cultural Expressions/Expressions of Folklore Prepared at IWG 1' (World Intellectual Property Organization 2010) WIPO Doc WIPO/GRTKF/IC/17/9 Annex Page 8.

1310 Frankel (n 788) Page 453.

what sets GIs apart, the verification of this link and causally related product qualities calls for greater scrutiny and public oversight during the registration process."[1311] In contrast, others have discussed how the exclusive use of the GIs occurs prior to their registration. They present the exclusive use of the GI 'Champagne' worldwide as evidence that registration is not the fundamental requirement for the protection of GIs.[1312]

Under the Paris Convention, the TRIPS Agreement and the Madrid Agreement, there is no registration requirement. However, according to Article 23 of the TRIPS Agreement, members are required to negotiate for establishment of a registration system for GIs concerning wines and spirits.[1313]

> With a view to completing the work started in the Council for Trade-Related Aspects of Intellectual Property Rights (Council for TRIPS) on the implementation of Article 23.4, we agree to negotiate the establishment of a multilateral system of notification and registration of geographical indications for wines and spirits by the Fifth Session of the Ministerial Conference. We note that issues related to the extension of the protection of geographical indications provided for in Article 23 to products other than wines and spirits will be addressed in the Council for TRIPS pursuant to paragraph 12 of this Declaration.[1314]

Some States have already been using the registration of GIs for the protection of TK-RI. For example, in Mali, traditional fabrics known as 'Bogolan' or 'Mud cloth' are registered as AO and GIs.[1315] Also, in the Czech Republic, the traditional art of Bohemia crystal, which is a product of the region with the same name is registered and protected as GIs.[1316] In the Russian Federation, ancient industries of "Velikiy-Ustyug niello, Gorodets painting, Rostov enamel, Kargopol clay toy, and Filimonov toy" are registered and protected as AO.[1317] In

---

1311 Dev S Gangjee, 'Introduction: Timeless Signs or Signs of the Times?' in Dev S Gangjee (ed), *Research Handbook on Intellectual Property and Geographical Indications* (Edward Elgar Publishing 2016) Page 2.

1312 Frankel (n 788) Page 453.

1313 Oskari Rovamo, 'Monopolising Names? The Protection of Geographical Indications in the European Community' (University of Helsinki 2006) Page 23.

1314 WTO, 'Doha Ministerial Declaration' (n 110) Paragraph 18.

1315 WIPO, *Intellectual Property Needs and Expectations of Traditional Knowledge Holders* (n 166) Page 153.

1316 ITC and WIPO (n 869) Page 10.

1317 IGC-GRTKF Secretariat, 'Consolidated Analysis of the Legal Protection of Traditional Cultural Expressions' (n 800) Page 50.

Slovakia, the GI 'Modranská Majolika' (meaning 'pottery from Modra') is registered in the IP Office database.[1318] Also, as shown in Table 10 below, by 2021, the titles of 62 PCs had been nationally registered as GIs at the IPC in Iran.

TABLE 10 Registration of PCs under Iran National GIs System

	No.	Appellation	Translation
1.	GI 1	فرش اصفهان	Isfahan/Esfahan Carpet
2.	GI 2	فرش قم	Qom/Qum/Ghom Carpet
3.	GI 3	فرش ماهی خوی	Khoy Fish Design Carpet
4.	GI 4	فرش افشار تکاب	Afshar Takab Carpet
5.	GI 6	قالی تبریز	Tabriz Carpet
6.	GI 7	فرش بخش خواجه	Khajeh District Carpet
7.	GI 8	فرش آذرشهر	Azar Shahr Carpet
8.	GI 9	فرش سراب	Sarab Carpet
9.	GI 10	فرش بخشایش	Bakhshayesh Carpet
10.	GI 11	فرش هریس	Heris/Heriz Carpet
11.	GI 12	فرش مهربان	Mehraban Carpet
12.	GI 15	فرش ترکمن گلستان	Torkman Carpet of Golestan
13.	GI 16	فرش مشهد	Mashad/Mashhad Carpet
14.	GI 17	فرش کرمان	Kerman Carpet
15.	GI 19	فرش اردکان	Ardakan Carpet
16.	GI 20	فرش اردبیل	Ardabil/Ardebil Carpet
17.	GI 21	فرش همدان	Hamedan Carpet
18.	GI 22	فرش کاشمر	Kashmar Carpet
19.	GI 23	فرش یزد	Yazd Carpet
20.	GI 24	فرش کاشان	Kashan Carpet
21.	GI 25	فرش نایین	Naein Carpet
22.	GI 26	فرش ساروق	Sarough Carpet
23.	GI 27	فرش سردرود	Sardroud Carpet

1318 ITC and WIPO (n 869) Pages 121–122.

TABLE 10 Registration of PCs under Iran National GIs System (*cont.*)

	No.	Appellation	Translation
24.	GI 28	فرش قهستان	Ghohestan Carpet
25.	GI 29	فرش مود بیرجند	Birjand Mood Carpet
26.	GI 30	فرش سنقر وکلیایی کرمانشاه	Kermanshah Songhor and Koleyaye Carpet
27.	GI 31	فرش شربیان	Sharabian Carpet
28.	GI 33	بختیاری فرش چهار محال و	Chaharmahal and Bakhtiari Carpet
29.	GI 34	گبه فارس	Gabbeh of Fars
30.	GI 35	فرش قشقایی فارس	Qashqaie Carpet of Fars
31.	GI 36	فرش ایلام	Ilam Carpet
32.	GI 37	فرش سیستان	Sistan Carpet
33.	GI 38	فرش لرستان	Lorestan Carpet
34.	GI 39	فرش کردی خراسان شمالی	Kordi Carpet of north Khorasan
35.	GI 40	فرش ورامین	Varamin Carpet
36.	GI 41	فرش ترکمن جرگلان و بجنورد	Torkman Carpet of Jarglan and Bojnord
37.	GI 46	گلیم نمین	Namin Kilim
38.	GI 47	جاجیم خلخال	Khalkhal Jajim
39.	GI 49	گلیم هرسین	Harsin Kilim
40.	GI 50	گلیم ارداق	Ardak/Ardagh Kilim
41.	GI 54	گلیم سنه	Senneh Kilim
42.	GI 70	فرش جوشقان	Joshegan Carpet
43.	GI 71	فرش بیدگنه	Bidgeneh Carpet
44.	GI 72	فرش کلاردشت	Kelardasht Carpet
45.	GI 73	فرش قلتوق	Qoltuq Carpet
46.	GI 74	فرش خمسه زنجان	Khamseh Carpet of Zanjan
47.	GI 75	فرش بیجار	Bijar Carpet
48.	GI 94	گلیم شیرکی پیچ سیرجان	Sirjan's Shirakipich Kilim
49.	GI 117	فرش سنه	Senneh Carpet

TABLE 10 Registration of PCs under Iran National GIs System (*cont.*)

	No.	Appellation	Translation
50.	GI 118	فرش درخش	Dorokhsh Carpet
51.	GI 119	فرش یلمه علی آباد دهاقان	Yalameh/Yahlameh Carpet of Ali Abad Dehaghan
52.	GI 120	فرش نهاوند	Nahavand Carpet
53.	GI 121	فرش دویدوخ	Dvydvkh Carpet
54.	GI 122	فرش یلمه بروجن	Yalameh/Yahlameh Carpet of Broujen
55.	GI 123	فرش شهربابک	Shahre Babak Carpet
56.	GI 126	گلیم لرستان	Lorestan Kilim
57.	GI 128	گلیم هزارجریب	Hezar Jarib Kilim
58.	GI 130	جاجیم آلاشت	Alasht Jajim
59.	GI 131	گلیم نقش برجسته ایلام	Ilam Contoured Kilim
60.	GI 133	گلیمچه متکازین	------
61.	GI 135	جاجیم لرستان	Lorestan Jajim
62.	GI 137	گلیم تالش	Talesh Kilim

Under Iran's GIs Law, the registration of GIs is not a prerequisite for protecting them. In other words, a GI must enjoy protection regardless of whether it has been formally registered or not. The registration of GIs merely raises the legal assumption that such an indication "identifies a good as originating in the territory, a region or locality of the country, provided that the quality, reputation or other characteristics of the good is essentially attributable to its geographical origin."[1319]

However, during the IGC's meetings, the view was expressed that the registration of TK under GIs law at the national level seems insufficient for protecting TK-RI. Thus, it is necessary to establish a specific international registration mechanism such as the Lisbon Agreement. Such an international system could assist TKHs to extend the protection to the international level.

1319 Iran – Act for Protection of Geographical Indications Article 3(a).

Nevertheless, to reach such an agreement would necessitate to a pre-decision on the role of formality on protecting TK.[1320]

Gupta believes registration of GIs on TK-RI must be subject to international negotiations. He argues that while the TRIPS Agreement has fundamentally accepted the need to create a notification and registration of GIs for wine, such an agreement could "be broadened to include TK, as well as contemporary innovations of local communities and individuals."[1321] Some states support this idea. During the WTO ministerial meeting of 2008, countries like Switzerland, Brazil and India, together with the EU, proposed the extension of the protection of GIs and the creation of a multilateral system of notification and registration.[1322] In the view of the author, although, registration of TK-RI as GIs could be a useful tool for the protection of PCs, as explained in Chapter 2, Section 3.1 of this study, registration shall not be a precondition for the protection of TK, including PCs because such a requirement would diminish the idea and possibility of protecting TK, as it places more barriers in front of the TKHs.

5 Challenges of Protection

While the legal regime of GIs seems to be a reasonable basis for protecting PCs, there are severe doubts as to its effectiveness in extending the protection to international markets. These challenges include the following:

Firstly, the protection of PCs under GIs laws is hampered by a lack of consensus among countries on the scope of protection for GIs and the different mechanisms regarding the protection of GIs within different national laws.[1323] Although there are many countries that, according to their national laws, have been able to protect GIs; these countries do not use a harmonized protection system. This is true even though their protection systems have generally been established to prevent the misappropriation of GIs and to avoid the public being misled by third parties about the exact origin of the GIs. For example,

1320 IGC-GRTKF Secretariat, 'Report of Intergovernmental Committee on Intellectual Property and Genetic Resources, Traditional Knowledge and Folklore' (n 1290) Paragraph 150.

1321 Gupta, *WIPO-UNEP Study on the Role of Intellectual Property Rights in the Sharing of Benefits Arising from the Use of Biological Resources and Associated Traditional Knowledge* (n 363) Page 47.

1322 IGC-GRTKF Secretariat, 'Report of Intergovernmental Committee on Intellectual Property and Genetic Resources, Traditional Knowledge and Folklore' (n 1197) Paragraph 141.

1323 WIPO, *Intellectual Property Needs and Expectations of Traditional Knowledge Holders* (n 166) Page 39.

some countries protect GIs through collective and certification marks within trademarks law.[1324] Therefore, the diverse forms of protection concerning GIs in different national laws are the most critical barriers within the international community.[1325] Those national laws even use different terms relating to the protection of GIs. As Cottier and Müller point out "while trademarks are the broadest and least specific ones, indications of sources are less specific than GIs, and these, again, are less specific than Appellations of Origin."[1326] These diverse approaches of countries might make the protection even further out of reach for TKHs.[1327]

Secondly, Although GIs appear to have a high potential to protect PCs; at the international level, they fail to prevent misuse of products other than for wines and spirits. Many national laws include some effective protection of GIs for all products within their territory. Nevertheless, such national laws are not competent to protect their products overseas. As discussed earlier in this Chapter, the Paris Convention and the Lisbon Agreement are two major international treaties on international protection of Indications of Source and AO. The Paris Convention has not provided a harmonized system for the protection of GIs. And, the Lisbon Agreement failed to attract many countries to join its international system for the registration of AO. Even though the TRIPS Agreement obliges its members to protect GIs, many members of the WTO consider that such an obligation for protection of GIs is not enough. They even doubt that the additional protection for wines and spirits under Articles 23 and 24(4) of the TRIPS Agreement is effective and adequate. For this reason, the need to establish a notification and registration system for wines and spirits, as well as the extension of protection of GIs to other commodities, has been a central feature of the Doha Declaration under which a mandate to further pursue the matter is given to the TRIPS Council:

> With a view to completing the work started in the Council for Trade-Related Aspects of Intellectual Property Rights (Council for TRIPS) on the implementation of Article 23.4, we agree to negotiate the establishment of a multilateral system of notification and registration of geographical indications for wines and spirits by the Fifth Session of the Ministerial

1324 WIPO, *Protect and Promote Your Culture* (n 664) Page 48.

1325 IGC-GRTKF Secretariat, 'Report of Intergovernmental Committee on Intellectual Property and Genetic Resources, Traditional Knowledge and Folklore' (n 1290) Paragraph 150.

1326 Cottier and Müller (n 140); in Cottier, *Trade and Intellectual Property Protection in WTO Law: Collected Essays* (n 140) Page 436.

1327 Vivas-Eugui (n 1189) Page 715.

> Conference. We note that issues related to the extension of the protection of geographical indications provided for in Article 23 to products other than wines and spirits will be addressed in the Council for TRIPS pursuant to paragraph 12 of this Declaration.[1328]

Many members of the WTO, including the EC, Switzerland and many developing countries, support the proposal for the extension of protection beyond wines and spirits. The debates on this proposal have been an essential part of the TRIPS Council meetings.[1329] The main reason for the interest of the European and developing countries in the subject of the extension of protection of GIs is the importance of agricultural products for their economies. The EU's efforts were in line with their internal regulations concerning the protection of agricultural products under the GIs law.[1330] For developing countries, as Blakeney points out, the extension of the GIs protection regime to agricultural products could have a positive impact on economic conditions. Any adverse reaction to such an extension could carry the message that the real policies of IPRs within the TRIPS Agreement will not be of any benefit to them.[1331] According to these groups of countries, GIs could be used as a tool for the promotion of exports as well as to prevent misappropriation and maintain the fairness of trade and IPRs beyond the protection for alcoholic beverages.[1332] Still, the efforts to extend the GIs regime to other products have not been successful because of the rejection by some significant exporters of agricultural products such as the USA, Australia and New Zealand. These countries argue that such an extension would impose additional trade barriers, including administrative costs and an unbalanced benefit for some Member

1328 WTO, 'Doha Ministerial Declaration' (n 110) Paragraph 18.

1329 See: WTO, 'The Extension of the Additional Protection for Geographical Indications to Products Other than Wines and Spirits' (n 1196).

1330 See: Council Regulation (EEC) No 2081/92 of 14 July 1992 on the Protection of Geographical Indications and Designations of Origin for Agricultural Products and Foodstuffs 1992 (OJ L 208); and Council Regulation (EC) No 692/2003 of 8 April 2003 amending Regulation (EEC) No 2081/92 on the protection of geographical indications and designations of origin for agricultural products and foodstuffs 2003 (OJ L 099) Regulation (EC) No 692/2003 has been repealed and replaced by Regulation (EU) No 1151/2012. Most recently, Regulation (EU) No 2024/1143 of May 2024 repealed Regulation (EU) No 1151/2012.

1331 Michael Blakeney, 'Proposals for the International Regulation of Geographical Indications' (2001) 4 Journal of World Intellectual Property 629, Page 652.

1332 Dwijen Rangnekar and International Centre for Trade and Sustainable Development, *Geographical Indications: A Review of Proposals at the TRIPS Council, Extending Article 23 to Products Other than Wines and Spirit* (ICTSD and UNCTAD 2003).

States.[1333] In 2008, a coalition of the WTO Members from all continents communicated a draft modality text to negotiate *inter alia* the extension of the protection of GIs to products other than wines and spirits.

> GI – Extension: draft Modality text
>
> 7. Members agree to the extension of the protection of Article 23 of the TRIPS Agreement to geographical indications for all products, including the extension of the Register.
>
> 8. Text based negotiations shall be undertaken, in Special Sessions of the TRIPS Council and as an integral part of the Single Undertaking, to amend the TRIPS Agreement in order to extend the protection of Article 23 of the TRIPS Agreement to geographical indications for all products as well as to apply to these the exceptions provided in Article 24 of the TRIPS Agreement mutatis mutandis.
>
> 9. Special and Differential treatment shall be an integral part of negotiations in the three are as above, as well as special measures in favour of developing countries and in particular least developed countries.[1334]

It is doubtful that the deadlock in the negotiations at the TRIPS Council on the revision of the TRIPS Agreement for the extension of GIs to other products will break any time soon. Any progress in the negotiations will depend on the interaction between several countries. In particular, countries like Switzerland and Bulgaria, as well as the European Union, clearly link the debates to the talks on agricultural products at the TRIPS Council and Agriculture Committee.[1335] Such deep divisions among Member States of the WTO concerning the extension of the protection of GIs to all goods makes it extremely difficult to assume that an extended, effective and enforceable GIs system under the TRIPS Agreement might be available in the near future to grant protection for the TK-RI including PCs.

Thirdly, it is doubtful whether the GIs regime could protect the cultural aspects of TK. There are two different views concerning this challenge. According to the first, GIs would be a right choice for protecting TKHs' cultures.

1333 Cottier and Müller (n 140); in Cottier, *Trade and Intellectual Property Protection in WTO Law: Collected Essays* (n 140) Pages 438–439.

1334 Communication from Albania, Brazil, China, Colombia, Croatia, Ecuador, the European Communities, Georgia, Iceland, India, Indonesia, the Kyrgyz Republic, Liechtenstein, the Former Yugoslav Republic of Macedonia, Moldova, Pakistan, Peru, Sri Lanka, Switzerland, Thailand, Türkiye, the ACP Group and the African Group. See: WTO, 'Draft Modalities for TRIPS Related Issues' (2008) WTO Doc Trade Negotiations Committee, Page 3.

1335 'Intellectual Property Rights' (2003) 1 ICTSD and IISD 4, Page 3.

The reason is the essential role of GIs in promoting the commercial value of the artistic works and the traditional methods which TKHs use in given geographical areas.[1336] Culture is always strongly linked with a specific region or regions. The existence of such a link means that GIs can be explicitly used for tangible cultural goods, such as handicrafts, that have characteristics derived from their geographic origin.[1337] Addor and Grazioli, supporting this view point out that GIs are means of expressing the cultural identity of a nation and represent the skills of local populations.[1338] In the same vein, Lamy stated, during his term as EU Trade Commissioner, that names and products "contribute to the identity of the heritage" and "image and prestige" of countries of origin and regions. He believes GIs "form part of the culture and national and regional identity" and are the "commercial flags of" countries. He highlights some terms, such as 'Parma' from Italy, 'Cognac' from France, 'Basmati' from India, 'Antigua' from Guatemala and 'Jasmine' from Thailand.[1339] Moreover, GIs can act as a "guardian of cultural identity and a defence against homogeneity brought about by globalization."[1340] Lamy's opinion is strongly supported by the EC, which has been the leading proponent of cultural features of the GIs. They claim GIs are crucial to "cultural heritage, traditional methods of production and natural resources."[1341]

> The laws on geographical indications could be applied to certain tangible folklore products (such as carpets, textiles or figures) as protection can be assigned to a territory rather than a natural or legal person. However, this protection does not grant exclusive rights as regards the actual good or service itself and will only prevent others from using the indicator: the same folklore could still be reproduced or performed under a different name. The concepts of unfair competition or unfair trade practice may provide, where they exist, protection against wrongful commercial use

1336 O'Connor, *The Law of Geographical Indications* (n 373) Page 373.

1337 WIPO, *Intellectual Property and Genetic Resources, Traditional Knowledge and Traditional Cultural Expressions* (n 231) Page 33.

1338 Felix Addor and Alexandra Grazioli, 'Geographical Indications beyond Wines and Spirits – A Roadmap for a Better Protection for Geographical Indications in the WTO/TRIPS Agreement' (2002) 5 The Journal of World Intellectual Property 865, Page 865.

1339 Pascal Lamy, 'Creation of the Organization for an International Geographical Indications Network' (2003) Speech 03/292.

1340 Rovamo (n 1313) Page 14.

1341 European Commission, 'Why Do Geographical Indications Matter to Us?' (2003) MEMO/03/160.

> and their scope could be used against industries, which profit from folklore but disregard its traditional nature.[1342]

In practice, many communities use the GIs regime for the protection of their TK-RI. For instance, in Slovenia, laces which are produced in the Idrija have protected by GIs since 2000. These laces are deeply incorporated in the cultural, social and educational life of the local community which holds the Idrija Festival every June. The first event of this kind was documented in the 17th century.[1343]

In contrast, a second point of view is expressed by Frankel who argues that, although given geographies in many cases are associated with given cultural identities, "cultural identity is not always a question of geography." She believes that geographical cultural identity is parallel to other cultural identities. In her opinion, GIs "do not have more credibility than indigenous cultural property claims." So other cultural identities are not protectable under the GIs regime.[1344] It seems that the GIs law itself does not recognise any cultural characteristics for the products. For example, in Iran's GIs law, the definition of 'goods' refers only to natural products, agriculture, handicrafts and industrial products, and does not take into consideration the cultural aspects of goods. In other words, the law only mentions material and tangible elements of goods.[1345]

In the view of the author, although Frankel's claim that GIs are not designed to protect TKHs' culture seems right; other IPRs also fail to provide such protection. However, GIs could indirectly assist TKHs to prevent some aspects of their TK including TK-RI from being misappropriated by third parties. Therefore, TKHs should use the potential protection offered by the GIs regime for protecting their products.

Fourthly, as a substantive challenge, GIs are not applicable for protection of TK as 'knowledge.'[1346] Riffel points out that GIs "do not protect knowledge as such, i.e. its content, and for this reason cannot prevent the misappropriation of traditional knowledge by third parties if these should use another indication."[1347] Despite this criticism, GIs could prevent misleading references

---

1342 The European Community and its Member States, 'Expressions of Folklore' (World Intellectual Property Organization 2002) WIPO Doc WIPO/GRTKF/IC/3/11 Annex Page 2.

1343 WIPO, *Intellectual Property and Folk, Arts and Cultural Festivals* (n 692) Page 21.

1344 Frankel (n 788) Page 453.

1345 Iran – Act for Protection of Geographical Indications Article 1(B).

1346 IGC-GRTKF Secretariat, 'The Protection of Traditional Knowledge: Updated Draft Gap Analysis' (World Intellectual Property Organization 2018) WIPO Doc WIPO/GRTKF/IC/37/6 Annex II Page 4.

1347 Riffel (n 3) Page 146.

to a knowledge system through the certification and protection of unique reputation, marks and signs associated with that knowledge.[1348]

6 Who Are the Beneficiaries of the GIs?

TKHs have the right to be recognized as the real source of TK and to object against any "false, confusing or misleading indications which, in relation to goods or services, suggest any endorsement by or linkage with" the TKHs.[1349] Therefore, identification and recognition of the TKHs, including the individuals and communities who must be entitled to enjoy protection under the GIs regime, are the most fundamental issues regarding the protection of PCs under the GIs regime. Like the collective marks regime within trademark law, the GIs regime has the potential to protect the interests of the groups as well as those of individuals,[1350] which is line with the interests, collective rights and entitlement of TKHs.

The GIs protection system is known as the IP *sui generis* regime for the protection of specific types of signs and marks. However, it is essential to consider the differences between GIs and trademarks to recognize the beneficiaries under each of them. A trademark is a sign used by a natural or legal person to distinguish the goods and services of one enterprise from goods and services provided by others.[1351] GIs are "names and symbols which indicate a certain geographical origin of a given product." In the trademark regime, enterprises are the main element of the system and play a significant role in supplying products in markets. These enterprises are the owner of the marks. The GIs is a different system of identification of a geographical place in which certain types of goods originate and are produced by a handful of enterprises. Thus, these enterprises are not the owner of the GIs; however, they have the right to use GIs for the products merely because they are located in the same given geographical area.[1352] Having considered the lack of ownership links between

1348 IGC-GRTKF Secretariat, 'The Protection of Traditional Knowledge: Updated Draft Gap Analysis' (World Intellectual Property Organization 2018) WIPO Doc WIPO/GRTKF/IC/37/6 Annex I Paragraph 87.

1349 See draft articles of the open-ended informal drafting group of IGC 17: IGC-GRTKF Secretariat, 'Draft Report of Intergovernmental Committee on Intellectual Property and Genetic Resources, Traditional Knowledge and Folklore' (n 241) Annex II, Article C.

1350 WIPO, *Intellectual Property Needs and Expectations of Traditional Knowledge Holders* (n 166) Page 219.

1351 WIPO, *WIPO IP Handbook* (n 450) Page 68.

1352 *ibid Page 121.*

GIs and enterprises,[1353] it is reasonable to look at what the legal relationship between GIs and persons is.

International documents addressing GIs, AO and indications of source have adopted different approaches concerning the subject of the beneficiaries, as summarized in Table 11 below:

TABLE 11 GIs beneficiaries in the international treaties

Regime	Rule	Beneficiaries
GIS	Geneva Act of the Lisbon Agreement Article 1(xvii)	"beneficiaries" means the natural persons or legal entities entitled under the law of the Contracting Party of Origin to use an appellation of origin or a geographical indication
	Article 22.1 of TRIPS	Not mentioned
	Article 2 of Regulation (EC) No. 510/2006	Group (associations of producers etc.)
AO	Article 2 of Lisbon Agreement	Subject to the national law and regulation all persons who have the right to use the Appellation
	Geneva Act of the Lisbon Agreement Article 1(xvii)	"beneficiaries" means the natural persons or legal entities entitled under the law of the Contracting Party of Origin to use an appellation of origin or a geographical indication
	Article 23.1 of TRIPS Agreement	Not mentioned
	Article 2 of Regulation (EC) No. 510/ 2006; (for wines and spirits)	Group (associations of producers etc.)
Indication of Source	Madrid Agreement on Repression of False Indications	Not mentioned

1353 Despite this fact, In the Indian law the concept of owning GIs is accepted. It stipulates: "any association of persons or of producers or any organisation for the time being entered in the register as proprietor of the geographical indication" is recognized as 'registered proprietor.' See: India – Geographical Indications of Goods (Registration and Protection) Act 1999 (Act No 48 (entered into force on 15 September 2003)) Article 2.

According to the Lisbon Agreement "any natural persons or legal entities, public or private, having, according to their national legislation, a right to use such appellations" are entitled to apply for registration of the AO.[1354] Hence, the Agreement has laid down the identification of rightful users of AO in the national laws. In the same manner, although the Geneva Act of the Lisbon Agreement defines beneficiaries, it leaves the recognition of the authorized persons who are entitled to use GIs and AO to the legislation of the contracting parties of origin:

> "beneficiaries" means the natural persons or legal entities entitled under the law of the Contracting Party of Origin to use an appellation of origin or a geographical indication.[1355]

In both documents of the Lisbon Agreement and its Geneva Act, the concept of the authorized user is the critical element for determining beneficiaries of GIs and AO. Therefore, it is necessary to analyze who might be identified as the authorized user of TK-RI as GIs concerning PCs.

In the Iranian GIs law any producer whose place of activity is the given geographical area "shall be allowed to use a registered geographical indication."[1356] Such a producer who is "engaged in the production of the goods indicated in the application in the geographical area specified in the application"[1357] is known as an authorized user[1358] and has the right to apply for registration of the GIs. The law also specifies who producers are:

> "Producer" means any person who is engaged in production and processing of agricultural, livestock and food products or manufactures and produces industrial tools and handmade articles or manipulates natural materials for the purpose of production or a trader of the said products.[1359]

It can be seen from the above extract that, under the Iranian GIs Law, the term 'producers' is used to refer three groups as the authorized users:

1354 Lisbon Agreement Article 5(1).
1355 Geneva Act of the Lisbon Agreement Article 1(xvii).
1356 Iran – Act for Protection of Geographical Indications Article 10.
1357 *ibid Article 7.*
1358 Iran – By-Law subject of Article 16 concerning Protection of Geographical Indications 2005 (Approved by Head of Judiciary) Article 1(C).
1359 Iran – Act for Protection of Geographical Indications Article 1(d).

- persons who are engaging in the production and processing of agricultural, livestock and food products or manufacturers and producers of industrial tools and handmade articles, or
- persons who manipulate natural materials for producing mentioned products, or
- merchants of the said products.

Indian law has adopted the same policy. Under the Indian GIs Act, persons who claim they produce the good as designated by the registered GI may apply to be registered as an authorized user.[1360] It seems that the Iranian GIs law categorises beneficiaries in line with the Paris Convention rules concerning false indication of source, which stipulates:

> Any producer, manufacturer, or merchant, whether a natural person or a legal entity, engaged in the production or manufacture of or trade in such goods and established either in the locality falsely indicated as the source, or in the region where such locality is situated, or in the country falsely indicated, or in the country where the false indication of source is used, shall in any case be deemed an interested party.[1361]

In short, the Paris Convention considers producers, manufacturers and merchants as beneficiaries whose rights are interested parties and entitled to ask for preventing false indications of source.

Notwithstanding the above mentioned, users are not the only beneficiaries of legal protection for GIs. Under Iran's GIs law, as well as authorized users, "any competent authority in production, distribution or policymaking for the goods being registered" may file an application for the registration of the GIs.[1362] In the same manner, in Switzerland, specific groups or institutions may request registration of GIs. These include:

> a. the group which registered the designation of origin or the geographical indication, or where such group no longer exists, the representative group which has assumed the role of protecting this designation of origin or geographical indication;

1360 Pradyot R Jena and Ulrike Grote, 'Changing Institutions to Protect Regional Heritage: A Case for Geographical Indications in the Indian Agrifood Sector' (2010) 28 Development Policy Review 217, Page 9.

1361 Paris Convention Article 10(2).

1362 Iran – Act for Protection of Geographical Indications Article 7.

b. the Swiss canton that protects the registered designation of origin or the foreign authority responsible for the regulation of wine designations corresponding to Article 63 AgricA22, as well as the group that obtained the protection of such a foreign wine designation;

c. the umbrella organization of an economic sector for which the Federal Council has enacted an ordinance based on Article 50 paragraph 2 or which acts on the basis of on an equivalent foreign regulation.[1363]

In the EU, the GIs registration system has recognized provisions for granting some exclusive rights over GIs for communities. Frankel points out that this approach has led to a significant common interest between the EU and TKHs on the use of GIs for protection of TK-RI.[1364]

The GIs regime enables communities and groups to attribute their goods to their specific geographical locations.[1365] Therefore, the TKHs who produce, manufacture or trade PCs would have right to use GIs.[1366] Such a capability of the GIs matches the TIP-rights theory, in which the right holders would be "communities or even regions concerned."[1367] This theory applies to the beneficiaries of PCs in the rural and urban areas, as geographical regions, and nomad peoples as communities who, as the producer of PCs, would be permitted to use the GIs regime for the protection of their rights.

7 Duration of Protection

TK-RI date back to the beginning of communities' settlement in different geographical areas. On the other hand, there are timeless and deep relations between these communities, their geographical area and local materials, which are well reflected in the PCs. As explained previously in Chapter 2, Section 4 of this study, TKHs' right over their carpet indications should survive in perpetuity. Thus, any protection mechanism for TK-RI shall last indefinitely. It also explained how two main approaches regarding the concept of the unlimited period of protection are predominant. While according to the first view TK shall enjoy protection without time limits, under the TIP-rights theory

1363 Swiss – Federal Act on the Protection of Trade Marks and Indications of Source Article 27(b).
1364 See: Frankel (n 788) Pages 452–453.
1365 Abbott (n 799) Page 30.
1366 ITC and WIPO (n 869) Page 86.
1367 Cottier and Müller (n 140); in Cottier, *Trade and Intellectual Property Protection in WTO Law: Collected Essays* (n 140) Pages 448–449.

the protection shall be continued without limit as long as the specific criteria for protection are met. It is crucial however to assess which of those strategies is compatible with the approach of the GIs regime concerning the duration of the protection of TK-RI.

In principle, the duration of protection under the GIs regime is supposed to be indefinite.[1368] In this regard, GIs mirror trademark law in which the unlimited duration of protection is acceptable. Notwithstanding this fundamental principle, international binding instruments and national laws have adopted different rules concerning the validity period of a registered GI.

According to the first approach the period of protection would begin from the date of registration and would be valid as long as the conditions that create the GI exist and as long as GIs are valid in the country of origin.[1369] This is the approach of the international registration system under the Lisbon Agreement:

> An appellation which has been granted protection in one of the countries of the Special Union … cannot, in that country, be deemed to have become generic, as long as it is protected as an appellation of origin in the country of origin.[1370]

Moreover, it stipulates that the renewal of the registration is not a condition for continued validity and protection of the international registration:

> Registration effected at the International Bureau … shall ensure, without renewal.[1371]

In the same manner, the GIs provisions in the European Union requires one-time registration, and there is no need for renewal. It recognizes the indefinite duration of protection provided that the conditions of the specification for a given product protected by a GI are ensured.[1372]

1368 WIPO, *Intellectual Property Needs and Expectations of Traditional Knowledge Holders* (n 166) Page 32.

1369 See: Sophie Reviron, 'Geographical Indications: Creation and Distribution of Economic Value in Developing Countries' (World Trade Institute 2009) 2009/14 Pages 24–25; and Bernard O'Connor, 'Geographical Indications and TRIPs: 10 Years Later … A Roadmap for EU GI Holders to Get Protection in Other WTO Members – Part I' (European Lawyers Insight Consulting 2008) Page 4.

1370 Lisbon Agreement Article 6.

1371 *ibid Article 7(1)*.

1372 See: Regulation (EU) No 2024/1143 of the European Parliament and of the Council of 11 April 2024 on geographical indications for wine, spirit drinks and agricultural products,

Some countries such as Switzerland and Iran have adopted similar provisions. In Switzerland the validity of registration of a name as a GI is indefinite;[1373] and it would remain valid if:

- all users, the cantons or related authorities are interested in maintaining the name;
- the product's specifications are guaranteed;
- the name is protected in the origin country.[1374]

Iran's law protects GIs regardless of whether they are registered or not. The registration of GIs is valid just as circumstantial legal evidence that the Act formally recognizes such indications by the provision of the "Act for Protection of Geographical Indications." The Act does not require renewal of a registered GI. However, the GIs which are abandoned or not protected in their country of origin are not protectable in Iran either.[1375]

According to the second approach although the duration of protection of GIs is unlimited, the registration must be renewed for certain periods of years. For example, in India "the registration of a geographical indication shall be for a period of ten years, but may be renewed from time to time."[1376] Similarly, in Republic of Azerbaijan, registration of GIs might last for an indefinite period. However, the rights to use of GIs are valid for ten years and are conditioned to renewal for ten-year periods.[1377]

The third approach for duration of protection is followed by those countries that protect GIs under trademark law. The USA and Nepal, as two main consumer and producer of hand-woven carpets, are good examples of this group of countries. In the USA GIs might be protected as collective marks. Like other registered marks, collective marks' registrations are valid for ten years and are renewable for successive ten-year periods.[1378] In Nepal, the registration of a trademark is valid for seven-year periods and it is possible to renew

as well as traditional specialities guaranteed and optional quality terms for agricultural products, amending Regulations (EU) No 1308/2013, (EU) 2019/787 and (EU) 2019/1753 and repealing Regulation (EU) No 1151/2012 2024 (OJ L 1143/1) Article 67.

1373 Swiss – Ordinance on the Register of Designations of Origin and Geographical Indications for Non-Agricultural Products 2015 (232/112/2 (Status as of 1 January 2017)) Article 12.

1374 *ibid Article 13.*

1375 Iran – Act for Protection of Geographical Indications Articles 3 and 5.

1376 India – Geographical Indications of Goods (Registration and Protection) Act Article 18(1).

1377 Azerbaijan – Law on Trademarks and Geographical Indications as amended on November 22, 2013 1998 (504-IQ) Article 21.

1378 See: The US – Trademark Act Sections 8 and 9.

registration for the periods of the same length.[1379] The period of protection of trademarks was discussed in Chapter 3, Section 6 of this study.

In all of the three approaches described above, the duration of protection of the GIs is unrestricted, provided that their use continues. Therefore, all three approaches are compatible with the theory of TIP-rights. Contrary to TIP-rights theory, however, the second approach, which demands timeless protection without restriction does not seem to be eligible to provide the legal basis for using the GIs regime for the protection of TK-RI. This theory might be useful only if the stakeholders agree to amend the existing GIs in such a way as to lift the use requirement as a condition for continuing the protection. Of course, it does not seem to be likely to be welcomed by all relevant parties in the international community. Comparing these two competing theories, I may conclude that the TIP-rights theory promoted by Thomas Cottier and Marion Panizzon is more appropriate for defining the duration of protection of GIs.

Moreover, there is a fundamental difference between the first approach on the one hand and the second and third approaches on the other. According to the first approach, the only condition for the continuation of the protection of GIs is the sustained use of those indications. This situation is entirely in line with the theory of TIP-rights. It is also in line with TKHs, and countries that demand that protection should last as long as the TK-RI continue to meet the criteria for protection.[1380] Unlike the first, the second and third approaches consider registration renewal as the condition for maintaining the protection of the GIs. Firstly, such a formality is fundamentally against the wishes of TKHs who oppose the imposition of formalities to protect TK.[1381] Secondly, this formality is contrary to the essence of the GIs regime, which has – as mentioned earlier in this Chapter – an enduring connection with the TKHs and their places; and the imposition of artificial formalities may not alter the fact of this traditional and customary relationship. Thirdly, international norms and rules of the Lisbon and Madrid Agreements require no obligation concerning the renewal of registrations.

1379 Nepal – The Patent, Design and Trade Mark Act 1965 (15 (entered into force 1965)); also see: Bernard O'Connor, 'Geographical Indications and TRIPS: 10 Years Later ... A Roadmap for EU GI Holders to Get Protection in Other WTO Members – Part II' (European Lawyers Insight Consulting 2008) Pages 426–430.

1380 See IGC-GRTKF Secretariat, 'The Protection of Traditional Knowledge: Draft Articles' (World Intellectual Property Organization 2018) WIPO Doc WIPO/GRTKF/IC/37/4 Annex Article 10 on Term of Protection/Rights.

1381 For example, Swakopmund Protocol stipulates that protection of traditional knowledge and expressions of folklore shall not be subject to any formality. See: Swakopmund Protocol Section 5 and 17.

8 Summary and Recommendations

Since the emergence of trade, merchants and consumers have been using some kind of GIs for the authentication of the source of the goods. The reputation of the TKHs' products, the high quality of the local materials, and the knowledge and know-how of the TKHs make the GIs regime one of the most effective IPRs for protection of TK. Therefore, many TKHs distinguish their local products by using their well-known indications, signs and symbols. The GIs regime might be used not only as a tool for safeguarding TKHs' cultural heritage. GIs are more predictable and less risky than the regulations on UC. GIs offer an appropriate tool for marketing locally produced products, including bio-products. Consumers are willing to pay higher prices for such products. In this regard, the GIs could help the rural population to increase their economic activities, generate employment and increase their income. The use of GIs would assist the promotion and protection of consumers' rights. Their use could also prevent confusion for consumers by clearly indicating the goods' origins, authenticity, quality and characteristics.

PCs have a clear and distinct connection with the GIs regime. Therefore, considerable efforts have been made by the Iranian authorities to develop the use of GIs. Unfortunately, despite these efforts, these actions have not prevented the abuse and misappropriation of TK-RI of PCs. The TKHs are facing the active presence and UC from many rivals. These competitors have been supplying their fake products under the name of PCs' GIs either with or without mentioning the real place of production. Another popular way to misappropriate PCs is using GIs as trademarks for the third parties' products. Therefore, TKHs are calling for the protection of the reputation of their PCs' GIs. They demand the prevention of undue free-riding and UC, which misleads consumers about the origin of the goods. However, the question arises as to whether PCs could be protected adequately within the framework of the GIs legal regime.

Concerning the elements of protection: If the elements of quality, reputation and other characteristics of goods are attributable to a geographical origin, then those goods are the subject matter of the definition provided by the Iranian law and the TRIPS Agreement. Different approaches to the protection of GIs and the variety of terms used in various laws, as well as the differences in the national regulations and procedures, have made it very difficult to analyze the scope and the extent of these elements.

Concerning the quality, there are neither coherent nor comprehensive criteria nor a single interpretation. Hence, national authorities use various approaches to achieve qualified quality. Moreover, the evaluation of the qualitative connection between PCs and a geographical location is a challenging task. Such a test requires the precise judgement of the factors affecting quality and how those factors and the geographic area are linked. Besides, the requirement for the existence of a qualitative relationship between a specific geographical area and the production would weaken the position of those hand-woven carpets whose quality has no specific relation with the geographical area. Concerning the PCs' reputation, there are no unique legal models relating to the element of reputation within the GIs regimes. Some legal systems follow the TRIPS model, and others abide by the Lisbon model. In the former model the element of reputation matters while the Lisbon model does not take reputation into consideration.

GIs could help consumers find out about the origin of PCs, as they inform the consumers that a product with a specific quality has been produced in and originates from a specific location. Such a GI may include the name of a geographical place, whether the name of an area within the country, a place that is divided into official subdivisions of the country or a traditional denomination. The essential role of a given place has been central to the debates concerning the protection of GIs. In this regard, all elements must originate from a specific place, and there should be an active link between PCs and the geographical area in which the PCs originate. Although GIs can identify and protect PCs through their places, they fail to prevent the use of PCs' GIs when the actual locations of manufacturing are indicated. Therefore, in order to avoid such misappropriation, there is a need to extend additional protection to TK products.

Moreover, according to the principle of territoriality of the protection of IPRs, the protection of GIs is governed by the law of the country in which the protection is sought, and not according to the laws of the country of origin. Therefore, the determination of the elements of the quality, reputation and other characteristics should be based on the perspective of the designated country of the protection.

Concerning protection of GIs under trademarks law: Some national laws have been using trademarks for the protection of GIs. Although both trademarks and GIs law are able to convince the potential consumers that a product has a specific characteristic because it is from a particular source, there are differences between GIs and trademarks. First of all, trademark protection is about distinguishing and protecting one enterprise from others, while protection of GIs is about distinguishing the products. Secondly, the primary use of the collective mark is to show specific characteristics such as nature, properties or quality of the products. Similarly, for the certification mark, the main feature is the technical content of the knowledge which was used to produce the goods, regardless of the geographical link of the products to a particular location. Both differ fundamentally from GIs, for which a link to a geographic location is essential. Thirdly, the owner of the collective or certification marks would have the right to prevent the use of the marks if the user is no longer meeting specified requirements. In contrast, GIs have no specific owner, and all persons located in the given geographic location are allowed to use the GIs. Finally, collective and certification marks cannot prevent their subject matters from becoming generic while, the GIs regime prevents or at least limits its subject matters becoming generic or entering in the public domain.

Concerning the registration requirement: As to positive protection, GIs is not subject to any registration requirement under the Paris Convention, the TRIPS Agreement or the Madrid Agreement. Some argue that the registration of GIs could be useful to find the beneficiaries of TK-RI. Moreover, there is a need for registration of defining criteria of GIs in the relevant contexts to examine users' consistency with them. By contrast, some hold the opinion that the exclusive use of GIs occurs prior to registration of it and registration is not the fundamental requirement for the protection of GIs. It seems that the registration of TK under GIs law at the national level is not likely to be sufficient for protecting TK-RI. Thus, it is necessary to establish a specific international registration mechanism. Such an international system could assist TKHs to extend the protection to the international level. Nevertheless, to reach such an agreement is contingent to a pre-decision on the role of formality on protecting TK. Many TKHs believe the protection of TK shall not be conditioned on any formalities, including registration of TK. A third opinion is that registration of TK-RI as GIs could be useful as a subsidiary tool for the protection of PCs. However, registration shall not be a precondition for the protection of TK because such a requirement would diminish the idea and possibility of protecting TK, as it places more barriers in front of the TKHs.

Concerning other challenges: One of the challenges to the protection of PCs under GIs laws is the lack of consensus among countries on the scope of GIs protection and the different mechanisms regarding the protection of GIs within different national laws. Secondly, although GIs appear to have a high potential to protect PCs, at the international level, GIs fail to prevent misuse of products other than wines and spirits. Many national laws include adequate protection of GIs for all products within their territory. Nevertheless, such national laws are not competent to protect their products overseas. Thirdly, it is doubtful if the GIs regime could protect cultural aspects of TK.

Concerning the beneficiaries: The GIs regime has the potential to protect the interests of the TKHs as a community, or individuals as members of the community or even representatives of the TKHs. The purpose of the GIs system is the identification of a geographical location from which certain types of goods originate and are produced by a handful of enterprises. Thus, these enterprises are not the owners of GIs; however, they have the right to use GIs for the products merely because they are located in the same given geographical area. In the Lisbon Agreement and its Geneva Act, and under the Iranian Act, the concept of the authorized user is the critical element for determining beneficiaries of GIs and AO. Any producer whose place of activity is the given geographical area qualifies as an authorized user. The term 'producer' has a broad meaning and may include not only the manufacturer but also the persons who manipulate natural materials for the production of the mentioned products, or merchants of the said products. In addition, competent authorities involved in the production, distribution or policymaking related to the goods may be recognized as interested parties.

Concerning duration of protection: TKHs' right over PCs should survive in perpetuity. Thus, any protection mechanism for TK-RI shall last indefinitely. In principle, the duration of protection under the GIs regime is supposed to be indefinite. Notwithstanding this fundamental principle, international binding instruments and national laws have adopted different rules concerning the period of validity a registered GI. There are three approaches to duration of validity of GIs. According to the first approach, the period of protection would begin from the date of registration and would be valid as long as the conditions that create the GI exist and as long as GIs are valid in the country of origin. The renewal of the registration is not a condition for continued validity and protection of the international registration. According to the second approach, although the duration of protection of GIs is unlimited, the registration must be renewed after a certain number of years. The third approach to the duration of protection is followed by those countries that protect GIs under trademark law. Like other registered marks, collective marks' registrations are valid for ten years and are renewable for successive ten-year periods. Under all three approaches, the duration of protection of the GIs is unrestricted, and all of them are compatible with the theory of TIP-rights. However, the second approach, which demands timeless protection without restriction, does not seem to be eligible to provide the legal basis for using the GIs regime for the protection of TK-RI. Moreover, there is a fundamental difference between the first approach on the one hand and the second and third approaches on the other. Under the first approach, the only condition for the continuation of the protection of GIs is the sustained use of those indications. This is entirely in line with the theory of TIP-rights. Unlike the first, the second and third approaches consider registration renewal as the condition for maintaining the protection of GIs, which is against the international norms and rules of the Lisbon and Madrid Agreements and against the wishes of TKHs who oppose the imposition of formalities to protect TK.

Conclusions

Maintenance and protection of TK is a vital principle for many indigenous and local communities around the world. Several international instruments have addressed and recognized the critical role of TK in local and indigenous communities' economic, social and cultural life and have called for respect and protection communities' rights over their TK.

TK possesses a dynamic nature. Multiple stakeholders in the various areas have particular interests concerning TK. But reaching an agreement on the abstract definition of TK will not necessarily help TKHs to reach an agreement on how to protect TK at the national and international levels. TKHs are the only eligible group who may legitimately provide the definition of TK which could serve their needs and expectations. Therefore, it is almost impossible to reach an agreement on a comprehensive legal definition for TK that could cover and represent all aspects of the TK. Instead, it is better to identify subject matters of TK that can be considered as the protectable issues rather than defining TK itself.

Two competing ideas have been expressed regarding the identification of TK subject matters, namely TK subject matters in a narrow sense, and TK subject matters in a broader sense. The second seems more reasonable and comprehensive. TK, GRs and TCEs are deeply integrated and inseparable. Accordingly, they shall be treated and protected under the general umbrella of the TK protection regime. Concerning PCs, only a broader identification of TK subject matters would serve the needs and expectations of TKHs.

PCs are one of the most significant and distinctive manifestations of TK in Iranian historical, social, cultural and economic life. However, PCs' TKHs face challenges and difficulties because of UC with third parties who misappropriate and misuse PCs. These competitors are producing their carpets using the designs, styles and methods of PCs and sell them under the name and reputation of PCs. These competitors do not use the necessary required original material or knowledgeable people in the process of producing their hand-woven carpets. They mislead the consumers about the carpets themselves by pretending that their products possess the quality and stability of PCs. Use of cheaper, non-original and low-quality materials, unfamiliarity with the spiritual and cultural context of the designs and signs, and employing less knowledgeable workers mean that these competitors' products are of poor quality and much cheaper than the original products. These imitated carpets have competitive prices lower than those of PCs, and consumers are led to believe that they are purchasing the original goods or using the reliable services of TKHs. However, in the long run, these pretend products would lose their quality and beauty, and in return project a bad image on PCs in the consumers' mind. Consequently, TKHs are struggling with grave problems such as decreasing exports, job cuts and immigration of community members to big cities, loss of knowledge and disappearance of cultural and spiritual ritual. Therefore, local communities are asking for legal protection for their TK on PCs to prevent competitors from using the PCs' reputation in unfair ways and without their prior consent.

Various suggestions have been made on how to provide legal protection of PCs to prevent their misuse, misappropriation, or other kinds of illegal exploitation. Among other legal regimes, such as customary law or contract law, it has been suggested that IP law in its existing format could be applied for the protection of PC. IPRs include different legal platforms, yet none of which would provide a one-size-fits-all solution to protect all angles of the TK as well as PCs needs and expectations. This in particular is true for copyright, unfair competition and undisclosed information. They could not serve as an adequate tool for granting TKHs full control over their TK and for preventing third parties from misfeasance with respect to TKHs' rights. Trademarks and GIs, in particular, attract more attention. Some TKHs believe they may rely on these regimes for the recognition and the protection of their interests and to halt misuse and misappropriation of PCs.

Regarding trademark law: TK in its broadest sense, among others, refers to TK-RS. These aspects of TK are tied to the reputation and distinctive character of TK incorporated in the product concerned. Trademark law serves different needs of TKHs. It protects goodwill and the reputation of producers, designers, artists and the commercial value of PCs as well as preventing confusion among consumers concerning genuine products. Moreover, it acknowledges TKHs' exclusive rights over TK-RS and helps them to preserve, recover and sustain TK-RS and TKHs' cultures. Trademark law is a reliable and precise legal regime for protecting PCs. Different types of trademarks including service marks, collective and certification marks and trade names provide a comprehensive platform for protection of different beneficiaries of PCs. Trademark regime may help TKHs to prevent misuse and misappropriation of TK either by registration of their TK-RS under trademark law or through stopping third parties' claims over marks which are identical with or similar to their TK-RS. In this regard, trademark law cannot only help TKHs to commercialise certain elements of TK, but it can also provide protection against UC.

Notwithstanding the benefits of positive protection and registration of TK-RS, some challenges remain. The first challenge relates to descriptive characteristics of PCs' marks, which will increase the risk of refusal of registration and the threat of litigation against TKHs by competitors worldwide. Using collective and certification mark might be helpful to overcome such a challenge. However, international trademark law does not provide a comprehensive and harmonized system for protection of collective and certification marks. Besides, individual members of communities have to rely on the trade name regime for enjoying protection under trademark law. Therefore, recognition of descriptive feature of TK-RS and PCs, and more harmonization in the international registration system of collective and certification marks are necessary to meet this challenge. The second challenge is the necessity for active use of registered TK-RS in the target markets. TKHs or their representatives have to maintain their rights over registered TK-RS through sustained and continuous use of their marks on PCs. In many instances, TKHs have no representatives or are not active in the target markets. This challenge may lead to cancellation of their rights over registered TK-RS. Expanding the concept of use beyond its existing notions of genuine use or use in commerce, and recognition of cultural and social activities as active use and accepting regional use will help TKHs to face this challenge. The third challenge originates from the classification system of trademark law. TKHs must decide on their strategy for determination of the number of classes that they want to register for their PCs' marks. Applications for registration of TK-RS for many classes may increase the risk of refusal of the applications or of cancellation of registration because many TKHs would not be able to afford the use requirements in many of those classes. Therefore, concerning the existing classification system of trademark law, TKHs are strongly recommended to register their marks only for those goods and services which they are able to use in the target markets. At the same time, TKHs should call for amendments to the international trademark classification under the Nice Agreement in such a way as to cover TK-RS as a whole new class or classes of goods and services. Another challenge of positive protection under trademarks is the expense of acquiring exclusive rights through registration of TK-RS at national and international levels. The financial capacity of TKHs is very limited and most of the PCs communities could not afford to pay the fees for registration of their TK-RS. Therefore, there is a strong need for establishing a specific financial package to assist TKHs to pay the cost for registration and the renewal fee for their marks. In particular, TKHs must be careful about renewal fees. If they fail to pay renewal fees, third parties can assume that they have abandoned their registered marks and would be permitted to use these marks.

It seems that positive protection under the trademark law, despite its benefits, would not be strong enough to protect the TK-RS and PCs or to prevent third parties (either companies or individuals) from misuse and misappropriation of TK. Hence, it is necessary to use a defensive mechanism under trademark law to prevent parties other than TKHs from registering and using marks similar or identical to those of TK-RS. It is important to note, however, that under current international trademark law there are specific grounds for refusal of applications for the registration of marks. One crucial function of trademark law is to prevent the marketing of products and services which are deceptive to consumers or mislead the market about the authenticity, origin, manufacturing method or style of a product or service. In this regard, trademark law may prevent registration of marks that are confusingly similar to the signs and symbols of PCs and falsely suggest that there is a connection between PCs and the applicant for the registration. Certain signs and symbols such as Olympic signs or armorial bearings, flags and State emblems, official signs and hallmarks, and international organizations' names and abbreviations are not allowed to be registered as trademarks. Although some national laws in the USA and Switzerland include such a prohibition regarding their TK-RS, relying on this mechanism for PCs at an international level is challengeable. The fact that it does not apply to those marks which are already misused or misappropriated is one challenge. Another challenge is the possibility of objection to and rejection of such a prohibition by the authorities of designated countries. And the third challenge is that only national authorities and institutions are allowed to categorise TK-RS as certain marks which are not allowed to be registered and TKHs have no power influence such decisions. Therefore, to meet this challenge at national level, Iranian national institutions such as INCC must provide a list of non-registrable PCs signs and symbols as trademarks and negotiate to insert such a list into bilateral and international instruments. Also, the states should try to establish an internationally binding instrument which recognizes TK-RS as non-registrable signs and symbols. Another defensive mechanism within trademark law is the prevention of registration and use of marks which are contrary to the public order or morality. This mechanism might appear useful for protection of TK-RS of PCs because PCs' symbols and signs also consist of sacred and holy elements and beliefs of TKHs. Some national laws, like the trademark law of the USA and New Zealand, have prohibitions on marks or signs, which include sacred elements of TK-RS, that are recognized as culturally offensive and are therefore non-registerable as a trademark. This mechanism is doomed to failure because, at best, it could only provide local or national protection of sacred PCs' signs, as the concept of morality and public order is tightly bound up with the societies' norms and values, and the opinion of authorities and national institutions. Therefore, one could not expect that their sacred sign or mark would command the same respect from other societies. PCs, in comparison with many other TK-RS worldwide, enjoy the advantage of being well-known, whereas most other TKHs and their TK-RS are less well-known around the world, PCs are famous for their unparalleled excellence and elegance. Under trademark law, use or registration of marks which are identical or similar to well-known marks is prohibited. It seems that protection of PCs under the well-known marks regime might be available. However, there are some impediments to the full enjoyment of such a legal mechanism. The lack of a uniform definition and interpretation of the well-known concept, the absence of harmonized standards, the variety of decision-making authorities, and different implementation procedures are the best-known barriers to the efficient protection of well-known PCs despite the WIPO recommendation document and a non-exhaustive list of elements concerning the protection of well-known marks. However, this document is not an internationally binding instrument, and therefore only serves as a guide, and countries have no obligation to accept it for harmonization of their laws.

Although the period of protection is limited, these periods are extendable indefinitely. This feature of trademark law is in line with TKHs expectations concerning the duration of protection and they will be able to continue their use of TK-RS. However, TKHs should realise that they have to meet deadlines for the extension of the registration; otherwise, they would lose their rights over TK.

Notwithstanding the facts mentioned above, TKHs may use trademark law to obtain protection for their TK-RS. However, trademark law could have an effect on the protection of TK opposite to the one that is expected. It may increase the threat of the misappropriation of TK-RS through the registration system. Moreover, grounds for refusal under the trademark law are not designed for defensive protection of TK. Consequently, appropriate amendments and improvements to trademark law are necessary to meet the TKHs' expectations and prevent misappropriation of TK-RS. Although redesigning the national legal system to fill the trademark law gaps is an appropriate step, these efforts must be supported by updating of international trademark law. In this regard, it is necessary to amend and establish norms and rules to meet the specific needs for protection of TK-RS based on the TIP-rights principle.

Concerning GIs: PCs have a definite and well-defined connection with the GIs regime. The reputation of the PCs, the excellent quality of the local substances, and the knowledge and experience of the TKHs make the GIs regime one on the most effective IPRs for protection of PCs. Despite the active use of the GIs regime at the national and international level, the abuse and misappropriation of TK-RI of PCs continues. The TKHs are still facing ongoing UC and undue free-riding, which misleads consumers about the origin and quality of the PCs. However, the question arises as to whether PCs could be protected adequately within the framework of the GIs legal regime.

The required elements of the quality, reputation and other characteristics of goods attributable to a specific geographical origin are well-fitted to the situation pertaining to PCs. However, national laws and authorities make different interpretations concerning the scope and extent of these elements in their jurisdictions. There is no consistent or generally acceptable concept of quality, reputation and other characteristics. Therefore, national authorities use various approaches to attain qualified concepts. Moreover, they evaluate the qualitative connection between those elements and geographical location based on their social practices, while such connections should be evaluated based on the practices of the country of origin. Furthermore, even binding instruments on international industrial property have no harmonized approaches regarding the concept of these elements.

Some national laws use a collective and certification marks system within their trademarks law to extend the protection to the GIs. Such an approach would force TKHs to register their PCs' TK-RI as a trademark. However, trademark law has fundamental differences with the GIs regime. Trademark law protects the enterprise's rights, while the GIs protects the products. Secondly, the collective marks and certification marks refer to specific features of the product, such as its nature and quality, or technical content of the knowledge used to produce it regardless of the geographical link of the product to a special place. Both differ fundamentally from the GIs for which a link to a geographic location is needed. Thirdly, the owner of the collective or certification marks would have the right to prevent the use of marks by third parties. In contrast, GIs do not recognize specific owners. Instead, they recognize the concept of authorized users, which are all users located in the given geographic location. They are all allowed to use GIs as long as they are domiciled in that geographic location. Finally, collective marks and certification marks increase the risk of their subject matter becoming generic or entering the public domain. In contrast, the GIs regime prevents or at least reduces the chances of its subject matters becoming generic or entering the public domain.

Although international GIs law does not require registration of the GIs, there are different approaches to the registration of GIs at national laws. It seems that registration of TK-RI as GIs could be beneficial as a subsidiary tool for the protection of PCs. However, registration shall not be a precondition for the protection of TK because such a requirement would decrease the possibility of protecting TK, as it places more restrictions before the TKHs.

There are further challenges concerning the use of the GIs regime for the protection of PCs. The first is the lack of accord among countries on the scope of protection under GIs. Secondly, at the international level, GIs fail to prevent misuse of products other than wines and spirits. Thirdly, it is doubtful if the GIs regime could protect the cultural aspects of TK.

The GIs regime has the potential to protect the interests of the TKHs as a community, or their dependents as beneficiaries of the TK. However, these beneficiaries are not the owners but authorized users of GIs. These beneficiaries have the right to use GIs for the products merely because they are in the same given geographical area.

Under the GIs, a wide range of legal entities or natural persons might be known as beneficiaries. They include local producers, persons who manipulate natural materials to produce local goods, or merchants of the said products. Besides, competent authorities regarding the production, distribution or policymaking for the goods may be recognized as interested parties.

In principle, the duration of protection under the international GIs regime is infinite. Therefore, the GIs system supports the idea that TKHs' claim over PCs should last indefinitely. Notwithstanding this fundamental principle, international binding instruments and national laws have adopted different rules concerning the validity period of a registered GI. According to one strategy, the period of protection would be valid as long as the conditions that create the GI exist and as long as GIs are valid in the country of origin. Under such a strategy, there is no need for renewal of the registration. According to the second approach, although the duration of protection of GIs is unlimited, the registration must be renewed for specific periods. Under the first approach, the only condition for the maintenance of the protection of GIs is the sustained use of those indications. This setting is entirely compatible with the theory of TIP-rights and harmonized with the international norms and rules of the Lisbon and Madrid Agreements.

From the author's point of view, the GIs system could potentially be an appropriate model for protecting PCs. However, the existing challenges as described need to be addressed, and operational solutions for them must be planned. Given the diversity of countries' laws and practices for the protection of GIs, and the conflicts between legal systems regarding the subject matters and the scope and extent of protection of GIs, it seems that the best way to overcome these challenges is to enter into bilateral or regional agreements concerning the protection of GIs. In such treaties, it is possible to identify members' intentions from the scope and extent of protection as well as the protected subjects matters.

The Importance of International IP Treaties for the protection of PCs is undeniable. One significant issue regarding the use of existing IP regimes for the protection of PCs is Iran's membership in the International IP treaties. Iran has joined many WIPO-administrated treaties regarding the protection of trademarks, GIs and acts against UC. However, such engagement has little effect on providing international protection of the PCs. Tables 4 and 5 show the membership of seven world-leading carpet producers (namely, Iran, Afghanistan, China, India, Nepal, Pakistan and Türkiye) and Twelve main PCs consumers (USA, Germany, Lebanon, the United Kingdom, Japan, the UAE, Pakistan, South Africa, Italy, Australia, Canada and Switzerland) in the relevant IP treaties. As outlined in these tables, even though Iran and all significant producers and consumers of hand-woven carpets are members of the Paris Convention, Iran has not joined the WTO and the TRIPS Agreement, which is the most important international trade agreement regarding implementation and enforcement of IPRs. By contrast, all countries which are the main markets for PCs as well as all six leading producers are members of this agreement.

To maximise its benefit from international IP law, Iran had joined the Madrid System regarding registration of marks, the Lisbon Agreement concerning protection of appellations of origin and the Madrid Agreement regarding protection of indications of source.

Concerning registration of TK-RS under the Madrid System, as of April 2024, among consumer countries, only Lebanon and South Africa have not joined the Madrid System. This suggests that there is an opportunity to apply positive protection of PCs' TK-RS through the Madrid System.

Regarding the protection of GIs, none of the main carpet producers has joined the Lisbon Agreement, and only Türkiye is a member of the Madrid Agreement (Indications of Source) which means Iran may not enjoy these two agreements' legal regime for protection of its PCs' GIs in the territories of those countries.

The need for establishing the TIP-rights is inevitable: The detailed assessment of the potential of the existing trademark and GIs rules to offer protection of PCs strengthened the hypothesis that even though the existing IPRs could support some elements of TK. The current IP law does not appropriately meet the protection needs regarding TK and innovations of TKHs. Furthermore, the application of trademarks and GIs for protecting PCs is severely challengeable. While TKHs should fully understand and maximise their use of the legal capacities of these regimes for the protection of PCs, they must address and solve these challenges. In this regard, the TIP-rights shall be used as a normative principle to guide the reform of international and national IPRs for the protection of TK and PCs. The author of this study recommends that the establishment of TIP-rights is needed to overcome these challenges.

Bibliography

Abbott FM, Cottier T and Gurry F, *International Intellectual Property in an Integrated World Economy* (2nd edn, Wolters Kluwer Law & Business 2011).

Abbott R, *Documenting Traditional Medical Knowledge* (WIPO 2014).

'About Cowichan Tribes' (*Cowichan Tribes*, 1995) <http://www.cowichantribes.com/about-cowichan-tribes/>.

'About Us | Farrahi' (*Farrahi Carpet Co. – Farrahi Group*, 2016) <http://farrahicarpet.com/EN/about_us/>.

Addor F and Grazioli A, 'Geographical Indications beyond Wines and Spirits – A Roadmap for a Better Protection for Geographical Indications in the WTO/TRIPS Agreement' (2002) 5 The Journal of World Intellectual Property 865.

Addor F and Grazioli A, 'Agreement on Trade-Related Aspects of Intellectual Property Rights: Section 3: Geographical Indications' in Thomas Cottier and Pierre Véron (eds), *Concise International and European IP Law: TRIPS, Paris Convention, European Enforcement and Transfer of Technology*, vol 4 (2nd edn, Kluwer Law International 2008).

'Admission of the Republic of Azerbaijan to Membership in the United Nations' (1992) Res 742, UN SCOR, 3052nd mtg, SC Res S/RES/742(1992).

Afrough M, 'نمادگرایی ونشانه شناسی درفرش ایرانی (Symbolism and Semiotics in Persian Carpets)' (2011) 10 Journal of The Iranian Studies 13.

Aguilar G, 'Access to Genetic Resources and Protection of Traditional Knowledge in the Territories of Indigenous Peoples' (2001) 4 Environmental Science & Policy 241.

'Akbar Mahdiei – The Creator of Colorful Gardens in Persian Rugs' (*Percarin – Persian Carpet Industry*, 2024) <https://percarin.com/bignames/akbar-mahdiei> accessed 24 April 2024.

Alexander M and others, 'The Role of Registers and Databases in the Protection of Traditional Knowledge: A Comparative Analysis' (Institute of Advanced Studies, United Nations University 2004) UNU-IAS.

Alexiades MN and Laird SA, 'Laying the Foundation: Equitable Biodiversity Research Relationships' in Sarah A Laird (ed), *Biodiversity and Traditional Knowledge: Equitable Partnerships in Practice* (Earthscan Publications 2002).

Allen S and Xanthaki A, *Reflections on the UN Declaration on the Rights of Indigenous Peoples* (Hart Pub 2011).

Anderson J, 'Indigenous/Traditional Knowledge & Intellectual Property' [2010] Center for the Study of the Public Domain, Duke University School of Law 82.

Annas M, 'The Label of Authenticity: A Certification Trade Mark for Goods and Services of Indigenous Origin' (1997) 3 Aboriginal Law Bulletin 4.

ARIPO, 'About Us | ARIPO' (*IP ARIPO*, 2017) <https://www.aripo.org/member-states>.

Azarpad H and Heshmati Razavi F, فرش نامه ایران (*Persian Carpet-Nama*) (Institute for Humanities and Cultural Studies (IHCS) 2005).

Bashir I, 'About Us | Bioresources' (*Bioresources Development and Conservation Program*, 2014) <http://bioresources.org/about/> accessed 24 May 2018.

Berkes F, 'Traditional Ecological Knowledge in Perspective' in Julian T Inglis (ed), *Traditional Ecological Knowledge: Concepts and Cases* (International Program on Traditional Ecological Knowledge: International Development Research Centre 1993).

Biber-Klemm S, 'Origin and Allocation of Traditional Knowledge and Landraces' in Susette Biber-Klemm and Thomas Cottier (eds), *Rights to Plant Genetic Resources and Traditional Knowledge: Basic Issues and Perspectives* (CABI 2006).

Biber-Klemm S and Berglas DS, 'Problems and Goals' in Susette Biber-Klemm and Thomas Cottier (eds), *Rights to Plant Genetic Resources and Traditional Knowledge: Basic Issues and Perspectives* (CABI 2006).

BIRPI, *Model Law for Developing Countries on Marks, Trade Names, and Acts of Unfair Competition* (BIRPI Publication 1967).

Blackshaw IS, *Sports Marketing Agreements: Legal, Fiscal and Practical Aspects* (Springer Science & Business Media 2012).

Blakeney M, *Intellectual Property Aspects of Ethnobiology* (Sweet & Maxwell 1999).

Blakeney M, 'What Is Traditional Knowledge? Why Should It Be Protected? Who Should Protect It? For Whom? Understanding the Value Chain' (World Intellectual Property Organization 1999) WIPO Doc, WIPO/IPTK/RT/99/3.

Blakeney M, 'Proposals for the International Regulation of Geographical Indications' (2001) 4 Journal of World Intellectual Property 629.

Bodenhausen GHC, *Guide to the Application of the Paris Convention for the Protection of Industrial Property, as Revised at Stockholm in 1967* (WIPO 1968).

Bouchoux DE, *Intellectual Property: The Law of Trademarks, Copyrights, Patents, and Trade Secrets* (4th edn, Cengage Learning 2012).

Boyle J, *The Public Domain: Enclosing the Commons of the Mind* (Yale University Press 2008).

Brascoupé S and Endemann K, 'Intellectual Property and Aboriginal People: A Working Paper' (Research and Analysis Directorate, Department of Indian Affairs and Northern Development 1999).

Brazell L, *Intellectual Property Protection and Enforcement* (Thorogood Ltd 1998).

Bretzke JT, *Consecrated Phrases: A Latin Theological Dictionary; Latin Expressions Commonly Found in Theological Writings* (3rd edn, Liturgical Press 2013).

Burge DA, *Patent and Trademark Tactics and Practice* (John Wiley & Sons 1999).

Burri M, 'Cultural Heritage and Intellectual Property' in Francesco Francioni and Ana Filipa Vrdoljak (eds), *The Oxford Handbook of International Cultural Heritage Law* (Oxford University Press 2020).

Burri M, 'The Protection of Cultural Heritage by Trademarks' in Irini Stamatoudi (ed), *Research Handbook on Intellectual Property and Cultural Heritage* (Edward Elgar Publishing 2022).

Canada Trademark Office, 'COWICHAN Certificate Mark' (*Canadian Trademarks Detail*, 6 November 1996) <https://ised-isde.canada.ca/cipo/trademark-search/pdf/0792173?lang=eng>.

Carpenter KA, Katyal SK and Riley AR, 'In Defense of Property' (2009) 118 The Yale Law Journal 1022.

Chair of the IGC Mr. Ian Goss, 'Chair's Text of a Draft International Legal Instrument Relating to Intellectual Property, Genetic Resources and Traditional Knowledge Associated with Genetic Resources' (2022) WIPO Doc WIPO/GRTKF/IC/43/5.

Chambers R, *Rural Development: Putting the Last First* (Longman 1989).

Chitsazan A and Pour Jafar MR, 'تاثیرپذیری طراحی فرش کاشان ازنمادها (The Influence of Symbols on the Design of Kashan Carpet)' (2004) 40 & 41 *Tandis*.

Choi S, 'Indigenous Intellectual Property and the Law: Navajo Nation v. Urban Outfitters' (2018) 1 Culture 91.

CIP – The Anton Mostert Chair of Intellectual Property, 'The Winning Choice For Traditional Culture' (20 July 2013) <http://blogs.sun.ac.za/iplaw/2013/07/20/the-winning-choice-for-traditional-culture/> accessed 21 December 2017.

Cirlot JE, 'Dictionary of Symbols' 451.

'Committee of Experts of the Nice Union' (*World Intellectual Property Organization*, May 2018) <https://www.wipo.int/meetings/en/details.jsp?meeting_id=46428>.

Condä HV, *A Handbook of International Human Rights Terminology* (University of Nebraska Press 2004).

Conrad A, 'The Protection of Geographical Indications in the TRIPS Agreement' (1996) 86 The Trademark Reporter 11.

Conway-Jones D, 'Safeguarding Hawaiian Traditional Knowledge and Cultural Heritage: Supporting the Right to Self-Determination and Preventing the Co-Modification of Culture' (2005) 48 Howard Law Journal 737.

Cordero SM, 'Cocaine-Cola, the Velvet Elvis, and Anti-Barbie: Defending the Trademark and Publicity Rights to Cultural Icons' (1998) 8 Fordham Intellectual Property, Media and Entertainment Law Journal 599.

Correa CM, *Intellectual Property Rights, the WTO and Developing Countries: The TRIPS Agreement and Policy Options* (Zed Books; Third World Network 2000).

Correa CM, *Traditional Knowledge and Intellectual Property – Issues and Options Surrounding the Protection of Traditional Knowledge* (The Quaker United Nations Office 2001).

Cottier T, 'The Protection of Genetic Resources and Traditional Knowledge: Towards More Specific Rights and Obligations in World Trade Law' (1998) 1 Journal of International Economic Law 555.

Cottier T, 'Chapter 22 – The Agreement on Trade-Related Aspects of Intellectual Property Rights' in Patrick FJ Macrory, Arthur E Appleton and Michael G Plummer (eds), *The World Trade Organization: Legal, Economic and Political Analysis*, vol 1 (Springer 2005).

Cottier T, 'Trade and Intellectual Property: Background Paper' in Thomas Cottier, Matthias Oesch and Thomas M Fischer (eds), *International Trade Regulation: Law and Policy in the WTO, the European Union and Switzerland: Cases, Materials and Comments* (Staempfli Publishers 2005).

Cottier T, *Trade and Intellectual Property Protection in WTO Law: Collected Essays* (Cameron May 2005).

Cottier T, 'Introduction' in Susette Biber-Klemm and Thomas Cottier (eds), *Rights to Plant Genetic Resources and Traditional Knowledge: Basic Issues and Perspectives* (CABI 2006).

Cottier T, 'WTO Negotiations on Environmental Goods and Services: A Potential Contribution to the Millennium Development Goals' (United Nations 2009) UNCTAD/DITC/TED/2008/4.

Cottier T and Germann C, 'Agreement on Trade-Related Aspects of Intellectual Property Rights: Part I. General Provisions and Basic Principles' in Thomas Cottier and Pierre Véron (eds), *Concise International and European IP Law: TRIPS, Paris Convention, European Enforcement and Transfer of Technology*, vol 4 (2nd edn, Kluwer Law International 2008).

Cottier T and Germann C, 'Agreement on Trade-Related Aspects of Intellectual Property Rights: The TRIPS Agreement Is Annex 1C of the Marrakesh Agreement Establishing the World Trade Organization, Signed in Marrakesh, Morocco on 15 April 1994.' in Thomas Cottier and Pierre Véron (eds), *Concise International and European IP Law: TRIPS, Paris Convention, European Enforcement and Transfer of Technology*, vol 4 (2nd edn, Kluwer Law International 2008).

Cottier T, Lalani S and Temmerman M, 'Use It or Lose It: Assessing the Compatibility of the Paris Convention and TRIPS Agreement with Respect to Local Working Requirements' (2014) 17 Journal of International Economic Law 437.

Cottier T and Müller AN, 'The Case for Protecting Geographical Indications and Traditional Knowledge in Agricultural Trade.'

Cottier T, Oesch M and Fischer TM, *International Trade Regulation: Law and Policy in the WTO, the European Union and Switzerland: Cases, Materials and Comments* (Staempfli Publishers 2005).

Cottier T and Panizzon M, 'Legal Perspectives on Traditional Knowledge: The Case for Intellectual Property Protection' (2004) 7 Journal of International Economic Law 371.

Cottier T and Panizzon M, 'Legal Perspectives on Traditional Knowledge: The Case for Intellectual Property Protection' in Keith E Maskus and Jerome H Reichman (eds), *International Public Goods and Transfer of Technology under a Globalized Intellectual Property Regime* (First, Cambridge University Press 2005).

Cottier T and Panizzon M, 'A New Generation of IPR for the Protection of Traditional Knowledge in PGR for Food, Agricultural and Pharmaceutical Uses' in Susette Biber-Klemm and Thomas Cottier (eds), *Rights to Plant Genetic Resources and Traditional Knowledge: Basic Issues and Perspectives* (CABI 2006).

Crespi RS and Straus J, 'Intellectual Property, Technology Transfer and Genetic Resources: An OECD Survey of Current Practices and Policies' (OECD Publishing 1996).

Cullet P and others, 'Intellectual Property Rights, Plant Genetic Resources and Traditional Knowledge' in Susette Biber-Klemm and Thomas Cottier (eds), *Rights to Plant Genetic Resources and Traditional Knowledge: Basic Issues and Perspectives* (CABI 2006).

Curci J, *The Protection of Biodiversity and Traditional Knowledge in International Law of Intellectual Property* (Cambridge University Press 2009).

Curtis GE and Hooglund E, *Iran: A Country Study* (5th edn, Government Printing Office 2008).

Dadvar A and Momenian HR, 'عوامل موثر بر شکل گیری و پیدایش نقوش گلیم قشقایی (Factors Influencing the Formation and Development of Qashqai Kilim Motifs)' (2006) 2 Goljaam, Iranian Carpet Scientific Society Quarterly 47.

Daes E-I, 'Principles and Guidelines for the Protection of the Heritage of Indigenous People' (1995) UN ESCOR, 47th sess, Agenda Item 15, UN Doc E/CN.4/Sub.2/1995/26 Annex.

Daes E-I, 'Principles and Guidelines for the Protection of the Heritage of Indigenous People' (UN Commission on Human Rights, Sub-Commission on the Promotion and Protection of Human Rights 2000) UN ESC Doc E/CN.4/Sub.2/2000/26.

Daes E-I, 'Principles and Guidelines for the Protection of the Heritage of Indigenous People' (UN Commission on Human Rights, Sub-Commission on the Promotion and Protection of Human Rights 2000) UN ESC Doc E/CN.4/Sub.2/2000/26 Annex I.

Damdin T, 'Chapter 75 – Mongolia' in Patrick FJ Macrory, Arthur E Appleton and Michael G Plummer (eds), *The World Trade Organization: Legal, Economic and Political Analysis*, vol 3 (Springer 2005).

Daneshgar A, فرهنگ جامع فرش یادواره – دانشنامه ایران (*Yadvareh Comprehensive Encyclopaedia of Carpet – Iran Encyclopaedia*), vol 1 (2nd edn, Yadvareh Asadi 2011).

de la Cruz R, 'Customary Law in the Protection of Traditional Knowledge' (Quito 2006).

Dhir RK, 'Sustainable Development Goals: Indigenous Peoples in Focus' (ILO 2016).

Dinwoodie GB, 'Trademarks and Territory: Detaching Trademark Law from the Nation-State' (2004) 41 Houston Law Review 885.

Dinwoodie GB, 'Developing a Private International Intellectual Property Law: The Demise of Territoriality?' (2009) 51 William and Mary Law Review 711.

Dogan B and Gokovali U, 'Geographical Indications: The Aspects of Rural Development and Marketing Through the Traditional Products' (2012) 62 Procedia – Social and Behavioral Sciences 761.

Downes DR and Laird SA, 'Community Registries of Biodiversity-Related Knowledge-The Role of Intellectual Property in Managing Access and Benefit Sharing' (UNCTAD Biotrade Initiative 1999).

Drexl J and others (eds), 'Intellectual Property Chapters in Free Trade Agreements: Their Significance and Systemic Implications,' *EU Bilateral Trade Agreements and Intellectual Property: For Better or Worse?* (Springer 2014).

Dutfield G, 'TRIPS-Related Aspects of Traditional Knowledge' (2001) 33 Case Western Reserve Journal of International Law 233.

Dutfield G, 'Harnessing Traditional Knowledge and Genetic Resources for Local Development and Trade' (WIPO 2005).

Dutfield G, 'Legal and Economic Aspects of Traditional Knowledge' in Keith E Maskus and Jerome H Reichman (eds), *International Public Goods and Transfer of Technology under a Globalized Intellectual Property Regime* (First, Cambridge University Press 2005).

Elias S and Stim R, *Trademark: Legal Care for Your Business & Product Name* (9th edn, Nolo 2010).

Encyclopaedia Britannica, 'Knowledge,' *Britannica Online Encyclopaedia* (2014) <http://www.britannica.com/bps/dictionary?query=knowledge> accessed 23 January 2014.

Esmaili A, 'Understanding Symbolism in Persian & Other Antique Rugs' (*Esmaili Rugs and Antiques*, 14 October 2016) <https://www.esmailirugs.com/index.php?dispatch=pages.view&product_id=75> accessed 17 November 2018.

Espanani MA, 'آسیب شناسی احیای طرح ها و نقشه های قالی عشایری و روستایی (Difficulties in Reviving the Designs and Patterns of Nomadic and Rural Carpets)' (2007) 6 and 7 Goljaam, Iranian Carpet Scientific Society Quarterly 35.

Etheredge L, *Iran* (Britannica Educational Pub in association with Rosen Educational Services 2011).

European Commission, 'Why Do Geographical Indications Matter to Us?' (2003) MEMO/03/160.

FAO, 'FAO Statement on Biotechnology' (*Agricultural Biotechnologies in Crops, Forestry, Livestock, Fisheries and Agro-Industry*, 2000) <http://www.fao.org/biotech/fao-statement-on-biotechnology/en/> accessed 13 August 2014.

Farley CH, 'Protecting Folklore of Indigenous Peoples: Is Intellectual Property the Answer?' (1997) 30 Connecticut Law Review 1.

Ferrier JP, *Voyages et Aventures en Perse* (Dentu 1870).

Ficsor M, *Guide to the Copyright and Related Rights Treaties Administered by WIPO and Glossary of Copyright and Related Rights Terms* (WIPO 2003).

Forsyth M, 'Lifting the Lid on "The Community": Who Has the Right to Control Access to Traditional Knowledge and Expressions of Culture?' (2012) 19 International Journal of Cultural Property 1.

Fowler BJ, 'Preventing Counterfeit Craft Designs' in J Michael Finger and Philip Schuler (eds), *Poor People's Knowledge, Promoting Intellectual Property in Developing Countries* (The World Bank and Oxford University Press 2004).

Frankel S, 'Trademarks and Traditional Knowledge and Cultural Property Rights' in Graeme B Dinwoodie and Mark D Janis (eds), *Trademark Law and Theory: A Handbook of Contemporary Research* (Edward Elgar Publishing 2008).

Frankel S, 'Using Intellectual Property Rules to Support the Self-Determination Goals of Indigenous Peoples,' *Research Handbook on Human Rights and Intellectual Property* (Edward Elgar Publishing 2015).

Gangjee DS, 'Introduction: Timeless Signs or Signs of the Times?' in Dev S Gangjee (ed), *Research Handbook on Intellectual Property and Geographical Indications* (Edward Elgar Publishing 2016).

Garner BA, 'Black's Law Dictionary.'

Gervais D and Studer M, 'Agreement on Trade-Related Aspects of Intellectual Property Rights: Part II. Standards Concerning the Availability, Scope and Use of Intellectual Property Rights' in Thomas Cottier and Pierre Véron (eds), *Concise International and European IP Law: TRIPS, Paris Convention, European Enforcement and Transfer of Technology*, vol 4 (2nd edn, Kluwer Law International 2008).

Gervais DJ, 'Feist Goes Global: A Comparative Analysis of the Notion of Originality in Copyright Law' (2001) 49 Journal of the Copyright Society of the U.S.A. 949.

Gervais DJ, 'The Internationalization of Intellectual Property: New Challenges From the Very Old and the Very New' (2002) 12 Fordham Intellectual Property, Media & Entertainment Law Journal 929.

Gervais DJ, 'Spiritual but Not Intellectual? The Protection of Sacred Intangible Traditional Knowledge' (2003) 11 Cardozo Journal of International and Comparative Law 467.

Ghaderi E, 'فروش فرش چینی و هندی به نام فرش ایرانی (Selling Chinese and Indian Carpets under the name of Persian carpets)' *Iranian Students' News Agency* (7 July 2016).

Ghasem Nejhad A, 'قالی بیجار (Bijar Rugs)' (*Iran National Carpet Centre*, 1 December 2018) <https://www.incc.ir/knowing/فرش-بیجار>.

Gibson J, 'Knowledge and Other Values – Intellectual Property and the Limitations for Traditional Knowledge' in Guido Westkamp (ed), *Emerging Issues in Intellectual*

Property: Trade, Technology and Market Freedom: Essays in Honour of Herchel Smith (Edward Elgar Publishing 2007).

Gilbert A, 'Intellectual Property & Traditional Knowledge and Traditional Cultural Expressions' (Workshop on Intellectual Property and Traditional Knowledge for Economic Development: Empowering Local Communities of Uganda, Kampala, Uganda, 4 July 2017).

Githaiga JW, 'Intellectual Property Law and the Protection of Indigenous Folklore and Knowledge' (1998) 5 Murdoch University Electronic Journal of Law 53.

Goebel B, 'Trademarks as Fundamental Rights – Europe' (2009) 99 The Trademark Reporter 931.

Goldstein P and Hugenholtz PB, *International Copyright: Principles, Law, and Practice* (4th edn, Oxford University Press 2019).

Goodenough U, 'Naturalizing Morality' in Charles R McManis (ed), *Biodiversity and the Law: Intellectual Property, Biotechnology and Traditional Knowledge* (Earthscan 2007).

Goswami KK, 'Developments in Handmade Carpets: Design and Manufacture' in KK Goswami (ed), *Advances in Carpet Manufacture* (Woodhead Publishing Limited 2009).

Government of Switzerland, 'Draft Guidelines on Access and Benefit Sharing Regarding the Utilisation of Genetic Resource' (World Intellectual Property Organization 2001) WIPO Doc WIPO/GRTKF/IC/1/9.

Graber CB and Girsberger MA, 'Traditional Knowledge at the International Level: Current Approaches and Proposals for a Bigger Picture That Includes Cultural Diversity' in Jörg Schmid and Paul Richli (eds), *Recht des ländlichen Raums: Festgabe der Rechtswissenschaftlichen Fakultät der Universität Luzern für Paul Richli zum 60. Geburtstag* (Schulthess 2006).

Greaves T, *Intellectual Property Rights for Indigenous Peoples: A Source Book* (1st edn, Society for Applied Anthropology 1994).

GRULAC, 'Traditional Knowledge and the Need to Give It Adequate Intellectual Property Protection' (World Intellectual Property Organization 2001) WIPO Doc WIPO/GRTKF/IC/1/5 Annex II.

GRULAC, 'Traditional Knowledge and the Need to Give It Adequate Intellectual Property Protection' (World Intellectual Property Organization 2001) WIPO Doc WIPO/GRTKF/IC/1/5 Annex I.

Gupta AK, 'The Honey Bee Network: Linking Knowledge-Rich Grassroots Innovations.'

Gupta AK, 'Rewarding Traditional Knowledge and Contemporary Grassroots Creativity: The Role of Intellectual Property Protection,' *A Seminar at Kennedy School* (Harvard University 2000).

Gupta AK, *WIPO-UNEP Study on the Role of Intellectual Property Rights in the Sharing of Benefits Arising from the Use of Biological Resources and Associated Traditional Knowledge* (World Intellectual Property Organization 2004).

Gupta AK, 'From Sink to Source: The Honey Bee Network Documents Indigenous Knowledge and Innovations in India' (2006) 1 Innovations: Technology, Governance, Globalization 49.

Hansen SA and van Fleet JW, 'Traditional Knowledge and Intellectual Property: A Handbook on Issues and Options for Traditional Knowledge Holders in Protecting Their Intellectual Property and Maintaining Biological Diversity' (American Association for the Advancement of Science 2003).

'HARIS ORIENT TEPPICHE in New Delhi, Delhi, India – Company Profile' (*Tradeindia*, 16 March 2005) <https://www.tradeindia.com/Seller-1030976-HARIS-ORIENT-TEPPICHE/> accessed 23 March 2019.

Harris Tweed Authority (HTA), 'Brand Use Rules' (Harris Tweed Authority 2017) Version 2.

Heald PJ, 'The Rhetoric of Biopiracy' (2003) 11 Cardozo Journal of International and Comparative Law 519.

Helfer LR, *Intellectual Property Rights in Plant Varieties: International Legal Regimes and Policy Options for National Governments* (FAO 2004).

Hennessey WO, *Toward A Conceptual Framework for Recognition of Rights for the Holders of Traditional Knowledge and Folklore* (University of New Hampshire School of law 2002).

Heri S and others, *International Instruments Influencing the Rights of People Facing Investments in Agricultural Land* (ILC 2011).

Hilty R, 'Rationales for the Legal Protection of Intangible Goods and Cultural Heritage' (Max Planck Institute for Intellectual Property, Competition & Tax Law 2009) Research Paper 9 <http://papers.ssrn.com/abstract=1470602> accessed 1 November 2014.

'History | Iran Carpet Co.' (*Iran Carpet Co.*, 2015) <http://en.irancarpet.ir/IranCarpetCo/History.aspx>.

Hofman J, *Introducing Copyright: A Plain Language Guide to Copyright in the 21st Century* (Commonwealth of Learning 2009).

Holcombe S, 'Confidential Information and Anthropology: The Politics of the Digital Knowledge Economy' in Matthew Rimmer (ed), *Indigenous Intellectual Property: A Handbook of Contemporary Research* (Edward Elgar Publishing 2015).

Horwitz E and Levi B, 'Fifty Years of the Lanham Act: A Retrospective of Section 43(a)' (1996) 7 Fordham Intellectual Property, Media & Entertainment Law Journal 59.

Houghton Mifflin Company, 'The American Heritage Dictionary.'

Huang J, *Tribeswomen of Iran: Weaving Memories among Qashqai Nomads* (IB Tauris 2014).

Hughes J, 'Traditional Knowledge, Cultural Expression, and the Siren's Call of Property' (2012) 49 San Diego Law Review 1215.

IFAD, 'Engagement with Indigenous Peoples: Policy' (The International Fund for Agricultural Development 2009).

IGC-GRTKF Secretariat, 'Report of Intergovernmental Committee on Intellectual Property and Genetic Resources, Traditional Knowledge and Folklore' (World Intellectual Property Organization 2001) WIPO Doc WIPO/GRTKF/IC/1/13.

IGC-GRTKF Secretariat, 'Survey of Existing Forms of Intellectual Property Protection for Traditional Knowledge' (World Intellectual Property Organization 2001) WIPO Doc WIPO/GRTKF/IC/2/5.

IGC-GRTKF Secretariat, 'Report of Intergovernmental Committee on Intellectual Property and Genetic Resources, Traditional Knowledge and Folklore' (World Intellectual Property Organization 2001) WIPO Doc WIPO/GRTKF/IC/2/16.

IGC-GRTKF Secretariat, 'Review of Existing Intellectual Property Protection of Traditional Knowledge' (World Intellectual Property Organization 2002) WIPO Doc WIPO/GRTKF/IC/3/7.

IGC-GRTKF Secretariat, 'Traditional Knowledge – Operational Terms and Definitions' (World Intellectual Property Organization 2002) WIPO Doc WIPO/GRTKF/IC/3/9.

IGC-GRTKF Secretariat, 'Report of the Thirty-First Session of the Committee of Experts of the Special Union for the International Patent Classification – Present Status of TKDL Project' (World Intellectual Property Organization 2002) WIPO Doc WIPO/GRTKF/IC/3/13 Appendix II of Annex I.

IGC-GRTKF Secretariat, 'Report of Intergovernmental Committee on Intellectual Property and Genetic Resources, Traditional Knowledge and Folklore' (World Intellectual Property Organization 2002) WIPO Doc WIPO/GRTKF/IC/3/17.

IGC-GRTKF Secretariat, 'Elements of a Sui Generis System for the Protection of Traditional Knowledge' (World Intellectual Property Organization 2002) WIPO Doc WIPO/GRTKF/IC/4/8.

IGC-GRTKF Secretariat, 'Overview of Outcomes and Activities of the Intergovernmental Committee' (World Intellectual Property Organization 2003) WIPO Doc WIPO/GRTKF/IC/5/12.

IGC-GRTKF Secretariat, 'Consolidated Analysis of the Legal Protection of Traditional Cultural Expressions' (World Intellectual Property Organization 2003) WIPO Doc WIPO/GRTKF/IC/5/3.

IGC-GRTKF Secretariat, 'Consolidated Analysis of the Legal Protection of Traditional Cultural Expressions' (World Intellectual Property Organization 2003) WIPO Doc WIPO/GRTKF/IC/5/3 Annex.

IGC-GRTKF Secretariat, 'Report of Intergovernmental Committee on Intellectual Property and Genetic Resources, Traditional Knowledge and Folklore' (World Intellectual Property Organization 2003) WIPO Doc WIPO/GRTKF/IC/5/15.

IGC-GRTKF Secretariat, 'Report of Intergovernmental Committee on Intellectual Property and Genetic Resources, Traditional Knowledge and Folklore' (World Intellectual Property Organization 2004) WIPO Doc WIPO/GRTKF/IC/6/14.

IGC-GRTKF Secretariat, 'Draft Policy Objectives and Core Principles: Background Information and Discussion' (World Intellectual Property Organization 2004) WIPO Doc WIPO/GRTKF/IC/7/5 Annex II.

IGC-GRTKF Secretariat, 'Draft Report of Intergovernmental Committee on Intellectual Property and Genetic Resources, Traditional Knowledge and Folklore' (World Intellectual Property Organization 2004) WIPO Doc WIPO/GRTKF/IC/7/15 Prov.

IGC-GRTKF Secretariat, 'Revised Draft Provisions for the Protection of Traditional Knowledge: Policy Objectives and Core Principles' (World Intellectual Property Organization 2005) WIPO Doc WIPO/GRTKF/IC/8/5 Annex.

IGC-GRTKF Secretariat, 'Second Draft Report of Intergovernmental Committee on Intellectual Property and Genetic Resources, Traditional Knowledge and Folklore' (World Intellectual Property Organization 2005) WIPO Doc WIPO/GRTKF/IC/8/15 Prov 2.

IGC-GRTKF Secretariat, 'Revised Provisions for the Protection of Traditional Cultural Expressions/Expressions of Folklore – Policy Objectives and Core Principles' (World Intellectual Property Organization 2007) WIPO Doc WIPO/GRTKF/IC/12/4(c) Annex.

IGC-GRTKF Secretariat, 'Revised Draft Report of Intergovernmental Committee on Intellectual Property and Genetic Resources, Traditional Knowledge and Folklore' (World Intellectual Property Organization 2008) WIPO Doc WIPO/GRTKF/IC/11/15 Prov 2.

IGC-GRTKF Secretariat, 'Draft Gap Analysis on the Protection of Traditional Cultural Expressions' (World Intellectual Property Organization 2008) WIPO Doc WIPO/GRTKF/IC/13/4(b) Annex I.

IGC-GRTKF Secretariat, 'Report of Intergovernmental Committee on Intellectual Property and Genetic Resources, Traditional Knowledge and Folklore' (World Intellectual Property Organization 2008) WIPO Doc WIPO/GRTKF/IC/12/9.

IGC-GRTKF Secretariat, 'Report of Intergovernmental Committee on Intellectual Property and Genetic Resources, Traditional Knowledge and Folklore' (World Intellectual Property Organization 2009) WIPO Doc WIPO/GRTKF/IC/13/11.

IGC-GRTKF Secretariat, 'Draft Articles on the Protection of Traditional Cultural Expressions/Expressions of Folklore Prepared at IWG 1' (World Intellectual Property Organization 2010) WIPO Doc WIPO/GRTKF/IC/17/9 Annex.

IGC-GRTKF Secretariat, 'Revised Provisions for the Protection of Traditional Knowledge: Policy Objectives and Core Principles' (World Intellectual Property Organization 2010) WIPO Doc WIPO/GRTKF/IC/17/5 Annex.

IGC-GRTKF Secretariat, 'List and Brief Technical Explanation of Various Forms in Which Traditional Knowledge May Be Found' (World Intellectual Property Organization 2010) WIPO Doc WIPO/GRTKF/IC/17/INF/9 Annex.

IGC-GRTKF Secretariat, 'Revised Provisions for the Protection of Traditional Knowledge: Policy Objectives and Core Principles' (World Intellectual Property Organization 2011) WIPO Doc WIPO/GRTKF/IC/18/5 Annex.

IGC-GRTKF Secretariat, 'Draft Report of Intergovernmental Committee on Intellectual Property and Genetic Resources, Traditional Knowledge and Folklore' (World Intellectual Property Organization 2011) WIPO Doc WIPO/GRTKF/IC/17/12 PROV. 2.

IGC-GRTKF Secretariat, 'Glossary of Key Terms Related to Intellectual Property and Genetic Resources, Traditional Knowledge and Traditional Cultural Expressions' (World Intellectual Property Organization 2014) WIPO Doc WIPO/GRTKF/IC/28/INF/7 Annex.

IGC-GRTKF Secretariat, 'The Protection of Traditional Knowledge: Draft Articles Rev. 2' (World Intellectual Property Organization 2014) WIPO Doc WIPO/GRTKF/IC/28/5 Annex.

IGC-GRTKF Secretariat, 'The Protection of Traditional Knowledge: Draft Articles' (World Intellectual Property Organization 2016) WIPO Doc WIPO/GRTKF/IC/31/4 Annex.

IGC-GRTKF Secretariat, 'Glossary of Key Terms Related to Intellectual Property and Genetic Resources, Traditional Knowledge and Traditional Cultural Expressions' (World Intellectual Property Organization 2017) WIPO Doc WIPO/GRTKF/IC/34/INF/7 Annex.

IGC-GRTKF Secretariat, 'The Protection of Traditional Knowledge: Draft Articles' (World Intellectual Property Organization 2017) WIPO Doc WIPO/GRTKF/IC/34/5 Annex.

IGC-GRTKF Secretariat, 'Report of Intergovernmental Committee on Intellectual Property and Genetic Resources, Traditional Knowledge and Traditional Cultural Expressions' (World Intellectual Property Organization 2017) WIPO Doc WIPO/GRTKF/IC/33/7.

IGC-GRTKF Secretariat, 'Report of Intergovernmental Committee on Intellectual Property and Genetic Resources, Traditional Knowledge and Traditional Cultural Expressions' (World Intellectual Property Organization 2018) WIPO Doc WIPO/GRTKF/IC/34/14.

IGC-GRTKF Secretariat, 'The Protection of Traditional Knowledge: Draft Articles' (World Intellectual Property Organization 2018) WIPO Doc WIPO/GRTKF/IC/37/4 Annex.

IGC-GRTKF Secretariat, 'The Protection of Traditional Knowledge: Updated Draft Gap Analysis' (World Intellectual Property Organization 2018) WIPO Doc WIPO/GRTKF/IC/37/6 Annex II.

IGC-GRTKF Secretariat, 'The Protection of Traditional Knowledge: Updated Draft Gap Analysis' (World Intellectual Property Organization 2018) WIPO Doc WIPO/GRTKF/IC/37/6 Annex I.

Ilanah Simon F, 'Introduction' in Fhima Ilanah Simon (ed), *Trade Mark Law and Sharing Names: Exploring Use of the Same Mark by Multiple Undertakings* (Edward Elgar 2009).

Indian Council of Scientific & Industrial Research, 'About TKDL' (*Traditional Knowledge Digital Library*, March 2012) <http://tkdl.res.in/tkdl/langdefault/common/Home.asp?GL=Eng>.

Ingrassia A, Manzella D and Martyniuk E, *The Legal Framework for the Management of Animal Genetic Resources* (Food and Agriculture Organization of the United Nations 2005).

'Intellectual Property Rights' (2003) 1 ICTSD and IISD 4.

InterCEDD Health Products, 'About Us | Intercedd Health Products' (*Intercedd Health Products*, 2007) <http://intercedd.com.ng/about-us/> accessed 24 May 2018.

International Classification of Goods and Services for the Purposes of the Registration of Marks (*Nice Classification*), vol II (8th edn, World Intellectual Property Organization 2001).

'International Registration of Marks – Fee Calculation' (*World Intellectual Property Organization*, 2018) <https://madrid.wipo.int/feecalcapp/> accessed 22 October 2018.

Interview with Gholamreza Bayat, 'Interview with Mr. Gholamreza Bayat, Head of Trademarks division of the Iranian Intellectual Property Centre' (2 September 2018).

'Iran Handmade Carpet Exhibition Kicks Off in Tehran' (*Islamic Republic News Agency*, 25 August 2018) <http://www.irna.ir/en/News/83011584/> accessed 17 January 2019.

Iran Intellectual Property Centre, 'جستجوی علامت فرش – صیرفیان (Search for Carpet Trademark – SEIRAFIAN)' (*Trademark National Database*, 18 November 2002) <http://ip.ssaa.ir/BSigns/SearchResult.aspx?DecNo=108618&RN=105642>.

Iran Intellectual Property Centre, 'جستجوی علامت فرش – فرش یعنی فرهی (Search for Carpet Trademark – Carpet Means Farrahi)' (*Trademark National Database*, 20 December 2016) <http://ip.ssaa.ir/BSigns/SearchResult.aspx?DecNo=139350140001036412&RN=227565>.

Iran National Carpet Centre, 'آمار صادرات فرش دست باف ایران در سال ۱۳۹۶ (Export Statistics of Iran Handmade Carpets in the year of 1396)' (*Data System of the Iran National Carpet Centre*, 2018) <http://www.incc.ir/آمار-و-اطلاعات>.

Iranian Company of Breeding of Silkworm, پرورش کرم ابریشم (*Silkworm Breeding*) (Iranian Company of Breeding of Silkworm 1997).

IRNA News Agency, 'Japanese researchers document the tradition of dyeing Chaharmahal and Bakhtiari hand-woven carpets' (*Database of the Iran National Carpet Centre*, 28 May 2011) <https://www.irna.ir/news/4044758/پژوهشگران-ژاپنی-سنت-رنگرزی-فرش-چهارمحال-وبختیاری-رامستندسازی>.

'Islamic Republic of Iran – Bilateral Investment Treaties (BITS)' (*UNCTAD Investment Policy Hub*, 25 October 2016) <http://investmentpolicyhub.unctad.org/IIA/CountryBits/98#iiaInnerMenu>.

ITC and WIPO, *Marketing Crafts and Visual Arts: The Role of Intellectual Property – a Practical Guide* (World Intellectual Property Organization 2003).

Jacob R, Alexander D and Fisher M, *Guidebook to Intellectual Property* (A&C Black 2014).

Janke T, *Minding Culture: Case Studies on Intellectual Property and Traditional Cultural Expressions* (World Intellectual Property Organization 2003).

Jena PR and Grote U, 'Changing Institutions to Protect Regional Heritage: A Case for Geographical Indications in the Indian Agrifood Sector' (2010) 28 Development Policy Review 217.

Jolly A and Philpott J, *The Handbook of European Intellectual Property Management: Developing, Managing and Protecting Your Company's Intellectual Property* (2nd edn, Kogan Page 2009).

Kallinikou D, 'Protection of Traditional Cultural Expressions or Expressions of Folklore' (International Council of Museums 2005).

'Karastan Rugs – Vintage & Antique Wool Carpets for Sale Online' (*Jewel Rugs*) <https://jewelrugs.com/collections/karastan-rugs> accessed 12 December 2024.

Kelley D, *The Art of Reasoning* (Norton 1988).

Keon J, 'Intellectual Property Rules for Trademarks and Geographical Indications: Important Parts of the New World Trade Order' in Carlos María Correa and Abdulqawi Yusuf (eds), *Intellectual Property and International Trade: The TRIPS Agreement* (2nd edn, Kluwer Law International 2008).

Khodadad Hosseini SH and Sham Abadi MA, 'Export Marketing of Persian Hand-Woven Carpet, Analysing Impact Factors and Damages' (2007) 43 Iranian Journal of Trade Studies 1.

Khor M, *Intellectual Property, Biodiversity and Sustainable Development: Resolving Difficult Issues* (Zed Books; Third World Network 2002).

Kilpatrick B, Kobel P and Këllezi P (eds), *Antitrust Analysis of Online Sales Platforms & Copyright Limitations and Exceptions* (Springer 2018).

Knobloch C and Savitri Reni D, 'Using "Batikmark" as a First Step to Extend Protection of Indonesian Javanese-Batik Patterned Textile in Foreign Countries.' (5 February 2009) <https://www.usptclaw.com/pdfs/Batikmark_Article.pdf>.

Kugelmann D, 'The Protection of Minorities and Indigenous Peoples Respecting Cultural Diversity' in Armin von Bogdandy, Rüdiger Wolfrum and Christiane Philipp (eds), *Max Planck Yearbook of United Nations Law*, vol 11 (Max-Planck-Institut für Ausländisches Öffentliches Recht und Völkerrecht 2007).

Kur A and Dreier T, *European Intellectual Property Law: Text, Cases and Materials* (Edward Elgar 2013).

Lahiji A, 'دعوی عدم استفاده ازعلامت تجاری (Trademark Non-Use Litigation)' (1973) 124 Iranian Central Bar Association Law Review 80.

Laird SA and Rachel W, 'Institutional Policies for Biodiversity Research' in Sarah A Laird (ed), *Biodiversity and Traditional Knowledge: Equitable Partnerships in Practice* (Earthscan Publications 2002).

Lamy P, 'Creation of the Organization for an International Geographical Indications Network' (2003) Speech 03/292.

Le Gall SB, 'Intellectual Property and Indigenous Arts and Cultural Expressions' (Virtual Seminar on Promoting and Protecting the Arts and Cultural Expressions of Indigenous Peoples: Perspectives on the Canadian Experience Organized by the World Intellectual Property Organization (WIPO), Geneva, Switzerland, 4 May 2022).

Lewinski SV, 'Introduction' in Silke von Lewinski (ed), *Indigenous Heritage and Intellectual Property: Genetic Resources, Traditional Knowledge, and Folklore* (2nd edn, Kluwer Law International 2008).

Li L, *Intellectual Property Protection of Traditional Cultural Expressions: Folklore in China* (Springer Science & Business 2014).

Lockie S and Carpenter D, 'Agriculture, Biodiversity and Markets' in Stewart Lockie and David Carpenter (eds), *Agriculture, Biodiversity and Markets: Livelihoods and Agroecology in Comparative Perspective* (Earthscan 2010).

Long DE, 'The Impact of Foreign Investment on Indigenous Culture: An Intellectual Property Perspective' (1997) 23 North Carolina Journal of International Law and Commercial Regulation 229.

Long DE, 'Trade Secrets and Traditional Knowledge: Strengthening International Protection of Indigenous Innovation' in Rochelle C Dreyfuss and Katherine J Strandburg (eds), *The Law and Theory of Trade Secrecy: A Handbook of Contemporary Research* (Edward Elgar 2011).

Lorentz JH, *Historical Dictionary of Iran* (Scarecrow Press 2007).

Lutzker A, *Content Rights for Creative Professionals: Copyrights and Trademarks in a Digital Age* (Focal Press 2003).

'Madrid Monitor' (*WIPO*, 2006) <http://www.wipo.int/madrid/monitor/en/index.jsp?search=MARK_ALL,HOL:qashqai>.

Mantrov V, *EU Law on Indications of Geographical Origin: Theory and Practice* (Springer 2014).

Marcantonio S, 'What Is Commercial Speech? An Analysis in Light of Kasky v. Nike' (2003) 24 Pace Law Review 357.

Mariana Bernal F, 'Controversial Trademarks: A Comparative Analysis' in Jamar Steven D. and Lateef Mtima (eds), *The Cambridge Handbook of Intellectual Property and Social Justice* (Cambridge University Press & Assessment 2024).

May CJD, *How to Identify Persian Rugs and Other Oriental Rugs: A Text Book for Collectors and Students* (Bell 1952).

McKeown JS, *Canadian Intellectual Property Law and Strategy: Trademarks, Copyright and Industrial Designs* (Oxford University Press 2010).

McManis CR, 'Biodiversity, Biotechnology and Traditional Knowledge Protection: Law, Science and Practice' in Charles R McManis (ed), *Biodiversity and the Law: Intellectual Property, Biotechnology and Traditional Knowledge* (Earthscan 2007).

Mead ATP, 'Intellectual Property, Genetic Resources and Associated Traditional Knowledge: Sharing Indigenous and Local Community Experiences' (Intergovernmental Committee on Intellectual Property and Genetic Resources, Traditional Knowledge and Folklore, Thirtieth Session, Geneva, Switzerland, 30 May 2018) <www.iucn.org/ceesp>.

'Members and Observers' (*World Trade Organization*, 1 April 2024) <https://www.wto.org/english/thewto_e/acc_e/a1_iran_e.htm>.

Merryman JH, 'The Public Interest in Cultural Property' (1989) 77 California Law Review 339.

Miller WJ, *Dictionary of International Commerce* (Chapman and Hall 1985).

Mirhosseini SH, حقوق علائم تجاری (*The Law of Trademarks*) (4th edn, Mizan Legal Foundation 2016).

Mitchell AD, *Legal Principles in WTO Disputes* (Cambridge University Press 2008).

Mojabi SA, *An Introduction on the History of Persian Carpet – Since Genesis until the Late 19th Century* (1st edn, Persian Carpet Research Centre (PCRC) 2003).

Motamedi G, 'تبیین نظام ملی حمایت حقوقی از دانش سنتی در پرتو حقوق بین الملل (Identification of the National Regime for the Legal Protection of the Traditional Knowledge in Light of International Law)' (Master Thesis, Islamic Azad University – Tehran Central Branch 2005).

Mugabe J, 'Intellectual Property Protection and Traditional Knowledge, an Exploration in International Policy Disclosure,' *Intellectual Property and Human Rights* (World Intellectual Property Organization 1999).

Munzer SR, 'Commons, Anticommons, and Community in Biotechnological Assets' (2008) 10 Theoretical Inquiries in Law 271.

Munzer SR and Raustiala K, 'The Uneasy Case for Intellectual Property Rights in Traditional Knowledge' (2009) 27 Cardozo Arts & Entertainment Law Journal 37.

Nafziger JAR, Paterson RK and Renteln AD, *Cultural Law: International, Comparative, and Indigenous* (Cambridge University Press 2010).

Nagan W and others, 'Misappropriation of Shuar Traditional Knowledge (TK) and Trade Secrets: A Case Study on Biopiracy in the Amazon' (2010) 15 UF Law Faculty Publication 9.

Nategh H, ایران در راهیابی فرهنگی (*La Perse tiraillée entre deux cultures 1834–1848*) (2nd edn, Khavaran 2001).

New Zealand Intellectual Property Office, *Protecting Intellectual Property with a Māori Cultural Element: User Guide* (Ministry of Business, Innovation & Employment 2016).

New Zealand Intellectual Property Office, 'Search Trade Mark Case(s)' (2018) <https://app.iponz.govt.nz/app/Extra/IP/TM/Qbe.aspx?sid=636629099839050546>.

Nims HD, *The Law of Unfair Competition and Trade-Marks* (Baker, Voorhis 1917).

Nissan, 'The Qashqai Story: Necessity Is The Mother of Innovation' (*NISSAN INSIDER*, 1 February 2017) <http://nissaninsider.co.uk/the-qashqai-story-necessity-is-the-mother-of-innovation/>.

Nouraie F, 'ریشه‌یابی وسبک شناسی طرح ونقشه درقالی ترکمن (Origins and Stylistic Features of Designs and Motifs in Turkmen Carpets)' (Iran National Carpet Centre 2009).

O'Connor B, *The Law of Geographical Indications* (Cameron May 2004).

O'Connor B, 'Geographical Indications and TRIPs: 10 Years Later ... A Roadmap for EU GI Holders to Get Protection in Other WTO Members – Part I' (European Lawyers Insight Consulting 2008).

O'Connor B, 'Geographical Indications and TRIPs: 10 Years Later ... A Roadmap for EU GI Holders to Get Protection in Other WTO Members – Part II' (European Lawyers Insight Consulting 2008).

Office of the Chief Financial Officer, 'USPTO Fee Schedule' (*The USPTO*) </learning-and-resources/fees-and-payment/uspto-fee-schedule> accessed 22 October 2018.

Oguamanam C, 'Localizing Intellectual Property in the Globalization Epoch the Integration of Indigenous Knowledge' (2004) 11 Indiana journal of global legal studies 135.

Osei-Tutu JJ, 'Harmonizing Cultural IP across Borders: Fashionable Bags & Ghanaian Adinkra Symbols' (2017) 51 Akron Law Review 1051.

Pacón AM, 'The Peruvian Proposal for Protecting Traditional Knowledge' in Sophia Twarog and Promila Kapoor (eds), *Protecting and Promoting Traditional Knowledge: Systems, National Experiences and International Dimensions* (United Nations 2004).

Pager SA, 'Traditional Knowledge Rights and Wrongs' (2016) 20 Virginia Journal of Law & Technology 82.

Pasha N, 'مطالعه ویژگیهای اجتماعی شیوه تولید خانگی وکارگاهی در تولید فرش دستباف در استان همدان (A Study on Social Features of Domestic and Workshop Production Methods in Producing Hand-Woven Carpets in Hamadan Province)' (Iran National Carpet Centre 2003).

Pflüger M, 'Paris Convention for the Protection of Industrial Property' in Thomas Cottier and Pierre Véron (eds), *Concise International and European IP Law: TRIPS, Paris Convention, European Enforcement and Transfer of Technology*, vol 4 (2nd edn, Kluwer Law International 2008).

Pires de Carvalho N, 'From the Shaman's Hut to the Patent Office: A Road Under Construction' in Charles R McManis (ed), *Biodiversity and the Law: Intellectual Property, Biotechnology and Traditional Knowledge* (Earthscan 2007).

Popova-Gosart U, *Traditional Knowledge & Indigenous Peoples* (World Intellectual Property Organization 2009).

Posey DA, *Indigenous Peoples and Sustainability: Cases and Actions* (International Books 1997).

Posey DA and Dutfield G, *Beyond Intellectual Property: Toward Traditional Resource Rights for Indigenous Peoples and Local Communities* (International Development Research Centre 1996).

'Process of Weaving' (*Iran Carpet Co.*, 2015) <http://en.irancarpet.ir/CarpetEncyclopedia/TheProcessofWeaving.aspx>.

Rahimpour S, 'سنت شفاهی و توسعه مدیریت فرهنگی فرش (Oral Tradition and Development of Carpet Cultural Management),' *Contemporary Challenges and Needs in the Economics and Management of the Handwoven Carpets* (Islamic Art University of Tabriz 2018).

Rangnekar D and International Centre for Trade and Sustainable Development, *Geographical Indications: A Review of Proposals at the TRIPS Council, Extending Article 23 to Products Other than Wines and Spirit* (ICTSD and UNCTAD 2003).

Raustiala K and Munzer SR, 'The Global Struggle Over Geographic Indications' (2007) 18 European Journal of International Law 337.

'Report of the UNCTAD-Commonwealth Secretariat Workshop on Elements of National Sui Generis Systems for the Preservation, Protection and Promotion of Traditional Knowledge, Innovations and Practices and Options for an International Framework, Geneva, 4–6 February 2004.' (United Nations 2005) UNCTAD/DITC/TED/2005/18.

Reviron S, 'Geographical Indications: Creation and Distribution of Economic Value in Developing Countries' (World Trade Institute 2009) 2009/14.

Riccheri M, 'The Importance of "Distinctive Signs" for the Handmade Carpet Sector: Trade Marks, Collective Marks and Certification Marks (Main Features)' (Seminar on 'The Use of Industrial Property for the Protection of Iranian Handmade Carpets,' Tehran, Iran, 26 April 2011).

Ricketson S, *The Paris Convention for the Protection of Industrial Property: A Commentary* (Oxford University Press 2015).

Ricketson S and Ginsburg JC, *International Copyright and Neighbouring Rights: The Berne Convention and Beyond*, vol 1 (Oxford University Press 2006).

Riffel C, *Protection Against Unfair Competition in the WTO TRIPS Agreement; the Scope and Prospects of Article 10bis of the Paris Convention for the Protection of Industrial Property* (BRILL | NIJHOFF 2016).

Roberts JN, *International Trademark Classification: A Guide to the Nice Agreement* (OUP USA 2012).

Rostami F, 'بررسی رقبای بین المللی برای صادرات فرش دست باف (A Study on International Competitors in the Export of Persian Hand-Woven Carpets)' (Science and Art University of Ardakan 2015).

'Roundtable' (1998).

Rovamo O, 'Monopolising Names? The Protection of Geographical Indications in the European Community' (University of Helsinki 2006).

Samuelson P, 'Enriching Discourse on Public Domains' (2006) 55 Duke Law Journal 783.

Sandler FAB, 'Music of the Village in the Global Marketplace: Self-Expression, Inspiration, Appropriation, or Exploitation?' (PhD Dissertation, University of Michigan 2001).

Scafidi S, 'Intellectual Property and Cultural Products' (2001) 81 Boston University Law Review 793.

Schmitt R, *Compendium Linguarum Iranicarum* (L Reichert 1989).

Schwabach A, *Intellectual Property: A Reference Handbook* (ABC-CLIO 2007).

Science Policy Research Group, 'Social Values, Science and Technology' (European Commission 2005) EUR Series 22062 EN.

SCP Secretariat, 'Dissemination of Patent Information' (2009) WIPO SCP, 13th sess, Agenda Item 6, WIPO Doc SCP/13/5.

SCT Secretariat, 'Geographical Indications' (World Intellectual Property Organization 2003) WIPO Doc SCT/10/4.

SCT Secretariat, 'Summary of Replies to the Questionnaire on Trademark Law and Practice (SCT/11/6)' (World Intellectual Property Organization 2005) WIPO Doc SCT/14/5.

SCT Secretariat, 'Article 6ter of the Paris Convention: Legal and Administrative Aspects' (World Intellectual Property Organization 2005) WIPO Doc SCT/15/3.

SCT Secretariat, 'Technical and Procedural Aspects Relating to the Registration of Certification and Collective Marks' (World Intellectual Property Organization 2010) WIPO Doc WIPO/STrad/INF/6.

Secretariat of the Convention on Biological Diversity, *Bonn Guidelines on Access to Genetic Resources and Fair and Equitable Sharing of the Benefits Arising out of Their Utilization* (Secretariat of the Convention on Biological Diversity 2002).

Secretariat of the Convention on Biological Diversity, Global Mechanism of the United Nations Convention to Combat Desertification, and OSLO consortium, 'Valuing the Biodiversity of Dry and Sub-Humid Lands' (Secretariat of the Convention on Biological Diversity 2013) Peer reviewed 71.

Secretariat of the Pacific Community, *Guidelines for Developing National Legislation for the Protection of Traditional Knowledge and Expressions of Culture Based on the Pacific Model Law 2002* (Secretariat of the Pacific Community 2006).

Secretariat of the Permanent Forum on Indigenous Issues, 'Who Are Local Communities?' (UNEP 2006) UNEP Doc, UNEP/CBD/WS-CB/LAC/1/INF/5.

Sehat S and Farajlou Motlagh M, 'بررسی وآسیب شناسی صادرات فرش دستباف ایران (An Analysis and Critical Assessment of Persian Carpet Exports)' Allameh Tabataba'i University 23.

Sell SK, *Private Power, Public Law: The Globalization of Intellectual Property Rights* (Cambridge University Press 2003).

Senftleben M, 'No Trademark Protection for Artworks in the Public Domain – A Practical Guide to the Application of Public Order and Morality as Grounds for Refusal' (2021) 71 Journal of European and International Law 3.

Shams'Oldini S, 'Iran Place in Hand-woven Carpets Global Exports' in Iran National Carpet Centre (ed), *1st National Seminar on Researches of Persian Hand-Woven Carpets*, vol 2 (Iran National Carpet Centre 2003).

Sharoni S, 'The Mark of a Culture: The Efficacy and Propriety of Using Trademark Law to Deter Cultural Appropriation' (2016) 26 Federal Circuit Bar Journal 407.

Sheff JN, 'Misappropriation-Based Trademark Liability in Comparative Perspective' in Irene Calboli and Jane C Ginsburg (eds), *The Cambridge Handbook of International and Comparative Trademark Law* (Cambridge University Press 2020).

Sherman B and Wiseman L, 'From Terroir to Pangkarra: Geographical Indications of Origin and Indigenous Knowledge' in Dev S Gangjee (ed), *Research handbook on intellectual property and geographical indications* (Edward Elgar Publishing 2016).

Shilling D, *Essentials of Trademarks and Unfair Competition* (John Wiley & Sons 2002).

Simon J, 'Agreement on Trade-Related Aspects of Intellectual Property Rights: Section 2: Trademarks' in Thomas Cottier and Pierre Véron (eds), *Concise International and European IP Law: TRIPS, Paris Convention, European Enforcement and Transfer of Technology*, vol 4 (2nd edn, Kluwer Law International 2008).

Sirinelli P, 'Exceptions and Limits to Copyright and Neighbouring Rights' (WIPO 1999) WIPO Doc WCT-WPPT/IMP/1.

Stevenson MG, 'Indigenous Knowledge in Environmental Assessment' (1996) 49 Arctic Institute of North America 278.

Stoll P-T and Hahn A von, 'Indigenous Peoples, Indigenous Knowledge and Indigenous Resources in International Law' in Silke von Lewinski (ed), *Indigenous Heritage and Intellectual Property: Genetic Resources, Traditional Knowledge, and Folklore* (2nd edn, Kluwer Law International 2008).

Stone PF, *Oriental Rugs: An Illustrated Lexicon of Motifs, Materials, and Origins* (Tuttle Publishing 2013).

Swiss Federal Institute of Intellectual Property, 'How Much Does It Cost to Protect a Trade Mark in Switzerland? Costs and Fees' (*IGE / IPI*) <https://www.ige.ch/en/protecting-your-ip/trade-marks/national-applications/costs-and-fees.html> accessed 16 October 2018.

Tambutoh DJ, Sardjono A and Dabiri M, 'Traditional Medicine and Intellectual Property Rights – a Move Towards Protection in Developing Countries' (WIPO Specialisation Course on Intellectual Property, Turin, 2011).

Taromsari M, حمایت حقوق بین المللی از طرح ها و نقش ها و سایر ویژگی های فرش دست باف ایرانی در مقابل تقلید خارجیان (*Legal Protection of Persian Carpets at National and International Levels Against Unauthorized Imitations: An Analytical Study*) (1st edn, Institute for Trade Studies and Research 2006).

Taubman A and Leistner M, 'Traditional Knowledge' in Silke von Lewinski (ed), *Indigenous Heritage and Intellectual Property: Genetic Resources, Traditional Knowledge, and Folklore* (2nd edn, Kluwer Law International 2008).

Te Awekotuku N, 'Ta Moko: Maori Tattoo' in Roger Blackley (ed), *Goldie* (Auckland Art Gallery; David Bateman 1997).

Tehran Chamber, 'چرا فرش ایرانی آب رفته است؟ (The Shrinking Trade of Persian Carpets: What Went Wrong?)' *Fasleqtesad* (Tehran, Iran, 14 May 2018).

Tehrani PM and Manap NA, 'Urgency and Benefits of Protecting Iranian Carpets Using Geographical Indications' (2013) 18 Journal of Intellectual Property Law 72.

The Andean Community, 'Decision 486 – Common Intellectual Property Regime' (World Intellectual Property Organization 2001) WIPO Doc WIPO/GRTKF/IC/1/11 Annex IV.

The Committee of Governmental Experts, 'Tunis Model Law on Copyright for Developing Countries.'

The Committee of Governmental Experts and WIPO, 'Model Provisions for National Laws on the Protection of Expressions of Folklore Against Illicit Exploitation and Other Prejudicial Actions' (UNESCO, WIPO 1983) UNESCO/WIPO/FOLK/AFR/2.

The Delegation of Portugal, 'Ministry of Agriculture, Development and Fisheries, Decree-Law No. 118/2002' (World Intellectual Property Organization 2005) WIPO Doc WIPO/GRTKF/IC/8/13 Annex.

The European Community and its Member States, 'Expressions of Folklore' (World Intellectual Property Organization 2002) WIPO Doc WIPO/GRTKF/IC/3/11 Annex.

The German customs, 'Customs Online – Bilateral Agreements and Treaties' (*Zoll*) <https://www.zoll.de/EN/Businesses/Movement-of-goods/Import/Restrictions/Goods/Protection-of-industrial-property/Indications-of-geographical-source/Protected-rights/Bilateral-agreements-and-treaties/bilateral-agreements-and-treaties_node.html> accessed 19 March 2019.

The Permanent Delegation of the European Union in Geneva, 'Proposal for the Terms of Reference for a Study' (World Intellectual Property Organization 2016) WIPO Doc WIPO/GRTKF/IC/31/9 Annex.

Thual D and others, 'Study on the Protection of Geographical Indications for Products Other Than Wines, Spirits and Agricultural Products or Foodstuffs' (Insight Consulting, Origin, Agridea 2009).

Toensing GC, 'World Intellectual Property Organization Blasted for "Misappropriation" of Indigenous Knowledge, Resources' (*Indian Country Today Media Network.com*, 16 May 2012) <available at: http://indiancountrytodaymedianetwork.com> accessed 2 October 2013.

Torsen M and Anderson J, *Intellectual Property and the Safeguarding of Traditional Cultures – Legal Issues and Practical Options for Museums, Libraries and Archives* (World Intellectual Property Organization 2010).

'Trade Mark Number UK00000319214' (*Intellectual Property Office of UK*) <https://trademarks.ipo.gov.uk/ipo-tmcase/page/Results/1/UK00000319214> accessed 25 May 2018.

'Transforming Our World: The 2030 Agenda for Sustainable Development' (2015) GA Res 70/1, UN GAOR, 70th sess, 4th plen mtg, UN Doc A/RES/70/1.

UNCTAD-ICTSD, *Resource Book on TRIPS and Development* (Cambridge University Press 2005).

UNDP, *Human Development Report 1990* (Oxford University Press 1990).

UNDP, 'The UNDP and Indigenous Peoples: A Policy of Engagement' (United Nations Development Program 2001).

UNEP, *Glossary of Terms for Negotiators of Multilateral Environmental Agreements* (UNEP 2007).

UNEP-CBD, 'Decisions Adopted by the Conference of the Parties to the Convention on Biological Diversity at Its Fifth Meeting' (2000) UNEP Doc UNEP/CBD/COP/5/23 Annex III.

UNEP-CBD, 'Report of the Meeting of the Group of Technical and Legal Experts on Traditional Knowledge Associated with Genetic Resources in the Context of the International Regime on Access and Benefit-Sharing' (2009) CBD AHWG, 8th mtg, Agenda Item 32, UNEP Doc UNEP/CBD/WG-ABS/8/2 Annex.

UNEP-CBD, 'Report of the Meeting of the Group of Technical and Legal Experts on Traditional Knowledge Associated with Genetic Resources in the Context of the International Regime on Access and Benefit-Sharing' (2009) CBD AHWG, 8th mtg, Agenda Item 32, UNEP Doc UNEP/CBD/WG-ABS/8/2.

UNEP-CBD Executive Secretary, 'Development of Elements of Sui Generis Systems for the Protection of Traditional Knowledge, Innovations and Practices' (UNEP 2005) CBD WG8J, 4th mtg, Agenda Item 8, UNEP Doc, UNEP/CBD/WG8J/4/INF/18.

UNEP-CBD Executive Secretary, 'Identification of Common Characteristics of Local Communities' (UNEP 2011) UNEP Doc, UNEP/CBD/AHEG/LCR/INF/1.

UNESCO, 'World Conference on Cultural Policies Final Report' (1982) UNESCO Doc CLT/MD/1.

UNESCO, 'Universal Declaration on the Human Genome and Human Rights' (1997) GA Res 53/152, 26th mtg, UN Doc.

UNESCO, 'DRAFT GLOSSARY – Proposed by a Group of Dutch Experts Convened by the Bureau of the Netherlands National Commission for UNESCO' (2002) International Meeting of Experts on Intangible Cultural Heritage: Establishment of a Glossary UNESCO Doc, TER/CH/2002/WD/4.

'United Nations Declaration on the Rights of Indigenous Peoples' (2007) GA Res 61/295, UN GAOR, 61st sess, 107th plen mtg, Supp No 49, UN Doc A/RES/61/295.

United Nations, 'The Universal Declaration of Human Rights' (1948) UN Doc GA Res 217 A (III), 3rd sess, UN Doc A/RES/3/217 A.

United Nations, 'What Can We Do? Activity Guide for the Implementation of the Second International Decade of the World's Indigenous People, 2005–2014' (Department of Economic and Social Affairs 2010).

United States Patent and Trademark Office, 'USPTO Establishes Database of Official Insignia of Native American Tribes' (29 August 2001) </about-us/news-updates/uspto-establishes-database-official-insignia-native-american-tribes> accessed 22 December 2016.

'Universal Declaration on Bioethics and Human Rights' (2005) GA Res, 33rd session, UNESCO Doc.

USPTO, 'Report on the Official Insignia of Native American Tribes' (United States Patent and Trademark Office 1999).

Varadarajan D, 'A Trade Secret Approach to Protecting Traditional Knowledge' (2011) 36 *Yale Journal of International Law* 371.

Verma SK, 'Protecting Traditional Knowledge, Is a Sui Generis System an Answer?' (2004) 7 The Journal of World Intellectual Property 765.

'Vicious Circle' (*Islamic Quest Net*, 16 March 2013) <http://www.islamquest.net/en/archive/keyword/vicious%20circle> accessed 17 March 2014.

Visser CJ, 'Making Intellectual Property Laws Work for Traditional Knowledge' in J Michael Finger and Philip Schuler (eds), *Poor People's Knowledge, Promoting Intellectual Property in Developing Countries* (The World Bank and Oxford University Press 2004).

Vivas-Eugui D, 'Negotiations on Geographical Indications in the TRIPS Council and Their Effect on the WTO Agricultural Negotiations-Implications for Developing Countries and the Case of Venezuela' (2001) 4 The Journal of World Intellectual Property 703.

Wendland W, 'Intellectual Property, Genetic Resources, Traditional Knowledge and Traditional Cultural Expressions' (Workshop on Intellectual Property and Traditional Knowledge for Economic Development: Empowering Local Communities of Uganda, Kampala, Uganda, 4 July 2017).

Wendland W, 'Is an International Agreement on IP, Genetic Resources and Associated Traditional Knowledge Finally in Sight?' [2023] *WIPO Magazine*.

'What Is the Attitude the Use of Māori Images for Artistic or Commercial Purposes?' (*Māori Information Sources*) <http://oil.otago.ac.nz/oil/module11/Scenarios/Maori-images.html>.

WIPO, *Model Law for Developing Countries on Appellations of Origin and Indications of Source* (WIPO 1975).

WIPO, *Guide to the Berne Convention for the Protection of Literary and Artistic Works* (WIPO 1978).

WIPO, 'Copyright Monthly Review' (World Intellectual Property Organization 1990) 120-1990-09.

WIPO, *Protection Against Unfair Competition: Analysis of the Present World Situation* (WIPO 1994).

WIPO, *Intellectual Property Reading Material* (2nd edn, WIPO 1998).

WIPO, 'Joint Recommendation Concerning Provisions on the Protection of Well-Known Marks' (World Intellectual Property Organization 2000) 833(E).

WIPO, *Intellectual Property Needs and Expectations of Traditional Knowledge Holders: WIPO Report on Fact-Finding Missions on Intellectual Property and Traditional Knowledge (1998–1999)* (WIPO 2001).

WIPO, *Consolidated Analysis of the Legal Protection of Traditional Cultural Expressions/Expressions of Folklore*. (World Intellectual Property Organization 2003).

WIPO, *Making a Mark – An Introduction to Trademarks for Small and Medium-Sized Enterprises* (WIPO 2006).

WIPO, *Intellectual Property and Traditional Cultural Expressions/Folklore-Booklet N°1* (World Intellectual Property Organization 2007).

WIPO, *Intellectual Property and Traditional Knowledge* (World Intellectual Property Organization 2008).

WIPO, *WIPO Intellectual Property Handbook: Policy, Law and Use* (2nd edn, World Intellectual Property Organization 2008).

WIPO, 'The World Intellectual Property Organization Traditional Knowledge Documentation Toolkit' (World Intellectual Property Organization 2012).

WIPO, *Intellectual Property, Traditional Knowledge and Traditional Cultural Expressions / Folklore: A Guide for Countries in Transition* (1st edn, World Intellectual Property Organization 2013).

WIPO, *Summaries of Conventions, Treaties and Agreements Administered by WIPO* (World Intellectual Property Organization 2013).

WIPO, *Intellectual Property and Folk, Arts and Cultural Festivals: Practical Guide* (World Intellectual Property Organization 2014).

WIPO, *Intellectual Property and Genetic Resources, Traditional Knowledge and Traditional Cultural Expressions: Overview.* (World Intellectual Property Organization 2015).

WIPO, 'Traditional Medicine as a Tonic for Development' (World Intellectual Property Organization and Bioresources Development and Conservation Programme 2015) Project Report.

WIPO, 'Madrid Monitor' (*WIPO Madrid System*, 2 July 2016) <http://www.wipo.int/madrid/monitor/en/#>.

WIPO, *Protect and Promote Your Culture: A Practical Guide to Intellectual Property for Indigenous Peoples and Local Communities* (World Intellectual Property Organization 2017).

WIPO, 'WIPO Project: Collective Mark for Kenyan Basket Weavers' (2017) <http://www.wipo.int/cooperation/en/funds_in_trust/japan_fitip/news/2017/news_0001.html>.

WIPO, *Documenting Traditional Knowledge – A Toolkit* (World Intellectual Property Organization 2017).

WIPO, 'WIPO-Administered Treaties: Members of the Paris Convention for the Protection of Industrial Property, Stockholm Act (1967)' (*World Intellectual Property Organization*, January 2019) <https://www.wipo.int/export/sites/www/treaties/en/documents/pdf/paris.pdf> accessed 12 June 2018.

WIPO, *Guide to the Madrid System* (WIPO 2022).

WIPO, 'WIPO Lisbon Express Search' (*World Intellectual Property Organization*, 20 April 2024) <https://www.wipo.int/cgi-lis/bool_srch5?ENG+17> accessed 20 April 2024.

WIPO, 'Customary Law and Traditional Knowledge' (World Intellectual Property Organization) Background Brief No. 7.

WIPO, 'Intellectual Property & Traditional Handicrafts' (World Intellectual Property Organization) Background Brief No 5.

WIPO and UNEP, 'The Role of Intellectual Property Rights in the Sharing of Benefits Arising from the Use of Biological Resources and Associated Traditional Knowledge: Selected Case Studies' (WIPO 2001).

WIPO Secretariat, 'Matters Concerning Intellectual Property and Genetic Resources, Traditional Knowledge and Folklore' (2000) WIPO GA Dec WO/GA/26/6.

WIPO Secretariat, 'Report' (World Intellectual Property Organization 2000) WIPO Doc WO/GA/26/10.

WIPO Secretariat, 'Report of General Assembly' (2000) WIPO GA Dec WO/GA/26/10.

WIPO Secretariat, 'Report of the Assemblies of the Member States of WIPO' (2017) WIPO GA Doc A/57/11 ADD.6.

WIPO Secretariat, 'Report on the Intergovernmental Committee on Intellectual Property and Genetic Resources, Traditional Knowledge and Folklore (IGC)' (World Intellectual Property Organization 2021) WIPO GA Doc WO/GA/54/10.

WIPO Secretariat, 'Proposal to Advance WIPO Normative Agenda on the Subjects of Genetic Resources Associated with Traditional Knowledge, and the Design Law Treaty' (World Intellectual Property Organization 2022) WIPO GA Doc WO/GA/55/11 Annex.

WIPO Secretariat, 'Summary Report of Assemblies of the Member States of WIPO' (2022) WIPO GA Doc A/63/9.

Woodward R, *The Organization for Economic Co-Operation and Development* (OECD) (Routledge 2009).

World Bank, 'Indigenous Peoples' (2005) Operational Policies: OP 4.10.

WTO, 'Compilation of Written Submissions and Oral Statements' (World Trade Organization 1988) Special Distribution MTN.GNG/NGll/W/12/Rev.l.

WTO, 'Review of Article 27.3(b)' (World Trade Organization 2000) WTO Doc IP/C/W/228.

WTO, 'Review under Article 24.2 of the Application of the Provisions of the Section of the TRIPS AGREEMENT on Geographical Indications' (2001) WTO Doc IP/C/W/253.

WTO, 'The Protection of Traditional Knowledge and Folklore: Summary of Issues Raised and Points Made' (2006) WTO Doc IP/C/W/370/Rev.1.

WTO, 'Draft Modalities for TRIPS Related Issues' (2008) WTO Doc Trade Negotiations Committee.

WTO, 'Doha Ministerial Declaration' WTO Doc WTO Doha Ministerial Conference, 4th sess, WTO Doc WT/MIN(01)/DEC/1 (20 November 2001 Adopted on 14 November 2001).

WTO, 'The Extension of the Additional Protection for Geographical Indications to Products Other than Wines and Spirits' WTO Doc IP/C/W/353.

Yasavoli J, مقدمه ای بر شناخت قالی ایران (*An Introduction to the Study of Persian Rugs*) (2nd edn, Farhangsara 1996).

Yazdani A, 'عملکرد صنعت فرش ماشینی در سال ۱۳۹۵ (Performance of the Machine-Made Carpet Industry in 2015–16)' *Donya-e-Eqtesad* (Tehran, Iran, 5 September 2017).

Yozo Yokota, 'Standard-Setting: Future Priorities for Standard-Setting Activities; Draft Guidelines on the Protection of the Cultural Heritage of Indigenous Peoples' (UN Commission on Human Rights, Sub-Commission on the Promotion and Protection of Human Rights, Working Group on Indigenous Populations 2006) UN ESC, 24th sess, Item 5(a), UN Doc E/CN.4/Sub.2/AC.4/2006/5.

Zent S and Zent EL, 'On Biocultural Diversity from a Venezuelan Perspective: Tracing the Interrelationships among Biodiversity, Culture Change and Legal Reforms' in Charles R McManis (ed), *Biodiversity and the Law – Intellectual Property, Biotechnology and Traditional Knowledge* (Earthscan 2007).

Zhao N, 'Choice-of-Law in Cross-Border Copyright and Related Rights Disputes: Comparative Inspiration for the PRC' (Doctor of Philosophy, Rijksuniversiteit Groningen 2012).

Zografos D, *Intellectual Property and Traditional Cultural Expressions* (Edward Elgar Publishing 2010).

'تاریخچه سازمان امور عشایر ایران (History of Iranian Nomad Affairs Organization)' (*Iranian Nomads Affairs Organization*, 2008) <http://ashayer.ir/index.aspx?fkeyid=&siteid=1&pageid=135>.

'جمعیت عشایری ایران (The Nomadic Population of Iran)' (*Organization for Nomads Affairs*, 2024) <https://ashayer.ir/جمعیت-عشایر-کشور>.

'دانشنامه فرش ایران (Encyclopedia of Persian Carpets)' (*Iran Carpet Scientific Association*, May 2014) <http://icsa.ir>.

'Interview with Mr. Mahdiei,' (3 February 2024).

National Legislations and International Instruments

Agreement between Austria and France on the Protection of Indications of Source, Appellations of Origin and Denominations of Products of Agriculture and Industry 1974 (entered into force on 24 September 1975).

Agreement between Costa Rica and France on the Reciprocal Protection of Industrial Property and Appellations of Origin 1933 (entered into force on 23 July 1935).

Agreement between Spain and Portugal on the Protection of Indications of Source, Appellations of Origin and the Denominations of Certain Products 1970 (entered into force on 23 August 1972).

Agreement between the Czechoslovak Socialist Republic and the Republic of Austria on the Protection of Indications of Source, Appellations of Origin and Other Geographical Denominations (entered into force on 26 February 1981).

Agreement between the Federal Republic of Germany and France on the Protection of Indications of Source, Appellations of Origin and Other Geographical Denominations (entered into force on 7 May 1960; amendments entered into force on 1 November 1969).

Agreement Between the World Intellectual Property Organization and the World Trade Organization 1995 (35 ILM 754 (entered into force 1 January 1996)).

Agreement on Trade-Related Aspects of Intellectual Property Rights 1994 (1869 UNTS 299 (entered into force 1 January 1995)).

Andean Decision No. 344 – Common Regime on Industrial Property 1993 (entered into force 1 January 1994).

Andean Decision No. 391 – Common Regime on Access to Genetic Resources 1996 (entered into force 17 July 1996).

Australia – Competition and Consumer Act 2010 (Cth) 2010.

Australia – Copyright Act 1968.

Australia – Trade Practices Act 1974 (Cth) 1974.

Azerbaijan (Republic of) – Law on Trademarks and Geographical Indications as amended on November 22, 2013 1998 (504-IQ).

Bangui Agreement Relating to the Creation of an African Intellectual Property Organization, Constituting a Revision of the Agreement Relating to the Creation of an African and Malagasy Office of Industrial Property 1977 (entered into force on 8 February 1982).

Basel Convention on the Control of Transboundary Movements of Hazardous Wastes and their Disposal 1989 (1673 UNTS 57 (entered into force 5 May 1992)).

Berne Convention for the Protection of Literary and Artistic Works, as revised at Paris 1971 (1161 UNTS 3 (entered into force 15 December 1972)).

Bonn Guidelines on Access to Genetic Resources and Fair and Equitable Sharing of the Benefits Arising out of their Utilization 2002 (CBD COP Dec VI/24, Item A, 6th mtg, UNEP Doc UNEP/CBD/COP/6/20 Annex).

Canada – Trademarks Act 1985 (RSC, 1985, c T-13).

Convention between El Salvador and France of concerning the Protection of Appellations of Origin 1932.

Convention between France and Italy on the Protection of Appellations of Origin, Indications of Source and Denominations of Certain Products 1964 (entered into force on 24 April 1969; additions and modifications agreed through an exchange of letters of 6 May 1969 and 13 February 1970).

Convention Concerning Indigenous and Tribal Peoples in Independent Countries (ILO No. 169) 1989 (1650 UNTS 383 (entered into force 5 September 1991)).

Convention Establishing the World Intellectual Property Organization 1967 (828 UNTS 3 (entered into force 26 April 1970)).

Convention for the Safeguarding of the Intangible Cultural Heritage 2003 (2368 UNTS 3 (entered into force 20 April 2006)).

Convention on Biological Diversity 1992 (1760 UNTS 79 (entered into force 29 December 1993)).

Convention on the Protection and Promotion of the Diversity of Cultural Expressions (CPPDCE) 2005 (2440 UNTS 311 (entered into force 18 March 2007)).

Council Regulation (EC) No 692/2003 of 8 April 2003 amending Regulation (EEC) No 2081/92 on the protection of geographical indications and designations of origin for agricultural products and foodstuffs 2003 (OJ L 099).

Council Regulation (EEC) No 2081/92 of 14 July 1992 on the Protection of Geographical Indications and Designations of Origin for Agricultural Products and Foodstuffs 1992 (OJ L 208).

Directive 96/9/EC of the European Parliament and of the Council of 11 March 1996 on the Legal Protection of Databases 1996 (OJ L 077).

Directive 98/44/EC of the European Parliament and of the Council of 6 July 1998 on the Legal Protection of Biotechnological Inventions 1998 (OJ L 213/13).
Directive 2011/77/EU of the European Parliament and of the Council of 27 September 2011 amending Directive 2006/116/EC on the term of protection of copyright and certain related rights 2011 (L 265/1).
Directive 2015/2436 of the European Parliament and of the Council of 16 December 2015 to Approximate the Laws of the Member states Relating to Trade Marks 2015 (OJ L 336/1).
Economic Cooperation Organization Trade Agreement (ECOTA) 2003 (entered into force 24 April 2008).
Finland Toiminimilaki 1979 (128).
General Agreement on Tariffs and Trade 1947 (55 UNTS 194 (entered into force 1 January 1948)).
Geneva Act of the Lisbon Agreement on Appellations of Origin and Geographical Indications 2015 (3384 UNTS (entered into force 26 February 2020)).
India – Geographical Indications of Goods (Registration and Protection) Act 1999 (Act No 48 (entered into force on 15 September 2003)).
India – Trade Marks Act 1999 (Act No 47 of 1999 (entered into force on 15 September 2003)).
International Convention for the Protection of New Varieties of Plants, as last revised at Geneva 1991 (1861 UNTS 281 (entered into force 24 April 1998)).
International Convention on the Elimination of All Forms of Racial Discrimination 1966 (660 UNTS 195 (entered into force 4 January 1969)).
International Covenant on Civil and Political Rights (ICCPR) 1966 (999 UNTS 171 (entered into force 23 March 1976)).
International Covenant on Economic, Social and Cultural Rights (ICESCR) 1966 (993 UNTS 3 (entered into force 3 January 1976)).
International Treaty on Plant Genetic Resources for Food and Agriculture (ITPGRFA) 2001 (2400 UNTS 303 (entered into force 29 June 2004)).
Iran – Act for Protection of Authors, Composers and Artists' Rights 1970.
Iran – Act for Protection of Geographical Indications 2005.
Iran – Act for Supporting Artists, Artisans, and Handicrafts Practitioners 2018.
Iran – Act for Supporting Establishment and Administration of Large and Centred Carpet Weaving Complexes 2002.
Iran – Act for the Establishment of Village Association and Village's Governor 1975.
Iran – Act on Country's Guild System 2004.
Iran – Act on Establishment of the Country Islamic Councils 1982.
Iran – By-Law of the Act for Supporting Establishment and Administration of Large and Centred Carpet Weaving Complexes 2006 (A Decree of Iran Council of Ministers).
Iran – By-Law subject of Article 16 concerning Protection of Geographical Indications 2005 (Approved by Head of Judiciary).

Iran – Civil Code 1928.
Iran – Commercial Code 1932.
Iran – Decree on Establishment of Iran's Nomads High Council 1986 (A Decree of Iran Council of Ministers).
Iran – Designating June 10th as the National Day of Hand-Woven Carpets 2021 (Resolution 753).
Iran – Executive Regulation of Patents, Industrial Designs and Trademarks Registration Law 2009.
Iran – Law for the Fourth Development Plan of the I.R. Iran 2004.
Iran – Law for the Third Development Plan of the I.R. Iran 2000.
Iran – Law on Definitions and Criteria of Country Divisions 1983.
Iran – Law on Organization, Duties and Election of the Islamic Councils of the Country and Assignment of Mayors 1996.
Iran – Law on Registration of Marks and Inventions 1931.
Iran – Law on Standing Rules of the Country Development Program 2017.
Iran – Law on the Rules of Medical and Pharmaceutical Affairs and Eatable and Drinkable Materials 1955.
Iran – Patents, Industrial Designs and Trademarks Registration Law 2007.
Iran – Reconstruction of Iran High Council of Nomads in the Ministry of Internal Affairs 1980 (A Resolution of Iran Revolutionary Council).
Iran – Regulation of Law on Definitions and Criteria of Country Divisions 1984 (A Decree of Iran Council of Ministers).
Iran – Resolution on Increasing of Production, Enhancing of Quality and Organizing Hand-Woven Carpet Industry 2003 (Resolution of High Council of Administrative Affairs).
Iran – The Constitution of the Islamic Republic of Iran 1979.
Lisbon Agreement for the Protection of Appellations of Origin and their International Registration. 1967 (923 UNTS 205 (entered into force 31 October 1973)).
Madrid Agreement Concerning the International Registration of Marks 1979 (828 UNTS 389 (entered into force 23 October 1983)).
Madrid Agreement for the Repression of False or Deceptive Indications of Source on Goods 1958 (828 UNTS 165 (entered into force 1 June 1963)).
Malta – Crafts Council Act 2020.
Nagoya Protocol on Access to Genetic Resources and the Fair and Equitable Sharing of Benefits Arising from Their Utilization to the Convention on Biological Diversity 2010 (3010 UNTS 118 (entered into force 12 October 2014)).
Nairobi Treaty on the Protection of the Olympic Symbol 1981 (1863 UNTS 367 (entered into force 25 September 1982)).
Nepal – The Patent, Design and Trade Mark Act 1965 (15 (entered into force 1965)).
New Zealand – Fair Trading Act 1986.

New Zealand – Trade Marks Act 2002.

Nice Agreement Concerning the International Classification of Goods and Services for the Purposes of the Registration of Marks 1977 (1154 UNTS 89 (entered into force 6 February 1979)).

Panama – Regulating Law No. 20 of June 26, 2000, on the Special Intellectual Property Regime Governing the Collective Rights of Indigenous Peoples for the Protection and Defence of their Cultural Identity and their Traditional Knowledge, and Enacting Other Provisions 2001 (Executive Decree No 12).

Panama – Special System for the Collective Intellectual Property Rights of Indigenous Peoples 2000 (Act No 20, Published in Gaceta Oficial (Official Gazette) No 24,083 of June 27, 2000).

Paris Convention for the Protection of Industrial Property, as last revised at Stockholm 1967 (828 UNTS 305 (entered into force 26 April 1970)).

Peru – Law Introducing a Protection Regime for the Collective Knowledge of Indigenous Peoples Derived from Biological Resources 2002 (Peruvian Law No 27811).

Protocol Relating to the Madrid Agreement Concerning the International Registration of Marks 2007 (entered into force 1 September 2008).

Regulation (EU) 2017/1001 of the European Parliament and of the Council of 14 June 2017 on the European Union Trade Mark 2017 (OJ L 154/1).

Regulation (EU) No 2024/1143 of the European Parliament and of the Council of 11 April 2024 on geographical indications for wine, spirit drinks and agricultural products, as well as traditional specialities guaranteed and optional quality terms for agricultural products, amending Regulations (EU) No 1308/2013, (EU) 2019/787 and (EU) 2019/1753 and repealing Regulation (EU) No 1151/2012 2024 (OJ L 1143/1).

Singapore Treaty on the Law of Trademarks 2006 (2633 UNTC 3 (entered into force 16 March 2009)).

Sri Lanka – A Legal Framework for the Protection of Traditional Knowledge 2009.

Swakopmund Protocol on the Protection of Traditional Knowledge and Expressions of Folklore 2010 (entered into force 11 May 2015).

Swiss – Civil Code 1907 (210 (entered into force 10 December 1907)).

Swiss – Federal Act on Copyright and Related Rights 1992 (231/1 (Status as of 1 January 2022)).

Swiss – Federal Act on the Protection of the Swiss Coat of Arms and Other Public Signs 2013 (232/21 (entered into force 1 January 2017)).

Swiss – Federal Act on the Protection of Trade Marks and Indications of Source 1992 (232/11 (entered into force 1 April 1993)).

Swiss – Federal Law on Unfair Competition 1986 (entered into force 01 March 1988).

Swiss – Ordinance on the Register of Designations of Origin and Geographical Indications for Non-Agricultural Products 2015 (232/112/2 (Status as of 1 January 2017)).

The Comprehensive Economic and Trade Agreement (CETA) between Canada, of the one part, and the European Union and its Member States, of the other part 2016 (OJ L 11/1).

The International Convention for the use of appellations d'origine and denominations of cheeses 1951 (entered into force on 12 July 1953).

The North American Free Trade Agreement 1992 (32 ILM 289 (entered into force 01 January 1994)).

The Pacific Regional Framework for the Protection of Traditional Knowledge and Expressions of Culture 2002.

The United States – Colombia Trade Promotion Agreement 2006 (entered into force 15 May 2012).

The United States – Panama Trade Promotion Agreement 2007 (entered into force 31 October 2012).

The United States – Peru Trade Promotion Agreement 2006 (entered into force 14 December 2007).

The US – Copyright Act 1976.

The US – Indian Arts and Crafts Act of 1990 as amended as at September 2003 1990 (PL 101-644).

The US – Trademark Act 1946 (Pub L No 79-489, 60 Stat 427,).

The US – Uniform Trade Secrets Act 1985 (14 ULA 529).

Trade Agreement between the government of the Islamic Republic of Iran and the government of the Republic of Cuba 2008.

Trademark Law Treaty 1994 (2037 UNTS 196 (entered into force 1 August 1996)).

Treaty between the Swiss Confederation and the Federal Republic of Germany on the Protection of Indications of Source and Other Geographical Designations 1967 (entered into force on 30 August 1969).

Treaty between the Swiss Confederation and the Spanish State on the Protection of Indications of Source, Appellations of Origin and Similar Designations 1974 (entered into force on 10 March 1976).

United Nations Convention to Combat Desertification in those Countries Experiencing Serious Drought and/or Desertification, Particularly in Africa (UNCCD) 1994 (1954 UNTS 3 (entered into force 26 December 1996)).

Vienna Agreement Establishing an International Classification of the Figurative Elements of Marks 1973 (1863 UNTS 317 (entered into force 9 August 1985)).

Washington Treaty on Intellectual Property in Respect of Integrated Circuits 1989 (Not yet in force).

WIPO Copyright Treaty 1996 (2186 UNTS 121 (entered into force 3 March 2002)).

WIPO Performances and Phonograms Treaty 1996 (2186 UNTS 203 (entered into force 20 May 2002)).

Index

www.ingramcontent.com/pod-product-compliance
Lightning Source LLC
Chambersburg PA
CBHW071335230926
51849CB00002B/399
* 9 7 8 9 0 0 4 7 2 1 3 5 7 *